PIMLICO

7 2

VIENNA

Ilsa Barea, a Viennese born and bred, studied political sciences at Vienna University and was a leader of her generation in the stormy Twenties and Thirties. From Czechoslovakia, where she had emigrated for political reasons, she went to Spain on the Republican side early in the Civil War. With her husband, the celebrated Spanish writer Arturo Barea, she settled in England and became naturalised. During the Second World War she worked in the BBC Monitoring Service. She translated more than twenty books into English, edited a paperback series of international classics and lectured and broadcast in several languages. She died in Vienna while working on her autobiography.

VIENNA

Legend and Reality

ILSA BAREA

PIMLICO

PIMLICO

20 Vauxhall Bridge Road, London SW1V 2SA

London Melbourne Sydney Auckland Johannesburg
and agencies throughout the world

First published by Secker & Warburg Ltd 1966
Pimlico edition 1992

Printed and bound in Great Britain by
Mackays of Chatham PLC, Chatham, Kent

ISBN 0-7126-5579-4

To the memory of my parents,
DR. VALENTIN POLLAK
and
ALICE VON ZIEGLMAYER

Acknowledgements

THE AUTHOR and publishers are grateful to S. Fischer Verlag for permission to quote Hugo von Hofmannsthal's "Ballade des äusseren Lebens",* nine lines from his "Prolog zu dem Buch *Anatol*",† and four lines from his "Manche Freilich . . .";* to the Bollingen Foundation and Routledge & Kegan Paul Ltd. for permission to the author to use her own translations of the above (though in the case of "Manche Freilich . . ." borrowing the fourth line from the version by Vernon Watkins in their editions of Hofmannsthal's *Poems and Verse Plays*); to Professor O. E. Deutsch and A. & C. Black Ltd. for permission and courtesy in making available the block for plate 4c; to Oskar Kokoschka for permission to reproduce plate 16a; to the Historische Museum der Stadt Wien for plates 5, 7, 8c, 9d, 10b, 11, 12 and 15b; to the Bildarchiv der Wiener Nationalbibliothek for plates 1, 4a, 4b, 8a, 8b, 9a, 9b, 10a, 13, 14a, and 15a, and also the engraving used for the jacket; and to Marlborough Fine Art Ltd. for permission to reproduce plate 16b.

* Copyright 1946 by Bermann-Fischer Verlag AB., Stockholm; all rights reserved by Insel-Verlag, Frankfurt am Main.
† Copyright 1946 by Bermann-Fischer Verlag AB., Stockholm.

Contents

repertory—French occupations of 1805 and 1809—submerged discontent—
music and theatre as compensation and escape—the case of the poet Franz
Grillparzer in his youth—survival of Josephinian ideas and the impact of
Napoleon—a popular hit at the Leopoldstädter Theater—disillusion and war-
weariness—sceptical patriotism—Beethoven's great years—first performance of
Fidelio—the Peace of Paris and the Congress of Vienna.

2. VIENNA BECALMED   130

Metternich after the Congress—his collaborator Friedrich von Gentz—censorship—Captain von Paumgartten and his album of water-colours—his com-
memoration of the Baumann family—Christmas, New Year's Eve, family
outings—Schubert and his circle—other musical circles—the Fröhlich sisters—
Grillparzer and Katty Fröhlich—a brilliant group—Schubert's anti-clericalism
—his intellectual curiosity and courage—his illness, death and funeral—
comparison with Mozart's—an increasing population and growing unrest—
the rôle of the theatre—the tragic life of a great dramatist and actor, Ferdinand
Raimund—and of a great actress, Therese Krones—growing police vigilance
—the political poems of "Anastasius Grün".

3. TOWARDS THE IDES OF MARCH   158

Travellers' tales of the gay city—Mrs. Frances Trollope and Peter Evan Turnbull, F.R.S.—the reverse side of the medal—overcrowding, harsh laws and
long hours—rival musicians: Lanner and the ebullient Strauss—rival actor-
playwrights: Raimund and Nestroy—Raimund and the fairy-tale play—
The Spendthrift—Nestroy the satirist and his first comedies—abuse of the
"ennobling" particle von—Fanny Elssler, Gentz's mistress and a dancer of genius
—Joseph Schreyvogel, a great theatrical producer—King Lear's impact on the
youthful Stifter—Grillparzer's plays—a disastrous première—rise of a new
bourgeoisie and new professional classes—growth of scientific research—
political stagnation and economic development—Bauernfeld the mouthpiece
of an evolving bourgeois society—his satire on Metternich's system—how the
censorship was fooled—a prophetic poem of Grillparzer.

IV. Revolution and Counter-Revolution   189

The revolutionary year of 1848—nationalist movements in the Polish and
Italian provinces—industrial unrest in the Czech regions—Vienna startles the
world—the rising of 13 March—Metternich resigns—the May revolt—the
events of October—insurgent Austria keeps faith with insurgent Hungary—
court and Government flee—short-lived triumph—retribution—an echo of
1848 in the 1920s—1848 a watershed in many lives—contrasting behaviour
of Johann Strauss father and son—undertones in Strauss operettas, Die
Fledermaus and Die Zigeunerbaron—poems and pamphlets of 1848—Ferdinand
Sauter—Bauernfeld and the demand for a Constitution—a naïve poster—his
subsequent rôle as licensed entertainer of good society—the complex case of

Grillparzer—growing Catholic influence after 1848—a revolution without leaders—the legend of the Good Emperor Joseph—Nestroy epitomises the spirit of 1848—his *Freedom in Krähwinkel* a triumphant success—his continued courage in the period of reaction—*Judith und Holofernes* an impudent skit—the young Emperor Franz Joseph—gradual easing of repression—new fortification or a new Vienna?

V. *Imperial City*

1. THE NEW FACE OF VIENNA   238

An age of rebuilding—the Ringstrasse as hub—the new Opera House, House of Parliament, Town Hall, Burgtheater, University—imitative styles—pomp and circumstance—an era of Constitution-making—political stresses—the war of 1866—a "compromise" with Hungary—Liberal reforms of 1868—compulsory schooling to 14 introduced in 1869—large-scale immigration—the young Masaryk in Vienna—Liberals and liberals—catastrophe on the Stock Exchange—unsettled economic conditions—and bad working ones—pressure for legislation—Taaffe declares a state of emergency—Vienna of a jubilee exhibition as described by Adolf Loos.

2. THE RULERS   258

The rôle of the Emperor—Hermann Broch's vision of "Vienna's gay apocalypse around 1880"—the prevalent image of Franz Joseph as an aloof, inflexible philistine—his domestic difficulties—the Empress Elizabeth and Archduchess Sophie—Crown Prince Rudolph and his political entanglements—his neurotic behaviour and suicide pact with Mary Vetsera—the Baltazzi-Vetsera clan—repercussions of the Mayerling tragedy—Franz Joseph becomes the Old Gentleman—the real man behind the mask—his *amitié amoureuse* with Katharina Schratt—Elizabeth's remarkable rôle in the relationship—her assassination.

3. NEW BOURGEOISIE AND OLD MIDDLE CLASS   281

Palais for the *nouveaux riches*—barons of finance as patrons of the arts—eclipse of the older painters—the case of Ferdinand Waldmüller—Hans Makart, the apotheosis of an age of exhibitionist décor—a typical example of his influence on interior decoration—the other stream: proud craftsmanship—the Lobmeyrs and their glassware—Bösendorfer and his pianos—his concert hall—the salon of the Wertheimstein ladies—young Hofmannsthal and his background—the rise of antisemitism—Pan-Germanism of Schönerer—the students' corps—the case of Freud's academic career reconsidered—links between Freud and the Wertheimstein circle—Theodor Gomperz, historian and philosopher—Franz Brentano, neo-Aristotelian—Ernst von Fleischl, scientist, stoic and buffoon—Theodor Meynert, psychiatrist—Victor Adler, socialist and physician—Karl Renner, future President of Austria, on the first May Day demonstration in Vienna—official panic—the career of Karl Lueger, Mayor of Vienna and admired by Hitler—birth of a lower-middle-class party, the Christian-Socials—

ambiguous rôle of immigrants to Vienna—the cult of *Gemütlichkeit* and the commercial legend of Vienna—the comedian Girardi—Vienna at the turn of the century—*art nouveau*—paintings of Klimt—essays of Hermann Bahr—the genius of Schnitzler: psychological diagnosis—the myth of *das süsse Mädel*—dissection of army mentality in *Leutnant Gustl*—of tensions caused by anti-semitism in *The Road into the Open.*

Illustrations

9(a). Therese Krones, the leading actress of Biedermeier Vienna, in her most
      famous part as Youth in Raimund's fairy-tale play *Der Bauer als Millionär*,
      first staged in 1827
      Lithograph by Kriehuber after a drawing by M. von Schwindt

  (b). The dancer Fanny Elssler
      Steel engraving by Carl Mahlknecht, undated

  (c). The actor-dramatist Ferdinand Raimund
      Drawing and lithograph by Kriehuber, 1829

  (d). The actor-dramatist Johann Nestroy
      Lithograph by Kriehuber

10(a). Franz Grillparzer, 1841
      Lithograph by Kriehuber

  (b). Grillparzer's "eternal fiancée", Kathi Fröhlich
      Water colour by Hähnisch

11.   1848: the outbreak of 13 March
      Coloured lithograph by O. Albrecht

12(a). 1848: the climax. The students' barricade on 18 May
      Chalk lithograph, unsigned

  (b). 1848: the end. Croat troops storming the main barricade in the Leopold-
      stadt suburb on 28 October
      Chalk lithograph by J. Lanzedelly

13.   The painter Hans Makart riding at the head of the festival procession
      which he designed to celebrate the silver wedding of Franz Joseph and
      Elisabeth in 1879
      Engraved from a drawing by Sigmund L'Allemand

14(a). "Makart" architecture: the pavilion and stand erected on the Ring-
      strasse for the guests of honour at the silver wedding celebrations, 1879

  (b). Ringstrasse: the new Town Hall of Vienna with the Rathauspark as
      projected in 1870
      Wood engraving by F. W. Bader

15(a). Dr. Karl Lueger, Mayor of Vienna, 1897–1910
      Lithograph by R. Fenzl

  (b). Victor Adler, leader of the Social-Democratic Party
      Coloured lithograph by Otto Friedrich, (?) 1900–05

16(a). Karl Kraus, by Oskar Kokoschka
      Undated, about 1909

  (b). Self-portrait by Egon Schiele
      Water colour and pencil, 1911

Preface

IT IS easier to say what this book is not, than what it is intended to be. Though a historical essay based on research, mostly that of others but to some extent my own, it is not a straight history of Vienna nor of Viennese civilisation. I have tried to sort out the elements that have gone into the making of Viennese society and of Viennese attitudes, the influences which helped to shape the architecture, the cultural atmosphere, and the speech of my native city. Doing this I hoped that the many lines I was drawing backwards and forwards in time, upwards and downwards at any given period, would in the end merge to form a portrait of Vienna—or at least the sketch for a portrait, with many angles traced separately on every plane.

Years ago I wrote an article about Arthur Schnitzler's prose for the *Times Literary Supplement*, and called it "Viennese Mirage", because even then I was obsessed with the way in which popular legend and poetic legend overlaid reality, and reality in its turn both created and imitated legend in the history of Vienna. Out of that article arose my first impulse to write a book about Vienna—an impulse fostered by my friend Mr. A. G. Weidenfeld, whose stimulus I gratefully acknowledge. At that stage I had in mind a book limited to the last quarter of the nineteenth century and the first decade of the twentieth, a period during which the contrast between Vienna's intellectual vigour and the disintegration of its established society became acute, with only the popular myth of a gay Imperial City, and the international fairy-tale of a Viennese never-never-land to bridge the rift. Presently, however, I found that I could not write more than glorified journalism unless I attempted to trace the origin of aspects of Viennese life and culture which are usually taken for granted as though they were immutable or a gift of the *genius loci*. I imagined that I would find comprehensive surveys based on modern research. In fact there exists no social and no economic history of Vienna. There are any number of chronicles and specialised monographs, as well as popular histories of the city, but I discovered that only the most recent monographs, a small number of historical studies, and none of the chronicles, were completely reliable in their use of the sources; not a few mistakes and misstatements have been repeated time and again. In short, I had to devise my own method to check and counter-check, and to use memoirs and literary works as evidence for the points I wished to make.

Geologists identify strata of certain periods by the fossils which are typical of them and can serve as guides. In a similar fashion, I have been using certain types of art and literature, music and architecture, politics and statistics, to bring out the character of the different phases and facets of Viennese civilisation. Indeed, for each period, individuals who have either left memoirs or about whom there is ample documentation have served me—I hope without distortion of their personalities—as incarnations, or as guides: Schubert, Johann Strauss father and son, the poet Grillparzer, young Hofmannsthal, Freud in his early career, Franz Joseph I, and several politicians are cases in point. However, I have tried to give each era the solid bones of economic and social fact, which were clothed in the soft—and occasionally flaccid —tissue of cultural life.

Among the raw material of which I have made use are my own impressions and experiences, and those of my family on both sides. This seemed to me legitimate, because my purpose was, after all, to portray the criss-cross of traditions, the influence of long-past epoch on later generations, and the way in which both legend and reality make an impact on the individual mind, so that a common attitude arises. I will not hide, however, that to some extent this book has helped me to clarify my personal development. In trying to find the roots of both positive and negative Viennese traits, in assessing our common heritage, I could not but uncover some of my own roots and realise what I owe to my heritage. In this sense, there is an element of autobiography in my book. I have also given rein to my prejudices, beliefs and convictions, but I have tried to make it clear what they are, so that any reader should be able to take them into account. It was my firm intent not to let any bias influence me in the method of my research; that one's bias influences the selection of material is inevitable, but even so I have mistrusted my own partisanship at every step and checked on it.

A great number of people have helped me by advice and criticism, whom I shall not even try to enumerate. If I have not always taken a piece of advice, I have never disregarded it. In the end the mistakes are mine, and I do not wish to spread the blame by a long list of good names. I can only thank those friends, in the hope that they will not misunderstand my not mentioning them singly as they deserve. There is one exception: I want to put on record my most sincere thanks to Professor Otto Erich Deutsch, who very kindly checked my section on Schubert, in spite of his heavy engagements, since I was leaning so much on his authoritative researches that I could not risk any factual blunders; the interpretation, however, and with it the risk of error, remains my own. In two other cases where I have had direct advice on a particular point from research scholars, it is recorded in the appropriate section of the text.

Of the many institutions and libraries which I have bothered over the years, there are in particular two which I would like to thank: the Archives of the City of Vienna, and the Austrian Institute in London. Without the help of their libraries I should have found my work infinitely more difficult. In the City Archives I was granted access to unpublished manuscripts and documents. Also, I had expert guidance in selecting illustrations at the Historical Museum of the City of Vienna. Contrary to custom, I feel that it is to the bodies rather than the individuals that recognition should be expressed, but this in no way reduces my private debt of gratitude to every single generous helper.

Finally I have to put in a plea for myself. This book, long as it is, has had to be condensed from a staggering wealth of material. Many extracts from diaries or memoirs, many episodes and, not least, further excursions into the history of the Habsburg empire, without which the rôle and problems of Vienna are so difficult to understand, have had to be sacrificed. No doubt I shall be plagued by the conviction that I have omitted the wrong guiding figure here or there. Yet on the other hand the fact that I have rarely followed through a literary career from beginning to end is not a symptom of excessive condensation: it was never my intention to write literary history. Rather I wanted to reveal the soil, milieu, or social sphere and situation, from which the contributions of Vienna to European civilisation have sprung, and so to explain the changes that have occurred.

In the end, this is no more than a "sketch" of an infinitely rich urban civilisation. I hope it is not my incurable love for my native city which makes me believe that Vienna is still important in the world of today, through all that is alive in its past, its present and its future.

I

The Casting of the Mould

DOZENS OF books have said it, dozens will say it again, but it is no less true for being a literary commonplace that the easiest approach to an understanding of Vienna is to look down on the Danube valley and round the horizon from one of the hills west of the city, and translate the message of the landscape into terms of history.

The hill may be the Leopoldsberg, the last escarpment of the range, with its steep drop to river, great abbey and famed vineyard. It was on this crest that Leopold, Margrave of Babenberg, lord of the Austrian March, built a castle at the turn of the eleventh century. Vienna—the successor to the small Roman outpost, Vindobona—was then at best a village of fishermen and vintners, but within forty years the Babenbergs made it a border fortress and their ducal residence. It became the town of Wien. Five hundred years later Vienna was the most solid obstacle in the path of the Turkish invaders of Europe. On 12 September 1683, thirty-three princes and generals in command of an international army heard Mass in front of the Leopoldsberg castle ruins before they led their motley troops down the slopes against the Turks, and broke the siege of Vienna. The Turks turned back eastward for good.

Or the hill may be the Cobenzl, a mere shoulder of the range, named after Philip Count Cobenzl who did better as a protector of Mozart than as Austrian Foreign Secretary at the time of Napoleon's rise. The Count bought the estate from the Jesuits shortly before their eclipse, and converted one of their houses into a château with a fashionable "English" park. Up there Mozart spent his last carefree days in the summer of 1781, when he had broken away from servitude in the retinue of the Prince-Archbishop of Salzburg and was about to plunge into insecurity and glory in the warren of Vienna. Much later the little castle became a hotel and was re-modelled out of recognition as a tourists' paradise, but in its terraces some of the old grace lingers, and below it the tapestry of Vienna is spread out.

Or the observation post may be the Kahlenberg itself, Vienna's domestic mountain, nearly as much part of its tradition as St. Stephen's spire, to quote a very Viennese autobiography (Rosa Mayreder's). The Kahlenberg wears its own patchwork cloak of local history. A monastery on its top was burnt by the Turks in 1683; it was restored, only to be closed by the Emperor Joseph II a hundred years later and to be sold by auction. An entrepreneur turned the cells of the Camaldolensian monks into guestrooms for sophisticates who wished to retire to a cosy hermitage and enjoy the spectacle of simpler Viennese picnicking under the beech trees. In 1795, one of the guests was the society painter Madame Vigée-Lebrun, a refugee from the French Revolution and its wars, who admired not only the vast view of the Danube with its "flowered islands", but also the taste of the old monks—and that of the great gentleman who had recommended the idyllic retreat to her. He was Prince de Ligne, the same Belgian grandee, Viennese by adoption, unsuccessful general of three generations of Habsburgs in unsuccessful campaigns, who spent his strength up to the eve of his death on coining *bon mots*, among them the over-quoted epigram on the Congress of Vienna: *Le congrès danse, mais il ne marche pas*. The Prince lived out his impoverished, brittle old age near the centre of social life and gossip, in a pink-stuccoed rococo town house overlooking Vienna's western ramparts, but had a small country place as well—on the slope of the Kahlenberg, for he was a connoisseur.

A generation later, the greatest Austrian poet, Franz Grillparzer, wrote a mediocre couplet in a friend's album, which no book on Vienna can by-pass:

> Hast du vom Kahlenberg das Land dir rings besehn,
> So wirst du, was ich schrieb und was ich bin, verstehn.

> If you survey from Kahlenberg the land,
> My writings and my self you'll understand.

This is not simply the condensation of a facile sentiment or a personal half-truth. It said something that is not easy to convey about Vienna and the Viennese. Nobody was more painfully conscious of the conflicting elements in his city and country than was Grillparzer. It shows in his fierce diaries, unpublished during his lifetime and insufficiently explored even now, and in the plays he kept locked up in his desk. He recognised the conflicts in his own complex nature, he diagnosed them in the tensions below the smooth surface of bureaucracy and middle-class comfort in which he had his share; and he saw the contrasts dissolved into the harmony he craved when he looked out over the cherished landscape.

These elements, contrasting yet fused, are still there to see from the top of the hills near the Kahlenberg.

To the south, on the far rim of the shallow basin, are Alpine peaks so distant that their grey limestone looks smoke-blue, so near that their patches of perpetual snow glitter in the sun on dry, clear days. The ancient roads to Styria, Carinthia and Italy lead in this direction. From there the leaven of Mediterranean civilisation was brought to Vienna by Italians who, once they had made their new home in the German-speaking but wine-growing town, quickened its sluggish pace. Yet there is another, more elusive message spelt out on the southern horizon: the presence of high mountains within sight is a reminder of solitude and grandeur. A glimpse of the distant Alps had the power to open a gap in the snug, smug enclosure of Old Vienna.

In Adalbert Stifter's novel *Der Nachsommer* (*The Indian Summer*), which opens in the becalmed eighteen-thirties, the apogee of Viennese middle-class domesticity, the young hero receives the impact of such glimpses long before he sets out to conquer rocks and glaciers:

At one place on the bastions of our town it is possible to see, between the trees and houses, a patch of blue of those mountains. I often walked on the bastion, often gazed at the small patch of blue. . . .

For many generations, Viennese children have had their first glimmer of great mountains—more, though, than a "small patch of blue"!— from the Kahlenberg during a tame family excursion, and never lost their longing for them.

To the south the mountains, to the east the plains. On both sides of the Danube with its islets and tangled waterside copses, the lowlands stretch eastward into Hungary, disappearing in a haze that never lifts. Out of it rose wave upon wave of invaders from Asia, Huns, Avars, Magyars, Turks, till the Magyars settled in these rich plains and the Turks were thrown back from the walls of Vienna, never to return to the attack on western Europe. Afterwards Hungary sent fat cattle, the whitest flour, strong wines and strange fish, red pepper—paprika —syncopated rhythms and eastern musical instruments, fine horses, and clans of Magyar nobles who served the Habsburgs at court, in the army and in the chanceries without turning Austrian; who built baroque houses in Vienna and dominated its high society without becoming Viennese—quite. The Danube is Europe's traditional trade- and war-route to the Near East. In Metternich's time, no more than 120 years ago, it was still a pointed joke to say that the Orient began on the other side of Vienna's last toll-gate.

North-east of the Danube—which here ploughs a straight furrow towards the south-east—lies a corn-growing plain, the Marchfeld, bounded by the faint blue line of the Low Carpathians and the Mora- vian Hills. In the Marchfeld, Rudolf, Count of Habsburg, who had been elected king of the disunited German realm by the German princes, defeated a great king of the Czechs, Przemysl Ottakar II of Bohemia, in 1278; this battle is of European importance, for it decided the future of the Holy Roman Empire—of Germany—and incidentally determined the allegiance of Vienna. (*König Ottokars Glück und Ende —King Ottakar's Fortunes and Fall*—was the first of Grillparzer's controversial "patriotic" plays which brought him into disfavour at court.) From Bohemia and Moravia peasants and artisans came to Vienna in a steady trickle, until the Industrial Revolution turned the trickle into a powerful stream. The immigrants from the Slavonic north brought with them their sly sense of fun, their fiddles, songs in the minor key, a capacity for hard work, a taste for beer and stodgy, floury dishes, the inflections of their speech, and their names.

Due west, the trough of the Danube valley is hidden by hills, up- stream from the point where the river makes a sharp bend at the foot of the Leopoldsberg and enters, divided into several arms, the "basin" of Vienna. Much that went into the making of the town—men, goods, and ideas—came down the river from the west. It was the waterway of the legendary Nibelungs and their historic counterparts, of colonising or plundering feudal lords and their followers, of priests and monks from rich, learned, civilised abbeys upstream, of the merchants and journeyman-craftsmen from Bavarian or Franconian cities who shaped the urban beginnings of Vienna. After the mid- eighteenth century, most of the students in search of public employ- ment came from inner-Austrian towns and took the mail boat for Vienna (the "water-ordinary") at the provincial capital of Upper Austria, Linz. This was the way Leopold Mozart travelled in 1762 with his two children and a piano, intending to launch the child prodigies at the court of Vienna; and little Wolfgang so charmed a Viennese customs official at the quayside of the Danube Canal by playing

a minuet on his fiddle, that the man waved the piano on through
the toll barrier. A very different kind of music was imported into the
capital by the boatmen who took huge rafts down the Alpine tributaries
of the Danube and the Danube itself, with timber for the buildings and
firewood for the households of Vienna: the stamping whirling dances
of their mountains, out of which the waltz evolved on Viennese soil.

The hills that hide the upstream valley from sight are a barrier, not
only against north winds but also against traffic. The old pack roads
had to skirt them on either side, and only small hamlets and scattered
cottages subsisted in the quiet valleys between the endless woods. From
the tapered spur of the Leopoldsberg-Kahlenberg, beech-grown ridges
fan out and curve south-west along a level plain until they meet the
chain of the Alps, whose last eastern foothills they are. All this is the
Wienerwald, the Vienna Forest or, better, Viennese Wold, usually
mistranslated as Vienna Woods. No other part of the chequered landscape has had so great an influence on the imagination of the Viennese
as the Wienerwald on their doorstep.

The city lies between the Wienerwald slopes and the Danube. At
least the older part of the city does, and only the modern industrial
districts have spilled across the main river on to the dusty, windswept
plain to the north-east. This is the plain where Napoleon lost his first
battle to an Austrian army led by the brilliant Archduke Charles, at
Aspern in 1809; whereupon he fell back on Vienna which his troops
already occupied, won the campaign and the peace, and in due course
married the Austrian Emperor's coy, foolish daughter, Marie Louise.

The Danube gave Vienna its strategic and commercial position, and
its links with West and East. It was turned into a vastly different asset
when the Viennese legend of the Imperial City on the Danube began to
grow, especially after Johann Strauss the Younger, by picking a catchy
title for a beautiful waltz, had turned its yellow-green waters into
magical blue, the blue we all have seen in rare flashes on enchanted
autumn afternoons. But the Danube has never been to Vienna what the
Thames is to London, the Seine to Paris, the Tiber to Rome—or the
Danube itself to Budapest. It does not flow through the city. No one
would have thought of building the houses of the great along its banks.
Old Vienna developed south of the southernmost arm of the river (it
was to become the Danube Canal), on a useful waterway, but far from
the devastating floods on the main bed. Fishermen would bring their
boats to the foot of a steep staircase leading down from the ramparts;

their coveted freshwater fish would be taken to markets within the
walls; but larger boats did not enter the narrow channel. Their
passengers had to disembark higher upstream and pass through all the
cordons of safety before reaching the town proper. So it was during the
centuries of Vienna's growth, and so it was still under Metternich's
régime: long enough to have contributed to the peculiar insularity of
the Viennese, to their conservative self-sufficiency, and to their addiction to the hills rather than the plains on the far side of the rivers,
whatever the landscape of their origin.

The oldest core of buildings, the *Innere Stadt* or City, was crammed
into the area constricted and protected by the town walls. It still shows
a tight cluster of church towers, domes and ornamental roofs round
the tall gothic spire of St. Stephen's Cathedral. The old city borough is
hemmed in by a wide boulevard further widened by many public
gardens; it is surrounded by a double horseshoe of boroughs, and the
opening of this horseshoe is barred by a stretch of the Danube Canal
and a densely populated island opposite. The inner zone of this double
belt is formed by the ancient *Vorstädte*, the *faubourgs* or suburbs—I
use this English word with reluctance because of the associations and
connotations it has accumulated—which developed between the
inner and outer lines of fortifications. The outer zone is a looser girdle
of equally old, originally rural parishes—*Vororte*, the different term
indicating a status different from that of a *Vorstadt*—long since engulfed by industrial and residential settlements, some of them truly
"suburban". They reach into the foothills of the Wienerwald, into that
semicircle which swings away from the Danube and leaves a wedge of
flat ground between itself and the river.

Many years before factory districts and the vast municipal cemetery
pushed forward into that bleak moorland where the winds from north
and east never cease, Vienna began to enclose the eighteenth-century
"summer" mansions of the aristocracy outside the city ramparts in a
network of countrified middle-class houses and to creep up the lower
steps of the Wienerwald hills. Yet even now spinneys, meadows,
lanes, and vineyards tilted to catch the full force of the sun, break
through the furthest edge of urbanised villages or colonies of villas,
and peter out lower down between the dusty streets. About 1820, when
Beethoven, Schubert and Grillparzer went hunting for summer
quarters in those old villages (they seem to have preferred low whitewashed houses curtained by twisting vines), the fields reached down as

far as the Line Wall, the outer fortification built in 1704 at the request of Prince Eugene of Savoy, to protect at least the suburbs, though not the more exposed outlying villages, from marauding Hungarian insurgents. In those years the view from the Kahlenberg would have shown—as paintings and drawings of the eighteen-twenties do—a town pattern not unlike a dartboard or rifle target: the walled city as the bull's eye; around it a green band, the ramparts converted into promenades, and the Glacis, the broad stretch of open ground below the walls, tied together by a short loop of the Canal; a wider circular zone—if one took in the island opposite the city, to complete the horseshoe to a ring—where houses were massed between spoke-like arterial roads but broken up by the green patches of parks and gardens; around it the narrow ribbon of the Line Wall, no longer a fortification but a toll and police boundary; then a wide belt of fields and vine-yards, merging with barren land to the east and south-east, but richly cultivated on the lower slopes of the curving hills, and in each fold or valley a village round a rustic, whitewashed church with an onion-shaped steeple; and finally the great sweep of the woods. The pattern is thickly overlaid by now, but it is still there underneath the sprawl of houses and streets.

As a child I thought of the landscape and the parks of Vienna as mapped out by wild flowers and trees. I still do. On the limestone cliffs of the south-eastern Wienerwald ledge grew black pine and tufts of the crimson spring heather (*erica carnea*). In the short sweet grass of its steeply sloping heaths bloomed strange orchids, bee-orchids, snake-orchids, and a sulphur-yellow wild rose, less lovely but more exciting than briar or dogrose a month later. And at Easter the pasque-flower opened its silky petals. I knew the exact spot on Perchtoldsdorf Heath, where the darkest purple, almost black blooms hid themselves.

Before the vineyards near the Kahlenberg showed the first leaf, the grass verges of their paths were lined with the tiny suns of coltsfoot flowers (but it was no good picking them, they folded up at once), and peach and apricot trees planted between the vines cast a pale pink veil across the gray or rust-red soil. Before the pointed leaf buds unfurled in the beech-woods higher up, further west, primroses and lavender-blue liverwort (*hepatica*) pushed their posies through last year's dry leaves.

In June, a marshy meadow by a small stream deep in the hills stood knee-high with glistening yellow globe-flowers (*trollius*). Under

certain clumps of silver poplars in the wilder part of the Prater, close
to a rookery, snowdrops and starry blue scillas flowered a few minutes'
walk from the old tram terminus, near an ancient hunting pavilion of
the Habsburgs called *das Lusthaus*, the Pleasance. The first horse-chest-
nut tree to light its white chandeliers stood not, as other people said,
in the great avenue of the Prater, but behind the yellow wall of the
Convent of Salesian Nuns, in front of a verdigrised baroque cupola.
The very first March violets, blue and white, opened at the foot of
clipped maple hedges along the formal parterre in the park of Schönbrunn Palace; but the old park-keeper had to turn his back before one
dared pick them.

North of the Danube, facing the Leopoldsberg across the river, is a
low whale-backed hill, the Bisamberg, where the alien flora of the
Hungarian plains had planted their vanguard, cushions of short-
stemmed iris (*iris pumila*) in purple, pale yellow, and creamy white;
later in spring you might find a few lady's-slipper orchids, such as grow
high up in Alpine clearings, if you knew the secret places of the Bisamberg: Alpine and Sarmatian flora met on that lonely, unbeautiful hill.

Not many Viennese children can have grown up so much in love
with flowers as I did, but all must have seen the public gardens and
parks of Vienna overhung with lilac and golden-rain—laburnum—in
the last days of April and first days of May, their stronger tints repeating the colours of a Wienerwald spring: blue, white, purple and gold.

The first painting I ever coveted was Ferdinand Waldmüller's
"Early Spring in the Wienerwald". At six, I was too young to know,
or care, that Waldmüller was the strongest of the early nineteenth-
century painters of Vienna—an imaginative naturalist. (His studio oils
of landscapes around Vienna are filled with a warm golden light, but
he also painted the most sombre of Beethoven portraits; and a likeness
of his wife in a sweetly pretty off-the-shoulder dress shows not the
simper à la mode, but the ruthless beauty of a mature woman.) I saw
"my" picture on a rainy Sunday morning when I could not play in the
wet sanded walks of the Belvedere Park and my father took me to a
gallery of nineteenth-century paintings then lodged in the Lower
Belvedere. The Wienerwald picture bewitched me with its lacework
of leafless branches against a bright windy sky, and with the pale
bunches of primroses breaking through dry coppery beech leaves. I
didn't like the village children in the foreground—in which I was right,
because they are coy. But for years I longed to be able to paint bare

branches with the delicate firmness of Waldmüller. All I dared paint with my water-colours were insipid primroses. Yet between the Wienerwald and its glistening image, my taste in landscape painting was committed for a long time, for better or worse.

These childhood fancies have no significance beyond the personal, except as an example of the influence the landscape of Vienna can have on its addicts. To each it speaks in a different language, but—whether they realise it or not—it is part of all their lives. It doesn't even matter whether they enjoy it or not. In every big town, different quarters breed different outlooks, and the distance from the open country has definite psychological effects. In Vienna it is not so much the distance from the open country as that from the Wienerwald which matters. When I grew up I was to discover with a shock, and with a sense os guilt, that the workers of the new eastern and southern factory beltt hardly ever took their children to the woods on Sundays, because if seemed too far and was too expensive for them. Those east of the city would most often picnic in the coarse grass of the inundation area along the Danube, those of the outlying southern districts on plots of waste ground near disused clay pits and brick kilns, where the eternal winds blew gritty dust on their sandwiches. However, it may have immunised them, to a certain extent, against the mawkish Viennese sentimentality which flourished best in the old suburbs and one-time villages near the hills, near the vineyards, and near the traditional wine-gardens.

For half a century the combination Vienna-Wienerwald-Wine has been so glaringly exploited by the tourist trade and the musical export industry that it has become even more suspect, at least in the eyes of those who refuse to fall for it, than it was while it was designed mainly for home consumption. In innumerable songs, more or less familiar place names (e.g. Prater, Kahlenberg, Grinzing, Sievering, Nussdorf, and above all the name of Vienna itself) are brought in to evoke idyllic memories, while the mention of spring is supposed to create a mood of sweet sadness, that of wine one of rakish gaiety. For listeners who know neither the places nor the taste of the local grapes, a lilting tune in waltz-time sets the appropriate mood. For instance:

> Im Prater blühn wieder die Bäume,
> In Sievering grünt schon der Wein . . .

> In the Prater the trees are in flower,
> At Sievering the vineyards show green . . .

which ends on the triumphant line:

> Und Frühling ist's wieder in Wien!
>
> And springtime is back in our Wien!

or the tipsier one:

> Ich muss wieder einmal in Grinzing sein,
> Beim Wein, beim Wein, beim Wein . . .
>
> I've got to be back in Grinzing again
> With the wine, the wine, the wine . . .

And, of course, the ubiquitous, vulgar and irresistible

> Wien, Wien, nur du allein
> Sollst stets die Stadt meiner Träume sein . . .
>
> Wien, Wien, you, only you,
> Shall be the town where my dreams come true . . .

Here, as in the first quotation, I have replaced the correctly English Vienna, which is used in broadcasts, on records, and no doubt in printed translations, by the native name of Vienna, *Wien*. The reason is that the long monosyllable Wien, pronounced Veen, plays a fatal rôle in such rhymes and rhythms. Rhymable as it is, and capable of being made to fill a whole 3/4 bar (perhaps with quivering violins as a background), the sound seems to have had an irresistible attraction for writers of popular songs in the German language, an attraction scarcely attributable to the corresponding "Vienna". The few genuinely lyrical lines built round the sound as well as the image of Wien— they do exist—defy translation into English because of the discrepancy of stress and tonality. (After all, the word-sounds *Paris* and *London* have each created their distinctive rhyme or verse pattern, of which "Sous les toits de Paris" and "Billy Brown of London Town" are trite examples. And the sound Wien in Viennese dialect, spelled "Wean" and too hard to convey to an English ear, produced in its turn different rhymes, styles and rhythms—because it has no long-drawn single vowel.) In short, the way in which the sound of Wien has been applied in a spate of songs, for more than 150 years, has contributed to the legend, to the myth, of a dream city called Wien and existing in Never-Never-Land. It has affected—but this is another story—the image the Viennese themselves wish to have of their Wien. Hence this digression.

The modern songs of Wien and Wine are mostly cheap and cloying, and when their vogue began they were not much better. Still, when the layers of sticky sentiment are scraped off, there remain one grain of irreducible fact and one grain of irreducible feeling, which survive any dosage of acid or caustic. Both fact and feeling are nearly as old as the hills on which they grew.

The plain economic fact is that the vineyards in the lee of the Wienerwald were of the greatest importance for Vienna's everyday life, from the earliest beginnings—modern scholarship has established that vines were grown there even before the Roman legionaries introduced their more refined stock—up to the transformation of Older Vienna into Old Vienna in the course of the eighteenth century. In 1524, a charter of Archduke Ferdinand called wine "the principal nourishment of the city of Vienna" and recast ancient regulations of wine-growing and wine-trading. At least a quarter of the property-owning citizens grew their wine in vineyards outside the town walls; most of them pressed their own grapes, stored the wine in deep cellars of their town houses (these cellars influenced the technique of building), sold it in bulk to foreign merchants, in retail to any comer—and drank it. All sovereigns of Austria protected and controlled the Viennese wine industry as a prime object of taxation. Imports of wine from other Austrian regions, let alone from Italy, Hungary or Spain, were restricted to a minimum; for centuries beer-brewing was prohibited within the city, and at all times licences for either beer-brewing or the sale of foreign wines were rare and very expensive.

Any society of wine-growers and wine-drinkers will develop particular habits, cookery, singing, jokes, social codes and tempers, a rhythm of life and use of the seasons unlike those of a beer- or spirit-drinking community. Customs of a strictly practical origin will be handed on as unquestioned rites and hallowed traditions, and largely survive the conditions whence they have sprung. Something of this kind happened with the vinous part of Viennese civilisation. As long as the vineyards were cultivated around and between the *Vorstädte*—the last suburban vineyard was registered till the end of the eighteenth century—the interest of the Viennese in the quality of the new wine, the *Heurige*, was matter-of-fact. It was no more than natural that the pleasantest, most popular wine-gardens were set up in the wine-growing villages outside the Line Wall, near the edge of the woods and in the garden or yard of the vintner himself. There they stayed even

when the vineyards began first to shrink and then to disappear; they
became stations on the roads into the Wienerwald. And in still later
years, the cult of the Wienerwald and the cult of drinking new wine
under spreading walnut or chestnut trees merged.

A little water-colour by the Viennese painter Moritz von Schwind
(see Schwind's ink-and-wash cycle *Die Lachner-Rolle*, Munich, 1862)
catches the spirit of that time of transition. Painted thirty-five years
after the incident, out of Schwind's memories of his early youth, and
far from his native town, it inevitably romanticises reality, but this
makes it an even better illustration of my point. The scene shows Franz
Schubert and two others in a Grinzing wine-garden: a bower-like vine
trellis, a small table with three glasses and a flagon; at the back, rising
from a fold between the vineyards, the village church of Grinzing with
its bulbous steeple; the line of Kahlenberg and Leopoldsberg, with its
abrupt drop from castle ruin to river, cutting across the sky and the
sinking sun; at the table the painter's three intimate friends, the
conductor Lachner, the playwright Bauernfeld, gayest rebel in Metternich's Vienna, and Franz Schubert in full face, round and tubby, his
hair in untidy tufts. It is very peaceful, as if floating in the warm air of a
summer evening.

This small water-colour is already part of the legend of Wien and
Wine, such as it was when the genuine feeling underneath was not
excessively tainted by false sentiment, and before it was commercialised. Sentimental the feeling certainly was, and nostalgic for a youth
which in retrospect appeared simpler than it had been, as anybody's
youth is apt to do at any time, in any place. What is important,
however, is the ageless quality of that feeling, and its share in the
reality as well as the legend of Vienna. It has little to do with wine-
drinking as such, though it encompasses the pale heady wine grown on
the slopes where town and countryside meet. It has everything to do
with the fusion of hill, town, river, plain, woods and houses, which stirs
the imagination. Not for nothing have so many Viennese writers,
whether Viennese-born or Viennese-made, tried to make others see
what they had seen when looking down on the city from a Wienerwald ridge. And this did not start with the self-conscious and nature-
conscious nineteenth century either.

Outside the fields of music, landscape gardening, and possibly the
more intimate type of architecture, the eighteenth century was more
unlyrical in Vienna than elsewhere. It produced no poet worth the

name. From my fairly comprehensive reading, I have retained no more than three lines of verse—and their subject is the view of Vienna from a hill.

Their author was a man of letters under Maria Theresia and Joseph II, by the name of Michael Denis. He was a kindly Jesuit and teacher at the *Theresianum*, the Theresian College for Young Noblemen. After the dissolution of the Society of Jesus and the temporary closure of the college, Denis lived quite happily as a librarian, freemason, and self-appointed "bard". He published a much read and indeed readable translation of "Ossian", which found only too many imitators in Germany; dedicated pompous Latin odes to the Empress; and would have been even more thoroughly forgotten than he is, had not Mozart tried to set an ode of his to music and mentioned the fact in a famous letter to his father, in 1782:

I am busy with a very difficult job, the music for a bard's ode on Gibraltar, by Denis. . . . The ode is magnificent, beautiful, anything you like, but too high-falutin for my finicky ears. But what can you do? The golden mean, the true essence in everything, is no longer known or appreciated. If you want to be applauded you must write stuff either so easily intelligible that any fiacre coachman can catch and sing it, or so unintelligible that people like it precisely because no sensible person would be able to understand it. . . .*

All the same, the highfalutin bard Denis once wrote a poem entitled "On Looking down on Vienna from a Hill behind the Village of Ottakring", in which he apostrophised the town:

> Wie glühet deiner Türme Gold,
> O Vindobona, durch die Schleier
> Der leichtgeschürzten, blauen Luft . . .

> Your golden spires, how they glow,
> O Vindobona, through the veils
> Of this blue, lightly-gathered air. . . .

This passage seems to me memorable for the sake of a single descriptive word—which I have not been able to translate adequately. It is the word *leichtgeschürzt*, "lightly-gathered" in my dull version. The German epithet, very much a word of rococo letters, belongs to

* This letter is included in Mr. Eric Blom's selection *Mozart's Letters*, Penguin Books, pp. 204–5, but I have used my own translation. The letter has long been famous. In 1842, Grillparzer quoted Mozart's two sentences about the golden mean and the need to write "stuff", etc., with the introductory remark: "It has been the same at all times"—a consolation intended for his own benefit.

shepherdesses, nymphs, and the gayer muses; Thalia, the Muse of Light Comedy, is called *die leichtgeschürzte Muse* in an outworn tag that was fresh once. Thalia was seen as gaily and innocently wanton, not dressed in flowing garments with austere folds like her graver sisters, but showing dimpled knees under coquettishly tucked-up skirts. That Michael Denis, worthy poet laureate and ex-Jesuit, should have thought of this image in describing the air of Vienna—that he stood on a hill overlooking Old Ottakring (long since swallowed up by a busy working-class district), saw the light draperies of clear, soft air veil and unveil the gilded spires of the walled town below, and invented this *leichtgeschürzte, blaue Luft*—all this says much about his Vienna.

Fifty or sixty years later, under Prince Metternich's tutelage, the Viennese cultivated the virtue of quiet respectability and arranged the surface of their existence as though they were painting a likeness of their orderly living-rooms on the surface of a mirror, in the then modish technique. Beethoven and Schubert were dead. The freakish Grillparzer was silent. The censorship was effective. A younger generation was trying to escape from the beaten track, though not yet into a new awareness of reality. Adalbert Stifter, a student from a village on the border of Bohemia and Upper Austria, dreamed of becoming a great landscape painter rather than a sensible minor civil servant. He fell in love with Vienna; in later years, in Linz, he was to feel exiled from it as from his spiritual home. When he started to write, he poured into these first literary efforts his pent-up romantic longings and the exact detail his painter's eye had observed. One of those early short novels, *Feldblumen* (*Wild Flowers*), is written in the form of letters from a young painter who lives in Vienna, in an attic room somewhere outside the ramparts. He describes what he sees from his window in spring, 1834—and indeed there exists such an oil study of suburban roofs, clouds and light by Stifter:

To the south, small puffs of clouds are gathering, with the sweet colour only spring can give; the metal roofs of the town shine and shimmer, and at times a distant flock of pigeons cuts white wheeling curves into the blue. . . .

He walks in a public pleasure ground on one of the town ramparts, the Paradise Garden, and looks into a convex mirror set on a stand:

Part of the town, and the green trees and the rose parterre in front of it, and the rings of the suburbs, are caught in neat smallness, swimming in a kind of sombre dusk through the black of the looking glass. . . .

He takes a walk in the fields just outside town and suburbs, under a bright, cloud-flecked April sky:

... the brooding spring warmth aquiver on the bare black fields—between them the beautiful green strips of winter corn—and then the dun and russet woods on the hillsides, and everywhere people in their finery walking on the fallow. ...

Franz Schubert had felt the same glad tenderness when, on a June evening of 1816, he had gone for a walk with his brother and found the green fields outside the toll-gate of his suburb very beautiful. "In the uncertain twilight ... my heart warmed within me", he wrote in the diary which he usually neglected, having other means of expression than words.

Michael Denis, or Franz Schubert, or Adalbert Stifter—and how many more greater and lesser names—it was always the same response to this union of landscape and town. Literary or intellectual fashion has had scant influence on this feeling. The words which writers of different generations chose to express sensations they shared with less articulate people show surprisingly little variation even if the style betrays the period.

Stifter, for instance, was under the spell of the German proto-romantic Jean Paul when he wrote *Feldblumen*, as much as he was under the spell of the Viennese atmosphere. Somewhere in the story he sent his other self, the painter, to a small village in the heart of the Wiener-wald, sat him at a wooden table in the shade of beech trees, a few dry biscuits and a bottle of Nussberger at his elbow, green-gold flashes of sunlight in his eyes, the not unpleasing noises of other trippers reaching his ears from the nearby inn; and then Stifter made the young man write an intense letter to his friend:

... Or I chose a night to climb one of Vienna's western hills, and saw the dawn rise over the big town: first a faint strip of light unfolding in the east, white fog banks glimmering along the Danube, then the town lifting out of the night haze in massed bulk, partly set aflame, partly still struggling with a sombrely golden, billowing smoke, and the whole prospect strewn with gold stars that sparkle from windows, metal roofs, steeples, lightning rods, while out there on the horizon a pale green ribbon gently, softly draws its gossamer across the sky.

Arthur Schnitzler was the novelist—and satirist—of the sophis-ticated, doubt-ridden intellectuals before and after the turn of the last

century, seemingly worlds apart from Adalbert Stifter. But Schnitzler
was a Viennese. In his novel *Der Weg ins Freie* (*The Road into the Open*,
1908) he too sent his protagonists on walks in the Wienerwald, just
beyond the margin of the town which had climbed up the slopes in
the meantime. Inevitably, what they saw was in its essence the same
picture their predecessors had seen; but they also felt essentially the
same, and this was not inevitable:

From the wood-clad ridge to the left came no shade yet, only a mild breath of
air that had been asleep among the leaves. On the right, the green slope
descended to the long furrow of the valley where roofs glinted through tree-
tops and branches. Across the valley, behind garden fences, vineyards and
arable land led up to pasture and to quarries overhung by glistening bushes and
shrubs. At the far end of the valley the view was blocked by meadows and
wooded heights, but the mirror of the air reflected a message of new valleys
and hills in the distant dusk. . . .
They looked down across the city, to the plain where vapour rose like an
exhalation and the river ran its shimmering course, to the faraway mountain
ranges veiled by a delicate haze. . . .

This is not a set piece of description inserted in the novel to counter-
balance an intricate psychological plot and the portrait of an over-
ripe urban society. It is necessary because it belongs to the lives of
Schnitzler's modern, citified human beings, even should they choose to
destroy their own mood by a tart joke before plunging back into the
coffeehouse fug. It was no great distance, either in miles or in sentiment, from the path called Sommerhaidenweg (a charming name:
Summer Heath Lane) which was the favourite walk of Schnitzler's
unheroic heroes, to the hill above Old Ottakring where Michael Denis
had snatched at a draught of air to carry into the stuffy cubicle of his
verse. Nor, for that matter, was it far to the small stream at Heiligenstadt where Beethoven conceived the Pastoral Symphony, listening to
the birds in old walnut trees without quite hearing them.

From Beethoven to Sigmund Freud there were many who rebelled
against the complacent lethargy of only too many Viennese—and not
all were born elsewhere like these two—but even the rebels surrendered to the Wienerwald. Which meant that it helped them to stay
and work in Vienna, to be at home there in spite of themselves and
others, because it would have been impossible to draw a sharp dividing
line between the town and its landscape.

The surroundings of Vienna are not the only reason, nor are they the main reason, why so many uprooted or restless people from outside made Vienna their adopted home; rather, it has been the city's specific mixture of national and cultural ingredients which favoured such a "naturalisation". All the same it was that other mixture, that of town, suburbs, villages, wooded hills, plains, river and distant mountains, which by providing imaginative outlets saved not a few from a sense of claustrophobia and isolation. Johannes Brahms is a case in point. When he settled in Vienna in 1865 he was a mature man; he never lost his Hamburg accent; yet he came to feel as though he were Viennese. Of course Vienna was to him the "sacred city of musicians", and it was the memory of the great composers who had lived, worked and died there, as much as hopes for his own future, which drew him to the town. Still, his friend and biographer Max Kalbeck thought that Brahms made up his mind in favour of Vienna among various possibilities, because it offered him the attractions of a big city, a small town (in the suburbs), and the loveliest open country in one.

These were intellectuals, artists, men of genius. But what about the masses of people who came to Vienna to find work, and had to live in a mean tenement, or in a backyard room of a small, untended suburban house? And what about those born in a dark narrow street, growing up in one of the old inner boroughs or in the near-slum of a decaying residential quarter? It is, and always has been, fatally easy to surround the existence of artisans and labourers in Old Vienna with an idyllic halo, for no better reason than that they could drink their glass of wine, if any, somewhere near a wood, or at least near the tall poplars of the Prater, and because they too could walk on Sundays in the park of Schönbrunn, or the hills near Grinzing and Ottakring, or the willow copses along the Danube. Yet they could, and did, do one or the other of those things, and it made a difference, in spite of the dark shadows that fall on the bright picture.

Even newcomers in the factory zone quickly took their pick of the existing habits, if or as far as their working hours and wages allowed. Those who stuck to beer and a beer-garden, whether out of preference or because it was nearer and cheaper, instead of sampling the local wine in one of the old *Heurigen* wine-gardens as the elder artisans would, tended to feel disprivileged or scornful. In most cases, however, the tradition of evenings under trees, from spring to autumn, and of Sunday picnics in the grass, set a pattern, or at least the pattern of an ideal. Where it survived the years of industrial expansion and crude exploitation, it delayed the development of a slum atmosphere. To be robbed, say by Sunday work, of something that was considered a birthright of the Viennese, was felt to be an enormity, even by workers who were neither Viennese by birth nor traditionalist by inclination. Later, when time for leisure had been won for industrial workers by their trade unions, the old pattern still influenced the use of free time at weekends. The good-natured gaiety of Viennese crowds at a fair or in a dance hall, commented upon by foreign visitors ever since the early eighteenth century, has always had a rural, open-air tinge. I also believe, though this could hardly be proved, that it was the Wienerwald habit which saved the average Viennese from wanting to spend his holidays (once paid holidays for wage-earners became law) in an overcrowded "resort". There is no parallel to Blackpool or Brighton for the Viennese, and not only because there is no coastline. . . .

A nineteenth-century writer on Old Vienna, Wilhelm Kisch, censured the common people for all wanting to go holiday-making to the country, in the decades following the revolutionary year of 1848, but even he admitted that they at least dispersed decently to small villages and farmsteads. Generation after generation, groups of friends and young couples had wandered off the road, along quiet paths and through unfenced woods of the Wienerwald. The taste for independent pleasures, tempered by the enjoyment of company, survived for a long time after the advent of popular mass entertainments, because its roots were old and tough. It is hard to say whether these roots are quite withered by now; they may not be. And until it became industrialised, the music that went with it all was neither loud nor shrill.

There exist in German literature two endlessly quoted poetic definitions both of which use a classical metaphor to attack the self-indulgent, unintellectual habits of Old Vienna. One is a distich by Schiller, in which he lets the River Danube say:

Mich umwohnet mit glänzendem Aug' das Volk der Phäaken.
Immer ist Sonntag, es dreht immer am Herd sich der Spiess.

Round me abide with lustrous eyes the Phaeacian people.
Ever is Sunday, the spit turns without cease on the hearth.

The Phaeacians, the people of King Alcinous and Princess Nausicaa, are the friendliest, most hospitable and most human crowd in the whole

Odyssey, if great gourmands and gourmets, but the educated Viennese resented Schiller's sally (more so as he had never been to Vienna), and earnest souls have argued against it ever since. The hint that the Viennese only know how to eat and feast, but not how to think and work, has rankled, foolishly but understandably.

The second classical quip occurs in a poem by the eminently Viennese Grillparzer. Before his journey to Greece in 1843 he wrote a poem entitled "Abschied von Wien" (Farewell to Vienna). In it he called his native town the "Capua of the mind". In Capua, Hannibal's soldiers lost their fitness for battle because they let themselves be seduced by the town's soft beauty and rich pleasures. Grillparzer felt, or wished to feel, that, if he had ceased from mental strife and let the sword sleep in his hand, it was because his creative energies had been numbed by the enchantment of the Viennese air. His criticism of the town, as a cloak for self-reproach, was far bitterer and more ambiguous than Schiller's quick, unsubstantial epigram. Since I am unable to translate Grillparzer's poem into English verse and rhyme without turning his poetry into quarter-poetry, his quarter-poetry into padded prosiness— some of those simple rhymes fall flat even in the original—I transcribe it here in undisguised, almost literal prose:

You are beautiful [Grillparzer addresses Vienna], but dangerous too, for the pupil as for the master. Your summer air saps strength, you Capua of the mind. Soft it is to tread your ground, and hills and forests spread about you a magic land through which the waters glide. Music all round, as when the choir of birds wakes in the trees. One does not speak, one scarcely thinks, and feels what is half thought. And then your people: staunch of heart, with healthy commonsense, they have wreathed truth's image with fairy tales and jests. One lives in a half-poetry, dangerous to whole art, and is a poet though one never dreamt of rhyme or stanza. But since, where all is full of beauty, we have but to breathe, we forget to exhale again what has swelled our hearts: tablet and canvas stay empty. Away, then, from your confines, to see whether through the stress of travel firmer images take shape.

Twenty-one years earlier, in 1822, when he was at the height of his fame as a dramatist, Grillparzer had quoted in his diary from a letter of the German historian Johannes von Müller, written in Vienna in 1793: "I have never been in a place where I was so little known, so incapable of working and—forgive this mystical expression—so spiritually fettered—I should be quite unable to do my writing— and yet so *content*." To this extract Grillparzer added: "This is how every literary man is bound to feel in Vienna, and the marvel of it is that one really feels content, perhaps not with one's self, but with the town and its people. They have a kindliness and warmth which command love. They do not admire and praise all the time, one is pestered with few literary importunities, and if they are lacking in education, it is all the rarer to meet with mis-education or over-education."

This sounds too good to be true, too like the later legend of Old Vienna and the Heart of Gold of the Viennese. Also, it is a period piece. In France, the post-rationalists admired the noble savage; in Vienna of the Romantic era, his place was taken by the unspoilt native, the simple man of the people. Grillparzer, whose sharp sardonic eyes saw much to displease him in the higher spheres and his own social group, longed to find the virtues of the Age of Innocence in "the people". Such an interpretation of motive does not however invalidate the judgement itself; a similar reaction to the Viennese was much too widespread to be glibly dismissed. Even a sober, dour man like Mozart's father wrote in 1762 to his Salzburg correspondent: "Are all people who come to Vienna bewitched so that they have to stay here? It rather looks like it." And his son was to stay in Vienna in the teeth of petty misery and constant irritation, as though both the good and bad qualities of the Viennese were necessary to him, and the city the best of all his possible worlds.

Some of it may have been that "blue, lightly-gathered air", the atmosphere in both meanings of the word. Yet it was the living organism of the city, and the individuals who were the "people" of Vienna, whose way of existence provided the recurrent pattern of disenchantment and enchantment.

What had made the Viennese what they were—and are? Here is the core of the matter, difficult of approach. At best it is possible to identify the main elements that went into the making: the fusion of ever shifting national groups in the urban melting-pot; the border fortress confronting the East, belonging to the West; the centuries-old tradition of living at the centre of political storms, as on an island with precarious privileges; the anti-heroic object lessons of long-drawn battles of conscience throughout Reformation and Counter-Reformation; the disruption of a rising middle class on the verge of social, intellectual and economic expansion; the crippling of municipal freedoms, and in exchange a rich mess of pottage, the patronage of an international court; finally, the need of living one's private life fully under the permanent pressure of external insecurity.

Mediaeval Vienna developed on the site of a Roman camp, at the point where the transcontinental route from north to south, the ancient Amber Road, crossed the Danube. There, German, Slav and Magyar cultures touched, with an older Celtic stratum deeply embedded underneath. From all these separate worlds, and from Italy, Vienna drew not only people but, as I have mentioned before, customs, ideas, musical rhythms and mental associations. The main Viennese stock was of German-Austrian origin, coming from the hereditary Habsburg dominions (Lower and Upper Austria and Styria in the first line), but there was also immigration from Bavaria and Franconia. From the sixteenth century on, the typical Viennese surnames speak of peasant or at least country connections. To the group of German surnames there were added, over the centuries, others: Italian, Czech, Polish, Croatian, Hungarian, and (from about 1775) Jewish; together with a sprinkling of French, Belgian, Dutch and Greek surnames. The non-German immigrants came in increasing numbers, though in shifting proportions, and the list echoes the historic fluctuations of the Habsburg empire and the changes in Vienna's European status. On the other hand the names of aristocratic families with town houses and "summer" mansions in the outlying boroughs point the story of the Habsburg court's ramifications, political, diplomatic and military. And the names on more recent electoral rolls of wards and districts give a broad indication of the parochial mixture, social structure and industrial history of each urban sector.

The cliché of the melting-pot is as true of Vienna as of London or New York, but for Vienna it has been true over many more centuries. The ingredients of the mixture have changed periodically; the fact of the mixture has been constant. It has turned the city into a unit radically distinct from the surrounding country with its blocks of homogeneous population. This may well be the principal cause of the Viennese brand of insularity: the people of the town defended, as it were, their island of cosmopolitan civilisation against the tides from the peasant countryside. Behind the ramparts of the old fortress and, when these had been razed, in the houses, streets and suburbs of the expanding city, the second generation of immigrants would turn Viennese, occasionally with a sense of rebellion against the milieu or its traditions, more often accepting them comfortably, adopting the current dialect and subtly changing it with new words, accents and jokes. In self-defence such new citizens tended to reinforce the common feeling that Vienna was unique, a closed world of its own.

This small world was for many centuries set apart in another sense as well. Vienna was the eastern frontier fortress of the Holy Roman Empire—of the community of German states—and through it of western Christian civilisation. It was always the first important German-speaking town to be harassed by invaders from the Orient who had overrun the Hungarian plains. And once the Crusaders had passed Vienna on the overland route to the East, they also left behind them the world in which their code was accepted. It was entirely within that code, which admitted ransom, greed and diplomatic treachery, that Richard Cœur-de-Lion was imprisoned by a Duke of Austria.

To be citizens of a frontier fortress was a double-edged privilege.* Such as it was, however, it dominated the material existence of the Viennese from an earlier stage onward, for more generations, and with profounder psychological effects (acceptance of insecurity and built-in defences against it) than the fact that the Habsburgs set up their residence in the castle built by their predecessors in Austria, the Babenbergs. Vienna remained the foremost fortified town of the "Austrian March" from the twelfth to the beginning of the eighteenth century, when Prince Eugene of Savoy still found it advisable to build his additional Line Wall; that is to say, for about six centuries. During the greater part of that long stretch of time it was also the seat of a ruling prince who was often not only a Habsburg but also German emperor; but it was not always, not uninterruptedly, the capital of a great realm, let alone an empire.

It is wise to establish this, because the tag of Vienna the Imperial City, the Emperor's Own Town, is not only a powerful myth but at the same time an important truth for certain periods of history, a misleading slogan for others.

* In June 1546, Emperor Ferdinand I wanted to raise more money for the fortifications of Vienna because of the constant Turkish threat. His letter-patent argued flatteringly: "Considering that Our City of Vienna is almost a frontier town against them (the Turks) . . . and that Vienna is important and precious not only for the hereditary dominions, but for all Christendom and the German Nation . . .", and ended by decreeing a collection in the churches for the organisation of which the clergy were responsible. The Emperor's own exchequer was empty. (*Quellen zur Geschichte der Stadt Wien*, Part I, vol. 5, p. 104, Act No. 5351.)

As long as the hereditary dominions of Habsburg were ruled by different branches of the dynasty—till the end of the fifteenth century and then again for some time at the end of the sixteenth century—each Habsburg prince had his own capital, though Vienna was the most coveted prize. (Those princes had the title of duke until the Emperor Frederick III, father of the more famous Maximilian I, raised all members of his house to the rank of Archdukes and Archduchesses.) In the thirteenth century, Przemysl Ottakar II, King of Bohemia, resided in Vienna and was acknowledged as sovereign by the Estates of Lower Austria. In the fourteen-eighties, Matthias Corvinus, King of Hungary, occupied Vienna and established his cosmopolitan court there. Charles V, the Habsburg who ruled over his "empire on which the sun never set" from Spain unless he was on the move, and who was by language and education a Fleming, left the Austrian dominions to his Spanish-bred younger brother, Ferdinand. Ferdinand, who was not made welcome by the predominantly Protestant burghers of Vienna, moved his court and administration for years to a small town at some distance, Wiener-Neustadt—though it was the scorned greater fortress that had to hold and deflect the first, dangerous westward thrust of the Turks in 1529. Even when, after Charles V's death, the imperial crown fell permanently to the younger, Austrian branch of the House of Habsburg, it was not invariably Vienna, exposed, unruly and heretical, that was chosen as residence. The strangest of the line, Rudolf II, a mystic and alchemist, set up his court at Prague where the Luxemburg emperors had resided before him. In sum, throughout those centuries Vienna was not yet the proverbial *Kaiserstadt*, the Imperial City, but it was irrevocably and ceaselessly the fortress on the border.

Only when the Turkish threat receded at the end of the seventeenth century did the Habsburgs settle finally on Vienna for their court, administrative centre, and capital. Only then occurred the identification of their dynasty with the city, which was to play so great a part in the minds of later Viennese generations and in the world's imagination. And yet even then the city was the capital only of the Austrian provinces, not of the German Reich—which had no capital proper. When a Habsburg was elected emperor (this was the rule, but with an exception for the time between 1740 and 1743) Vienna was indeed his capital and residence, with all it entailed in prestige, diplomatic and commercial advantages, and economic burden. But the Reich, the Holy Roman Empire, was fast becoming a powerful political shadow, more than fiction, less than reality. It had no central government, administration, bureaucracy, judiciary or standing army. An Imperial Vice-Chancellor had his office and staff attached to the court and acted as the emperor's intermediary with the Estates of the Reich. This loose diplomatic link meant little in Vienna's everyday life. It was more important that noble Catholic families from every principality of the empire sent their sons to serve their greatest patron, the emperor, as courtiers, diplomats or soldiers—Metternich was one of the last of that stream. Some built sumptuous houses in or near Vienna, but left in due course for their family estates; others were absorbed and assimilated by the city. It influenced Vienna's social life, but scarcely added to its importance in German affairs. Even as the capital of the vast Habsburg realm Vienna was neither the richest nor the most important German-speaking town, though the largest and at times the grandest of them all. It remained tucked away, so to speak, on the margin of the German-speaking countries, it was cut off from their old cultural centres by distance, customs barriers and censorship policy, and yet it was the true centre of the multi-lingual Habsburg domains. Even while the emperor in the Vienna Hofburg, the Palace, wore the crown of "the Holy Roman Empire of the German nation", the city was more open to Italian and French influences than to German. This showed, and still shows, in the vocabulary and inflections of Viennese speech.

Throughout the late Middle Ages Vienna, like any other mediaeval town, was ruled by patrician burgesses, merchants and craftsmen. As long as the court was no fixture, few noble families had any incentive to build houses for their permanent personal residence inside the city walls. About 1550, only twenty-two are on record as having done so. Nor were there many of the higher clergy. Until 1480, Vienna had no bishop of its own, but belonged to the Bavarian see of Passau. Wealthy abbeys and priories owned large tracts of real estate in the city, freed from billeting duties and taxes which ordinary citizen-house-owners had to bear; the abbots or priors themselves, however, resided in the country. (An interesting exception was the ancient foundation called the *Schotten*—because of the Irish monks, or Scoti, who had established it—with its right of asylum and highly influential grammar school.) The hierarchy of the Church was not top-heavy in Vienna in the Middle Ages.

Such a social structure should have favoured urban self-government, but it failed to ripen. Vienna never (that is, with the exception of forty years when the privilege existed on paper only) attained the charter of civic autonomy of the type called *Reichsunmittelbarkeit*, which was granted directly by the emperor, by-passing the territorial sovereign— hence the German term, literally: Reich Immediacy. In this respect it was to the disadvantage of the city that its own territorial sovereign was no other than the emperor, most of the time. The history of Vienna's city charter is one of gradual retraction. Freedoms were granted or withdrawn, but over a longer period always reduced, in accordance with the part its leading citizens played in the many internal feuds of the Habsburg princes. Whenever an elder and a younger son of the House fought over the succession to the dukedom of Lower Austria, or a regency, both would try to enlist not only the Estates of the "Land"—their Diet had its seat in Vienna, the natural centre of the region—but also the city council which held the heaviest purse. This infallibly led to conflicts among the citizens, in which the dynastic and feudal issues barely overlaid clashes of interest between landed burgesses and newer guildsmen, or statutory citizens and lesser townsmen. Loyalty to the Habsburgs was, to put it mildly, fluctuating.

The town's civic position and civic pride suffered rather than gained through that series of struggles against different members of the House of Habsburg. Mayors, aldermen and councillors who supported one side would do so in the name, and occasionally even in the cause, of their city's freedoms; the most independent champions ended on the gibbet or an executioner's block; some made good martyrs, and in the liberal era of the nineteenth century their careers furnished the raw material for some bad, well-meaning local novels. But there were many recantations, much changing of sides, an endless confusion of loyalties; they created no great tradition.

These continual small-scale civil wars—which merged not infre- quently with external wars against the neighbouring states of Hungary and Bohemia as long as these were still independent—did considerable damage to Vienna's trade and its value as a trading post. Time and again, when commerce had suffered too badly, wealthy staplers from Germany had to be lured to Vienna by the grant of privileges which benefited the sovereign's exchequer but incensed the native Viennese merchants, and increased their inbred weaknesses. Only the wine industry, the vineyards and vines themselves, survived upheavals without major crises. Yet the guilds stagnated, printing developed tardily, the start of new crafts and manufactures was cut short more than once by war or the threat of war. The Turks first besieged Vienna in 1529, but the hundred years preceding their invasion had been overshadowed by the Turkish menace. The astonishing thing is not that Viennese civilisation developed fitfully, but that it developed so richly after all.

By the beginning of the sixteenth century a fairly homogeneous middle class, a *Bürgertum*, under the leadership of merchants had emerged and with it, as elsewhere, the spiritual unrest of the age of Humanism. It was a shortlived flowering, but a flowering it was, extending to the arts, to letters (somewhat more timidly), and to the refinements of life. The university—the second oldest in the Holy Roman Empire, thanks to the initiative of a gifted Habsburg prince, Duke Rudolf IV—attracted eminent scholars and young, lively students from abroad. St. Stephen's cathedral was magnificently completed. If lack of funds stopped the construction of the second great tower, the single tall spire seems today the only imaginable solution to Viennese eyes.

The standard of living must have been high. In spite of financial bloodletting through the unceasing loans and contributions for wars, Vienna lived well before and after the Turkish siege. Chroniclers of the times praised and exaggerated, or else, with a different bias, they censured and exaggerated, the worldly pleasures of the people and the luxury which wealthier citizens flaunted in their stone-built, glass-paned houses—then mostly of one or two floors with a gable, an indication that they could afford to be sole occupiers of their houses, though they had to put up with the court's right of billeting soldiers and other personnel. Overcrowding was not yet disastrous: the old maps and plans show that there were many small gardens left within the town walls.

"Bread is cheap, the meat, beef as well as veal, excellent, and there is wine in abundance, though dear," a Venetian envoy reported in 1528. In 1548, not quite twenty years after the Turkish siege, a teacher at the Benedictine *Schotten* grammar school named Wolfgang Schmeltzl put primitive statistics into doggerel verse: there were seventy-odd butchers (in a town of 1,200 houses) who dealt weekly with 300 bullocks, 800 calves, 1,000 sheep and 100 pigs; turnips, cabbage, lettuce and horseradish were on sale; 180 cartloads of river crayfish were sold daily during the right season. The dark side of the picture comes out not in these songs of praise with their whiff of primitive "hand-outs", but in the documents of the first Turkish siege which tell of the stampede of the court, the great and the rich, of muddle, hunger and demoralising despair. Contemporary descriptions of Viennese good cheer and of the underground city of wine cellars—"more buildings down below than above ground", as Hans Sachs the Master-Singer said in an obsequious homage—were copied many times and re-written with suitable adornment. This image was dominant for a couple of centuries, till the time of Schiller's dig at the "Phaeacians".

It was a frequent and popular device of sixteenth-century writers to describe the huge meals and extravagances of European capital cities, but the accounts of bucolic, gluttonous Vienna stayed in the imagination of posterity beyond and above many others. Because they were well founded in fact? Or because there was something unusually suggestive about them? Possibly. The more complicated their existence, the more the Viennese seemed to cling to the small, accessible pleasures of life. It came to be ingrained; it had a flourish to it—panache. To outsiders it may have appeared a piquant, noteworthy trait, especially while the story of Vienna's unlikely defence against the Turks was in circulation. Also, there were soon tragically few things to report on the cultural life of the city.

The disruption of the Viennese middle classes began almost immediately after their rise. It filled the sixteenth and seventeenth centuries. By the time of the second Turkish siege, in 1683, it was an accomplished fact. What had been a town dominated by the social groups of merchants and burghers interconnected with the gentry, and by the guildsmen, with an unruly intellectual life centred in the humanist sector of the university, was transformed into a city in the hands of officials directly or indirectly depending on court bureaucracy, and dominated by a powerful aristocracy. There were fewer houses and more palaces, fewer men of letters and more clergy than there had been at the beginning of the period. And no heretics were left. Or so it seemed. For this profound transformation of Vienna's whole structure was entirely bound up with the cold and hot wars of Reformation and Counter-Reformation.

When Archduke Ferdinand, brother of Charles V and favourite grandson of King Ferdinand of Aragon, left his Spanish homeland to take over the succession to the Austrian hereditary dominions, he clashed immediately with rebellious, predominantly Lutheran Vienna. The rebellion was led by the solidly Lutheran gentry of the Lower

Austrian Estates and by the City Council; it was directed against
encroachments on their self-government, borne up by the newly found
assurance of a rising social class, and stiffened by the discovery of a so
far unexplored freedom of conscience. The political mutiny was soon
crushed. This marked the virtual end of the City Charter of Vienna:
the beginning of municipal administration by officialdom. About the
same time, an insurrection of the Castilian Estates, of old and new
forces, was suppressed in Spain, yet the resistance of the *Comuneros*
lasted longer and violence was more brutal on both sides. In Austria,
Ferdinand began to organise his modern bureaucratic machine from
small, fortified Wiener-Neustadt where he felt less exposed to the
Turkish threat and somewhat removed from the pressure of his greatest
city. Ferdinand, who was also heir to the two kingdoms of Hungary
and Bohemia, thanks to the dynastic marriage contracts engineered
by his grandfather Maximilian of Habsburg, and who became Emperor Ferdinand I after the abdication of his brother Charles, was not a
bigot but a practical politician, not unlike his Aragonese grandfather
Ferdinand, and willing to make concessions to the Protestants if and
when it was unavoidable; among the Spaniards he had brought with
him were men touched by the humanist reform ideas of Erasmus of
Rotterdam. Yet both the prince and his Spanish advisers had, after all,
been trained in a country where even then the Inquisition was busy
stamping out the Erasmist influence together with all bolder heresies.
In 1527, an edict of the sovereign made it illegal for citizens of Vienna
to be witnesses in court, to establish a business, to make a valid last
will and testament, or to enter into an inheritance, if they were
Protestant heretics. In 1551 Ferdinand called the Jesuits to Austria and
installed them in Vienna. The battle between the sovereign and the
Estates was joined in Austria, as all over Europe. But, interlaced with
it, the battle for the religious and spiritual allegiance of Vienna had
started.

It lasted almost exactly a century, and it is my contention that the
experiences of that period had a decisive permanent effect on what is
called the Viennese character.

An essay in the interpretation of Vienna's civilisation, reality and
legend, has small room for details of remote struggles. But to the
people whose whole outlook was being twisted, pulled and hammered
into new shape, everyday details must have mattered at least as much
as explicit doctrines. The behaviour of leaders, the careers of converts

and re-converts, the price of strongly held convictions and, by contrast, that of prudent conformism: it is legitimate to assume that such was the substance of countless cautionary tales passed on from generation to generation, until the stories were forgotten while their impact remained, working in devious ways. No counter-tradition developed. Those who refused to give up or to hide their faith were not allowed to stay on in Vienna to embody heroic loyalty in the face of ruin.

There are recent examples to show how it would have worked. It is enough to look at post-Civil-War Spain. A thoroughly defeated libertarian mass movement leaves behind a thick sediment of cynicism and opportunism, covering a passive resentment which will dissolve into small-scale gestures of self-liberation without risk—in all but the small, dedicated minority groups.

This applies to Vienna for the long period of Reformation and Counter-Reformation. There had been a Protestant mass movement; it had had a libertarian tinge like any other Protestant movement in its early stages, and it had kindled hopes of an egalitarian freedom among the "lower orders". Among the first heretics to be burnt were, as elsewhere, Anabaptist preachers: "agitators".* These socially un-settling currents were most relentlessly squeezed out, so much so that evidence is scant and elusive. The mass movement as a whole was defeated and suppressed. It took more than a century, but defeat was complete: it sounds improbable that a mainly Lutheran Vienna ever existed, so triumphant is the legend of an innately pious Catholic population. Yet the tell-tale residues are there, and they are more easily accessible than the buried facts.

In my childhood and youth two idiomatic phrases were current, which used to puzzle me on the lips of staunch Viennese Catholics.

* The first Protestant with Anabaptist leanings was burnt in Vienna in 1524; he was followed by a famous preacher and his wife in 1528—a time overshadowed by the Peasant War of 1525 with its social-religious movements. In the second wave of persecution, directed against the Moravian Anabaptists after the crushing of the "communist" theocracy in Münster, twenty-three of the brethren were burnt, beheaded or drowned in Vienna. One of them escaped together with his wife during a fire, thanks to the help of a Viennese citizen—evidence of an undercurrent of sympathy. Also, the Chief Magistrate of the city pleaded with his superiors for a release of the prisoners who should only be expelled from the country. But Ferdinand I's decrees held good. See Adolf Mais: "Gefängnis und Tod der in Wien hingerichteten Wiedertäufer" in *Jahrbuch des Vereines für Geschichte der Stadt Wien*, 1963/64, pp. 87–182, which contains some texts of hitherto unpublished documents.

One, denoting exasperated impatience, ran: "*Das is ja zum Katholisch-werden!*"—That's enough to make one a Catholic! The other was a threat usually addressed to naughty children by a cross old nurse-maid: "*Wart' nur, ich werd' euch schon katholisch machen. . . .*"—You just wait, I'll make Catholics of you yet. I thought for a time that these phrases were off-shoots of modern popular anti-clericalism. I was wrong: they were much older. Rosa Mayreder, a Viennese born in 1858, mentions in her autobiography *Das Haus in der Landskrongasse* that her old family retainer would threaten the children with the same formula. "To make a Catholic of you" meant a severe beating. The author adds: "It seems to have come down to us as a relic of the Counter-Reformation, and the late descendants found the procedure of being turned into Catholics no less painful, on a small scale, than their forebears had done on a large scale."

When Ferdinand I set to work in 1527, with his ordinances, man-dates and letters-patent,* with executions and with missionaries, all social strata of Vienna were considered Protestant in their majority, but most conspicuously the upper classes. At least there exist docu-ments to prove it, while the lesser fry were inarticulate, and not caught in the net of official records. Most of the landed families, two-thirds of the nobility and gentry represented in the Lower Austrian Estates, and at least the same proportion of Viennese burghers, most of the privileged German staplers, and not a few of the educated clergy were Protestant or advocated a church reform on near-Lutheran lines. As long as the Protestants were entrenched in councils and corporations they could counter the pressure of the officials now moving into administrative posts. But as this bureaucracy increased its hold on municipal affairs, as jurisdiction was taken from the city magistrates, and as the university was purged of Lutheran influences, the counter-moves of the town council became more and more ineffectual.

The reigning archduke and his officials, not the citizens, operated the customs barriers, external and internal. Very soon after Ferdinand's arrival in Austria, booksellers were subject to heavy punishment if they had heretical literature on sale. Their stocks were confiscated. Contact

---

* For instance, 31 March 1528: "King Ferdinand I ordains, since the corrupting condemned doctrines, sects and opinions are increasingly taking root and prevail-ing, to institute a general visitation and investigation in Lower Austrian territory." K.K. Archive for Lower Austria, Act No. 5254, quoted from *Quellen zur Geschichte der Stadt Wien*, Part I, vol. 5, p. 88.

with the intellectual currents of the outside world was interrupted. Then the struggle was concentrated on education. A score of private Protestant schools sprang up, supported by patricians, the gentry, and the Estates. Those who could afford it sent their sons to the university of Wittenberg, Luther's university. But the Jesuits soon proved successful with their first two educational ventures, a free school and a boarding school for the sons of the nobility. When in 1578 all Lutheran preachers and teachers were banned from the city, the Jesuits were left in the field to instruct the youngest generation.

Later Catholic chroniclers told atrocity stories of Lutheran mob rule in Vienna: the faithful beaten up in taverns—priests prevented from saying Mass on weekdays—journeymen blasphemously insulting the Holy Host—no citizen free to take a Catholic as his servant—and so forth. Much of it may have happened. The strong social-revolutionary undertow in early Protestantism emerged here and there in Vienna too, even though the notion that evangelical freedom implied other freedoms as well was soon driven underground. Probably the moderate Lutherans, good substantial citizens, were shaken by any danger sign of rioting, much as Martin Luther was appalled at the great German peasant revolt. Law and order, represented by the Most Catholic Emperor and his officers, must have had a strong appeal for the luke-warm. Others followed the lure of German principalities with a Lutheran prince, where faith, fortune and career could be pursued in excellent harmony. The emigration from Vienna began. It waxed and waned, and waxed again, in step with the power of the Lutheran Estates; but in the long run it drained away the richest, the economically most active and the independent-minded among the new middle-class citizens.

In 1577, there were only two Catholic members among the twelve who formed the Inner Council of the city. Then Archduke Ernst, the regent of Lower Austria, increased his pressure by exercising his prerogative of endorsing or vetoing nominations; and one year later the Protestants were in a minority of five, although the larger Common Council and the city judiciary were still Protestant almost to a man. The next turn of the screw came in 1579. The government decreed that Lutheran city councillors had to recant or be dismissed. If the council had been a shadow before it now became a mere decoration. In future anyone applying for full citizenship (which entailed the right to own houses within the city walls and to belong to a guild) had to take an oath on the orthodox articles of faith. Lutherans could no longer obtain academic degrees. Upon this there followed a mass demonstration in front of the castle, but a riot was averted—characteristically—by temporising. In Vienna (though not in the provinces) the ceaseless skirmishes with the Turks across the border had caused successive Habsburg rulers to go slow with their anti-Protestant measures; several archdukes and at least one emperor, Maximilian II, inclined towards Lutheran beliefs; the engineers of the Counter-Reformation employed highly successful Fabian tactics, with hideous executions thrown in as a deterrent now and then. After the near-riot of 1579, five leaders, all well-to-do burgesses, were sentenced to death, reprieved, and banished. There was no rioting in protest. The Lower Austrian Estates, i.e. nobility and gentry, carried on their fight against the central authorities in both the religious and political field; the Lutheran merchants of Vienna were still strong enough, with the backing of the Estates, to circumvent many of the anti-Protestant measures. Yet among the lesser townsmen the war of attrition began to tell.

The archives of Lower Austria, explored by the Catholic priest and historian Dr. Richard Matt, have yielded two clumsy but moving appeals to the emperor by a Viennese tradesman who had been expelled from the city for having embraced the Lutheran creed (the "Augsburg Confession"). Caspar Huethofer, unable to find a place to settle and ply a trade, was doomed to beggary with his wife and children, and asked to be allowed to return to Vienna or at least to become a citizen elsewhere. His cry for mercy was turned down twice: "Refused"—"Earlier decision stands". This was, no doubt, a commonplace story, one that served as an object lesson to others. It is part of the background to the statement of another historian, Professor Grete Mezenseffy, that by the end of the sixteenth century Archduke Ernst had "accumulated experience in Vienna on how to deal successfully with a civic community which, though refractory, was not determined to the utmost".

Social conflicts were widening, and they split the ranks of the Protestants. In distant valleys of the Wienerwald and in the Alpine dukedoms, peasant risings were endemic. Within twenty miles of Vienna, peasants rose, first to drive out their parish priests, then to sack churches and monasteries, finally to attack manors. While their "army" was liquidated by a posse of soldiers mustered partly by the

Estates and partly by the sovereign, the Viennese burghers—just then claiming recognition as a fourth estate—kept their peace, though they had tried to mediate at first. Several peasant leaders were executed in the main square of Vienna; and the townspeople stayed quiet. The provost of the chapter of St. Stephen's organised the compulsory conversion of the surviving insurgents; his commissioners were successful. A few years afterwards, in 1597, labourers in the wine-growing villages south of Vienna (the same places where the *Heurigen* idyll is cultivated even now) massed together, refusing to work for last year's wages. They were also accused of being heretical rebels, and it is not unlikely that they were readier to defy the established order because of their new faith, which some of their social superiors wanted to take from them. The Englishman John Ball may have been the first to use the revolutionary jingle:

> When Adam dolve and Eve span,
> Who was then the gentleman?

Its German version, however, ran with a threatening rumble through every abortive peasant movement; the greatest Catholic preacher of Vienna, Abraham a Sancta Clara, still quoted it a hundred years later, though in a different spirit. The strikers near Vienna were promptly rounded up by a task-force of gentlemen and lords of the Estates, supported by a company of soldiers. A few were hanged on the spot, about fifty were taken to Vienna as prisoners to do forced labour on the new town moat. Once again the town stayed quiet. Too many citizens, of whatever denomination, were worried about the rising labour costs in their own vineyards, which were particularly precious after the imperial decree which forbade a conversion of arable land into vineyards, so as to keep down the price of bread cereals and the wages of vineyard labourers. Thus the vintner villages were quickly pacified, and the Protestant nucleus of the city was more isolated than before.

When the Thirty Years War began, in 1618, Vienna was by no means a Catholic town yet, though it had become very difficult for all but the most resolute Protestants to give their children religious tuition, while the Jesuits had made inroads through their schools and at the university. Yet the landed upper classes, organised for political action in the Estates, were again on the move and had wrung concessions from the Emperor Matthias; the Viennese merchants and tradesmen, a number of court officials, and, at the other end of the scale, groups of journeymen, were pressing for freedom of worship. The bewildering series of imperial decrees and mandates had not succeeded in breaking down the resistance of that refractory community, but it had produced evasions and unheroic devices galore. Among the last wills of Viennese citizens preserved from the years between 1578 and 1627, few risk an open declaration of Lutheran faith, but nearly half express their allegiance through bequests, legacies and turns of phrase—"Christian" standing in for Lutheran, for instance.*

One of the side-issues settled in the Thirty Years War was the long-drawn struggle between the Lower Austrian Estates and the sovereign. The central power won, though centralisation had to be shelved in favour of a loose form of regional self-government. Nobility and gentry lost their privileges of religious freedom. Those nobles who submitted, and above all those who served the emperor unswervingly during the war, were rewarded, not only by confiscated estates in the country (especially in the kingdom of Bohemia whose rebelling aristocracy had been virtually wiped out in the battle of the White Mountain), but also by real estate inside Vienna.

When the emperor Matthias was succeeded by the notoriously bigoted Ferdinand II, Protestant members of the Lower Austrian Estates refused to swear allegiance to him, preferring Frederick V of the Palatinate, the champion supported by the Bohemian nobles. Some, though not many, of the Viennese citizens followed their lead. It was first against the rebels, and not against the religious aspect of their rebellious attitude, that the new monarch took severe measures, even before the decisive battles in Bohemia were fought. Again, the non-Catholic part of the population was thrown into confusion. The emperor had a powerful ally in the selfish but human wish of the Viennese to be spared destruction; only the staunchest fanatics could want the town to be conquered by the emperor's Protestant enemies. If the multi-national imperial soldiery was bad, the Hungarians and Swedes might be worse. . . . In fact, the war moved up to the ramparts of Vienna only in the last stage of the thirty years. This gave the two Ferdinands, Ferdinand II and Ferdinand III, a long period in which to

---

* Dr. Richard Matt has examined these last wills and other documentary evidence in his unpublished thesis of 1935 (MS. at Vienna City Archive), which exists in a slightly condensed version in print, *Mitteilungen des Vereines für Geschichte der Stadt Wien*, vol. 17, 1938, both under the title *Die Wiener Protestantischen Bürgertestamente*, 1578–1628.

fulfil their Catholic mission. Even under the confusing conditions of war, and in an already demoralised community, it was not an altogether easy task.

First the estates, and in Vienna houses and vineyards, belonging to "rebels" were confiscated and sold; in the case of commoners, mostly rich merchants, heavy fines were imposed as well: the war was costly and the exchequer needed the money. Within a few years the economic power of the landed gentry of Lower Austria and of the rich merchant class of Vienna was broken. A change in house ownership began, which altered the social pattern of the city. Houses and housing sites were given to loyal aristocrats such as the Liechtensteins, or to religious bodies; others were bought by officials, and by a new type of merchant, purveyors to the armies, who made a fortune out of the war. The tradesmen and craftsmen, bereft of their former leaders, were submitted to sharper regulations. In 1623 a decree ruled that non-Catholics could neither be made citizens nor appointed to any civic post. In 1624 older bans on visits to Protestant chapels outside the city gates were renewed and made more stringent, not without provoking protests from the Estates and from the journeymen. In 1625 the Town Council, by then an obedient tool, decreed that all citizens had to profess their Catholic faith or emigrate. All inhabitants of Vienna had to accept religious instruction within four months, or else they would lose all their goods, trades and means of subsistence. They had, however, the right to sell all their possessions if they refused to be converted and were therefore obliged to leave. The great turnover of houses began, and so did the exodus. When all had settled down again, in 1633, the direction and administration of the university of Vienna were handed over to the Jesuits, together with the censorship of books.

It is impossible to say how many emigrated. The marginal entries of a Viennese tax official in a register of tenants who had failed to pay their taxes for 1625–29 list about 150 names of absentees: Lutherans who had gone away, openly or secretly. More than 100 men and women from Vienna turned up in the Regensburg district alone, according to the registers for the pertinent period. Dr. R. Matt, who gives these details, also examined the old municipal accounts to assess the sums of "exit money", i.e. of the payments of 10 per cent on all liquid assets, which every citizen had to make before his departure. To take two years only, the sum total in 1624 was 133 florins; in 1625, 24,446 florins. At the peak of the emigration well over 1,000 families left in a single year.

And they were families of moneyed citizens who took nine times as much with them, out of town and country. The purely financial loss Vienna and Austria suffered through the success of the Counter-Reformation was devastating; it was to affect the development of Viennese trade and industry and, more important still, the city's social fabric. But the loss in human substance was irreparable.*

One of the most revealing individual cases was that of Helmhart von Jörger. He was the lord of the castle and village of Hernals—now a crowded urban district of workers and small shopkeepers, among whom there is a strong Catholic tradition—including large, nearly unspoilt stretches of woodland on the Wienerwald slopes and many popular *Huerigen* taverns. In Helmhart's time Hernals was far away from the town, and under his jurisdiction as lord of the manor. He was a member of a powerful Protestant family, a rich man, owner of houses in the "Noblemen's Quarter" of Vienna, and a leading member of the Lower Austrian Estates. It was he who gave sanctuary to a famed Lutheran predicant from Swabia when no other was left in the district, and it was to his chapel in Hernals that the most stubborn Lutheran townsmen walked, rode or drove every Sunday in the teeth of the authorities. In 1620 the Jörgers were among the Protestant noblemen who refused the oath of allegiance to Ferdinand II, and were outlawed for high treason. Helmhart's fief fell back to the realm, his property was confiscated, and he had to flee the country, though he was able to return years later.

At the point where Helmhart II, Freiherr von Jörger, disappears from the Viennese scene there begins the major shift in house property which is bound up with the triumphant Counter-Reformation, the result of forced sales, confiscation and imperial favours, and which made the rise of aristocratic Vienna possible.

The Hernals estate and Jörger's own town house were both given to the Church, Hernals to the chapter of St. Stephen, the town house to the abbey of Kremsmünster. The abbey sold the house with its annexes, and it became one of the sites bought two generations later by noble-

---

* My personal opinions are bound to affect my interpretation of the facts. Yet an Austrian traditionalist who by no means shared my bias, my late friend Dr. E. H. Buschbeck, said in his valuable study *Austria*, London, O.U.P., 1949: "The number of those who preferred emigration to recantation was enormous; and it was the staunchest and most upright elements who chose exile rather than submission. Austria has probably never quite repaired this loss, it has left deep and permanent marks on her character."

men in the ascendant at court. Without mobile real estate in the hands of ecclesiastic bodies, the immense architectural change from narrow, gabled middle-class houses—*Bürgerhäuser*—to baroque mansions would have been slower and even more cramped in space. Citizens living in their own houses were loath to sell them, preferring to add new storeys and let apartments. Jörger's private catastrophe contributed, ironically, to the pomp and power of Vienna's Catholic aristocracy, deployed towards the turn of the century.

The former Lutheran church in the castle of Hernals became the centre of religious stage-management at its theatrical best. After it had been reconsecrated in the presence of court and emperor, the chapter of St. Stephen decided to build next to it a Holy Sepulchre on the model of that in Jerusalem.

A *via crucis* with seven stations was mapped out, starting from the door of St. Stephen's, passing through the city gate near the *Schotten* Abbey, leading to Mount Calvary and the Holy Sepulchre in Hernals. The city corporation paid for the first station, the others were built out of pious contributions. Every Friday before Palm Sunday, a penitentiary procession went from the cathedral to its goal in St. Bartholomew's Church, as it came to be called. Lay organisations called confraternities, a mediaeval tradition now refurbished by the Jesuits and giving the Viennese an outlet for their hierarchical ambitions, soon turned these processions into macabre carnivals, so that they had to be banned for some years, until shortly before the Turks burnt church and calvary during the siege of 1683. Later the *via crucis* was rebuilt with a more bizarre calvary, by the Brethren of the Seventy-Two Disciples, a suburban confraternity. The pilgrimages on penitential Fridays continued, but in the nineteenth century they acquired the atmosphere of tumultuous fairs, the taverns being too near. Still, the Hernals *via crucis* which had replaced the Protestant highroad was genuinely popular. It was in its baroque beginnings an offshoot of that strange Catholicism for the people and by the people, which filled the emptiness—not, I think, so much a spiritual emptiness as one of emotion and imagination—left behind by the slow crushing of Protestantism in Vienna.

It is impossible to doubt that the Jesuits were the main architects of this transformation. Between the years 1624 and 1627 they bought a dozen houses—apparently of Protestant absentees or exiles—to build their church next to the university. And as early as 1623 (according to

Dr. R. Matt) their other establishment in the heart of the city reported 2,200 brought back into the fold of the Catholic Church, among them 536 inside the walled city. Apart from the higher spheres of court society and bureaucracy they were most successful among the poorer population, among those who must have felt abandoned or tricked by the Protestant gentry and patricians, and saw at close quarters the unedifying spectacle of prospering converts. The Jesuits had mastered the mental idiom of the Viennese. It might also be said that Vienna domesticated their zeal. This shows best in the propaganda weapon they developed, the school drama enacted by their pupils. At its height, Jesuit dramaturgy included in the Latin text broad farce in the vernacular: all impeccable intention and doctrine, but also good fun with a double bottom. On the other hand the Jesuits dropped the idea, imported from Spain, of propagating flagellantism which failed to catch on. Also, such fanatics as they met or trained were better employed in pious witch hunts, at least during the decades after the expulsion of the Lutherans when heretical ideas lingered on.

For the Viennese were not the adaptable turncoats of another, darker version of the legend. In 1633 the Bakers' Guild listed the Viennese master-bakers in town, with riders on whether not only the master but also his family had duly returned to the Catholic faith. It turned out that twelve out of sixty-three families had emigrated, and that of the remaining fifty-one, eight had among their members one or more who were not yet Catholic, mostly because "the wife didn't want it".* And in 1630 an official was ordered to search for "non-Catholic persons" still living, illegally, in the town. The Emperor himself complained in a letter that only a few had submitted to his intentions, while the rest stayed stubborn and "reckless".

A tiny hard core survived even under the nose of the court (more remained here and there in the country), and secret Protestants used the privileged staplers as a cover for generations, until Joseph II's policy of religious tolerance made secrecy unnecessary. Then a surprising number of Lutheran sympathisers emerged from the dark. But in the meantime all the aristocratic families once leading the rebellious Protestant Estates had recanted, the Starhembergs, the Khevenhuellers, and even the Jörgers. In Vienna and its suburbs the flickering sparks of nonconformity died from lack of air; all was quiet

---

* Heinz Zatschek's research on the Bakers' Guild in *Jahrbuch des Vereins für Geschichte der Stadt Wien*, vol. 9, 1951.

on the intellectual front. The Jesuits were shaping the minds of students and scholars, the budding jurists, administrators, teachers, courtiers and priests. There were always exceptions, even at the court itself, but those were Protestant loyalists, prudent people. Merchants and tradesmen were subdued, made dependent on the official network. At worst they may have grumbled in the style of John Donne's London citizens, who, however, belonged to the beginning of the seventeenth century, and to a richer, expanding society:

> Our onely City trades of hope now are
> Bawd, Tavern-keeper, Whore and Scrivener.
> The much of Privileg'd kingsmen, and the store
> Of fresh protections makes the rest all poore. . . .

Indeed why should the Jesuits have whipped up Catholic fervour in Vienna, risking to cross the safety limit beyond which thought begins to move in unexpected directions?

It was neither a Jesuit nor a Viennese-born, but an Augustinian friar from Swabia who castigated the Viennese for their lax frame of mind, and recorded their modes of existence such as they really were underneath the conformist behaviour. He was Pater Abraham a Sancta Clara. When he came to Vienna in 1662, at eighteen, he was not yet ordained; when he died there in 1709 he was more Viennese than any Viennese, a preacher and a poet, the only strong, clear voice in that barren stretch of time.

There were few things from music to the Great Plague, from coffee-houses to the habits of young noblemen, about which Abraham a Sancta Clara did not vociferate, often in rough rhymes. His vigorous homilies, however, sprang from a current that ran counter to Jesuit opportunism, counter to the aristocratic code even then imposing itself. He was a belated humanist, and a satirist with a great love of life, but also with a burning concern for the souls of his people. What I have read of his works has left me with the vivid impression that among the ordinary Viennese at the end of the seventeenth century there were two tendencies at work which defied their spiritual advisers. One was an almost pagan enjoyment of every sensual pleasure, whether food or fine music, a Punch-and-Judy show, the spectacle of a religious procession, or the game of love. It was an attitude of "let us eat, drink and be merry, for tomorrow we die" with a vengeance. The burden of individual responsibility before God and one's own conscience, which

Protestant teachers had laid on the shoulders of their pupils, had been lifted from the Viennese; it was as if they had been glad to surrender all responsibility for their consciences to the new instructors. Yet a popular Catholicism without a strong sense of guilt and sin is an unorthodox thing. It seems to have anguished Abraham a Sancta Clara as a priest, even while it appealed to a lusty element in his own being.

The other tendency was a sly distrust of all authority and all heroics, so strong that it bordered on anarchism. Behind it lay not only the experiences of three or four generations with a succession of lip-servers, turncoats and spurious converts, but the much older legacy of the border fortress: a familiarity with civic muddle, military blunders, weakness of rulers, with camp-followers and racketeers, half-victories, half-defeats, and with the willy-nilly toughness of those not important, rich or lucky enough to get away from dangers.

When the Turks encircled Vienna with a network of trenches in 1683, and those inside the walls battled without the arms that should have been there, it was once again an experience of mixed courage and muddle; the great ones of the realm, with one notable exception, had escaped in good time. When the Great Plague of 1679 began and killed 70,000 people of Vienna—the official figure quoted by Abraham a Sancta Clara—not only the court, but the nobles, with one eminent exception, the high officials, and the wealthy citizens took to flight so that the best quarters of the city were deserted; the poor people in the slummy suburbs and in overcrowded, airless tenements of the town tried to get away, too, but most of them had to stay and see if they survived.

None of these things are specifically Viennese. But in the Viennese, in their peculiar historic situation, they strengthened attitudes and provoked reactions which have been a part of the pattern of the "Viennese character" ever since.

On the eve of the Great Plague, so Abraham a Sancta Clara told his flock afterwards (in *Mercks Wienn*), "ringing trumpets and music resounding everywhere from noblemen's houses and courtyards made such a noise that it was as if a hole had opened in the sky and joy were being poured down in the city in pecks". But horror had followed joy; Vienna should do penance. The preacher failed in his labours. The Viennese had no guilt feelings and no inclination towards austerity, whether of the Puritan or the Catholic brand. As soon as three outbreaks of the plague and the Turkish siege had passed, music again filled those mansions and courtyards. Unlike the Spaniards, the Viennese treated ever-present death with disrespect. Once the immediate threat had disappeared, they returned to their pleasures and their work, but saw no reason to intensify their faith.

The reigning Emperor, Leopold I, built a flamboyant baroque monument to commemorate the passing of the plague of 1679. Carved in white Salzburg marble, clouds billow upwards, populated by angels and demons, the emperor on his knees, Triumphant Faith with the Cross, and far above, too distant to hold attention, the Holy Trinity. But another lasting Viennese memorial to the Great Plague was a legend and tune about "Dear Augustin", a rascally piper who had tumbled, dead drunk, into a plague-pit filled with corpses, had survived to tell the tale, and gone on making music and drinking himself to death.

Those two symbols, the white marble writhing up to a remote religious effigy, and the half-legendary figure of a tough, coarse, ebullient street-musician, stand at the beginning of the great building boom which converted Vienna into a town of palaces.

The eighteenth century was to leave its indelible stamp on Vienna: Baroque, Rococo and Josephinian Classicism; great houses, tenements and benevolent institutions; formal parks and romantic wilderness; baroque opera, Gluck, Haydn, Mozart, and the young Beethoven; reason and sentiment; enlightened philosophy and despotic paternalism; aristocracy, bureaucracy, and a sceptical multi-national "nation"; ageing Prince Eugene of Savoy, two Habsburg reformers, and the pressure of the French Revolution; a whiff of Jacobinism at home, and the march of Napoleon Bonaparte's armies in the distance; the rhythm of stately buildings and the grace of small ornaments to develop a tradition of good and bad taste—all this, and more, but no home-grown poetry. Yet when this eighteenth century opened, the mould of the Viennese temper, of the collective attitude to life, was already cast.

II

The Legacy of Baroque

IN SEPTEMBER 1716, Mr. Edward Wortley Montagu, Ambassador Extraordinary of His Britannic Majesty King George I to the Ottoman Porte, broke his transcontinental journey to Constantinople at Vienna where he had tricky diplomatic business. The Habsburg Emperor Charles VI was again at war with the Turks whom his great general, Prince Eugene of Savoy, had driven out of parts of Hungary twenty years before, and who were on the warpath once more, encouraged by the statesmen of France. Britain, however, was interested in the restoration of normal commerce in the Near East—the Ambassador was also the representative of the Levant Company—and anything but interested in a further aggrandisement of the Habsburg realm which might upset the European balance of power, or in an engagement of the Austrian army that would upset it in the opposite sense by leaving a radius of free action to the French and Spanish bloc. Mr. Wortley Montagu had been appointed to prevent the outbreak of the war between Austria and Turkey by his diplomatic services; now, when war had overtaken his embassy, he was to attempt discreet mediation.

He spent thankless months in Vienna. Not only was the Turkish campaign going well for the Austrian arms (it was to end in 1718 with a peace treaty which for a short spell extended the Habsburg Empire into the Balkans), but a peace mission was also doomed to failure by the Emperor's attitude. In those years the imperial faction felt that the power of the Habsburgs was on the ascendant again, and its optimism had not yet overreached itself. Prince Eugene, above all, had an ambitious concept of the future of the Habsburg Empire in south-eastern Europe. As an agent of the Levant Company, the British envoy was immediately suspected of being pro-Turkish. Moreover, the peace treaties which had concluded the War of the Spanish Succession two years before, in 1713-14, had made Charles VI resentful of British diplomacy; while leaving the Habsburgs with the rich spoils of the formerly Spanish possessions in the Low Countries, these treaties had cost Charles the crown of Spain which he never ceased to consider his by the rights of legitimacy—an attitude viewed without sympathy by his Viennese subjects, who disliked the Spanish men and manners their sovereign had brought back from his war.

When Charles had succeeded to the Austrian dominions on the early death of his brother, the Emperor Joseph I, and was due to be elected German Emperor, his British allies had turned against his succeeding to the Spanish realm as well, and preferred to let it go to a branch of the Bourbons rather than tolerate the resurgency of a European–Trans-atlantic empire still more powerful than that of Charles V. Yet if it was British policy to maintain the balance of power on the European con-tinent, it was the dream of Charles VI to renew the universal Roman empire in the hands of a Habsburg. Checked in the West, he was bent on pushing forward to the Orient even while trying to strengthen his position among the German princes. Long before his death in 1740 his dream was shattered, some of the territorial gains of 1713 and 1718 lost, and the Austrian monarchy on the defensive mainly through his own dynastic schemes. In 1716, however, the grand design seemed possible to many, inside and outside Austria: Mr. Wortley Montagu came to Vienna under bad auguries, and could scarcely hope that the Viennese court as a whole would wish for a quick end to the war with-out decisive gains. He could do little more than establish contact with important people who were adverse to Prince Eugene and his strategy.

Some of these stresses affected the social round which the Am-bassador's young and brilliant wife, Lady Mary, was pursuing, and they gave an edge to her observations. Out of her ample corre-spondence, together with the journal she kept during the "embassy to Constantinople", Lady Mary later fashioned a manuscript, the so-called *Embassy Letters*, published only after her death. Touched-up though they are, a number of those partly-fictitious letters preserve Lady Mary's fresh, witty, sometimes unreliable and always illuminating impressions of baroque Vienna in its brief heyday. They deal mainly with the international set in which she moved, and with the official face of the town. In England, she was an unconventional wit, a minor satirical writer, as much in touch with leading men of letters as with the Whig aristocracy to which she belonged by birthright.* In Vienna,

* See Mr. Robert Halsband's *Life of Lady Mary Wortley Montagu*, London, O.U.P., 1956, which is a mine of factual information. I sometimes differ from Mr. Halsband in the interpretation of the couple's Viennese sojourn, and have here expressed my own opinions.

however, she showed no interest in people outside the *beau monde*, and none in the fine arts unless they added lustre to elegant living. That she met no poet in Vienna except the Frenchman Jean Baptiste Rousseau, a member of Prince Eugene's private court, was not her fault; there were no native writers to meet even had her noble friends been less exclusive. But her letters show no sign of her ever having been curious about the great architects who built the palaces she admired. Still, she did see those palaces when they were new. She did know their inhabitants in the first flush of splendour, and through her eyes we get a unique glimpse of their Vienna.

The first thing that struck Lady Mary on coming to Vienna was its smallness:

This town, which has the honour of being the emperor's seat, did not at all answer my idea of it, being much less than I expected to find it: the streets very close, and so narrow, one cannot observe the fine fronts of the palaces, though many of them very well deserve observation, being truly magnificent, all built of fine white stone, and excessive high, the town being so much too little for the number of people that desire to live in it, the builders seem to have projected to repair that misfortune by clapping one town on the top of another, most of the houses being of five, and some of them of six storeys. You may easily imagine, that the streets being so narrow, the upper rooms are extremely dark; and, what is an inconveniency much more intolerable, in my opinion, there is no house that has so few as five or six families in it. The apartments of the greatest ladies, and even of the ministers of state, are divided but by a partition from that of a tailor or shoemaker; and I know nobody that has above two floors in any house, one for their own use, and one high up for their servants. Those that have houses of their own let out the rest to whoever will take them; thus the great stairs (which are all of stone) are as common and dirty as the street.

All of this, whether blithe generalisation, acute observation or simple error, is relevant, because it conveys the immediate impact Vienna made on an intelligent stranger.

It was not true that "most" of the Viennese town houses had five storeys. Municipal records, and the stiff, prim engravings of the time, show that the bulk of the town consisted of four-storeyed and three-storeyed houses, while many older dwellings with two storeys and a gable survived in the shadow of taller neighbours. But it was true that Vienna had long been a town of flat-dwellers, not excepting house-owners who reserved only one storey, one more or less sumptuous

apartment, for their own use. And it was true that the newer thorough-
fares gave an impression of uniformly high rooflines, an illusion
that made it easy to speak of the old city as though it were all
palaces.

It was absurd to say that the upper rooms of tall buildings facing one
another across a narrow street were particularly dark: the high
windows of the first floor, the *piano nobile*, with its ornate balcony,
or of the almost equally high-ceilinged second floor, saw less of the
sun than the low windows of the top floors. And yet Lady Mary
was not quite wrong. Poky little rooms immediately under the massive
cornice of the roof had a better view, but away from the windows
they were dismally dark. After all they had been "clapped on" because
the house-owner knew that he would find tenants for the smallest hole.
Joseph Haydn lived in such a bare, unheated attic as a young man,
giving piano lessons to the Spanish ward of the court poet, Metastasio,
some floors lower down, to earn his food and quarter. The house still
stands, and a succession of engravings makes it possible to observe
what floors were built on at which time—with the religious order
which owned the Grosse Michaelerhaus making good use of the
valuable site.

Lady Mary admired the fine white stone of the new palaces. In
reality their brick walls were faced with fine stucco, which in those
days must have been painted white, not yet the utilitarian grey of the
Age of Reason under Joseph II, nor the strong yellow of still later eras.
To take stucco for stone was a blunder. But what Lady Mary saw,
unerringly, was that baroque Vienna was a light-coloured, a "white"
town. It was the same fifty-five years later when the celebrated Dr.
Burney noted the fact in his journal, long after the great building boom
and the elation of imperial success had come to an end.

Dr. Burney, otherwise little concerned with non-musical matters,
found it advisable to give a short description of Vienna because "it is
so remote from England, has been so imperfectly described by writers
of travel, and is so seldom visited by Englishmen": he might have said
because Vienna was no item of the Grand Tour. Here is a passage from
Dr. Burney's description in *The Present State of Music in Germany, the
Netherlands and United Provinces, Etc.*, quoted from the 2nd edition,
London, 1775:

The streets of Vienna are rendered doubly dark and dirty by their narrowness
and by the extreme height of the houses; but as these are chiefly of white stone

Lady Mary's mistake all over again] and in a uniform, elegant style of architecture, in which the Italian taste prevails, as well as in music, there is something
grand and majestic in their appearance, which is very striking; and even many
of those houses which have shops on the ground-floor, seem palaces above.
Indeed the whole town, and its suburbs, appear, at first glance, to be composed
of palaces, rather than of common habitations. . . .

This legend of Vienna as a town of palaces, an aristocratic city, soon
replaced the reality of the eighteenth century. It was constantly
reinforced by the visual impact of Vienna's façade. And it had a substantial core of truth. Grand—majestic—elegant in style—a town of
palaces in spite of dark, narrow alleys and of shops on the ground-floor:
this was the stamp the builders of the era of Charles VI wanted to
imprint on the small great town, and they succeeded. Yet because they
had to work within rigid space limits, they evolved architectural
solutions to the problem of how to convey dignified splendour without colossal proportions. This restriction compelled them to be
sparing with their ornamental devices; not for them the flamboyance
of the late, "Churrigueresque" Spanish Baroque. And because the
solutions for town palaces were restrained, lesser builders employed
by quite unaristocratic landlords were able to adapt those distinguished
patterns to the fronts—but only to the fronts, and occasionally the
staircases—of ordinary apartment houses. The driving force behind the
building and re-building was the pressure of a ceaseless stream of new
arrivals, ". . . the town being so much too little for the number of
people that desire to live in it . . ."

Compelling material factors, far more than an elusive *genius loci*,
made the Viennese Baroque something unmistakably local in spite of
Italian origins and French influences.

Within a cramped space the architects created the most ingeniously
curving, boldly suspended staircases fit for the grandest receptions.
But in very few palaces were they reserved for the owners and their
guests alone. By no means every nobleman's town house was exempted
from the onerous billeting duty which put whole storeys into the hands
of the court officials; far too many young gentlemen from abroad, and
too many relatives of successful courtiers, wanted apartments corresponding to their social ambitions, and found them in houses of their
equals who were glad of the rent to recoup themselves for building
expenses. Far too many humbler newcomers paid good money for
accommodation in backyard wings, basements or garrets, to make a

neat division of classes by housing profitable. As in many Paris *hôtels*
and Italian *palazzi*, noblemen and commoners, people of quality and
artisans, were living next door to one another under the same roof.

In the noblemen's quarter near the Imperial Castle, the most distinguished street was called the Herrengasse: two rows of palaces. In
1694, during the first wave of the great building boom, a German
journeyman-sculptor drifted into Vienna and worked forty-four
weeks in the workshop of a Viennese citizen and master sculptor—
who lived with all his journeymen in the Herrengasse. The five other
journeymen came from Upper Austria, Tyrol, Swabia, Bavaria and
Bohemia respectively. Not one Viennese! The young itinerant artisan
who recorded these facts in his journal soon left, but one or the other of
his mates is likely to have settled in the capital, as so many foreign
craftsmen did. New palaces were going up all the time, inside and
outside the city walls; they needed statues for their roofs and balconies,
figures to flank their portals, and sculpture for the niches of their
staircases, in common use though they might be. Where should the
craftsmen-decorators be housed but in the backyard outbuildings or
the attics of the mansions themselves?

The social medley was forced upon the nobility at a time when its
caste system was not quite so rigid as it became later, if only because
there were so many changes in the status of great families, and so many
newly ennobled favourites of the court. Somehow the reverential
separation of "orders" had to be expressed. Owners of great town
houses applied to the authorities for a licence to make the narrow
streets still narrower by a garland of heavy iron chains swinging from
stone posts in front of the white façades. Exalted position was proclaimed by a redoubled luxury inside the apartments (more important
still if these apartments were rented), and by pedantic attention to rank.
Again, Lady Mary is the most useful witness, virtually the only one to
put down descriptive detail:

'Tis true, when you have once travelled through them [i.e. the common stairs],
nothing can be more surprisingly magnificent than the apartments. They are
commonly a; *t ite* of eight or ten large rooms, all inlaid, the doors and windows
richly carved and gilt, and the furniture such as is seldom seen in the palaces of
sovereign princes in other countries—the hangings are the finest tapestry of
Brussels, prodigious large looking-glasses in silver frames, fine Japan tables,
beds, chairs, canopies, and window curtains of the richest Genoa damask or
velvet, almost covered with gold lace and embroidery. . . .

This is the first intimate description we have of the style of the high aristocracy at home in Vienna—impossible to call it "Viennese aristocracy", since at the beginning of the eighteenth century most families were relatively new in the town and might have their roots anywhere outside. Lady Mary, who was born Lady Mary Pierrepoint, daughter of the fifth Earl of Kingston, appreciated the setting and responded to the cosmopolitan air even while she made her critical comments:

It is true, the Austrians are not commonly the most polite people in the world, or the most agreeable. But Vienna is inhabited by all nations, and I had formed myself a little society of such as were perfectly to my own taste. And though the number was not very great, I could never pick up, in any other place, such a number of reasonable, agreeable people.

The very first prominent man mentioned (and mis-spelled) in the *Embassy Letters* is a good example of Vienna's cosmopolitan aristocracy, an adopted Viennese who went abroad again towards the end of his life but left his traces in the cultural pattern and on the stucco-and-stone face of the town: the Imperial Vice-Chancellor, Friedrich Carl Count Schönborn. He was a younger son of one of the greatest Catholic houses of western Germany, a family of rulers, diplomats, builders and connoisseurs, with at least one ecclesiastic prince-elector and one member in the emperor's service, generation after generation, for centuries. Count Friedrich Carl was absentee bishop of two Franconian dioceses, and a very gay secularist. His descendant, Sir George Franckenstein, says in his memoirs that his ancestor had built several palaces in Vienna "for magnificent balls and masquerades". Having retired to his see of Würzburg, to a famous and vast palace, he wrote plaintively to his brother: "I cannot get used to my princely cage and am very homesick for Vienna."

When the Count first arrived at the court of Emperor Leopold I, to serve as diplomatic intermediary between the crown and the German Estates, he brought rich culture and a refined western taste to Vienna, still a backward frontier town. He seems to have had little liking for ostentation. The town house in which he lived for some time before he bought it from Countess Batthyány was not large; about 1700 Fischer von Erlach had modernised it in the chastest, almost classicist version of Baroque, and Schönborn never had it changed to a newer fashion. There it is today: small and deep, fairly low, rusticated walls, simple columns flanking the finely curving door, above the window of the great reception room four panels in very shallow relief—from across the street they look as though designed by Flaxman for an early Wedgwood vase—and, as a counterpart, luxuriant arabesques flowing down from the capitals of six pilasters. It is perhaps the quietest and most timeless of Viennese town palaces.

More important for the evolution of the local style: Schönborn bought in 1706 an old country house and garden in the suburbs, which his favourite architect, Lucas von Hildebrandt, turned into a calmly graceful, almost intimate summer residence with a terraced park. Even between the two world wars, its stucco grey and flaking, it had an airy elegance without drama or pomp; at the time when it was gleaming white, it was a new departure of its kind. In 1716, Lady Mary Wortley Montagu dined there:

I was yesterday at Count Schönbrunn [sic], the vice-chancellor's garden, where I was invited to dinner, and I must say that I never saw a place so perfectly delightful as the Fauxbourgs of Vienna. It is very large and almost wholly composed of delicious palaces; and if the emperor found it proper to permit the gates of the town to be laid open, that the Fauxbourgs might be joined to it, he would have one of the largest and best-built cities of Europe. Count Schönbrunn's villa is one of the most magnificent. . . .

There were about 200 summer palaces and "villas" in the suburban belt of Vienna then, and Lady Mary saw them from a vantage point where they were clustered. After crossing the fields of the Glacis, the open space below the ramparts, she must have driven past Prince Trautson's summer residence, one of Fischer von Erlach's classicist masterpieces which was completed about that year. She probably skirted the park and riding school of Count Paar's villa; in an otherwise unattractive engraving of the period, its formal parterres are shown filled with be-wigged gentlemen and ladies in the stiffest of crinolines, looking at Spanish steeds, while a little negro slave bends to pick up a lady's handkerchief—he might have stood model to the little blackamoor who trips in and out at the end of *Der Rosenkavalier*. The summer palace of the Rofranos, later in rebuilt shape known as the Auersperg Palais, was not far away. Lady Mary would have looked across another formal garden filled with the colour of flowers, brocaded coats and crinolines, softened by the blue and golden air of a Viennese September, and as she walked up Schönborn's marble stairs her ready malice may have given way to exhilaration.

Gaiety and splendour, rather than pomp and splendour, had their ideal setting in the smaller garden palaces and villas, between jewelled flower beds, fountains, goldfish ponds, mildly sensual statuary, and walks bordered and bowered by trimly clipped yew, maple, hornbeam or lime, which led up to a whimsical pavilion and down to the shimmering, hospitable house. In town life was statelier and more tedious, except during the hectic weeks of carnival. The two "assemblies" which tried to approximate Paris, that of Countess Rabutin and that of Countess Althan, lacked the leaven of intellectual curiosity and general interests. Lady Mary's casual comments on her visits to the two salons convey a sense of emptiness relieved by ices, card games, and thin conversation with alchemy for its loftiest subject:

I don't find that learned men abound here: there is indeed a prodigious number of alchymists at Vienna . . . and those who have more reading and capacity than the vulgar have transported their superstition (shall I call it?) or fanaticism from religion to chymistry. . . . There is scarcely a man of opulence or fashion, that has not an alchymist in his service.

The ladies' dresses too earned Lady Mary's mocking censure:

. . . never in my life saw so many fine clothes ill-fancied. They embroider the richest gold stuff; and provided they make their clothes expensive enough, that is all the taste they show in them.

This cannot be taken at face value. The fact was that Viennese court society followed the stiff fashions of Spain, not yet those of France, let alone England. And Lady Mary's bad opinion was apparently reciprocated. Mr. Halsband quotes a letter written shortly before the Wortley Montagus' departure by the British Ambassador in Vienna, Stanyon, to his colleague in Paris:

Lady Mary is pretty much the subject of conversation here. She sticks to her English modes and manners, which exposes her a little to the raillerie of the Viennese ladies. She replies with a good deal of wit, and is engaged in a sort of petty war; but they own she is a witty woman, if not a well-dressed one.

If Mr. Stanyon was right about the "petty war" of the ladies, some of the observations Lady Mary recorded—on the ugliness of Viennese women, their erotic market value at an advanced age, the meretricious character of wives' love affairs, the chase for Counts of the Empire in the betrothed's pedigree, the excessive pride of caste, and so forth—are to be taken with more than a grain of salt. In any case they were sharpened by her need for self-assertion: Lady Mary was dissatisfied with her marriage, her intellect and her passions were in conflict, and in Vienna these strains made her generally bellicose. This is conjecture, of course. Yet I feel on safe ground in suggesting that one of the roots of the ladies' war, and a reason why some of Lady Mary's most stringent comments on Viennese matters and manners are not quite reliable, was the failure of her husband's mission in Vienna. She was disappointed; the failure was to cost them the continuation of their work in Turkey, which fascinated her; much later, when she edited her journal in the form of letters, she could give free rein, or almost free rein, to her impatience with the Viennese friends who had let her down. All the same she remains the most important eye-witness of that period —and it is a period that did more to shape the face of Vienna than the later periods which play more conspicuous rôles in the Viennese legend.

In the *Embassy Letters*, names turn up which stood for political cliques and currents. The Althans, hosts at the "gala" that provoked Lady Mary's strictures, were important through their connexions, being related to several princely houses in Bohemia; Count Michael III belonged to a family of great feudal lords in Moravia, was Master of the Horse and the Emperor's favourite; his Spanish-born wife was the Emperor's mistress. The Bohemian group was gaining ground in Vienna—an increasing number of the great palaces built round the turn of the century were owned by Bohemian aristocrats—and on the whole it was opposed to Prince Eugene of Savoy and his policies. Since Charles VI himself was not too fond of a man who outshone him and thus hurt his dignity as the new Caesar, court intrigues against the Prince became more and more successful, though not in time to further Mr. Wortley Montagu's diplomatic interests. It was only natural that he and his wife should hope to find common ground with the set assembling in the salon of "the Spanish Althan", as the Viennese called the Countess with the current undertones of dislike for the Emperor's Spanish entourage.

All Ministers who could be counted among Prince Eugene's adversaries are mentioned with words of praise by Lady Mary: their influence might have prevailed on the Imperial War Council to stop the offensive against Belgrade which made Mr. Wortley Montagu's peace feelers so ill-timed. In fact it did not prevail. Yet if the letters Lady Mary actually sent to London from Vienna were at all like their edited version, there was political design behind the seemingly artless pen portraits boosting the anti-Eugene faction. (An exception was her coy

account of the charming young Portuguese, Count Tarouca, whom
Viennese gossip called her lover—and whom she spelt Tarroco.)

Not once did Lady Mary refer by name to a woman, as important in
Vienna as the Countess Althan, but set apart as Prince Eugene's friend:
Eleonora Magdalena Countess Batthyány, "Lovely Lory", daughter
and heiress to Leopold I's chancellor Count Strattmann, widow and
heiress of General Adam Count Batthyány, a Hungarian magnate and
Lord Lieutenant of Croatia, Dalmatia and Slavonia. Yet Lady Mary
seems to have hinted at her when she refused to discuss the great Prince
by letter because

I am as unwilling to speak of him at Vienna, as I should be to talk of Hercules in
the court of Omphale, if I had seen him there. I don't know what comfort other
people find in considering the weaknesses of great men (because, it brings them
nearer to their level), but 'tis always a mortification for me to observe that there
is no perfection in humanity.

As a skilled lampoonist, Lady Mary whittled down the stature of
Prince Eugene in every slight reference, as when she discussed his
library in terms such as "finnikin and foppish taste" and "books . . .
pompously bound in Turkey leather". Indirectly, however, her terms
of grudging respect surround him with a sulphurous glory. He was a
lonely figure away from the wars, bizarre, serious, a creator of power
and tension in a town and society that liked to relax.

On the entirely different plane of architectural patronage, all the
names occurring in Lady Mary's text belong to the story of baroque
Vienna. It was the ups and downs in the material and political fortunes
of aristocratic clans that led to continual change in the ownership of
residential property. Each change in its turn led to commissions for
artists and artisans.

When thirty-year-old Johann Bernard Fischer, born in Graz but
trained in Rome by Bernini himself, at last came to Vienna in 1678,
the first important employers he found were the Liechtensteins,
Althans, Chancellor Count Strattmann—the great names of the court
of Leopold I.*

Johann Michael II Count Althan tracked down Fischer ("He's that
fellow who was sixteen years with Bernini, isn't he?", asks a letter)
when he was lodging with a sculptor in the oldest, darkest part of

* For facts about J. B. Fischer, his work and his circle, see Professor Hans
Sedlmayr's monograph, *Johann Bernhard Fischer von Erlach*, Vienna, 1958.

Vienna. Some years later Althan commissioned him to rebuild his ancestral castle in Moravia, with an immense oval hall and cupola dedicated to the glory of the house. About the same time another Althan, Christian Joseph, gave Fischer his first opportunity not to rebuild but to build from the foundation stone a country mansion outside the ring wall, in the lowest foothills of the western suburb of Vienna. Fischer devised a small dream palace with a flat Italian roof, an oval centre part, and four boldly jutting wings. It stood in the landscape as a stranger. Soon the rains and snows made it necessary to add pitched roofs which clashed with the classicist balustrade and statuary. Still, it was one of the earliest villas in the suburbs, and it set a fashion that lasted until Lucas von Hildebrandt, Count Schönborn's protégé, brought to the task a lighter style, more "Viennese" in its proportions. Perhaps it was the chain of italianate villas ringing the town which made the Venetian Niccolò Madrisio say in 1718 that anyone coming from Italy to Vienna would think "he was breathing a whiff of Italian air in the middle of Austria; a certain Nordic element noticeable in the architecture enhances rather than reduces its charm. . . ."

In a narrow street running at right angles to the Herrengasse, which was the axis of the noblemen's quarter, there are two long-fronted mansions which each replaced several older houses, each changed hands (commoners, speculators, a Jörger, forced sales, Althans and Chancellor Strattmann are only part of the sequence), and each owed their grand entrance to Fischer. Lory Strattmann, Count Batthyány's widow, bought three small middle-class houses and had them knocked into one in the style of 1718. The palace next door, belonging to Wolf André Count Orsini-Rosenberg, was built by Fischer. In the state rooms of Countess Lory's house, Prince Eugene used to play piquet with his old friend every night up to the eve of his death.

This small fact is the substance of an amiable little legend which may be of nineteenth-century vintage, to judge by its sentimental tinge. The story is that towards the end of his life Prince Eugene—who died at seventy-three, in 1736, as much in disgrace with the Emperor as the cabals of the "Spanish" faction at court had been able to achieve—was so frail that he often fell asleep on the way from his town palace in the Himmelpfortgasse to Countess Lory's. Coachman and lackey, almost equally aged, would doze as well, but the horses were familiar with the route and stopped of their own accord in front of the Batthyány palace. Then the three old men, with 210 years between them, would have their nap, the horses would stand at rest in well-bred composure, the Viennese passing by would grin affectionately, and upstairs the faded beauty would wait in patience for the spell to break.

It may provide a salutary astringent at this juncture to look at the documented life of the artist who designed those nobly structured fronts, portals and staircases for so many princes and counts of the empire, not to forget the works he created for the greater glory of three Habsburg emperors.

Johann Bernhard Fischer was in 1689 appointed teacher of architectural drawing to Archduke Joseph, King of Hungary, Emperor Leopold I's eleven-year-old son who was soon to be crowned King of the Romans (which meant King of the Germans, a formality of importance for his future election as an emperor). The assignment brought Fischer the title of Royal Court Engineer, and contacts of immense value. In 1690 he married the daughter of a Regensburg notary; this settled him more securely in the middle-class bay of the evolving social order. His pupil, the King of Hungary, stood godfather by proxy to Fischer's first son, who died of "bowel cramps", a fortnight old. The second child, a daughter without illustrious sponsors, died at six weeks of the same complaint. Then came Joseph Emanuel, godson of Count and Countess Strattmann, who lived to become his father's assistant and successor, a great and original talent without the older Fischer's genius. And the last child, a daughter born when Johann Bernhard Fischer had been ennobled, with the addition of *von Erlach* to his name —*von* being the operative particle denoting the lowest rank of nobility but not, in Austrian tradition, a place in the aristocracy—entered the register of St. Stephen's sponsored by three noble godparents, the widowed Countess Strattmann, the Bohemian Count Sternberg, and Countess Argenthin. The names are quoted not because they tell a success story, but because they speak of Fischer's struggle to find the right sort of protectors: in the "Vienna Gloriosa" of 1697 these had to be members of the great aristocracy.

During his first years in Vienna, when he was already sought after as the greatest architect in the German-speaking countries, Fischer lived on gratuities for commissioned work of every description. The Princes Liechtenstein, who soon reverted to strictly orthodox Italian masters for their palaces, paid Fischer 30 florins here, 300 there, and an entry in their estate ledger shows that he once received wine to the value of 201 florins 30 kreuzer. Two designs for triumphal arches dedicated to the King of the Romans on his entry in Vienna rated, one 300 florins, the other 200. Plans and a few sculptures he contributed to the Plague Memorial of Vienna, that white marble swirl of figures and theatrical clouds, earned Fischer 3,000 florins from the Court exchequer—in instalments.

There were serious setbacks. Fischer's project for an imperial summer palace vaster and more tension-laden than Versailles, the so-called first Schönbrunn project, remains on paper. He obtained the permit to print the engravings of his design, and that was all—except for the stimulus which the grandeur of this design gave to others. But the grand vision was unreal, not only in proportion to the financial means of the Habsburgs, but also in relation to Vienna and its landscape. When Schönbrunn was built, it was on a much smaller scale and with far less of Caesarean symbolism than Fischer had planned.

Another vast project of Fischer's, this time decidedly earth-bound, foundered as dismally: his proposal to regulate the dangerous narrows of the Danube in Lower Austria by blowing up the obstructing cliffs. The provincial administration even made a small money grant, but the resistance of the landowners was stronger. The regulation of the narrows was begun in earnest in 1956.

Even in the field of palace-building Fischer met with increasing difficulties. His strength was the modulation of masses of masonry, but he was mostly given façades to reconstruct, in streets too narrow to permit more than the faintest projection of wings. Outside the gates of Vienna he suffered from the rivalry of Hildebrandt who was miraculously adept at using the given landscape, not an Arcadia, for his formal parks, and at turning the restricted scale into an asset. Then, precisely when the War of the Spanish Succession enforced a pause in the Viennese building orgy, Fischer was rescued by a secure post at court. Joseph I, who became Emperor in 1705, made Fischer von Erlach the Superintendent of Imperial Court and Pleasure Buildings. (Another Althan, Count Gundaker, was Comptroller for all Imperial Court Pleasance, Civilian and Garden Buildings.) Fischer's salary started at 1,100 florins, then rose to 2,000, and finally to 2,500 a year. This was not munificent; for everything but food, Vienna was a very expensive city. To quote another salary in comparison: an Italian stucco craftsman who spent eleven months on the vaulting of the ground floor hall in the great Liechtenstein garden palace, in 1704-05, was paid 1,000

florins plus twenty bushels of wine. But possibly the Princes Liechtenstein were more generous employers than the court.

Still, Fischer was called in as an architect by great Bohemian families
for their houses in Vienna or Prague, or their seats in the country; his
influence reached to Warsaw, Dresden, Salzburg and Berlin. And
though Hildebrandt, not Fischer, built Prince Eugene's Belvedere, the
loveliest new palace of Vienna, it was Fischer who designed Vienna's
most impressive baroque church and the Emperor's magnificent
domed library. Indeed, the Emperor Charles VI, who followed
Fischer's protector Joseph I, not only confirmed him in his official
post but knew how to make use of a man whose ideas of building were
vast and, ideally speaking, on a Roman scale.

This point has been made, though overstated in what is very nearly a
historical caricature, by Mr. Sacheverell Sitwell in his *Southern Baroque
Art* (London, Grant Richards, 1923):

The Emperor Charles VI was a patron of everything that could support the
dignity of a Roman emperor. To this purpose colonnades and porticoes were
indispensable, and there was no lack of able designers of these state picture-
frames. Bernard Fischer von Erlach was the architect responsible for the
arrangement of stucco vistas down which, as through the wrong end of the
telescope, Charles can be seen, in pictures and prints, standing in the open under
a curtain, while Crown jewels and insignia lie in heaps around him like a
traveller's luggage in a celestial douane. . . . Von Erlach, a student of Bernini,
did his best to foster the Emperor's Caesarean affectations by building Vienna
into the semblance of an improved Rome.

Fischer von Erlach—it is against Austrian usage to call him Von
Erlach in the Prussian manner, as if the magic particle *von* were an
indissoluble part of the surname—was not a "student" of Bernini, but
Bernini's pupil; the least of his work was concerned with stucco vistas
for state occasions. When Charles VI became emperor Fischer had
already served his two predecessors and built most of the italianate
palaces; he had come to Vienna at a time when it was the high aristocracy even more than the ruling emperor which attempted to vie, in
Vienna, with the tremendous Roman palaces "out of their inflated
self-importance", in Professor Sedlmayr's words. Thus it was not a
single Habsburg's affectation, but a social and political revolution in
the wake of the religious wars, which lent impetus to Viennese
Baroque and converted the town—in harsh reality for no more than a
limited period, but in imagination for the two centuries that followed

—into the centre of an expanding supranational empire. All the same Fischer did draw his main inspiration from Italy, even though he welded old and new elements of art into a new synthesis; both sides to him are shown in his own engravings for his universal history of architecture. It is equally true that Fischer, like others of the thin layer of intellectuals, catered for Charles VI's high-flown imperial aspirations, and that this contributed to the shape of Vienna—which is why this relatively short period is of such importance.

In 1716, the same year in which the Wortley Montagus came to Vienna, Charles VI laid the foundation stone for a church on the outskirts of the Wieden suburb. It was dedicated to his patron saint, St. Charles Borromee. Johann Bernard Fischer von Erlach designed it after winning a competition in which his project won over the heads of Hildebrandt and of the Empire's pet artificer, the Italian theatre architect Galli-Bibbiena; Fischer's son Joseph Emanuel supervised the final construction. The intricate, learned symbolism of the ornamental features was the work of a Swedish convert to Catholicism, Hernaeus, the director of the Emperor's numismatic cabinet, author of most of the grandiloquent Latin inscriptions of those years, and a personal friend of Fischer. The philosopher Leibniz, the greatest mind in Germany, acted as adviser from afar, trying to infuse still more emphatic imperial symbols into the programme of his correspondent Hernaeus; Leibniz hoped that the Emperor would found an Academy of Art and Science at Vienna, and Fischer von Erlach was one of Leibniz's candidates for it.

The church is compact and looks vaster than it is. Fischer gave it aloof grandeur and bizarre exuberance, classical simplicity and dramatic flamboyance in an odd blending of forms. Behind a severe portico, looking like the entrance to a Roman temple, soars an oval dome whose copper roofing has turned a soft green. The portico is flanked by two free-standing columns decorated with spiral bas-reliefs. They recall minarets or triumphal columns of ancient Rome. More reconditely, as part of the complex programme of allusions, they were supposed to recall the Pillars of Hercules which are Spain's gate to the New World. All served the triumph of the Emperor, who saw himself as the protector of the Church Triumphant. The impression of victorious worldly power is not softened by the relative modesty of the spiralling bas-reliefs which represent the life of the Saint and not, as Leibniz had proposed, the deeds of Charlemagne and of a sainted Count of

Flanders, ancestor of Charles V and Charles VI. To make the message
clearer, the two columns are topped by the imperial crown of which
the Cross is only part and apex; the dome is crowned by a globe and
Cross, symbols of the universal empire and the universal church.
The two lateral bell-towers appear as oriental pavilions with open
gateways. The whole of the Karlskirche is a stage for the glitter and
colour of ecclesiastic displays, unexpectedly chill and rational inside
despite the gilt-stucco outburst of the altar and Rottmayr's immense
frescoes which convert the cupola into heaven, open to the glory of
the Saint. It has never been a place for simple souls at prayer. The
Emperor built it to fulfil his vow of the plague year 1713, but in fact
it is a show-place rather than a church, fitting perfectly into the
suburban belt of garden palaces: an end, not a beginning, of a religious-
political cycle.

Fischer von Erlach did not live to see his greatest building completed.
Though he had become affluent enough to own two small houses with
gardens in the Wieden, the suburb backing St. Charles Borromee
where, in between grander mansions and formal gardens, respectable
middle-class people began to own property (and Fischer remained a
member of the respectable professional middle class), he died in a
mediaeval corner of the old city. Brethren of St. Salvator accompanied
the coffin to St. Stephen's in a nocturnal cortège. The exact spot where
Fischer was buried in 1723 is as unknown and unmarked as Mozart's
grave. Then, as in the rationalist era of 1791, the Viennese at large, the
bereaved families and the exalted patrons of defunct artists alike, were
remarkably free of any emotional cult of funerals, unless it was a case
for deploying the pomp and powers of a royal or princely house. And
then it was a matter of pride of caste, not of sentiment.

When the Emperor Joseph I died in 1711, Fischer von Erlach
designed a show catafalque, a *castrum doloris*, for which he received a
fee of 500 florins from the imperial privy purse. When Fischer died
twelve years later, Charles VI granted to his son Joseph Emanuel an
ex gratia payment of 300 florins towards the costs of illness and funeral.
The scale of values was well defined and graduated.

Fischer's Viennese palace fronts helped to fix that social scale. They
also helped to preserve face when apartments were let. They gave the
greatest visual emphasis to the aristocratic rule, making it seem more
absolute than it was, and far more permanent. Like the Italian architects of his time, but in a subtly different idiom, Fischer created

examples of a style that could not be scaled down, even when put to humbler uses, and even where other buildings right and left showed that a compromise in design was possible to fit the needs of the new well-to-do middle class. Within the limits of Viennese material conditions, J. B. Fischer von Erlach upheld the architectural and the social ideals of an earlier palace-building generation. He was no modernist.

In the middle of the seventeenth century, when the first aristocratic town houses went up in the walled city, there was still space for free-standing, arrogantly austere blocks which proclaimed to the cowed burghers that they belonged to the new overlords. Churches built at the same time, in the prevalent Jesuit style, were theatrical and sump-tuous, but the palaces repeated the pattern of an earlier Roman fashion, without the convolutes and spirals called "Jesuit snails" by the Viennese, and with no concessions to the startling changes in contemporary, Italian architecture introduced by Bernini. Because of the time-lag in the absorption of foreign influences—a result of the long barren years when nothing important had been built in Vienna—different stylistic tendencies were jumbled. What was old-fashioned abroad, looked new here. And it always had some new element. After the Peace of Westphalia of 1648, which left the Habsburg dynasty in secure possession, secular and religious, of their hereditary lands, Emperor Leopold I added a long wing to his old castle, the Viennese Hofburg. It had a perfectly flat front of forty-four windows, imposing through clear proportions and lucid ornamental mouldings, but with-out columns or even decorated window frames. It was a residence suggesting withdrawn, severe, inaccessible power. The Italians who built it created in this Leopoldine wing a model of its kind which, by its few moulded lines in the plaster wall, became part of the distinct Viennese tradition.

Some years later one of the Emperor's foremost liegemen, Konrad Balthasar von Starhemberg, built his new town house in the centre of the noblemen's quarter. It is a high square block with an almost plain surface and massive, beetling eyebrow-roofs over the windows of the main storeys: a fortress standing all by itself in the midst of lessser dwellings. This, too, was the work of Italians, but to anyone coming from Rome or Milan it must have looked outdated even then, at the beginning of the 1660s. For Vienna it was new. But it was also some-thing of an alien body in the urban organism, which Leopold I's wing was not, thanks to the restrained grace of its sparse ornaments.

At the end of the 1670s Charles Eusebius Prince Liechtenstein wrote an architectural treatise for the benefit of his son, to whom he wished to bequeath the conviction that a grandee's station was best exhibited by grandiose palaces—and, next to them, by fine horses in fine stabling, a notion that was to secure for Fischer von Erlach the commission to build princely stables for the Liechtenstein stud. Prince Charles Eusebius laid down the law that "an edifice needs length to be splendid —the longer, the better—because it makes for renown and magnificence to see a great number of windows and columns". This could have led him to recommend adoption of the increasingly fashionable French style; Versailles, with 375 windows to its garden front, was almost completed and was moving every sovereign in Europe to some form of emulation. But the head of the Liechtensteins thought that the Italians held "the secret of majesty" in architecture. Indeed, when his son, Prince Johann Adam Andreas, decided on building a great summer palace at the gates of Vienna, and another great town house near the Hofburg, he commissioned the Italian Martinelli. Yet the cool, polished traditionalism of the italianate town palace, with its main front facing one of those narrow streets (the same in which Count Strattmann and his daughter had their houses, with Fischer's façades) and only one side standing free, conveys dignity no better than Fischer's more boldly articulated mansions, and looks heavy compared with its smaller neighbours.

One of these smaller neighbours was a house which Lucas von Hildebrandt created for Count Daun, Viceroy of Naples and later Governor of the Low Countries. It was so restricted in space as to be revolutionary: there were only seven windows to its front. Yet with its tapering pilasters and the web of flat arabesques on its walls it was a masterpiece of elegance and cool grace. This was a pattern—unlike Fischer's grandiose distribution of classical forms—which lesser master-builders could adapt, and did adapt for many ordinary citizens' houses in and around Vienna. The most attractive among them show the simplified features of Hildebrandt's smaller palaces or villas, from dignified entrance to discreet pilasters unifying the storeys, which are separated and at the same time classified by graduated window architraves. Hildebrandt designed the front of some middle-class apartment houses himself.

Lower down the scale of social standing and financial means, plasterers and stonemasons applied the skill they had acquired under the guidance of architects, and began to decorate the flat surfaces of small houses with scrolls above the windows or panels sunk into the plaster. Once the artisan tradition was established, this style of middle-class Rococo, with no more than a touch of fancy relieving an essential plainness, stayed popular for generations. It survived the wave of neo-classicism at the end of the eighteenth century, which apart from official buildings never thrived in Vienna, and merged into the small-scale cosiness of the next century, the "Biedermeier" era. It is the Viennese counterpart of English Georgian architecture, as distinct from it as plaster is from brick, or as an urban society dominated by a court aristocracy and bureaucracy is from one dominated by bankers and traders. Even from the old suburban tenements outside the old core of Vienna, from houses with only a few curlicues and moulded lines dug by a mason's thumb into the plaster to give the plain walls life through the play of light and shade, threads lead back to the palaces and villas which Fischer and Hildebrandt built into the narrow frame of the Viennese streets and the folds of the Wienerwald foothills.

Prince Eugene of Savoy was the most powerful of patrons, and in the country, or in his summer palace above the walled town, he built spaciously. But when he wanted to have a winter residence in the heart of the old quarter, he too had to bow to necessity and let his architects (first Fischer, then Hildebrandt) seek grandeur through restraint. In the dark Himmelpfortgasse near St. Stephen's he bought the house of a commoner, the outbuildings of a count's old mansion, and the small garden of another count's house. This site was hemmed in by two ordinary *Bürgerhäuser*, properties of middle-class people. The middle part of a low-slung palace was built, but with the first extension the Prince had to wait till Fauconet, the court hatter who introduced beaver hats in Vienna, was ready to sell the small house he had been using for profitable shows and games. The second extension followed when the neighbour on the other side, an usher at court, died and his daughters agreed to a sale. Then Hildebrandt carried the quiet rhythm of tall windows and pilasters further along the street, in the pattern which Fischer had devised to defeat the narrowness of the site. Dramatic fantasy was reserved for the state rooms and the wonderfully curving staircase, where writhing stone giants supported the weight of the landings. On the street side, the portals were flanked only by shallow bas-reliefs, not by the atlantean slaves testifying to the greatness of many other houses. As though an external show of power were not necessary in this case, art made a noble virtue out of material necessity. The reliefs show scenes of the myth of Hercules. Prince Eugene was Hercules to the Habsburgs' Olympus; no one else could dare to usurp his place and symbol. But the architectural idiom that served his dignity and the given conditions with such calm assurance was eminently fit to influence the taste of less exalted persons, above all of those adopting the façade of nobility.

The early eighteenth century saw the rise of rich merchants and financiers who seized the opportunities offered by military campaigns, standing armies in distant Habsburg dominions, fumbling mercantilist ventures of the sovereigns, corruption and muddle in high places, and the insatiable need for cash and credit of the whole court. There was no shortage of *bourgeois gentilhomme* types in Vienna, and they too were building palatial town houses with every refinement their money could buy. The social status of these upstarts was anything but secure, nor was their financial position very stable, but they did compete with wealthy aristocrats and religious bodies in amassing real estate, particularly in the suburbs. When one of the innumerable counts withdrew to his estates in the country or abroad, a freshly ennobled speculator would take the town house off his hands; the archives are full of documents to such transactions. And others built new houses in the very heart of the noblemen's quarter.

In his libretto to the opera *Der Rosenkavalier*, Hugo von Hofmannsthal created the comic figure of Herr von Faninal, father of the charming Sophie. Faninal has made his pile as contractor for the imperial army in Flanders, and is the proud possessor of a new patent of nobility, twelve rent-raising houses in the Wieden suburb, and a brand-new palace in town. Now he wants to marry his only daughter to a man with an old title and good connections at court. The story is set in the early days of Maria Theresia's reign, shortly after 1740, but it could as well have been set about the time, say, of Lady Mary's stay in Vienna.

Hofmannsthal was a good historian, even if he invented, very plausibly, the ceremony of the Silver Rose presented to a nobleman's chosen bride, which provides an opportunity for tangling the threads of the plot. In baroque Vienna there were thousands of Faninals, and there must have been hundreds of daughters of rich bourgeois who married younger sons of great families, just as Sophie von Faninal marries the young Count Octavian, brother to the Marchese di

Rofrano. Hofmannsthal did not even have to make up the name.
Geronimo Marchese di Rofrano, Imperial Privy Councillor and
member of the Supreme Spanish Council at Vienna, bought a garden
palace near that of Count Schönborn (bought it, of course, from
another count) and had it modernised, with a more elaborate middle
part, by an architect-contractor, although the original building had
been designed by Hildebrandt; a long wrought-iron railing inter-
spersed with twenty-three columns protected it on the side of the Glacis.
The lane outside the Rofrano Palace was a favourite spot for duels at
that time, the second decade of the eighteenth century. The Marchese
might well have been pleased to see a younger brother married to the
well-dowered daughter of an ennobled vulgarian. After all, as Baron
Ochs von Lerchenau says to the Marschallin in the opera: sons from
such a *mésalliance* as he then contemplated himself might be debarred
from wearing the golden key of a Lord-in-Waiting, since they would
not have the required immediate ancestors of impeccable lineage; but
twelve iron keys to profitable houses in the Wieden would compensate
them for this loss.

In another dark, narrow street close to Prince Eugene's winter
residence stands a tall house built by the man who modernised the
Rofrano palace. Johann Christian Neupauer, town councillor, militia
captain, architect, and a man with bold ideas, bought at an auction
three small houses that had belonged to the bankrupt Count de
Souches, and had them pulled down immediately: the year was 1715,
the peak of the influx of important foreigners into Vienna. On the
site of one of the houses Neupauer built a narrow-chested tenement for
ordinary tenants, but on the site of the other two he erected a mansion
on the model of Fischer's Bohemian Chancery, though every structural
device was simplified and slightly coarsened. The front was plain, but
distinguished by two barely receding wings, and the doorway was
flanked by two pairs of muscular atlantean figures; the balcony
resting on their shoulders was adorned with statuary, the windows had
heavily sculptured architraves. No provision was made for special state
rooms or for a great hall at the foot of the utilitarian staircase. In short,
it was a dignified apartment house for people of more pretensions than
means, hence its front promised far more than its interior fulfilled.

Neupauer petitioned the Emperor for exemption from billeting
duties as soon as the house was ready, saying that without such a
privilege he "would never in all eternity be able to let such a vast

building, constructed with so much travail; and thus he would lose his nerve for the future erection of new edifices in the place of old ones". Later he fell into debt and lost both his houses in the Singerstrasse to a gentlewoman who married a Count Breuner and so brought the property back into aristocratic ownership. The Neupauer-Breuner palace, to give it its courtesy title, changed hands repeatedly and shed its glamour. Lowly tenants invaded its high-ceilinged rooms. But it retained the hallmark of fine proportions and an imposing doorway. However bourgeois, petit-bourgeois or quite simply poor its inmates, it remained indelibly and deceptively aristocratic. It is so even now, when it is no more than an empty shell, its swarthy façade blistered and crumbling.

Of course not even the innermost core of Old Vienna under Charles VI was all dignified façades, counts, rich speculators and loyal lower orders, though the nineteenth century preferred to see nothing but a noble surface behind which to lodge the nostalgic legend of imperial greatness. Nor were those narrow streets exclusively filled with people riding in magnificent carriages or in the sedan chairs carried by men in red coats—whose privilege of 1703 had a clause forbidding them to transport sick persons, persons in livery, and Jews, as well as to have in their ranks any strangers to the city.

The walled town contained about 1,000 dwelling houses, in which some 80,000 people were living at the height of the baroque building boom. There was a criss-cross of social tensions below the upper crust, and these tensions too influenced the shape of Vienna's daily life. The large group of journeymen-artisans knew how indispensable they were, and tried to wrest concessions from the masters' guilds which upheld the patriarchal forms of production and exploitation. An imperial manifesto of 1718 prohibited their carrying swords with their Sunday best and indulging in "bloody rencontres". More than once the regulations for the closing of the city gates were made more severe, to prevent noisy brawls of journeymen on their way back from sprees in the suburbs. In 1715 a movement started among the journeymen-shoemakers. They demanded a say in the administration of their funds, abolition of compulsory boarding in guild hostels, and freedom of movement. This agitation was harshly suppressed and many journeymen were banished from Vienna. Rioting flared up again among the same professional group in 1722. Now the journeymen-shoemakers demanded the right to join a workshop of their own choice, not one allotted them by the guild, and they went on strike, almost to a man, to enforce their demand. The Emperor was quick to proceed against the rebels. When their tumults continued, the city guard opened fire on them. Two leaders were hanged, others sent to the galleys and forced labour.

Before long, however, the government again intervened, this time in favour of the journeymen, or rather, of the freedom of the craft, because it was useful to break the guilds' stranglehold on an expanding trade. The hostels were subjected to control, the journeymen authorised to seek work without direction by the guild (even in the workshops of "free" masters outside the guild), and four of their representatives admitted to the administration of a fund into which they paid their contributions as a mutual insurance. But first the mutineers against an existing order had to be punished.

I quote the account given in a contemporary chronicle by Matthias Fuhrmann, from Professor Hans Tietze's anthology *Alt-Wien in Wort und Bild* (Vienna, Schroll, 1926, part I, p. 38):

Since the Imperial Court understood, with the greatest displeasure, that in this Residence of Vienna the shoemakers' journeymen had culpably resisted the commands, regulations and orders decreed by the Sovereign for the maintenance of good policy and a safe general order, and gone so far as to leave and abandon their workshops and masters without the least cause, maliciously and in the dangerous intention to rob the public of the necessary workmen, thus disregarding and annulling the Sovereign's mandates and as it were perishing according to their own will; and since this kind of mischievous and, in the Imperial Residence, exceedingly offensive presumptions could in no way be tolerated by His Imperial Majesty, but had to be extirpated in good time with all seriousness and energy: it was graciously resolved, and made public in a Court Decree dated 21st October in this same month [of 1722], that pending a further decree no journeyman should leave his work and still less part from his master, and anyone who had already left should return without delay to his master's workshop. . . . However, when the journeymen-shoemakers insisted on their arbitrary acts and began to cause great disorder, another Patent of the Sovereign was published at the end of this month. . . . The journeymen-shoemakers who in this town and its suburbs assemble in numbers of ten or more, on whatever invented pretext, and have meetings and conferences, will be immediately arrested and court-martialled, and without investigation of any other crime punished in life and limb. . . . Moreover, such innkeepers and inhabitants who give shelter to those journeymen-shoemakers for their highly criminal assemblies . . . will be banished from the country and sent to the rowing-benches of galleys. . . .

One year after the first outbreak of the shoemakers' movement,
Lady Mary Wortley Montagu accompanied her husband on a trip
from Vienna to Hanover, where he had to consult King George I.
On the way she did some shopping at Leipzig:

... and I take this opportunity of buying pages' liveries, gold stuffs for myself,
etc., all things of that kind being at least double the price at Vienna; partly
because of the excessive customs and partly the want of genius and industry in
the people, who make no one sort of thing there: and the ladies are obliged to
send even for shoes out of Saxony.

It was a fact that not enough "gold stuffs" for the demands of high-
born ladies were being produced at Vienna, where industries and crafts
had only just emerged from a long paralysis and everything was
correspondingly dear. Fifty years earlier a silk company had been
founded, with foreign merchants who were to introduce the new
techniques developed in the less harassed towns of Italy and France.
But Vienna was still the frontier city then. In the course of their siege
the Turks had destroyed the first suburban silk factory, and the
foreign entrepreneurs had left, discouraged. After the turn of the
century more than two dozen silk master weavers, Italian, French and
Swiss, settled in Vienna, and soon the first native Austrian too became
a rich man by purveying silks to the court. In 1714—the year in which
the Peace of Rastatt gave Lombardy to the Habsburgs, and with it a
source of raw material and skilled craftsmen for the silk industry—
this *nouveau riche* already owned a big house with a garden in a suburb
which later was to be known as the *Brillantengrund*, Diamond Field,
because of the many millionaire silk manufacturers who lived there.
Yet his gold stuffs were presumably not up to the taste of the international aristocracy—and very expensive indeed. The ministers of the
Crown had no choice but to import experienced men from abroad and
subsidise them; the alternative was to allow great sums to go out of the
country, in the manner recorded by Lady Mary. Foreigners, however,
came only if they were granted special privileges, a charter to set up
workshops that otherwise would have been a monopoly of Viennese
citizens, and the precious freedom to practise the Protestant faith
if this happened to be their denomination.

At first there was an uneasy truce between the quickly established
Viennese citizen-guild of silk weavers—the Brotherhood of Citizen
Manufacturers of Velvet, Gold, Silver and Part-Silk Stuffs—and the

privileged intruders. Later unrest broke out, and in 1732 the government made it an excuse to whittle down the guild. From then on, a
state-aided silk and ribbon industry developed at Vienna, training
native apprentices, and in time creating something like Viennese
patterns and a Viennese taste. And in 1756, when the journeymen
silk weavers went on strike against low wages, Maria Theresia had
them all arrested.*

"Want of genius and industry in the people", as in Lady Mary's
verdict? Say rather that the traditions of craftsmanship and the
beginning of manufacture had been deeply upset by the upheavals of
the Counter-Reformation and the wars. In spite of this, the foreign
immigrants who came to fill the gaps once the Turkish threat was
removed were time and time again assimilated by the Viennese, and
their skill was being naturalised. Unless such facts are fitted into the
picture, the image of eighteenth-century Vienna remains unreal, no
more than a shell in the shape of a baroque façade filled by music.

There is for instance the case of porcelain manufacture. Right after
the start of the great Meissen enterprise, two middlemen of the court,
one of them with the French name of du Pasquier, went in company
with a Viennese merchant to set up the second china factory of Europe
in Vienna. They stole at least one important artist-artisan from Meissen,
who knew the secret of porcelain alchemy. In 1718 they obtained the
privilege of manufacturing fine china, and established a workshop in
the suburb near Prince Liechtenstein's and Count Althan's summer
residences. The venture was completely new, so that no fossilised guild
was there to hamper it, but also no body of journeymen on which to
draw. After some years of experimenting the firm was heavily in
debt and appealed for help to the City Corporation; in 1744 the State
took it over, and it was run by court employees, though with du
Pasquier as the manager. Slowly colours and patterns and shapes were
emancipated from foreign models and attained distinction. The
products of the Viennese porcelain factory showed a frank pleasure
in gilt and gingerbread colours which had charm, but possibly fitted
the simpler Viennese homes better than the lustre of great houses. On
the continental market they could hardly compete with Meissen or
Sèvres, yet even the home market suffered under the new wars and the

* For details on the Viennese silk manufacture of the eighteenth and nineteenth
centuries, see contributions by Dr. Braun-Ronsdorf to the review *Ciba-Rundschau*,
Basle, April 1954.

insecure finances of State and public. By 1780 the factory had a small annual surplus, 300 workers, and a large, valuable, unsalable stock which rapidly depreciated and became outdated. Joseph II tried to sell the establishment to rid the exchequer of a liability (though he proclaimed that he wished "not to withhold any branch of industry from private enterprise"), and found no private buyer. For another three generations the bureaucratic management carried on.

This little case history illustrates the shortage of capital resources in eighteenth-century Vienna. By the time of the French Revolution, no industrial and financial bourgeoisie of any substance and cohesion had emerged. This circumstance had a profound and lasting effect on the ideas of incentives and rewards among the Viennese. All prosperity, even that of small tradesmen and merchants, was tied up with the expansion or retraction of court society in all its branches, and with the functioning of a vast officialdom, first of the court proper, then of the imperial administration. The success of a family was measured not so much in money as in signs that it was well-connected and accepted by those higher up. It was the reverse of the saying of Anita Loos's blonde: "Kissing your hand may make you feel good but a diamond bracelet lasts for ever." What seemed to last for ever in the eyes of the average Viennese was not money (ups and downs of fortunes, bankruptcies and forced auctions were too frequent for that, even in the best circles) but a title, preferably aristocratic, or at least the questionable knighthood of a newly conferred *von*. And what lasted for the rest of one's life, and was less difficult to get, was a court post of sorts (in a later epoch it would be a public post) with the corresponding official label, which was a compensation for the devastating shabbiness and irregular payment of the salary.

The importance of having a bureaucratic title, almost any title beginning with the formula K.K.—*Kaiserlich-Königlich*, "Imperial-Royal"—began to haunt many Viennese in the later years of Charles VI's reign, when the new aristocratic caste sealed itself off as best it could, when the new bureaucracy changed from a court retinue to a State machine increasing in size, power and stability, and when old forms of economic life broke up while new ones quickly came under the control of those very bureaucrats. A sense of social inferiority went with the material insecurity of the middle class; therefore the smallest official title that placed the bearer at a fixed point of the Establishment became a saving grace. There was a solid background of experience to an attitude which only too often turned into ludicrous or pathetic snobbery.

The composer Karl Ditters von Dittersdorf, a contemporary of Haydn, says in his autobiography:

I was born in Vienna on the second day of the winter month of 1739. My father, born at Danzig, was in the reign of Charles VI Imperial-Royal Court and Theatre Embroiderer; and as he was also a good draughtsman, he was elected First Lieutenant in the Citizens' Artillery and in the Bavarian war, which broke out after Charles VI's death, commanded the so-called Löbel Bastion with twenty cannons. His income was enough to permit him to give his five children a better education than was common among the middle class [bei Bürgerlichen]. We three sons, of whom I was the middle one, studied at the Jesuit grammar school, and moreover we had as a tutor a priest who received lodging, board and pay from my father. . . . In addition my father arranged it that the five of us were taught French, which he himself spoke very well. Since he had at the same time a taste for music, he employed a violin teacher for my eldest brother.

In this case, the rapid rise from the lower to the upper edge of the middle class within two generations was explained by the special quali-fications of father and son at the most propitious time. The father, one of the host of foreign master-craftsmen absorbed by Vienna, held his excellent post at court, with the letters, K.K., Imperial-Royal, preced-ing the prosaic description of his office, because his skill fitted in with the Emperor's passion for grandiose theatrical functions which con-sumed untold embroidered costumes. The son was awarded a title of gentility, which raised him to the status of a gentleman-commoner, because his compositions pleased Maria Theresia's music-loving court, and because he had led the private orchestras of influential grandees. But so had Joseph Haydn, incomparably the greater composer, without reaping a similar reward. Haydn, however, had had no K.K. court official as a father to launch him, and he was a genius.

The ascent of thousands of Viennese families began similarly, with an artisan or tradesman attached to the court of Joseph I or Charles VI, and rose in a slow curve to the patriciate without passing through the industrial or financial sphere from which other strata sprang somewhat later. As this sort of family tradition set its stamp on one "reference group" (to use a sociological tag) of the old middle class, the Bürgertum, I shall quote two more cases, which at the same time illustrate some national strands of the Viennese population.

Early in the reign of Charles VI the church of St. Peter at the centre of the town was at last completed and given its interior decoration. The stucco work was done by the Swiss-Italian Alberto Camesina. He stayed in Vienna, and later adorned the ceilings in his own house in the Schulerstrasse with the most graceful amoretti and nymphs, as though in preparation for the days when Mozart would be composing his *Figaro* in those very rooms. One of Camesina's sons became a lawyer, the grandson an art- and book-dealer, and the great-grandson an eminent art-historian and official, who carried the title Ritter von Camesina with a citizen's dignity. (*Ritter von* and *Edler von* were variants of the plain *von*, deriving from distinct procedures of ennoblement.) In this instance the family stayed within the liberal professions, but eventually touched the civil service, in the middle of the nineteenth century.

My other example comes from my mother's family, and I owe the details, in the most devious and ironical way, to the loathsome investigations into ancestry during the Nazi occupation of Austria.

The first in my maternal grandfather's male line about whom an entry was found in Viennese church records was Johannes Michael Zieglmayer, a "grower of flowers"—the surname hints at peasant origin. In 1704 he married the daugher of a K.K. court gardener and so entered the orbit of patronage at a time when a hundred new villas had to be supplied with bedding plants for the parterres of their formal gardens. His son Josephus (born in the reign of Joseph I!) was already a subordinate official, an Imperial tax- or toll-gatherer in Vienna; I like to imagine, without the faintest justification, that he was the customs man who waved Leopold Mozart and his two children past the barrier at Nussdorf, under the spell of the boy's fiddle. The nurseryman's grandson Carolus, dutifully named after Charles VI, was a clerk in the army pay corps; he married an Italian, daughter of another army clerk in the province of Venetia (then a Habsburg possession), and took her back to Vienna. The great-grandson was a civil servant in the financial administration with a title ending in "Councillor"; he brought a Pole from Cracow to Vienna as his wife. The great-great-grandson, my grandfather, was an officer in the regular infantry and served in the unlucky Italian campaign of 1859. There exists a portrait of him as a young lieutenant in which he looks (it must have been the fashion for loyal officers) like Emperor Franz Joseph in his early, clean-shaven days: slim, in a tight white tunic, hand on sword; a smooth, narrow, grave face; elegant, diffident and arrogant. He married a Lutheran—who retained her faith and brought her children up in it though he was a Roman Catholic—from a family of mixed Thuringian, German-Hungarian and Styrian origin, as though to make the blood richer in Old-Austrian ingredients and introduce a new strain at the same time. In middle age he headed the office of the Mayor of Vienna, was Warden of the Citizens' Old Age Home, Vice-President of the Citizens' Riflemen Club, and *Kaiserlicher Rat* (one of those titles ending with "Councillor" which had lost any meaning), and grew a moustache and tufted beard such as the emperor sported by then. By Imperial grant, which had to do with a romantic adoption story, my grandfather bore the complicated surname Zieglmayer-Hamman Edler von Hollenfeld, simplified it for everyday use, and called himself with pride a commoner. His cousin retired from active service with the rank of Colonel-General and a *von* to his name, the badge of distinction conferred on such occasions.

To sum up, after a slow, unspectacular progress in the imperial service through four generations this particular Viennese family, which stands for many others, reached the level of sub-nobility granted to well-merited officials and officers, the *Beamten-und Offiziersadel*, but remained staunchly middle-class. People reared in this tradition reacted against the growing sense of insecurity in the political machine, and against the onslaught of the new brash bourgeoisie and the new unruly working class, by defending their *Bürgertum* status, their old place in the older society. They did this, more often than not, by looking to the past and cherishing an idealised image of the period when the rise of "their" town, their social group and their own forebears had started: the eighteenth century. It offered to their imagination a safer refuge than the more popular era in the first half of the nineteenth century, when Metternich's system grew rigid, the sentimental cosiness of the suburban lower middle class predominated, and the stagnation of Austria was too noticeable to be disregarded even in retrospect.

I remember being shocked in the flush of my youthful republicanism by my mother's counter-attack: "But, after all, we and all Vienna owe everything to the Old Habsburgs. You know, to Charles VI and Maria Theresia. And of course to *Kaiser Joseph* most of all, because it was he who created the civil service and put the aristocracy in its place." When I wanted to seize upon this last point she hastily added: "And even the aristocrats were necessary in their time because without them we wouldn't have all the palaces, and Vienna wouldn't look like itself, and Haydn, Mozart and Beethoven would have had an even more difficult career."

Ingenuous though this vision was, I believe it to have been widespread. A benevolent emperor (hence certain reservations about the dull, arrogant Charles VI in Viennese tradition), a beautiful town frame built by an otherwise ungifted high aristocracy, and glorious music to fill the heart—God was in his heaven, all was right with that world. This, at least, was the picture a great many educated Viennese liked to conjure up. Even others, who were aware of deep shadows or of varnish, were influenced by this picture when they felt harassed by the reality of their own time.

The composite legend of eighteenth-century Vienna renewed itself, nourished by the view of baroque façades and gardens, whenever one of the recurrent crises of the Austrian State made the contradiction between Vienna's apparently brilliant growth and the Habsburg empire's dry rot more than usually evident. The eighteenth century was, after all, the only not-too-remote period in which the expansion of the city coincided with, and sprang from, an internal or external expansion of the State. Afterwards, from the Napoleonic Wars to the War of 1914-18 which altered everything, the centrifugal forces within the realm were felt increasingly at the centre, in Vienna, and most of all by the civil servants whose palliative, self-defeating task it was to render those centrifugal forces less harmful. No wonder they and those dependent on them looked back with nostalgic regret to the "enlightened despotism" of the eighteenth century, when a sense of widening horizons and constructive statesmanship was stronger than awareness of political ineptitude and social stress. It depended on political leanings which particular span of the era was seen in that alluring light. The sterner conservatives would choose Prince Eugene's design for Habsburg, and Charles VI's reign, when Austria expanded her territory, and the individual hereditary lands together with the annexed provinces were first welded into a coherent whole. Tolerant Catholic moderates and sceptical humanists would fasten upon the times of Maria Theresia, when the inner colonisation of the realm gained sufficient impetus to outweigh territorial losses, and when life in Vienna itself was being urbanised; liberals with a puritanical bent, and progressive civil servants with a sense of mission, would turn to the rule of Joseph II, when unification and modernisation were decreed from above, the new centralist bureaucracy was given dignity outside the feudal code, and the intellectual life of the capital was quickened by unorthodox ideas.

After the collapse of the Habsburg Monarchy in 1918, Robert Musil wrote his famous novel, *Der Mann ohne Eigenschaften* (*The Man without Qualities*). This intricate, convoluted satire was set in the preposterous upper-middle-class world of Vienna on the eve of war, but the hero— who, trying to be himself, appears to submit passively to the purpose- less flow of existence and people—had his home in a house rebuilt in a jumble of styles at various stages, from Rococo to nineteenth-century modernism, yet Baroque in its foundations and fabric. This is, I think, a neat image of the mental atmosphere in which the Viennese upper middle class lived at the time, which permeated Hugo von Hofmanns- thal's early poetry, and which explained the postures of many characters in Arthur Schnitzler's prose and plays. The edifice has collapsed, the baroque foundations have survived. And they belong to no single social group either.

Not far from the verdigrised cupola of St. Charles's Church there stands—or stood in 1964, when this was written—an ugly, dilapidated half-ruin, the last remnant of an old suburban "rent barracks" known as the Freihaus auf der Wieden. Though condemned for years, it is still inhabited by some thirty stubborn tenants. When I left Vienna at the end of 1934, the greater part of the vast block had been demolished already; what is left now looks like a decayed tooth and will soon have to go. But if any building in the whole town encompasses three centuries and a cross-section of the middle and "lower" orders it is the Freihaus.

In 1643 the Emperor Ferdinand III gave to Conrad Balthasar von Starhemberg a piece of land near the river Wien as a fief. Four years later Starhemberg paid to his liegelord 1,000 florins as the price of free tenure, and was granted perpetual exemption from all tax and quarter duties—hence the name Freihaus, literally "free house", a label used for every building relieved of those burdens. Conrad Balthasar's first house on the site burnt down. He built a palatial residence, added a chapel—he had returned into the fold of the Catholic Church, the first after four generations of Protestant Starhembergs—and leased small cottages along the walls of his park to little tradesmen.

During the Turkish siege of 1683, his son, Count Ernst Rüdiger, commander of the town and fortress of Vienna and a great man in his own right, ordered a scorched earth policy, and the Freihaus was burnt down with the rest of the suburb. It was rebuilt as soon as the Turks were beaten off, and for a time the Starhembergs themselves used it in season; they even had Peter the Great as their guest in the Freihaus when he visited Vienna, incognito, in 1698. Things changed with the more aristocratic eighteenth century. Count Georg Adam, raised to the status of prince as head of his house under Maria Theresia, no longer found the Freihaus a suitable abode. When he had to rebuild it again after its virtual destruction by a fire in 1759 which devastated the whole adjacent quarter—and which had started in the yard where timber and firewood from the Starhemberg estates were stored for sale to customers in half Vienna—he did it with a new purpose in mind. It became the biggest tenement house of Vienna, with small flats for modest, poorish people, except for the better-class wing near St. Rosalia's Chapel. Tradesmen, artisans, public employees, artists and persons living on scant private means, moved into flats consisting of one room and kitchen, or one room, cubicle and kitchen. In the vaults on the ground floor there were shops and workshops of every description. It was a suburban community of its own, self-contained but open to newcomers, outside the city gates yet belonging to the town—perhaps the most effective single melting-pot in the whole of Vienna.

The Freihaus that rose from the ashes in slow stages, but mainly between 1785 and 1793, preserved the endlessly long, shallow, irregularly curved front it had had ever since Conrad Balthasar had built his mansion. Meanwhile the houses that had forced this odd shape on his building had gone—legend has it, and many books have repeated it, that a rubbish dump had caused the unlovely curve, but there is no documentary evidence for this—and a fruit and vegetable market had taken its place. But the late-eighteenth-century front had a new feature: the plasterers had decorated the reconstructed walls, as though taking pity on their nakedness, with not unpleasing though clumsy curlicues above the windows. The old gardens were nearly swallowed up by the six courtyards, the thirty-two dark staircases, and the 300-odd poky flats which housed at that time between 1,000 and 1,500 persons, if not more. It was the largest rent-raising property in suburban Vienna up to the time after the First World War when the municipality erected the great blocks of flats for workers. And the foundations of its main façade were—still are in the squalid section left standing—the same as in the seventeenth century.

The Freihaus has so long been a precinct for tradesmen, artisans and the lonely poor that scarcely anyone thinks of it as a sample of Vienna's baroque heritage, but it belongs to it no less than the coldly grand, beetling Starhemberg town house.

Its congeries of passages, stairs, wings and courtyards remained virtually unchanged from the end of the eighteenth century to the beginning of their demolition between 1912 and 1914. Tallow lighting was replaced by candles and oil lamps, the oil lamps by gas—slowly and not in all rooms—while I am not certain that electricity was ever introduced in more than the best wings. At some stage of the nineteenth century water was piped into the passages. Otherwise little changed—for the better.

It must have been in the early 'twenties when I first explored the Freihaus. The dark stairs smelled dank, a smell shot with fumes from kitchens and lavatories. The room of the embroideress to whom I took a message was low and airless; she kept the gas lamp lit in daytime, and her begonias looked sickly. So did she. The curved wall of the long front was a patchy grey. The plaster had flaked off long ago and seemed to have been touched up with thin grey wash. But at the back of the labyrinth of wings and blocks there were unexpected little garden plots with a somnolent country air and coloured witch-balls on rosetree stakes, as quiet as if they were still giving on to the vineyards and market-gardens of the old suburb instead of a landscape of windowless back walls. Or has my memory tinted the picture? The space in front of the shallow curve of the façade was filled with the noise and colour of what was left of the fruit and vegetable market called the Naschmarkt. Open stalls under huge umbrellas, bleached canvas or red-and-white stripes, were heaped with goods still carted in by the old road from the south, from Italy, Carinthia and Styria. A formidable breed of women, notorious for their aggressive wit and gift of juicy insult, harangued the passers-by.

As a small girl I used to be frightened if my mother dared walk past without buying anything, while the women hawkers, the *Naschmarktweiber*, would stand arms akimbo, shrieking first compliments to the beautiful lady and the sweet little girl, and then behind our backs shrill remarks about stuck-up people who didn't even have the money to buy ripe cherries for their poor kids. But I didn't understand all they said, for they spoke the raciest old-fashioned Viennese, fitting well into the Freihaus climate.

In the last century a Prince Starhemberg sold the property to a bank, and the bank sold it to an industrial group. The unbroken tradition was henceforth represented by a family of oil merchants called Marsano, who had been Freihaus tenants from its inception to the start of its demolition, in a corner that had always miraculously escaped ruin and fire. The first signboard their Genoese ancestors hung out is dated 1662. Maria Theresia granted to the Marsanos, who were continually reinforced by nephews from Genoa, the privilege of wholesale merchants. The firm imported or pressed every sort of oil, including a fashionable hair-oil they called Maccanar but which I suspect of having been Macassar oil. Their original hydraulic press, a nine days' wonder at its installation in the seventeenth century, was still in use somewhere in the dark vaults towards the end of the Freihaus. And by that time the Marsanos had become Viennese and patrician. For, like the small town-within-the-town it was, the Freihaus had developed its own layer-cake society.*

The Freihaus had its brief time of glory in the dawn of an enlightenment that never saw its full noonday. In 1786, a year when the block was still being enlarged, the director of a troupe of strolling players set up a small barn-like theatre in the third courtyard. The stage-crazy Viennese then had no permanent theatre in the suburbs except that of Marinelli—for broad farce and comedy—in the Leopoldstadt, the borough on the island between Danube and Danube canal to the north-east of the city. Inside the town walls there were only the two court theatres, one reserved for Italian, the other for German performances.

Joseph II issued a licence to the Freihaus Theatre, stipulating exclusively German performances. It was one of his pet ideas to wean the Viennese from their addiction to Italian opera on the one hand, and coarsely irreverent impromptu farce on the other. After some years Schikaneder, a comic actor, hack playwright and theatrical entrepreneur, took over the Freihaus Theatre but found it difficult to make a financial success of it. He appealed to his brother-freemason Mozart who had, after all, provided the court theatre with its first German comic opera, or Singspiel, Die Entführung aus dem Serail (Il seraglio).

* On the Marsanos, see the firm's brochure L. B. Marsano's Sohn, Wien IV., Freihaus, 1682–1912. On the Freihaus, see Hermine Cloeter, Das Starhemberg'sche Freihaus auf der Wieden, Veröffentlichungen des Vereins für Geschichte der Stadt Wien, Nr.1/3, 1937. Also, under the same title, the account by Else Spiesberger in Jahrbuch der Geschichte der Stadt Wien, vol. 19/20, 1963/64, which incorporates original research and the latest findings. To Dr. Spiesberger I owe valuable personal advice on the subject.

Schikaneder wrote a libretto in German. It was derived from many sources, abstruse, stilted in parts, but also full of popular ingredients: fairy-tale, magic on the grand scale, slapstick comedy, highflown humanist tirades, and a double meaning to the plot, which tilted at obscuranticism in high places, in the best spirit of progressive free-masonry. "Mumbo-jumbo and buffoonery" were the terms by which Mr. Desmond Shawe-Taylor once characterised it. This was the libretto to *Die Zauberflöte* (*The Magic Flute*).

In a small "garden-house" belonging to Schikaneder, in the second big court of the Freihaus, Mozart occasionally sat and worked while the libretto was being produced in bits and pieces. (That he composed the whole opera there, is a nonsensical piece of early journalism.) The conductor Seyfried records in his memoirs that Haselbeck, the prompter, would come and help in putting Schikaneder's rough draft into verse. *The Magic Flute* had its first performance on the shabby stage of the Freihaus Theatre on 30 September 1791, and it was followed by twenty-three more up to the end of the year. To judge by his letters to his absent wife, Mozart enjoyed Schikaneder's *ad lib* jokes as Papageno with the same uninhibited glee as the audience, which loved not only the music but the story, and braved mud, stench and darkness on the banks of the river Wien to hear both.

It is easy now to scoff at text and plot, but even before the music raised them to another plane there was human life in them. When Papageno and Pamina (a surprising conjunction) sing their "Mann und Weib und Weib und Mann reichen an die Gottheit an"—"man and wife, and wife and man, to divinity attain"—it was not yet a hack-neyed message. It was a noble and fresh ideal. When Papageno, after his music-hall fooling, sings about his dream wife: "Sie schlief' an meiner Seite ein, ich wiegte wie ein Kind sie ein"—"She'd fall asleep by my side, I'd rock her to sleep like a child"—it was so simple and direct that every man and woman in an unsophisticated audience had to respond. These two lines with their faulty rhyme sound as though Mozart himself had written them to a dream-Constanze. And when Sarastro sang in deepest tones of those sacred halls where vengeance is unknown and fallen fellow-men are retrieved by love, a Viennese public of 1791 must have invested the words with a pointed meaning.

It was the third year of the French Revolution, the first of a new reign in Austria. Joseph II's experiments in enforced tolerance and reform from above were finished; he himself had revised them and his,

brother Leopold who succeeded him in 1790 began to reverse them.
Libertarians were prosecuted because they might carry the Jacobin
taint—later there was to be an ugly persecution and trial of Jacobin
conspirators in Vienna. The high clergy emerged from its temporary
eclipse and began a new offensive against the pervading Viennese laxity
in matters of faith. (When Pope Pius VI came to Vienna in 1782, in an
unsuccessful attempt to dissuade Joseph II from his radical secularising
reform, he blessed an enormous multitude from the balcony of a Jesuit
church; the irreverent poet Blumauer alone kept on his hat, and
nothing happened to him, which would have been unthinkable in a
Spanish or Italian or even Tyrolean crowd.) Court society, too, was on
the move to recover its political hold and social monopoly which
Joseph II had curtailed. Bureaucracy, no longer driven by Joseph's fierce
humanitarian doctrines, quickly turned into a frustrating machine at the
service of the powers-that-be. The new Viennese middle class was
leaderless, uncertain of its standing as a group and as individuals, without a strong economic basis or guiding ideas. The suburbs did not yet
develop into real slums, because the magnet of important industries was
lacking, but they were crowded with tradesmen, artisans and labourers
in close-knit local communities. The ferment of social change was
there. And in its own fashion *The Magic Flute*—absurd text and
sublime music—marked the exact stage in the disruption of the old
order as precisely as Beaumarchais's *Noces de Figaro* had done for
France in 1784.

The different state and structure of the two societies, one heading for
revolution and the other for a partial counter-revolution, show in the
contrast between the sharp satirical play and the evasive ironies of the
opera. (Mozart's *Figaro* had so little sting in its libretto that it passed
a suspicious court censorship, admittedly before the explosion in
France.) Even the milieu of each first performance illustrates the
contrast. *Figaro* was staged at the Comte de Vaudreuil's elegant
château, by the actors of the Comédie Française, in front of a select
audience disdainful of any criticism levelled at it. "Dialogue and
couplets, the whole piece in fact, was directed against the Court, of
which a great part was present, not to mention our excellent Prince
[i.e. the Comte d'Artois]. Everybody felt the inconvenience of this
lack of taste" — thus the somewhat foolish painter Madame Vigée-
Lebrun. *The Magic Flute* had a squalid makeshift stage in the backyard
of a gigantic suburban tenement, an uneven cast composed of

trained singers and rough barnstormers, and a public in which the musical élite was far outnumbered by people frankly out for enjoyment. In the French château, there was a blatant, fundamentally tragic contradiction between the manner and matter of the play, and the character of stage and audience; in the Vienna suburb, a hazy but powerful communion between the opera and its motley public. Beaumarchais's comedy sounded the tocsin for the old régime of France. Mozart's music dissolved tensions in beauty and gaiety, confirming the belief of the Viennese in their familiar world even as it changed.

Mozart himself, once petted by archduchesses and grandees, composer of perfect *divertimenti* for rococo summer villas, had broken out of the feudal frame and merged with the shifting, shiftless fringe of the Viennese "middling orders". No other of the great composers called "Viennese" because they lived and died in Vienna embodies so fully the social changes of the eighteenth century—not even Haydn, though he entered Prince Esterházy's service with the contract of a glorified valet ("... that he, Joseph Haydn, will daily appear in the ante-chamber before and after noon, whether here in Vienna or on the country estates, and ask to be admitted to receive renewed orders from His Serene Highness as to whether there should be music. . . ."), and died, greatly honoured, in a little suburban house he had bought from money earned in England, leaving the orderly last will of a substantial citizen. Mozart died in a mean two-roomed flat on 5 December 1791, while *The Magic Flute* was playing to full houses in the Freihaus Theatre, and was taken to St. Marx Cemetery in a third-class funeral (cost eight florins fifty-six kreuzer paid to the parish priest of St. Stephen) against the blast of wind and sleet that made the few mourners turn back at the city gate and leave the light coffin on the hearse (cost three florins) to hired men, to a priest at the graveside, and to a gravedigger who had no duty to mark the spot if no one else did.

A pauper is buried at the expense of the parish. A third-class funeral is just a fraction better, because the family pays a minimum of money for its self-respect. Surely the facts of Mozart's last journey are more poignant, even to people who have no belief in mourning rites, than the notion of "a pauper's funeral in the rain", as W. H. Auden put it in his *Metalogue to the Magic Flute* for the Mozart bi-centenary of 1956? Also, the facts are more illuminating than the tradition, especially when they are not merely used as a reproach against the Viennese contemporaries of the dead master, but as the raw stuff of social history.

Apart from books, music and personal belongings Mozart left 60 florins in cash; 133 florins 10 kreuzer in arrears of his salary as court composer, which was 800 florins per annum—or less than a third of Fischer von Erlach's salary as Imperial Superintendent of Works eighty years earlier; about 800 florins' worth of doubtful claims to fees; and a debt of roughly 3,000 florins. It was impossible to guess what his unpublished works would bring in; music publishing was in an embyronic stage. The long-suffering friend Michael Puchberg, who had lent his masonic brother Wolfgang money during the past four years, waived the considerable sum owed to him. Baron Gottfried van Swieten, the court librarian and diplomat whom Eduard Hanslick (in his *Geschichte des Concertwesens in Wien*) called "grave, tall and solemn, with the reputation of being a sort of musical high priest in Vienna", helped to organise a public concert for the widow's benefit to clear the pressing debts. The Emperor Leopold II sent a donation, but his sympathy was lukewarm: the exchequer granted to Constanze Mozart a pension of 200 florins 40 kreuzer a year, an exact third of her husband's salary. It was a pittance. About the same time, the exchequer granted a pension of 400 florins per annum to the widow of a rich Swiss silk manufacturer who had set up a factory in Vienna; but then her claims would have been considered greater than Constanze's as she had rescued the firm after her husband's death, and he had been enticed to Vienna by Maria Theresia to stimulate industry. Music, great or vulgar, was part of people's lives but not a matter of official interest, and no longer, by that time, an accepted feature of official display.

Even so Mozart's death must have commanded, did command, public sympathy, and the solidarity of friends. And yet, his funeral? When Gottfried van Swieten advised the widowed Constanze in favour of a third-class funeral, and a poor man's grave shared with a handful of strangers, it was a bleakly rational measure in the interests of the debt-ridden survivor, but this fails to explain the terrifying loneliness in which Mozart was sent to his grave and the well of silence in which he was buried. The Viennese people had not yet developed their ghoulish delight in a "lovely funeral"—*eine schöne Leich*—which was still considered a prerogative of the great and rich. Mozart's own family displayed a curious indifference to sentimental gestures, as had been proved by their earlier matter-of-fact attitude to mother Maria

Anna's death in Paris—in his moving letter to his father, Wolfgang had mentioned nothing about her burial place. But there were still Mozart's masonic friends, generally prone to sententious utterances. How to explain it all, except by the facile formula of Viennese callousness?

Franz Grillparzer, who was born in the year of Mozart's death, had an interpretation of his own. He saw in the neglect of Mozart, alive and dead, an example of the ugly trait he, and many after him, attributed to the Viennese: a resentment of any man of genius because he showed up the others' mediocrity. In 1844 Grillparzer spoke his mind in a scathing epitaph for Mozart's shy, unsuccessful composer-son Wolfgang:

> The Son of Great Mozart:
> The World neglected him as it did his Father,
> Although it had only Virtues to forgive him,
> And no Greatness.

Grillparzer judged out of the mood of his time and projected his personal experience back onto the past. In his generation, which was inspired by the Romantics, and had seen the rise and fall of Napoleon, the fierce struggle of Beethoven, and the intellectual sway of Goethe over the German-speaking élite, the idea that genius had a special place and special rights in society had won acceptance. In the eighteenth century not even genius itself, least of all in the person of Mozart, was certain of having rights that would upset the existing hierarchical values—Beethoven being the revolutionary exception. What Grillparzer said was, and remained, a useful thrust at the smug legend of Vienna as the "capital of Music", as though everyone shared in the highest understanding, and at the self-admiration to which his Viennese contemporaries inclined as much as their successors. It has become part of the anti-legend of Vienna, the reverse side to the rose-coloured legend, but this does not necessarily make it a true explanation.

While Mozart was laid out in that dingy room in the Rauhenstein-gasse, a certain Count Deym appeared and took a death mask in wax. (Constanze's copy of it was smashed in a domestic accident, not to her regret as she thought it an ugly thing.) Deym was a bizarre man who, after having to flee the town under Maria Theresia's reign because of a duel, had mastered the art of moulding in wax and plaster abroad. This was the era of neo-classicism and Winckelmann's popularisation

D

of "noble simplicity and quiet grandeur" in the shape of Greek
sculpture, and Count Deym made a small fortune out of plaster casts
of antique statues. In 1790 he returned to Vienna under the assumed
name of a commoner which deceived nobody, least of all the police,
but was a sop to Cerberus. He opened a sort of Madame Tussaud's
and turned it into a popular sensation. One vault was rigged out as a
mausoleum with the wax figures of Joseph II, who had died that year,
and of Laudon, the most famous among Maria Theresia's war lords.
There, a mechanical organ contrivance played a dirge which was one
of several pieces Deym had commissioned Mozart to write for that
curious instrument, the *Orgelwalze*.

When Count Deym was in possession of Mozart's death mask and a
set of his clothes, he invited the Viennese to come and "see Mozart in
his own dress". Many years later, long after the failure of his enterprise,
Deym endeavoured to slip back into his former social milieu by
marrying Josephine Countess Brunswik, the sister of Beethoven's pupil
Therese. But in 1791 he was still a businessman and showman. He
would hardly have invested in Mozart's wax effigy had he not been
certain of its appeal to a wide public. This appeal reached, of course,
circles other than serious music-lovers, but it was none the less remarkable. Its elements were no doubt mixed: anecdotes about the man
who had once been a child prodigy petted by princes, married into a
theatrical family, and played pranks at carnival dances; the popularity of melodies which Mozart might, half seriously, have included
among those "so inane that a fiacre coachman could sing them"—
perhaps "Non più andrai" and "Si vuol ballare signor contino", of
course with German texts, or folk-songs like "Komm, lieber Mai,
und mache Die Bäume wieder grün" or "Das Veilchen" with Goethe's
arch rococo text; and the lingering memory of serenades and dances
played at a wedding reception or a summer fête in the garden of a villa
like Dr. Mesmer's. The point is that the ordinary Viennese citizen did
know of a marvellous musician called Mozart, even if he hardly knew
his music; with the result that Count Deym could cash in on it in
a grotesquely macabre fashion. There was no unbridgable gulf between
the well-educated connoisseurs, the well-bred patrons and fastidious
musicians on the one hand, and the many, the very many, who merely
enjoyed melody on the other. This was one of the legacies the
eighteenth century left to the nineteenth in Vienna.

And though nobody, not even the widow, took the trouble to mark the exact spot where Mozart was buried—by the time this was felt to be shameful all traces were blurred—the love of Mozart in its simplest form survived among the people. O. E. Deutsch quotes, in his documentary biography of Schubert, an entry of August 1827 in a diary (Franz von Hartmann's) which describes a brief encounter with Schubert in a *Heurigen* tavern at Grinzing, where there was a solitary old violinist: "The old fiddler played Mozart. . . ."

In 1833, the Silesian writer Heinrich Laube, in later years director of Vienna's Burgtheater, came to Vienna in search of copy for amusing travel sketches. Beethoven had died six years ago, Schubert five; two years ago the German opera house had folded up, and Rossini was the rage; Vienna was filled with the fame and the tunes of Lanner and Johann Strauss the Elder. But Laube noted: "He [Mozart] is still the only one who fulfils the highest demands of the laws of art and yet delights the simplest understanding", and told the following story:

I went several times to the Spittelberg where Mozart had his daily game of skittles, and listened to stories about him. My informant was an old fellow who recalled the good times he had had with Mozart. "If you think he was one to mope, you're far out, sir." And he would start telling tales about the jokes and fun they'd had together. It always ended with the expression of the wish that he could see him again in his shirt sleeves and red waistcoat, both cheeks a-bulge with something he was chewing, his eyes full of laughter—and "making all nine, the rascal".

Laube loved to heighten the local colour, and to embellish or sentimentalise the traditions he observed. But why should his story not have been substantially true? By the time Laube had tracked it down, Mozart had become a legend among the Viennese, and somewhere at the back of this legend was a sequence of direct, genuine impressions: "He was one of us . . ." Down to the shabby way in which he was buried.

There is another thread which leads to the heart of the matter by helping to explain the neglect of Mozart's grave and the mental climate at the time of his death, all of which plays so considerable a part in generalisations about the Viennese.

The intellectual leaders of Vienna were still imbued with the ideas of the Enlightenment which rejected "superstitions", and with the austere, impersonal public ideals of Joseph II. It is fashionable to speak of rationalists as cold, sterile and so forth, and if the abstract formulas of those philosophising reformers are read by themselves they sound chilly indeed. But the rationalists of the second half of the eighteenth century were also sentimentalists. Their counterpart, Jean Jacques Rousseau, had taught them to exalt their emotions and to indulge in them. In Vienna, there was no fertile soil for sheer theory. Young Gottfried von Jacquin, Mozart's pupil, confidant, and companion in hilarious exploits, was a good Josephinian, but he wrote in his teacher's album: "Neither reason nor imagination—love, love, love is the soul of genius." That he didn't keep his emotions on this lofty peak all the time is evident from the playful, teasing nonsense Mozart wrote to him: "... dearest friend, dearest Hinkity Honk..." But when Mozart died, men like young Jacquin, or his father, the famous botanist and scientist, or the solemn Austrianised Dutchman van Swieten, who initiated the first performance of Handel in Vienna, would have thought it degrading and materialistic to pay attention to the poor body, emptied of the spirit.

In 1784, Joseph II issued a decree regulating funerals and interments. He was concerned about hygienic conditions in the overpopulated city and the preservation of useful materials in short supply like cloth and even timber. The decree stipulated that no one was to be buried in clothes and in a coffin; every parish was to have a stock of coffins in various sizes, available to all parishioners free of charge; once in the churchyard, the bodies were to be lowered, wrapped in a shroud, into a communal grave and covered with quicklime. There should be a single religious ceremony for all the dead of a day. Nobody was to be buried inside a church or within the city, all burials were to be in graveyards outside the town walls; monuments were to be erected not on graves but along the cemetery walls.

It was an imposition, offending against deep-seated notions, feelings and fears, and against ancient—though not early Christian—traditions. The immediate resistance was so great (of a score of pamphlets which were as outspoken as the temporary relaxation of censorship permitted, nearly all attacked the decree) that Joseph II had to retract his rescript, leaving everyone free to deal with dead relatives as he wished. However, the clauses prohibiting burials within the walled city or inside a church stood. An odd sequel to the episode was that it was followed, not by a wave of funerals with a surfeit of pomp and circumstance, but by a short period when the show, the social exhibition, was kept to a minimum, except in the sphere of the conventional aristocracy. Joseph II himself was, of course, buried in the great mausoleum of the Habsburgs at the Capuchin Church, in the heart of the city.

The people most likely to understand the purpose of the Emperor's ill-devised and unpsychological measure were cultured free-thinkers, sceptical scientists, and all those who satisfied their need of symbolic action by masonic rites. They would interpret it as an intent to deal with "dust, ashes and nothingness" in an uncompromisingly utilitarian fashion, to the greater benefit of the living. What they would fail to understand, since they themselves thought it crass materialism to make much of the human clay, was that most of the living (though not feather-brained, selfish Constanze Mozart) refused to reap benefit at the expense of their warm, muddled, comforting feelings. To free-masons, death was the key—one of their master words!—to liberation, and to the union of the liberated spirit with the Divine. It was to be celebrated in solemn gatherings of brothers, through a symbolic ritual and to strains of music such as Mozart's *Maurerische Trauermusik*, which he wrote for his Lodge to celebrate the memory of a Duke of Mecklenburg-Strelitz and a Count Esterházy of Galantha, who was christened Franz and familiarly called Quinquin—like Hofmannsthal's Octavian Count Rofrano in *Der Rosenkavalier*.

Shortly before the death of his father, Mozart wrote in a letter to him that he had learnt to understand death as "the key to our true life" and come to terms with it by thinking every night, before falling asleep, that he might not be alive the next day. "And all the same nobody who knows me can say that I'm gloomy or sad among people." The same integration is found in the music of *The Magic Flute*, the opera that is of all Mozart's works the most Viennese, in spite and because of its libretto.

The Magic Flute is also the work which integrates two strains in the theatrical life of Vienna—always a most significant part of the city's cultural and social life—and has influenced non-realistic Viennese play-wrights since, from Grillparzer and Raimund to Hofmannsthal. At the beginning of the baroque era, these two strains were running apart, as elsewhere, separated by language (Italian for the heroic, vernacular for farce), presentation and spirit: the high road and the low road. To gauge the depth of the popular tradition that went into *The Magic Flute* where the two roads merged, it is useful to return once more to Lady Mary Wortley Montagu's unique eye-witness accounts.

She tells in a letter purporting to be written to Alexander Pope that she has been to an opera performance in the garden of the Emperor's summer palace, the New Favorita, and on a Sunday too, *pace* the

Church of England. (Charles VI neglected Schönbrunn; the New Favorita is a building with a vast, unexciting, purely italianate front.) Lady Mary was staggered by the magnificence with which Fux's opera *Angela Vincitrice d'Alcina* was staged:

... I can easily believe what I am told, that the decorations and habits cost the emperor thirty thousand pounds sterling. The stage was built over a very large canal, and, at the beginning of the second act, divided into two parts, discovering the water, on which there immediately came, from different parts, two fleets of little gilded vessels, that gave the representation of a naval fight ... the story is the Enchantments of Alcina, which gives opportunity for a great variety of machines, and changes of the scene, which are performed with a surprising swiftness. The theatre is so large, that it is hard to carry the eye to the end of it; and the habits in the utmost magnificence, to the number of one hundred and eight. No house could hold such large decorations; but the ladies all sitting in the open air, exposes them to great inconveniences, for there is but one canopy for the imperial family; and the first night it was represented a shower of rain happening, the opera was broken off. ...*

This was the illusive world peopled by heroes, sorceresses and divinely inspired princes, in which the court liked to find its mirror image. The subjects were taken from the Italian Renaissance court poets, from Boiardo or Tasso or Ariosto, or from new versions of Greek and Roman myths; they were re-written and newly composed in every generation by an assorted pair of court poets and court composers. Sumptuous costumes (here Dittersdorf's father came in as K.K. court embroiderer), painted architectural scenes, limitless, ever changing vistas in cunning perspective, and the most ingenious machinery were deployed to present Olympus, or the Elysian Fields, or a magical Mediterranean Sea. The finest Italian singers achieved the height of beautiful unreality. And somehow it was always flattering to the monarch and his court. Even Gluck, who revolutionised the serious opera by giving it passion and cohesion, left the aristocratic Olympus serene, untroubled and beautified. Chevalier de Gluck—who unlike Mozart used the title of knighthood that went with his Papal order— died in a charming garden villa near the Freihaus, in 1784, honoured, safe and sated.

By way of contrast with the imperial opera, Lady Mary was taken

* Mr. Sacheverell Sitwell has given a marvellous description (in *Southern Baroque Art*, pp. 165 ff.) of a performance in baroque Vienna when the famous castrato Farinelli sang before Charles VI. Lady Mary's account is much drier— but she was there in person.

to the playhouse where German comedies were given, and found it disconcertingly low-ceilinged and dark. The boxes were full of "people of the first rank", yet the play itself, a Viennese version of Amphitryon, not only sent her into gales of laughter but also shocked her by its coarseness, or so she pretended. She had been wise enough to go with an Austrian lady who explained the meaning or *double entendre* of every word to her. Here is a passage of her "letter to Pope" dated 14 September 1716, but probably copied from her diary:

> . . . I never laughed so much in my life. It began with Jupiter's falling in love out of a peep-hole in the clouds and ended with the birth of Hercules. But what was most pleasant was the use Jupiter made of his metamorphosis; for you no sooner saw him under the figure of Amphitrion, but, instead of flying to Alcmena with his raptures Mr. Dryden puts into his mouth, he sends for Amphitrion's tailor and cheats him out of a laced coat, and his banker of a bag of money, a Jew of a diamond ring, and bespeaks a great supper in his name, and the greatest part of the comedy turns upon poor Amphitrion's being tormented by these people for their debts, and Mercury uses Sosias in the same manner. But I could not pardon the liberty the poet has taken of larding his play with not only indecent expressions, but such gross words as I don't think our mob would suffer from a mountebank; and the two Sosias fairly let down their breeches in the direct view of the boxes . . .

Here, then, is the soft underbelly of the baroque Olympus exposed to rude laughter. The passage is famous with Austrian scholars who, in the absence of any text of the farce *Amphitruo*, have used it to trace the pattern of Viennese popular comedy even at that early stage—the comic clash between an upper and a lower world, and the presentation of deities (or fairy kings) with every frailty of poor ordinary human beings. Literary history apart, I believe that it is equally interesting as a piece of evidence to show an ingrained attitude of the people of Vienna. At a time when the Viennese exhibited the most complete and apparently most genuine respect for the social hierarchy—at a time when this hierarchy seemed no less permanently established than the state balcony of a palace on the brawny shoulders of cyclopean slaves—popular farce expressed an utter lack of hero worship and reverence for an Olympic order.

The theatre, whether of barnstormers or of a company patronised by the court, was always a place where the Viennese could release suppressed judgement and half-conscious criticism, in safety and harmlessly. In the last analysis, unaffected bawdy, tolerant and self-indulgent laughter, realistic fantasy and home-grown satire, all revealed the disrespect underlying the Viennese submission to their "betters". This disrespect, however, was a symptom not of simmering rebellion but of disenchanted acquiescence. With the safety valves open, the gods of baroque Vienna were secure in their marble-and-gilt Olympus after all, even if the mass of the people refused to consider them beings made of a finer clay. A knowledge of their rulers' human shortcomings has never disturbed the allegiance of the Viennese, as long as there was no cold meanness in them.

The Magic Flute presented a different Olympus, beings ennobled by great ideals which they shared with searching, erring humans and taught to the most basely selfish. There was laughter and farce still, there was the machinery of black and white magic, but the deus ex machina was luminous, compassionate Reason. In the struggle against the powers of darkness not only Prince Tamino, but also the bumbling vulgarian Papageno had his part. With all the ingredients inherited from the baroque period absorbed and transformed by the music, it held out a promise of new vistas which would no longer be painted architecture.

In 1857 the Emperor Franz Joseph decreed the razing of the fortifications of Vienna, and the incorporation of the suburbs (Vorstädte) in the city, thus unleashing the second great wave of building. By then the aristocratic and absolutist system was in rapid decline. The palace gardens had shrunk to islets amid solid rows of humdrum houses, or had disappeared, or been turned into public parks where children played and nursemaids gossiped. Yet many of the summer palaces themselves still ringed the core of the old town, which contained the darker, heavier town palaces; and the mere presence of this double shell of baroque Vienna influenced the following generations more strongly and subtly than rearguard actions of the old aristocracy could have done.

The bourgeois promoters of modern Vienna in the eighteen-seventies and -eighties sought to set the pomp and colour of spacious residential quarters against the harmonious dignity of the great baroque houses round the corner; their architects strove at all costs to outshine the old palaces by the Renaissance-style buildings with which they lined the Ringstrasse, the wide boulevard that took the place of the Glacis between city and suburb.

The next generation of middle-class intellectuals shied away from

the blowsy eclecticism of their elders. Haunted by a sense of futility
in the present, they began to conjure up the mirage of rococo Vienna
as a backdrop to their sophisticated games of wit.

When Hugo von Hofmannsthal, still in his teens, wrote a verse
prologue to the published version of Arthur Schnitzler's satirical
society comedy *Anatol*, he started by painting the scenery of a formal
garden, now neglected:

> Hohe Gitter, Taxushecken,
> Wappen, nimmermehr vergoldet,
> Sphinxe, durch das Dickicht schimmernd . . .
> . . . Knarrend öffnen sich die Tore.
> Mit verschlafenen Kaskaden
> Und verschlafenen Tritonen,
> Rokoko, verstaubt und lieblich,
> Seht . . . das Wien des Canaletto,
> Wien von siebzehnhundertsechzig . . .

> Lofty railings, yew-tree hedges,
> Coats-of-arms no longer gilded,
> Sphinxes glimmering through the thicket . . .
> . . . Creakingly the gates swing open.
> With cascades in drowsy trickle
> And with drowsy lolling tritons,
> Graceful, powdery Rococo,
> See: the Vienna of Canaletto,
> Vienna of the seventeen-sixties . . .

This older Vienna, seen in the reality of formal gardens run to seed,
in the mirror of Bellotto-Canaletto's paintings, and in the tinted
looking-glass of a self-conscious imagination, was the background
which the adolescent Hofmannsthal imagined for the theatre of
"Young Vienna" in the 'nineties. In such a garden landscape they were
to play-act their own plays, "early ripened, sad and fragile".

Still later, after the turn of the century, when the tradition of Old
Vienna was being commercialised and cheapened, and the smell of
decay was getting more obtrusive, some leaders of the same generation, notably Hofmannsthal himself and the essayist Hermann Bahr,
went further back in their search for healthy roots, back to Prince
Eugene of Savoy and the symbols of the Church of St. Charles
Borromee. At the same time there had been all through the nineteenth
century, and beyond it, a minority of civil servants who felt themselves

heirs to the vision of Joseph II, of which the severely plain public buildings of his era, without the sculptured power of High Baroque, and without the grace of Rococo, but still with a grand secular sweep, were mute witnesses.

The attitude of the Viennese in general to this part of their town's tradition varied not only with each generation, but with every social layer, and almost every urban district. The eighteenth-century façades had become permanent symbols; the interpretation of the symbols changed time and time again.

In the 'sixties of the last century the German dramatist Friedrich Hebbel, who lived in Vienna for practical reasons without ever wanting to be a Viennese, seized upon the stone giants guarding palatial doorways as a poetic allegory. By then the belief in a permanently settled hierarchical world had gone, but some of it survived in the treacherous form of a national scale of values. To Hebbel those figures symbolised the "servant nations" (they sound much like Kipling's "lesser breeds without the law") which until then had carried on their backs the weight of German supremacy in Austria. He, the German, was afraid of their rebellion. It would bring down the ramshackle edifice—which it did. In a poem addressed to the King of Prussia in 1864, he wrote:

> Auch die Bedientenvölker rütteln
> Am Bau, den jeder tot geglaubt.
> Die Tschechen und Polacken schütteln
> Ihr strupp'ges Karyatidenhaupt.

> Even the servant nations make
> The structure stir which all thought dead.
> The Czechs and Poles begin to shake
> Each shaggy atlantean head.

After the First World War, when my own generation was very young and optimistically rebellious, I was not alone in thinking of those enslaved, tortured stone giants as symbols of social injustice. They were downtrodden and disinherited, still held subject but already vigorously stirring. Like Samson they would bring the whole building down in ruins, as they had done in the East. The stately beauty of Baroque seemed to enclose an ugly secret that marred it: the price for it was paid by the vanquished beasts of burden.

And yet it was impossible to deny the legacy of Baroque in that town of ours. I have only to recall my childhood in a district of many palaces, the old Landstrasse suburb. The borough had much else, a slum area of squalid cottages near the Canal, long shoddy streets of suburban tenements, and many pretentious apartment houses such as that in which I grew up, built in a bad imitation of late-Victorian Gothic. But when I was taken for a walk it was to the Botanical Gardens which Jacquin, the father of Mozart's friend, had founded, or more often to the park of Prince Eugene's Belvedere.

The Belvedere is a terraced garden with an upper and a lower palace. Johann Lucas von Hildebrandt built them, and planned the garden as well, between 1700 and 1724. It was a challenge to the French court, and the counterpart to the Duke of Marlborough's Blenheim Palace. But while Blenheim is the perfect example of exotic Baroque transplanted, fantastically, into an Oxfordshire landscape, the Belvedere fuses contemporary elements of international architectural art in such a manner that it seems to belong to the soil on which it rose. Prince Eugene, the puny, solitary, cantankerous Italian bred at Versailles who never learnt to speak German properly and signed his name in the trilingual version of "Eugenio von Savoye", was the architect of the regenerated Habsburg empire and therefore of Vienna's rise to the status of a true metropolis. Here he grew roots. He chose as the site for his summer residence a long slope overlooking Vienna from the south-east, so that the ridge of the Kahlenberg, bisected by the spire of St. Stephen's, bound the horizon. First the gardens were laid out by a Frenchman imported from the Bavarian court. Then Hildebrandt built at the foot of the hill a long, one-storeyed, outwardly simple edifice in which the Prince set up living quarters decorated with the most lavish extravagance of marble, stucco and gold; this was the Lower Belvedere. Finally the Upper Belvedere Palace on the hill crest was completed for great receptions and festivals.

Articulated by the copper-green roof, the jutting middle part, and four octagonal, domed corner pavilions, it seems an Arab tent out of the Thousand-and-One Nights, hovering weightlessly above the topmost terrace. Long clipped maple hedges lead down from it and meet below, on the level, in miniature mazes. Dark, low yew hedges, and balustrades with small statues along yellow-sanded walks link the two palaces, and on each side of the garden an imposing staircase, with a sloping pavement of huge stone flags set between twin stairs, marks the cut from incline to level. In the niches of the leafy walls stand sandstone figures with fluttering draperies. A great basin with leaping fountains, tritons and nereids breaks up the centre of the slope, and shallow basins are sunk into squares of lawn. High up, on the steps to the flagged ceremonial terrace, lie amiable sphinxes. From there Canaletto's nephew Bernardo Bellotto (whom likewise the Viennese insist on calling Canaletto) painted a view of the distant city, with the two great cupolas of St. Charles Borromee and the nearby Salesian convent church to the left and right in the middle distance.

For me it was a magic place, and I shall never be able to see it without a veil of enchantment. When I was playing at hoops or diabolo or "Who's afraid of the Black Man?" in those long sanded walks I saw, unthinkingly but with joy, the silhouettes and colours Bellotto had seen, the two verdigrised cupolas, the blue distant hills, and the needle of St. Stephen's. Turning round I would see the fine web of arabesques round the windows, and the rise and fall of the pitched tent roofs. I never saw the inside of the palace which then—to my precocious indignation—was the residence of the heir to the throne, Archduke Franz Ferdinand, whose heavy black moustaches I hated in the photographs. Even had I been able to see the vaulted garden hall, the *sala terrena*, where the elaborate stucco ceiling was supported by the most violently writhing, most desperately straining stone giants of that whole baroque tribe, I would not have believed that the whole weight of my fairy castle was crushing.

Later we were taken for longer walks, past more tall forged-iron gates and yellow garden walls behind which the fruit trees bloomed earlier than elsewhere, to another palace and garden, the Schwartzenberg Park. There, among the "English" boscages, stood statues of brawny young Romans with Sabine women in their muscular arms, their dramatic postures fixed in sandstone. The women were wringing their hands, or lifting their arms to show off beautiful naked breasts, giving lessons in deportment during a not altogether unwelcome rape. By the upper pond with its huge old carp, lilac and laburnum flowered in early May in front of one of the corner pavilions of the adjacent Belvedere. Their golden and violet sprays would half hide the copper-green little cupola and the pale, mellow stonework. But I could see the small ornaments on the domed roof tiles which were—who had told me?—tassels of the tent-ropes of Prince Eugene's tent-palace.

Still later, when I went to school, I had to go through dark narrow streets with old *Bürgerhäuser* whose window architraves were frowning at me, and palaces whose grey fronts were heavily scored with ornamental bands. I seem never to have looked at any newer house, though this is a trick of memory. It was then I began to dislike the male caryatids, supporting their balconies with so much effort. In terms of my priggish school lore I wondered why these old princes and counts had preferred them to the harmonious female caryatids—the newer Pallavicini Palace had them, in an insipid version of Greek models—who carried their burden proudly and effortlessly. And I began to love the stern front of the Hofburg's library wing on the Josefsplatz; this was, I thought, true dignity and gracious beauty in stone, unmarred by distortion. Every day I timed the last minutes of my walk to school by the milky-white or dapple-grey stallions of the Spanish Riding School which their grooms led through the archway at a quarter to eight. There was dignity and gracious beauty in living flesh. The horses figured in many of my daydreams, and even then I had the feeling that they belonged inseparably to those palace fronts.

All this was my Vienna when I was eleven years old. It fascinated me. It had an excessive influence on my taste. When the architect Adolf Loos built the first functional business and apartment house without any ornament, architrave or window frame, the "house without eyebrows", I was as childishly incensed as any grown-up philistine that he dared put it next to the Hofburg and the old Michaelerhaus. What specially annoyed me was the idea that it had no moulding or scroll in which the snow could settle in the gentle lines I loved. But it also stirred me to thought by the tremendous implied contrast. It is my belief that in many similar and different ways the visual image of baroque Vienna has been absorbed by generation after generation of adolescent Viennese of the middle classes. How they transformed its influence is another question.

I said: of the middle classes. There were also, more important in size, population and social impact, the ugly factory districts and new working-class suburbs where no mellow building or old park rested the eye. The people who lived and worked there, often recent immigrants to the town, had another picture of Vienna as it had been, as it was, and as they wanted it to be. Neither burdened nor enriched by the visual baroque heritage, they were free to work out their own tradition. And they did. If they loved the park of Schönbrunn, or looked at the pictures in the marble and stucco halls of the Liechtenstein Garden Palace, or simply wandered through the back-streets of the old city, they did so in unforced spontaneous appreciation. Otherwise they were inclined to be suspicious of the ancient, alien architecture from which they were excluded by taste and milieu, but above all by the undisputed circumstance that it was a class symbol they themselves rejected as such. Their strongest link with the past was an intrinsic part of their lives—the common speech of Vienna.

"We speak badly here in Vienna", Maria Theresia had said to the pedantic German grammarian and poet Gottsched who had come to pay court at what he termed "the new Rome on earth". The Empress was ruefully aware of her own idiomatic, ungrammatical way of talking and writing German. Indeed, the German spoken in Vienna is anything but pure, now as then. In the Viennese dialect, all the Austrian provinces of the old Habsburg realm (not least the Italian, French, and even the Spanish connexions) have left their traces, and the folklore of centuries its deposits. Much has been levelled out, much has been coarsened or turned artificial, much is overlaid by the slang of the day and by current idioms from abroad. But the baroque foundations of the language of Vienna survive in vocabulary and structure.

Hugo von Hofmannsthal wrote in his epilogue to the printed text of the *Rosenkavalier* libretto:

The language cannot be found in any book, but it is in the air, for there is more of the past in the present than we surmise, and neither the Faninals nor the Rofranos nor the Lerchenaus have died out, although their three liveries no longer sport gorgeous colours.

III

Biedermeier

1. BEFORE THE CONGRESS

IN THE first decade of this century the State printing works at Vienna, the *K.K. Hof-und Staatsdruckerei*, issued a set of fine reproductions in the new technique of heliogravure, all of them vistas of Viennese baroque palaces painted by Bernardo Bellotto "called Canaletto". In a note accompanying the folder, Alois Trost staked the claim for the supreme importance of eighteenth-century architecture in the image of Vienna, by first arguing against a popular attitude: ". . . if one speaks of Old Vienna, one thinks of the times of Schubert and Raimund, the Emperor Franz and Metternich. This era, however, left scarcely any trace." He meant visual trace.

It would be easy to attack this contention and show that even architecturally the period which the commentator defined through figures embodying its main concerns—music through Schubert, the popular theatre through Raimund, the patriarchal monarchy through the Emperor Franz I, and the all-pervading system of government through Metternich—has left its mark on the old suburbs of Vienna, though only a faint one on the inner core of the city. Indeed, scattered along streets and obscure side-streets, from the boulevard ringing the old city to the Wienerwald foothills, there still stand small middle-class houses with plain fronts and neat if playful ornamental panels, or sober, well-proportioned apartment houses with an unexpected group of stuccoed children at play over the doorway, or villas with a trace of the "Gothick" in the shape of their windows, all speaking the unobtrusive language of the eighteen-twenties or -thirties.

All the same the comment I have quoted was true when it was made, and is still true. In the imagination of the Viennese (and many non-Viennese) *Alt-Wien*, Old Vienna, stands for that particular period. Moreover, they mean by it not so much the façade, the style of buildings, as the mental climate, the domestic interior, and certain types of music ranging from Schubert's easier melodies to the waltzes of Lanner and the elder Johann Strauss. In the generally accepted usage, the period is limited by two decisive dates: 1815 and 1848, the end of the Congress of Vienna, and the outbreak of the revolution which shattered the old régime even though it was itself defeated.

Rather imprecisely the whole era is known as the Viennese Biedermeier. Biedermeier is the label given to these decades and their characteristic style all over the German-speaking countries, but it was in Vienna that its elements were most beguilingly fused.*

Later legends, whether springing from diffuse tradition or commercial revival, not least from sentimental operettas such as *Lilac Time*, have obscured the view of those complex years. In fact there exist a rose-tinted legend and a black-tinted counter-legend, each producing its mirage.

A symposium called *The Golden Ages of the Great Cities* (London and New York, Thames & Hudson, 1952) decided on the Biedermeier as Vienna's golden age. Alan Pryce-Jones's essay has the title "Vienna under Metternich". Though neither rose-tinted nor uncritical in description and characterisation, it argues the protective virtues of the paternal-authoritarian system under which there developed, as Vienna's "great contribution to European civilisation", an "extraordinary diffusion of kindly temper, of ease, of mutual confidence". The conclusion is that "we can say of the Viennese . . . that they were happy while it lasted". This is one view in its most urbane form.

Another view, diagnosing in the Biedermeier era an escapist stagnation-in-cosiness, was put by the modern Viennese poet Josef Weinheber in the deliberately simplified form of a poem called "Biedermeier". (Weinheber, it should be added, was deeply in love with "his" Old Vienna, with the old half-rural suburbs, the Wienerwald, the parks, the inflections of the dialect when it was genuine, but

---

* The explanation of the term Biedermeier offered in encyclopaedias is that it derived from the title of a series of humorous poems by an otherwise unknown German writer, L. Eichrodt. The satirical weekly *Fliegende Blätter* published them in 1850 under the title *Biedermayers Liederlust*; their fictitious author was presented as a comically naïve Swabian schoolteacher, by name Gottlieb Biedermayer [*sic*]. The name caught on, presumably because it conveys a little-man cosiness— for once the word *Gemütlichkeit* applies—which the younger generation was pleased to attribute, condescendingly, to their parents' world and style of living. As time went on, the word Biedermeier, usually in this spelling, was employed ironically or appreciatively, as the changing waves of taste and attitude to the past would have it.

he hated make-believe and was a satirist and grumbler in the best Viennese fashion.) The poem describes in flat verses a family of nice middle-class people: the father grafting yellow and red roses—the mother lovingly dusting her knick-knacks—auntie dozing in a garden corner—the girl dreaming of her young man, he of her, and the couple whispering across the garden fence at night—the clock striking under a glass dome, time itself vanquished by a figurine. Then a thunderstorm sweeps through the "junk shop", and the dream bubble bursts on the barricades—the barricades of 1848.

The surface of the Biedermeier was certainly glossy, well dusted and well polished, and well policed too; certainly the air was mellow, and the tone was one of sedate gaiety—with occasional outbursts of wild exuberance. It would be as fatuous to deny that a sense of well-being, at times of elation, pervaded the middle classes (they were coming into their own, it was their period more than that of any other group), as it would be to deny or ignore the tensions, fears and repressions which were tunnelling the Biedermeier society of Vienna and rising to the surface in the explosion of 1848. And because this is far more than a period with a pleasant, attractive, small-scale style in applied arts, more than a period in which Beethoven and Schubert worked, lived and died in Vienna—because it is a seminal era, its complexities are more interesting than its simplified traditional image.

The men who dominate an "age" (in itself a vague concept, defying sharp definition!) are more often than not children of an essentially different period. It is the members of a younger generation, born within the new framework of life, who express the period with greater truth, and transcend it either through personal evolution, or through the new beginnings contained in their work. This truism helps to elucidate the cross-currents of the Viennese Biedermeier.

One has only to take the four names mentioned in the superficial remark quoted at the beginning of this chapter, Schubert and Raimund, the Emperor Franz I and Metternich. The two rulers, the monarch as well as his Foreign Minister and all-powerful adviser, were firmly rooted in the aristocratic traditions of a semi-feudal régime: the Habsburg Emperor was born in 1768, Metternich, son of an old Rhineland family, in 1773. In both cases, though in different degrees, rationalist ideas tinted the childhood and early education; each in his different sphere was influenced by Joseph II's experiments in centralist absolutism and recoiled from his humanist doctrines. Both were profoundly shaken by the French Revolution when they were young men, and worked out what amounted to a trauma in their respective policies of government throughout their lives—not least during the Biedermeier years, when they were getting old. Neither of them can be called a Biedermeier character by any stretch of imagination, even though Vienna was truly "under" Metternich, and Franz I its reigning Emperor until his death in 1835. On the other hand the Emperor was essential to the image, because his fears contributed to it an element of pettiness, his appearance and behaviour an oddly middle-class model in high places, and his speech and manner at carefully staged audiences a cosy—*gemütlich*—veneer overlaying the frustrating methods of bureaucratic rule. At least he was a Viennese Habsburg, while Prince Metternich remained a German nobleman aloof in his classicist palace, even when he collected minor Biedermeier art.

Franz Schubert and Ferdinand Raimund belonged to the social groups which made, and indeed which were the Biedermeier, and expressed, each on his own level, moods of the people around them. But again, neither of them could be put under a glass dome, like a figurine, to represent the period. The glass would shatter.

Raimund, the actor and playwright, was the elder of the two. He was born in 1790. His hard childhood was spent in the unsettled years, and his character was already formed, for better or worse, when peace broke out after 1815. Nevertheless he caught, in the best-loved characters of his fairy-tale comedies, something of the essence of suburban Vienna in the eighteen-twenties: a peculiar contentment based on the rueful acceptance of things-as-they-were. His private life was involved and unhappy. In 1836 he committed suicide, from fear of dying insane.

Franz Schubert was born in 1797 in one suburb of Vienna, and died in 1828 in another. His childhood and early adolescence belonged to the uneasy, war-ridden years before the Congress of Vienna and the European peace; his musicianship burst into flower in the first flush of post-war elation, and he died before the political and intellectual climate changed, i.e. before the critical year of 1830. If any of the great Viennese can be said to have grown to full stature in and with the Biedermeier—if any of them can be taken as the embodiment of the town's time-bound civilisation and ageless atmosphere—it is Schubert. Schubert's life reflects not only the sentiment and sentimentality, the gaiety and ease of the Viennese Biedermeier, but also its deep shadows and sharp angles. His music should not be described in non-musical terms, but it had firm roots in the narrow world it transfigured and transcended.

The bare biographical data of birth and death, covering no more than these four key figures of Biedermeier Vienna, point to the importance of the period immediately before the Congress of Vienna. Its political impact on Europe is too obvious to demand explanation: England or Spain, Holland or Germany, Sweden or Russia—each country suffered a sea-change in its encounters with Napoleon's armies and with the ideas that followed in the wake of the French Revolution. Here, however, the question is not how those years affected the body politic of Austria, but how they affected the social and cultural structure of Vienna, and the minds of the individual Viennese. As the Biedermeier was first and foremost a post-war period, the experiences of the preceding war period lay buried in it. They have to be uncovered to explain the inner tensions of their sequel.

In 1797, the peace with victorious France concluded at Campo Formio cost the Habsburgs Lorraine and their possessions in Burgundy; it also cost them Lombardy. In June 1800, Napoleon Bonaparte defeated the Austrians at Marengo; the campaign, followed by the peace of Lunéville, cost the Habsburgs Tuscany. In 1805, the war was carried into the heart of Austria itself. The French occupied Vienna, and the peace treaty of Pressburg not only stipulated the surrender of the province of Venetia, but also the cession to the elector of Bavaria, Napoleon's ally, of the ancient Habsburg dominion of Tirol. Next came the disastrous war of 1809 with its one compensating victory for the Austrian arms at Aspern. Napoleon Bonaparte, no longer consul and generalissimo but the Emperor Napoleon I, dictated his conditions in the Palace of Schönbrunn and took Carinthia, Carniola, Friuli, Dalmatia and Galicia from the Habsburg crown. Immediately afterwards he became, with the able if double-edged assistance of Metternich, the son-in-law and temporary ally of the Head of the House of Habsburg, Emperor Franz I, and so gatecrashed the hallowed circle of "legitimate" sovereign families.

As early as 1804 Franz, then German Emperor with the title of Franz II, had assumed the crown of a hereditary emperor of Austria—which had never been an empire—and called himself Franz I in this capacity. In 1806 he accepted Napoleon's dismemberment of the old German

Reich by decreeing that the "Holy Roman Empire" has ceased to exist.

Yet in the early spring of 1800, when he was still Franz II, the Emperor spent much time over a difficult decision. It concerned Emanuel Schikaneder, the actor-manager who was clamouring for a permit to set up a new theatre in the suburbs of Vienna, on the left bank of the river Wien. Schikaneder had made (and quickly spent) fortunes out of drama and opera—above all *The Magic Flute*—which he staged in the little Freihaus Theatre. But he had been forced to sell out to a stage-struck merchant who was his main creditor, and now he wished to take up a privilege Joseph II had granted him far back in 1786 and Leopold II had endorsed in 1790. The times were favourable for the establishment of a more spacious and more modern theatre in the suburbs, and the building Schikaneder was proposing to use was under construction not far from the Freihaus, though on the other side of the river. Franz II, however, first studied dozens of reports and memoranda on the complicated legal position, as there existed another claimant; he was never capable of delegating responsibility or decision to others even in the case of domestic trivia.

(For instance, although this belongs to a later date, two days after the great battle of Leipzig in 1813, in which the allied Austrian, Prussian and Russian armies defeated Napoleon, the Emperor Franz I —as he then was—put his signature to an order deciding which three out of four Viennese scholarship choirboys whose voices had broken should receive an endowment for further grammar school studies; the emperor endorsed the choice of Franz Schubert, with the rider that good behaviour and industry were of primary importance, "singing and music a subsidiary matter". . . .)

What persuaded the Emperor in 1800 to grant Schikaneder's request, after much pondering, was a short passage in a report from the legal department of the Exchequer:

Finally the political consideration cannot be overlooked that those spectacles have come to be a need for a great part of the public in this town, and that a refusal of the Licence for the building would cause great discontent, particularly among the lower class of public.

When the large theatre in the classicist style then sweeping the continent in advance of the French armies—the style later labelled Empire—was inaugurated in 1801, everybody was ravished by the blue and silver décor, the arrangement of boxes and galleries and the sheer spaciousness: 700 seats and standing room for 1,500 people. It was far better value than the two outdated court theatres in town; the suburbs were getting fashionable, and also economically more important than the aristocratic quarters, just as the aristocratic mansions were being engulfed by a mass of new middle-class dwellings.

The stage curtain of the Theater an der Wien showed a vague romantic landscape with temples and Faërie, a bearded Sarastro, and Tamino pursued by a serpent. Viennese gossip maintained that this was not so much a homage to *The Magic Flute*, on which Schikaneder's fortune was founded, as an allusion to the worthy Zitterbarth who pursued his partner and debtor with demands for a cession of the precious imperial privilege. Schikaneder, however, was no noble Tamino. Over the portico of the entrance he enthroned himself as Papageno in the birdcatcher's feathery costume, playing the pipe of Pan and surrounded by small Papageno-amoretti.

Schikaneder did not last long as licensee of the playhouse. After three years he sold his share and all his rights for 100,000 florins to the persistent Bartholomäus Zitterbarth—a name that sounds as if a German Romantic poet had invented it in a satirical mood, for the surname means, literally, Tremblebeard; a man whose ambition in life it was to own and direct a theatre—but while Schikaneder was in power he offered an astonishing fare to his public. He billed, of course, dozens of his own hastily scribbled farces and comedies, effective tear-jerkers by the German dramatists Kotzebue and Iffland, parodies and musical comedies by forgotten teams. But he also produced *Hamlet*. He put on French plays, and French operas sung in German. He produced no less than four Mozart operas: *The Magic Flute, Don Giovanni* (in German, as *Don Juan*), *Il Seraglio*, and, surprisingly, the grand opera *La Clemenza di Tito* with a German libretto. (Its revival on the operatic stage in the nineteen-fifties was considered a remarkable feat.) Schikaneder did one more thing that should not be forgotten: he engaged Beethoven, with a fixed salary and a year's free lodging in the theatre building, to write an opera for him which, after many vicissitudes, turned out a failure on its first performance. It was *Fidelio*.

With money from the sale of the theatre to Zitterbarth, Schikaneder bought one half of a little baroque château in the suburban village of Nussdorf, had the Queen of the Night painted *al fresco* on one of its ceilings, and was soon forced to sell the property again. He was never able to hold on to money—he might have stood model for the character of the amiable spendthrift who turns up so frequently in Viennese popular tragi-comedy*—in spite of his fertile publicity ideas. One of his stunts was to cash in on the atrocious communications between the theatre and the city, which forced many people to make their way on foot in the dark and rain: he set up a stall for lending umbrellas to the public at a low rental combined with a high deposit. There were about 2,000 private carriages in Vienna, and over 600 fiacres for hire (for a population of round 80,000 in the city proper and nearly 200,000 in the adjoining suburbs) but the Theater an der Wien by no means catered for the well-to-do alone, and pedestrians might use umbrellas . . .

As a producer, in which capacity Zitterbarth retained him, Schikaneder was no less extravagant than in private life. Expenses quickly outpaced the excellent takings; the good businessman, deciding that he would not like to risk ruin after all, sold the theatre with all rights and privileges to a Bohemian nobleman and industrialist who was at the same time the lessee of the two court theatres. Yet the times were getting harder and the censors stricter. They made, for instance, difficulties about the libretto for Beethoven's opera *in statu nascendi* because it contained a Spanish minister as its villain. Joseph Sonnleithner, the author, a prominent member of a prominent patrician family—though a clumsy librettist—had to argue in letters and memoranda that the action in his text was set in the eighteenth century, and that the minister had, firstly, not acted politically but for private motives, and, secondly, was duly punished at the end. *Fidelio* was finally passed for performance.

It was more difficult with the dramas of the rebellious Schiller, not only on the plebeian stage in the suburbs but even in the court theatres with their—presumably—safer audiences. The Secretary of State for Foreign Affairs, Count Stadion, himself banned Schiller's *Don Carlos* because it presented a Spanish Habsburg as the sombre despot he was, and made the real hero, Marquis Posa, demand "freedom of thought" from his sovereign. The book to which I am indebted for nearly all the details in this context, *150 Jahre Theater an der Wien*, by Anton Bauer,

---

* Schikaneder's own end, however, was wholly tragic. He died insane, a pauper; his funeral in 1812 was indeed a pauper's funeral paid for by the parish, and his grave a mass grave. See Eugen Komorcynski, *Emmanuel Schikaneder*, 2nd edition, Vienna, Doblinger, 1951.

quotes a pathetic and significant passage from the diary of a Viennese civil servant, written in 1808:

At the present moment one is bound to remember the times of the unforgotten Emperor Joseph II, since free thought has been relieved from its fetters with the advent of the French; it is now once more permitted to sell political pamphlets and banned books. Schiller's works, too, can be found in several bookshops, and there is reason to hope that his *Wallenstein*, *Don Carlos* and *Maria Stuart* will again be allowed on the stage . . .

The two occupations of Vienna by the French, in 1805 and 1809, were not rich in dramatic conflicts. On the second occasion there was a brief bombardment of the walled city, but the citizens' militia which manned the ramparts did not go into action. On the whole the French forces had orders to behave considerately. There were isolated attempts at an underground resistance movement, for which the French executed Viennese patriots; Arthur Schnitzler used one of these incidents in his drama *Der junge Medardus*, and his portrait of the humorous, sceptical, spinet-playing artisan who quietly gives his life sounds intrinsically true. Of more lasting importance, I would suggest, were the conflicts created by the French occupation in the minds of many Viennese.

The Viennese might have hated being a conquered population at the mercy of the occupiers, but occasionally they felt envious of the greater intellectual freedom which the French officers took so readily for granted—as the quotation from the obscure civil servant's diary shows. They might have been loyal to their sovereign, but they could not help seeing him shrink into dull insignificance beside Napoleon's ruth-less personality. They might have been thrilled by the news of the one and only victory Archduke Charles won for the Austrian arms at Aspern in 1809, but they were shamefacedly relieved—as many decent British people were in 1938 when Mr. Chamberlain bought a brief spell of peace at Munich—when a year later the Emperor's daughter was married to the triumphant Napoleon. In the most sensitive minds, clashes of emotions like these must have left scars. Those to whom music was accessible, and they were the overwhelming majority in Vienna, found release from self-doubts or resentments in the serenity of Haydn (who finished *The Creation* in 1798, *The Seasons* in 1801, and died in 1809), the perfection of Mozart, the clarity of older chamber and vocal music, and the earlier symphonies of Beethoven. The history

of music-making in Vienna during those harassing years, of the many
private circles of cultured dilettanti even more than of fumbling
public performances, gives an idea of the immense rôle music was
playing then.* The other escape route was the theatre. And the experiences of the Viennese, especially of the educated middle class,
which they accumulated during the years of the Napoleonic wars and
the Napoleonic peace, were such as to condition them for the enjoy-
ments of a quiet, stagnant life when the upheavals were a thing of the
past. At least for a time.

Franz Grillparzer was eighteen years old in 1809 when the French
invested Vienna. He was the son of a hyper-sensitive mother, sister to
the *Fidelio*-librettist Joseph Sonnleithner. Her whole life was bound
up in music and in her son Franz—the other sons, less gifted, were
flawed in character—and she was prone to a melancholia that was to
lead to her suicide. His father was a lawyer, unbending rectitude itself,
and a patriotic puritan cast in the stern Josephinian mould. When the
son was Austria's most famous yet eternally frustrated poet he began to
write an autobiography which he never completed. Although it is far
more reticent and decorous than Grillparzer's occasional entries in his
journals, it demonstrates that his painful, life-long vacillation between
the rebel and the loyalist in himself was at least worsened, though not
caused, by the impact of the national catastrophe of 1809. His is an
exceptional case, yet in a heightened form it only makes explicit what
other people in Vienna had been feeling more dimly, and what impressions they carried with them into the piping times of peace after
the Congress.

Even the details of Franz Grillparzer's bleak childhood help to
illuminate the moods and the reactions that went into the chubby
pleasures of the Viennese Biedermeier later on. He grew up in the
high, bare rooms of a dismally sunless apartment connected with his
father's chambers, at the very centre of the old town. There were
occasional outings to the theatre, best of all to popular pantomimes,
and he staged little plays with his cousins; but every failure he had in
his studies led to an implacable veto from his father. Since the father
"had grown up in the Josephinian period", he had no liking for church
ceremonies, so that the boy found no emotional outlet in religious
faith; passed, indeed through an early crisis of belief. In his depression

*See Eduard Hanslick, *Geschichte des Concertwesens in Wien*, Vienna, 1869, for
details about this and the subsequent periods up to 1868.

and "need for some outside diversion" he turned to music—poetry meant as yet very little to him and would have demanded more sharply defined notions, so Grillparzer judged many years later—and for some time thought of nothing but music. The need for music was to stay with him. (Other young men, coming from similar cultured, austerely rational surroundings became, a decade later, Franz Schubert's companions, audience and propagandists.)

The foundations of the Grillparzers' respectable but frugal existence crumbled, as they did for countless other Viennese middle-class families. The inflation of those years, with its spiral of rising prices and steadily depreciating money, was caused by the fantastic rise of the public debt and the successive issues of paper money, all designed to cover the costs of war. It culminated in 1811 with a virtual declaration of bankruptcy by the State, when the existing paper money was devalued to a fifth of its nominal value. This created a new financial crisis and muddle, of course, and the after-effects lasted into the early 'twenties. But the worst times were, for many Viennese, those of the French occupation of 1809, when prices trebled between May and July.* What it meant in terms of human suffering is put baldly in Grillparzer's autobiography:

Then came the war events of 1809, the lost battles, the bombardment of the town, the entry of the French in Vienna, the paralysis of business, the billeting, the war tax and contributions; above all his [the father's] patriotic heart was suffering torment under all these humiliations. . . . While expenses continued to mount with the rising prices, incomes gradually fell to an insignificant amount, until in the last months the entry he made in the ledger, with an uncertain hand, was *Nihil*. He even had to take up a loan, he, to whom the terms contractor of debts and thief were synonymous. To know that the town was occupied by the enemy was abominable to him, and to see a Frenchman was like a knife-thrust. . . .

A few months later the Peace of Pressburg was concluded. Grillparzer's father was a sick man, with no hope of recovery, and was kept in bed for the greater part of the day, so that the news could be hidden from him. Somehow he heard it, angrily told his son to get him a copy of the printed text, and read it—the treaty in which "a third of the Monarchy was ceded to the French". The sick man turned his face to the wall. "From then on he hardly spoke another word." So his son wrote a lifetime later, adding in self-reproach:

* Josef Karl Mayr, *Wien im Zeitalter Napoleons*, Vienna, 1940, p. 110.

In truth I never felt any tender affection for my father. He was too harsh. By striving, most successfully, to lock up every expression of feeling within himself, he made it virtually impossible for anyone else's feeling to reach him. Only later when I had come to understand the reasons of many of his actions, and felt happy in the enduring renown of his almost legendary rectitude . . . did I pay the arrears to his memory. . . .

Wenzel Grillparzer was no doubt too humourless and inflexible to be a model Viennese—he sounds more akin to Mr. Barrett of Wimpole Street—but there have always been significant counter-types to the more popular Viennese attitudes, as a number of old popular plays show. That tribe of austere parents, together with the bewildering influence of the war years, explains the turning which the next generation took in reaction and evasion. Yet there is another side to it as well. Old Grillparzer belonged to the extremely important minority group of educated men who cherished and transmitted the ideals behind Joseph II's reforms when these reforms themselves had been largely revoked and the ideas anxiously emasculated by the ruling caste. Thanks to them and their heirs, Josephinian ideas subsisted as a strong undertow until the Revolution of 1848, and in altered shape beyond it. (I would count my own father, born in 1871, as a Josephinian at heart, and not at all unlike Wenzel Grillparzer in some of his civic principles and puritanical tenets.) In the years of Napoleon's unsettling progress, Josephinian beliefs alone gave to the Viennese a sense of cohesion and the hope of a new start, in defiance of the muddle at home and the forceful new ideas brought from post-revolutionary France by the victors.

Emperor Franz I, or his advisers, knew what they were doing when in 1807 they erected, as the first statue of a sovereign ever set up in Vienna, an equestrian effigy of Joseph II in bronze, in the middle of the beautiful square bounded on three sides by Fischer von Erlach's Imperial Library, and on the fourth by two noble palaces. A gesture towards democracy was needed to reduce complaints against an inept, corrupt aristocratic leadership, and to revive a people's faith in the future; the Emperor's ministers included in the project of reorganisation a plan to strengthen the rôle of the old Estates, and with them the new middle classes, the new Estate in the making. There could have been no better patron saint for the new venture than Joseph II, long since canonised in popular imagination.

Exactly thirty years later, in 1837, when Franz I was dead and

Metternich's rule had hardened, Franz Grillparzer wrote a political poem which he called "Des Kaisers Bildsäule" (The Emperor's Effigy). In it he let Joseph II address his faithless descendants: he would come down from his pedestal and pass judgement on them for having wrecked what he had built up. Another nine years later, in 1846, Grillparzer wrote a short, sharp poem entitled simply "Kaiser Franz". It opposed the plan to erect a statue to the late Emperor, Franz I, because the true monument was already there, in Joseph's Square; for when Franz I had been so hard pressed by Napoleon that, despairing of "the magic power of the Old", he had decided to make a new start, he had felt that he might break a promise given "from necessity alone, not from the heart", and so, to make his word binding, he had set up a bronze monument to his great uncle. These two poems were not written to be published, but they expressed the mounting rebellion felt by loyalists of a Josephinian stamp in the years of the inner disintegration of the Biedermeier. And the basic experience behind them went back to the years when Grillparzer's father and his contemporaries defied the pressure of the Napoleonic era by passing on their creed to their doubt-riddled sons.

It is again Franz Grillparzer who is the best witness to and best example of those doubts. In his autobiography he speaks caustically of his participation in the defence of Vienna in 1809, and self-consciously of his unwilling admiration for Napoleon:

During the siege I could not exclude myself from the students' detachment which manned a sector of the bastions. . . . As for my own conduct under the bombardment, it was neither conspicuously brave nor particularly cowardly. In the preceding days, while we walked the streets with badges on our hats, I even had bouts of heroism. The news of the town's surrender filled us with indignation. I vented mine in an outburst—only half sincere—against our citizens who cared more for their roofs than for their honour. At best, however, we were glad to get home, especially since we had not touched food for sixteen or eighteen hours. . . .

I myself was no less an enemy of the French than my father, and yet Napoleon fascinated me with a magic power. I had hatred in my heart, I had never been addicted to military displays, and yet I missed not one of his reviews of troops at Schönbrunn and on the parade ground of the so-called Schmelz. I still see him before me, running rather than walking down the open-air steps of Schönbrunn, behind him the Crown Princes of Bavaria and Württemberg as *aides-de-camp*, and then standing there cast-iron, hands folded behind his back, to survey his hosts on their march past with the unmoved look of the lord and master. His figure is present to me, his features have unfortunately merged with the many portraits of him I have seen. He put me under a spell as a snake does a bird. My father must have been little pleased at those unpatriotic excursions, but he never forbade them.

Here it is, the old Viennese mixture of self-mockery, anti-heroism, self-indulgence, fascination by the outstanding individual, and double-edged irony. Grillparzer's father was incapable of it, as the son well knew. The father would go for walks in the street every evening, against his custom, only to be able to help any fellow-countryman if there should be a clash between Frenchmen and Viennese; the son would go to Schönbrunn and gaze at the magic image of power—perhaps so as to confront his own weakness with the conqueror's masterful strength. On Napoleon's death in 1821, Grillparzer, then at the height of success and fame, published a poem in which he dared to question whether, with the removal of the dictator, thought, word and opinion had been set free "on the free earth", and to say that the dead adversary's life had shown that wholeness, majesty and grandeur were still possible "in our piece-meal world", *in unsrer Stückelwelt*. For the poet, his world had gone to pieces in his earliest youth, and unlike others he was never able to gloss over his own lack of integration.

The pattern which Grillparzer himself had traced in the self-debunking version of his juvenile exploits—"bouts of heroism" ending in bathos—was to persist. Whenever he wrote a patriotic poem out of a genuine impulse, the nagging doubt would lurk underneath, and there would be a tell-tale line to bring him into disfavour with the ruling powers. Either his greatest plays came into absurd, humiliating conflict with the authorities, or he hid them away in a drawer. And they all ended quietly, with an anti-climax or a question mark, thin cloaks to disturbing ideas.

An odd little story which Grillparzer tells of his adolescent years not cnly forecasts some of his special psychological twists, but also links his attitudes with those of less articulate and much less idiosyncratic Viennese during the pre-Biedermeier years. After Vienna's first occupation by the French in 1805, when he was fourteen, he felt so incensed about the blunders of the Austrian leaders which had led to the defeat that he vented his disgust in crudely satirical doggerel verses. His father blenched on hearing the poem, explained that it would cost the boy's future career if it became known, and ordered him not to show it to anyone. The boy, noting that he was not told to destroy it, which could only mean secret sympathy, obeyed; at least, this is what he later said in his autobiography. On the next day, the father returned from the wine-house very upset because a customer had recited the verses amid general applause. They were soon quoted "all over Vienna", because of their "coarse impudence" according to Grillparzer in his decorous statement, but "luckily no one guessed the author". This story is told stolidly as though the poem had escaped from its drawer by a miracle, not by an act of defiance. And before launching into his anecdote, Grillparzer took care to explain that he had at the time been as fervent a patriot as his father.*

Grillparzer's whole life proved that he had the right to call himself a patriot. However, in common with the ordinary people of Vienna he had the capacity for cheering the flag with sincere emotion even while noticing its every hole and stain. Only, what for him was a painful dichotomy was to most others the accepted state of things; for things were never quite what they seemed, neither in life nor in the theatre which in Viennese tradition was but a heightened form of life itself.

After 1809, during the short years of peace and recovery before a new war, Vienna was one of the focal points of anti-Napoleon Europe. The women still wore the French fashions of the Empire; but intellectual fashion was swayed by the German Romantics who flocked to Vienna, by admiration for the Spanish War of Liberation and Wellington's victories—Beethoven composed his Battle Symphony much as a poet laureate may write a poem on an official theme—and by dynastic loyalty, which at that time was a form of national self-assertion. Austrian poets and playwrights, not one of them of any true stature, were spurred to great bardic efforts, which rose in a patriotic crescendo when Austria joined the two continental countries already at war with Napoleon, Russia and Prussia. In October 1813, the three allied armies under the Austrian Prince Schwarzenberg defeated Napoleon at Leipzig.

A fortnight later, the most popular suburban theatre of Vienna, the

* The poem was published much later. It is a primitive expression of popular feelings, in stanzas which turn on the simplest of repeated rhymes. To quote a few: To fight a bold enemy and defeat him always—that would be good (*recht*); to take to flight without having drawn the sword—now that is bad (*schlecht*). If rogues get together and betray king and country—now that isn't good; but to pension them off instead of shooting them—now that is bad. If they reformed us and led us on a new road, that would be good; but everything stays as it is, the rogues are left in charge, and this is bad . . .

Leopoldstädter Theater, staged a topical comedy that became a sensational success. This theatre had been the main home of the fairy-tale musicals and burlesques which descended in an unbroken line from baroque comedy, and were written round a succession of much-beloved clown types, all drawn from Viennese folklore and speaking the Viennese idiom. But the familiar types, always types, never persons, had become stale. Now something entirely new yet still understandable appeared on the scruffy stage. Adolf Bäuerle, a clever journalist and theatre critic, gave to the Viennese the play *Die Bürger in Wien* (*The Citizens of Vienna*). Its plot was miserably thin as far as the couple of young lovers was concerned; but the "citizens" were shown on sentry duty and doing their best—not too badly, not too well—as officers of the Citizens' Guard; there were patriotic trimmings, slightly ridiculous but genuine; and there was a new comic character, a recognisable human being, named Staberl. Staberl, made flesh and blood by a dry-voiced, hunch-backed comedian of great natural gifts, was an umbrella-maker and incurable nitwit, the butt of his friends, the eternal "little man". His signature tune with which he ended every speech (and Staberl had to live on through thirty-odd plays, mere vehicles for his disarming innocence, before the public tired of him) was the cry: "I wish it did me any good . . ."

E. J. Hobsbawm, in *The Age of Revolution* (p. 121), calls the Viennese popular theatre "the faithful mirror of plebeian and petit-bourgeois attitudes" and says that in the Napoleonic period its plays had combined "*Gemütlichkeit*" with the naïve Habsburg loyalty". *Gemütlichkeit* and loyalty to "Father Franz" were there indeed, but so even then was an under-current of irony, of self-mockery. It speaks through Staberl, the innocuous blunderer who is so silly that no Viennese spectator would have recognised himself in him, yet so irrepressibly Viennese that he could not have been repudiated.

And Bäuerle, who was a lip-server and no hero, knew well enough what he was doing. On one occasion Staberl, who does everything wrong on sentry duty, tries to disperse a crowd by starting to drum. Bäuerle's stage direction is that the actor could, if he wanted to increase the noise, let off his musket, but "this wouldn't be plausible, since the citizens in Vienna never keep guard with their firearms loaded". No doubt Bäuerle would have denied, dead-pan, that his comment had any satirical edge, just as at a later date Grillparzer—though in every way to be placed on a different level—denied dead-pan that he had slipped out of his father's house with a rhymed lampoon as a young boy.

In the Napoleonic years the Viennese, high and low, patrician and plebeian, began to doubt themselves and one another. The traditional attitudes most of them shared, and the temper that had become inbred, helped them to absorb the impact of rapid social change, the shock of each defeat. Peter Toll, master carpenter and captain of the citizens' guard, and Jakob Eschenbacher, master harness-maker, who had been shot against the wall by the French in 1809, one because he had snapped the sword of a rude French officer in two across his knee, the other because he had hidden three Austrian guns in his back garden, were both buried in half-oblivion. "I wish it did me any good", was Staberl's *cri de cœur* every time he had entangled himself in his foolish excuses.

Yet those were also the great years of Beethoven. Not that it would be admissible to use his works as pegs on which to hang historical interpretations, or to weave fantasies about the impulses behind them. It is possible, however, to consider the changes in his public, and that public's response. This was something he himself observed attentively and took into account in his fight for material freedom and recognition.

His Third Symphony, the Eroica, was—according to Hanslick—first performed as a "totally new" work in the private circle of the banker Würth before invited guests, one Sunday morning in February 1804. Beethoven himself conducted it, the orchestra consisting mainly of amateurs. It was performed again by a private orchestra of a far more professional character in the palace of Prince Lobkowitz, a rather heavy baroque palace with a lovely slanted portal by Fischer von Erlach, near the Imperial Library; the Prince had bought the score, but was generous in admitting music-lovers from other social strata to his concerts. This was the last private performance of one of the great symphonies which could be counted as a first performance (Würth's circle having been exceedingly small), and was given by one of the last surviving private orchestras in the pay of aristocratic connoisseurs. Even though aristocratic patrons continued to be of the highest importance in Vienna's musical life (and one of Beethoven's main sources of income), the middle-class public, the well-to-do dilettanti among the upper bureaucracy and leaders of the new bourgeoisie, were gradually taking first place. When the Eroica was performed in public for the first time, in April 1805, it was in the Theater

an der Wien, which a memorandum of the Court Police Department
called in the following year the favourite diversion "of the higher and
middle orders; even the lower orders are interested"—in short, a
popular forum.

All Beethoven's symphonies with the exception of the Ninth were
composed, published and publicly performed in the course of the years
overshadowed by the Napoleonic Wars. It is almost impossible to
overstate what their revolutionary impact must have been, and yet
they reached from the first a public too wide to be exclusively composed of musical highbrows. Even the open-air concerts in the
Augarten, clearly designed to be entertainments, included Beethoven
symphonies. The master himself put his Viennese admirers to stiff
tests. The programme of his subscription concert of February 1807
included not only his new Fourth Symphony, but the three earlier
symphonies as well: it is hard to imagine people leaving it in any other
state than that of reeling intoxication, but it seems to have been a
success. In his benefit concert on 22 December 1808, at the Theater
an der Wien, Beethoven put on no less than two new symphonies
(the Fifth and the Pastoral), the Piano Concerto in G Major, the Choral
Fantasia Op. 80, and four shorter pieces. Hanslick quotes the German
conductor Reichardt as recording that they had stuck it out in the bitter
cold—the theatre was unheated—from 6.30 p.m. to 10.30 p.m.
Presumably not a few said, or felt, what Schubert at the age of eighteen
had expressed in his diary, under the influence of his teacher Salieri:
that there was an eccentricity "almost wholly due to one of our greatest German artists", which confused " . . . the agreeable with the
repulsive, heroism with howlings . . . so as to goad people to madness
instead of dissolving them in love". And yet two years before, in 1814,
Schubert had sold his school-books so as to be able to attend a performance of *Fidelio* in its final version.*

The fate of *Fidelio* in Vienna is often cited, usually to attack the
Viennese public and show up its lack of appreciation for Beethoven.
It is useful to recall the precise circumstances. The first performance of
Fidelio at the Theatre an der Wien, on 20 November 1805, was a sad
failure, and it would be facile to blame it entirely on the situation, the
recent occupation of Vienna by enemy troops, and the fact that the
theatre was sparsely attended—by French officers who were admirers

---

* Cf. O. E. Deutsch: *Schubert*, a documentary biography, Dent, 1946, p. 64
and p. 42 respectively.

of Beethoven. Joseph Sonnleithner's libretto seems to have been clumsy, un-theatrical, burdened by declamation and the worthiest sentiments; the music was suffering from *longueurs*, not wholly explained by the faults of the libretto either, or so one may infer, since Beethoven withdrew it, revised it, and withdrew the opera again when the second version was no more successful in 1806 than the first had been. There exists an account, by the tenor Joseph August Röckel, of an endless session in the salon of the Princess Lichnowsky, in which a few friends were trying to make Beethoven cut or condense the opera, while he defended every bar and note. Princess Christiane's appeal: "This is your greatest work . . ." helped a little; Beethoven had shaken off any trace of subservience, he was no chamber musician to his aristocratic protectors, but he responded as soon as he was treated as an equal. The second version, however, had not changed the structure, had not made an opera out of the symphonic sequence. When Beethoven was asked in 1814 to release *Fidelio* for a performance, he made, the condition that its text would first have to be recast by the experienced librettist of the court opera house, G. F. Treitschke. He had obviously considered the effect on the public—this was the time, moreover, when Cherubini's graceful and polished operas were fashionable—and demanded of Treitschke the text for an aria which the prisoner Florestan would have to sing. This was supplied by the librettist, unwillingly, and became the famous aria ending with the lines:

Ein Engel, Leonoren, der Gattin so gleich,
Der führt mich zur Freiheit ins himmlische Reich.

It was on the other hand Treitschke himself—as he claimed in an article in 1841 (quoted by Herbert Lengsheim, "Georg Friedrich Treitschke", published in *Studien aus Wien*, 1957)—who gave to the second act a finale in the sun, away from the shadows of the dungeon. This strengthened the theme of freedom from oppression which had been as much part of poor Joseph Sonnleithner's original concept as the "marital love" of the sub-title. The finale is Leonore's apotheosis, but in the chorus Beethoven touched upon the strain which was to swell to the great hymn of human hope in his Choral Symphony.

Fidelio had its first performance in the final version on 23 May 1814, and this time it triumphed.

The dark years had come to an end. In June 1814 Emperor Franz I

entered Vienna, having signed the Peace of Paris. Napoleon had ab-
dicated and was safely, it was hoped, in Elba. An international congress was about to meet in Vienna, and display the peacock's tail of
legitimate monarchy. In cheering their monarch, the Viennese could
surrender to the emotion of national unity that comes—briefly—at
the moment of a victorious peace. After long, weary years they felt
great and whole again, led by men who were capable of succeeding,
not only of weathering a storm. For the time being, Vienna, the
Kaiserstadt, the Imperial City, was the capital of Europe. They, the
people of Vienna, strutted the stage as if they had been extras in a vast
baroque State gala, acting as the foreigners expected them to act and
as they felt like acting in their relief and release. In the sound and
light, *son et lumière*, of the Congress they saw a mirage of their town.

2. VIENNA BECALMED

The purpose of the Congress of Vienna was the settlement of
European affairs on foundations that would be lasting and shock-proof.
After the violent interruption by Napoleon's lightning return, his
campaign, and its end at Waterloo—"The Hundred Days"—the
Congress finished its set task in 1815, under Metternich's sovereign
leadership. Working with or, as the case might be, against the other
statesmen (Castlereagh for England, Tsar Alexander I and his Minister
Nesselrode for Russia, Hardenberg and Humboldt for Prussia, Tal-
leyrand for France) he alone had the vision of an international defence
and restoration of the old order. This gave him his celebrated elasticity
in manœuvring and his freedom from narrow national considerations.
Whatever else he was, Metternich had fixed principles and was not
petty. He disliked the internal development of Prussia, and, though not
an Austrian, was not a north German either; but he agreed to Prussia's
huge expansion so as to gain her co-operation in the new Confederation of German States presided over by Austria, which took the place
of the defunct Holy Roman Empire. He was against a resuscitation of
the Empire as a unified State because it would have smacked of
Napoleon's new order. As Imperial Chancellor or Foreign Secretary,
he worked towards his ends through foreign cabinets and assemblies,
conferences and councils, in consistent attempts to make other states
adopt in their domestic government the ultra-conservative principles

which he believed imperative, if the spectre of subversion and revolution was to be banished. However, as Metternich was the Austrian spokesman, those principles naturally had to be reflected by administrative practice in Austria, and first of all in Vienna, to enable him to speak from a position of strength.

Metternich's most intimate collaborator was a brilliant intellectual, Friedrich von Gentz. Gentz was born as a commoner at Breslau in 1764—yet another man of enormous influence in Biedermeier Vienna who belonged by origin and early development to a vastly different period and country—and settled in Vienna in 1803. By the time of the Congress he had risen to the rank of Hofrat, or Aulic Councillor, had been ennobled, and was the principal publicity adviser to the cabinet. Some of his confidential memoranda had made so great an impression that he was asked to write the text of the Emperor's manifesto to his people in 1813. It is a lucid essay, justifying with great dignity and impeccable casuistry both Austria's apparent vacillations and the final decision to go to war. After the Congress, Metternich and Gentz made a formidable combination. Between them they gave a high gloss to official statements of reactionary thought. Gentz was an ambiguous character, to put it mildly, but his views—virtually the same as Metternich's—were strongly and sincerely held. The letters he exchanged with Metternich seldom touch on purely Viennese concerns, but all the same they throw a glaring light on the principles and attitudes behind the system by which the Viennese were kept in their state of officially attested harmlessness, and also on the reasons for certain distortions of intellectual life.

Between 1817 and 1820, one of the questions exercising Metternich and Gentz was that of the students' movement at the German universities, in which both saw a great potential danger. Metternich tried hard to make the representatives of other German states accept a general line, which they would have to implement by legislation, and he sought Gentz's advice. Gentz was against half-measures, including that of a police control of the universities, which the German Federal Assembly would not accept anyway. To get at the root of the trouble, he advocated the appointment of a comptroller for each university, and a discreetly executed purge of the holders of chairs— two steps which needed no formal negotiation but could be arranged by a gentlemen's agreement between the German states concerned. (Gentz to Metternich, 25 April 1819.)

Gentz also sent Metternich a copy of a long memorandum addressed to Adam Müller, a German scholar dabbling in conservative politics who was highly esteemed by Metternich and used as an expert adviser together with Gentz. This memorandum contains at least one essential passage: Gentz expressed his agreement with Müller on the point that the priority of "positive sciences" over "philosophical and critical sciences" should be vindicated. This would help to restore authority at the expense of bogus freedom, because "anyone could philosophise and criticise as the spirit moved him, but positive sciences had to be learned". And if youth decided to study in earnest, it would once more be capable of intellectual subordination. To admit only once, by silence, that—as some asserted—youth had to be educated to independence, and that the clash of opinions alone could lead to truth, amounted to underwriting any future revolution. . . . Austria had in this matter an "externally uncompromised" (*aüsserlich unbefangen*) position. In other words, all was quiet on the Viennese university front.

Metternich thanked Gentz for his memorandum and endorsed his and Müller's opinions fully. During the first half of the nineteenth century, and in particular during the Biedermeier era, natural sciences and technology were indeed officially promoted in Vienna. The Polytechnic was built between 1816 and 1818, and Metternich was one of its patrons. And philosophy atrophied.

When Metternich answered Gentz, on 17 June 1819, he spoke contemptuously of the academic agitators. "I have never feared that the revolution could be produced at the universities; yet I feel certain that a whole generation of revolutionaries is inevitably being bred there—unless the evil is contained. . . . This impression will not prevent me from intervening from above, and the only measures I deem possible have indeed been taken already. . . . The greatest and therefore the most urgent evil today is the press."

He was working out a scheme for the strict censorship of periodicals, pamphlets, leaflets, etc., which should be adopted by all German states. He would have preferred to propose a censorship for the printed word without exception, for every kind of book as well, but realised that this would meet with strong resistance from many German governments who had to abide by concessions they had made. Better to get their agreement on the necessary minimum precautions. Would Gentz help to formulate Metternich's ideas? In fact, the

German Ministers' Conference at Karlsbad accepted his (and Gentz's) proposals.

Gentz returned to the troublesome subject in a long letter of 11 August 1823, in which he referred, for once, to Austrian conditions by way of contrast and warning. "The severity of our censorship has up to a point—but only up to a point—protected our monarchy from being invaded by this pestilential poison [i.e. political journalism of a critical tendency]. And if it cannot be halted, it is difficult to gauge, judging the future by the present, to what degree of depravity even this State may come, which so far has remained so calm and happy in the paternal care of a virtuous sovereign."*

Calm and happy: those were the key words for the world of Old Vienna "while it lasted", to use Alan Pryce-Jones's formula, in the minds of its rulers as in the memoirs written much later, out of that fond remembrance which of all possible editors of raw material is the least reliable. And for a limited time there was much truth in the description. If Vienna was sealed off from any free exchange of opinions and from the "hideous spectre of the freedom of the press", as Gentz called it, the fact was noted but did not—yet—impinge on the general feeling that life was enjoyable. The natural reaction after the shocks of the Napoleonic decades, and in the case of many intellectuals the reaction to the first disappointment of a peace that quickly destroyed all hope of a new deal, was to turn to temperate pleasures in music, at the theatre, and above all at home.

The Historical Museum of the City of Vienna possesses a small album which, more intimately and directly than other documents, pictures the family life of a prosperous Viennese middle-class family about 1820. An article by Hubert Kaut in *Studien aus Wien*, a publication edited by the Museum in 1957, not only provides all available details but also a number of enchanting reproductions of amateur water colours—almost too Biedermeier to be true. The story of the album is itself a vignette of the times. It is a sort of memorial to years of friendly intercourse, in the shape of prints of the surroundings of Vienna and, more important, thirty-two water-colours by the compiler of the album. He came from the Styrian gentry, served in the Austrian regular army, and had taken part in all six campaigns against

* All quotations in connection with Gentz, including the passages from Metternich's letters, are taken from: *Friedrich von Gentz, Staatsschriften und Briefe*, 2 vols., annotated and introduced by H. v. Eckardt, Munich, 1921.

Napoleon between 1797 and 1815. His resounding name was Franz
Xaver Maria Nikolaus Andreas, Freiherr von Paumgartten. By the
end of the wars he held the rank of captain and was a seasoned, popular
officer, but his tastes were unmilitary. While in Vienna on a pro-
longed leave from his partially disbanded regiment, from 1817 to
1824, he made himself at home in the household of a family with
whom he seems to have fallen collectively in love in 1813, during a
pause between the campaigns. Thus, when he had to rejoin his unit in
a German garrison, he fashioned a little "book of remembrance" as a
gift to his friends the Baumanns, revealing his nostalgia in very bad,
explanatory couplets on the back of each of his water-colour evo-
cations.

The Baumann family was typical enough of a certain layer of the
Viennese upper middle class. At the time of their friendship, father
and mother were in their early forties, Paumgartten's own age; they
had four daughters and two small sons. Baumann had come from
western Germany and made good in Vienna. He was not only a
merchant—belonging to a select class of thirteen similar firms which
shared a complicated set of privileges—but became a manufacturer
as well. His wife, of Viennese patrician stock, was part-heiress to the
printing works which published the immensely important, and of
course semi-official, *Wiener Zeitung*, the Vienna Gazette. They lived
in the heart of the city, in a large flat on the first floor of an eighteenth-
century apartment house which no longer exists. Its baroque front was
plainer than most of its contemporaries', but the rooms were high and
well proportioned, as they show in Paumgartten's water-colours.

I shall translate a few of his paintings into words, because they
provide an inventory of a comfortable home and portray it as simple
and uncluttered, in a way that gives the lie to prettified notions of
Biedermeier Vienna. Two are also reproduced on Plate 5.

In one of the pictures, the family are holding hands round the
Christmas tree while the father, disguised as the popular sub-devil
called Krampus, stands at the door and the mother wears the robes of
Father Christmas, though to the Viennese the figure stood, and stands,
for St. Nicholas the Bishop. At that time the Christmas tree had been
recently introduced into Catholic Vienna from the Protestant North.
The custom spread quickly—when Mrs. Trollope came to Vienna ten
years later she saw one, glittering with candles and ribbons, in Princess
Metternich's salon—yet this little water-colour seems to be the first

record in painting of its appearance in a Viennese family. But then, Baumann had come from Germany. This tree is almost bare, its only decoration a few gingerbread mannikins. There are a few small presents. The floor of the room is of plain boards, the high windows have no curtains, only a white drapery in place of a pelmet. The walls are painted a soft green, the doors white. Two chairs are set against the walls, with plain dark seat covers and Regency backs—since the Congress Viennese cabinet-makers were adopting the designs of English furniture, with slight local variants.

Another painting shows the family at table, eating—we are told—fried sausages. The dining-room is larger, and clearly a reception room, in contrast to the back room with the Christmas tree. Its floor is tiled, there is not a single rug. Three doors show panels picked out in green against white; the walls are plain green once more. (Other pictures indicate that the painter would have tried to render patterns if they had existed.) Thanks to Paumgartten's device of presenting the four walls as if by opening out those of a doll's house, flush with the floor level, every piece of furniture is recorded: chairs, this time with embroidered seat covers, primly set against the walls; a console-table with a tall mirror; a round table with a fish bowl in front of one of the two windows; a very plain dresser; a cupboard with a latticed top; a round stove; two pictures and a birdcage on the walls; potted flowers—red geraniums?—outside the curtainless windows. That is all. The people sit stiffly at table, but Xaver von Paumgartten's accompanying couplet says (the translation follows the childish original as closely as possible):

> Love, friendship, concord, wit and pleasantry
> Gladden each heart in this delightful company.

Then follow pleasurable incidents. A New Year's Eve celebration disturbed, none too seriously, by the punch bursting into flames. Two *tableaux vivants*, one of them in the apartment of Frau Baumann's clever, popular sister. An amateur performance of an old one-act musical, a *Singspiel*, called *The Village Barber*. A series of family outings by carriage: place names in the surroundings of Vienna, boating and swimming in backwaters of the Danube, snacks in rural tavern gardens, ices in the garden of a coffee-house at Heiligenstadt where waiter, table and chairs are more sophisticated; and, in spite of the ladies' long dresses, even a climb to a ruin on top of a hill. There is some dancing in the house of Frau Baumann's sister, after games, supper and talk; one of the water-colours shows a couple in peasant costume dancing a *Ländler* to a zither. There is no mention of public dances. Everything that happens stays within the family circle.

The man who dreamed in his German garrison town of these friendly things and painted them with the directness, though not the skill, of the American primitive painter Grandma Moses, was forty-five at the time. He had been thirty-four when his friendship with the Baumanns began to flourish, and from that first encounter he had carried memories of an amateur pantomime with him. He never painted himself in uniform—though he was to rise to the rank of Colonel—but he painted a dress rehearsal of that pantomime from memory.

In the reduced scale of Paumgartten's convex mirror, the circle of the Baumann family looks even more self-contained and self-contented than it can possibly have been. Nothing of stress or problem mars the surface. We know so little of the individuals—though one of the boys became a popular writer of songs in the vernacular and a successful playwright—that the Biedermeier tag remains undisputedly accurate.

At a superficial glance a similar impression is produced, on a larger scale, by the group of friends revolving round Franz Schubert. The pictorial record of the Schubertians, although the work of gifted professional painters, is in spirit close to Xaver von Paumgartten's naïve portrayals of his friends—which is natural, since not only dates and place but also the cultural orbit coincide. The young girls' dresses, long, high-waisted, not yet *bouffant* as they were soon going to be, the excursions by carriage, the plain, light-coloured walls of the rooms, the air of friendly gaiety at a party game, were all much alike, in the two circles. Thanks to the labours of Professor O. E. Deutsch, a wealth of intimate detail is known about Schubert's friends from their letters and diaries, always with Schubert as the focus. The early years, from 1816 up to 1823, seem to confirm the general feeling of buoyancy; but then those men and women were very young still. They came to Vienna to study at the university (the whole skein started with Schubert's school-fellows who came from the provinces, mainly Upper Austria, and brought others in their wake), or to go through the first stages of a professional career, and found Viennese friends, Viennese girls they could court, and homes or at least rooms in which to talk, dance and hear music. Franz Schubert played dances for them, though he did not dance himself, read their own poems and those of others they might bring him, set to music whatever poem moved him—he was capable of quick response to a very wide range of poetry and thought, but the quality of the texts to his songs is frequently unrecognisable in translation—and roomed with one or another of his friends as often as not. Then a young man would write to his girl about the last *Lied* "our Schubert" had composed, and send her a copy to sing at home, say, at Linz. Within a short time there existed a circle meeting regularly, mostly in Vienna but sometimes at a country manor. It consisted of young people all more or less the same age: attractive young girls coming from cultured homes, poets, painters, students, a few drifters, officials, musicians, and Schubert. They had fun and games, outings and charades, but when they listened to music it was to Schubert's own. They called it a *Schubertiade* then.

Even Professor Deutsch's monumental documentary volume on Schubert—nearly a thousand pages—cannot fully elucidate his private life. It is strange to see the young composer drift away from home, without any quarrel, at the age of nineteen and after three years as his father's school assistant, and begin his wanderings from one friend's room as a guest to another's as a sub-tenant, never earning more than an occasional miserable fee but never quite destitute. He scarcely fought to get his works before the public, though some of his friends waged battles on his behalf. There was a small private orchestra in which he occasionally played the viola. It had started from the quartet his own father had formed together with three of his sons. When the schoolhouse proved too small for their bi-weekly chamber concerts their musical society, as it was called by then, moved first to the house of a friendly merchant, then to the apartment of the professional violinist Hatwig who had taken over the leadership of the orchestra. Here Schubert's first symphony was first performed, and for this circle Schubert wrote a symphony in C Major and an overture in the Italian style, at a time when it had found a new well-to-do patron and host in still another wholesale merchant (of much the same category, commercially and socially, as Baumann, Paumgartten's friend).

Yet though this and a host of similar private musical societies of amateurs mixed with a few professionals filled the gap left by the virtual withering-away of aristocratic patronage, before it was more effectively filled by public concert organisations such as the *Gesellschaft der Musikfreunde* (the Philharmonic Society), they could hardly afford to pay fees to composers. It was progress when Hatwig's orchestra members paid regular small quotas towards the expenses of their musical exercises. Schubert received his first fee, 100 florins, for his cantata *Prometheus* in 1816; it had been commissioned by students and friends of a popular, nonconformist university professor, Watteroth, in celebration of his name-day. The choice of the Greek myth of the rebel against Olympus, Prometheus, who stole the divine fire, shaped human beings in his own image, and defied—in Goethe's great poem—the punishment the Gods sent him, is evidence of an intellectual counter-current to the Metternich–Gentz Establishment.

The mesh of private musical entertainments which overlaid the social life of Vienna in the first decade after the Congress was closely knit. It encompassed several otherwise neatly compartmented groups: the rich bankers who were mostly ennobled, whatever their origins, and connected with the old Austrian aristocracy through intermarriage, but who represented the vanguard of the new bourgeoisie; the wealthier merchants and manufacturers, often caste-proud Viennese citizens with deeper roots in the old city and its suburbs than the leaders of finance; cultured K.K. officials from every part of the Habsburg dominions; university men, among them those who suffered most under the intellectual famine inflicted from above, and who usually had a following of lively students; and the lovers of music from the solid, unpretentious middle classes ranging from retail dealers to schoolteachers such as Schubert's own father.

Eduard Hanslick (*op. cit.*, p. 143) gives an incomplete list of regular musical circles, whose hosts included a university professor, a general, a civil servant without distinguishing rank, two high-ranking civil servants, a calligrapher, a brewer, a wholesale merchant, and three retail traders. From Hanslick's book, O. E. Deutsch's Schubert documentary, and Grillparzer's journals alone it would be possible to draw up an astonishing map of musical Vienna in those years. It would for instance mark the "historical" concerts in the home of Hofrat Rafael Georg von Kiesewetter, president of the Imperial War Council, in which early vocal music was performed by amateurs—Grillparzer was to hear a *Stabat Mater* by Astorga there in 1834, and record in his diary an odd outbreak against the mixture of poetry and music in modern song compositions, an impure form when compared with the old. The map would mark with a star the musical entertainments at Dr. Ignaz Sonnleithner's, an uncle of Grillparzer and brother of the *Fidelio* librettist, which helped to launch Schubert's songs and vocal quartets. Sonnleithner's son Leopold was so impressed by the first semi-public performance of *Erlkönig* at one of his father's soirées in 1820 (the famous song had been composed five years before, when Schubert was eighteen, and had become a favourite with private circles) that together with two friends he put up the money to publish it by subscription. No music publisher had wanted to take the risk with a piece by an unknown composer, and with a highly unusual, fiendishly difficult accompaniment. . . . Before the first printed copies were out, guests at another of Ignaz Sonnleithner's domestic concerts subscribed a hundred copies on the spot, which amounted to more than the money laid out by Sonnleithner junior and his friends. Op. 1, *Erlkönig*, appeared in April 1821, paired with Op. 2, *Gretchen am Spinnrade*. The second song (which Schubert had written when he was seventeen) was for once dedicated to one of the bankers-turned-aristocrat, the Swiss-born Count Fries, whose banking house was to fail and involve him in private ruin later on.

Schubert himself, his songs and a few of his other works, from waltzes to chamber music and vocal quartets, began to make the round of social gatherings where music was welcome. He played and sang his own songs at the home of a professor of theology, Vincentius Weintridt, who was so unorthodox a freethinker that his chair was taken from him in 1820, in the true Metternich–Gentz spirit. There Schubert met for the first time the young writer Bauernfeld, from whose translation of Shakespeare's *Two Gentlemen of Verona* (the first in German) he was to take "Who is Silvia?", transposed into fluid, faithful German rhyme and metre. He played the piano in the house of the banker Johann Heinrich von Geymüller, which contained— so it is reported—a piano for each one of his five daughters and provided a more luxurious frame for musical entertainment than Schubert's customary haunts. Perhaps this was one of the reasons why he never became a *habitué* there; every one of the reminiscences written by his friends after his death mentions his dislike of any occasion that smacked of snobbery and artificiality, and his tendency to shy away from highly placed patrons. The gatherings in Geymüller's house, however, were important as meeting places, even for Schubert, and the tinge of *parvenu* style, suggested by the five pianos, must have been faint, otherwise the difficult Grillparzer would not have been a frequent visitor. Thereby hangs a story which could be told with a romantic pseudo-Biedermeier coyness, and has often been told in such a manner, but which lights up the ramifications of cultured Viennese society in those years even if the tempting psychological issues are by-passed, and has certain links with Schubert as well.

It was at the Geymüllers' that Grillparzer fell in love with the woman to whom he was to be bound for life as to his "eternal betrothed" in an incomplete, unbreakable relationship, frustrating and at the same time satisfying. She was Katharina—"Kathi"—Fröhlich, the third of four exceptionally musical sisters, children of an impoverished suburban manufacturer, who seem to have been petted favourites in Vienna at the time, singly and jointly, not only because of their talents but also because of their unaffected charm. Two of them sang soprano, one mezzo-soprano, one contralto; Anna, the eldest, was the Geymüller girls' piano teacher, and became teacher of singing at the Philharmonic Society's conservatory; the second, the only one who married, turned from music to painting but had been a gifted professional, and retained her connections with music (and Schubert) through her flautist husband as well. The youngest, Josephine, was her sister Anna's pupil and became a successful contralto singer on the operatic stage and in the concert hall. Kathi was never a professional, but "she got herself drunk on good music as a drunkard does on wine", as Grillparzer recorded almost reproachfully, and held her own as second soprano when singing in a quartet with her sisters at church or in a salon. For Schubert, the most important of the four was Anna, one of the grey eminences in Viennese musical life during those years of transition from dilettantism to professional musicianship. But Grillparzer, who had long admired the intelligent, spirited singing of the two elder sisters and overlooked Katty, fell for her in the end, though he came to be wedded to the whole Fröhlich family instead of to the girl to whom he was engaged for a few stormy years.

Kathi Fröhlich must have been more representative of her generation than the sweet, meek-looking girls of the current Biedermeier portraits would lead one to expect. She was not beautiful, but at twenty she was entrancing: dark brown curls framing a mobile face dominated by dark, quick, expressive eyes, and a blend of hot temper and mischievous humour, independent spirit and frank tenderness.* And she

---

* Theodor von Karajan, Grillparzer's younger friend and colleague, described her in early middle-age as tall, very slim, with an oval face, and "immense eyes, bottomless, really unfathomable". Alfred Klaar, editor of one of the Grillparzer editions, saw her standing at the window next to the poet when he was seventy-

was naturalness itself—altogether the incarnation of Grillparzer's idea of the Viennese *persona*, but too strong an individual to fuse her life in his even had he been able to want it. In the first flush of his feelings for her, however, when he called her "the girl with the eyes" in a letter, he wrote a poem describing her "as she sat listening at the piano", too absorbed to let him speak to her. The little scene happened in the Geymüllers' music room, in 1821. The authority in these matters, O. E. Deutsch, dismisses the story that the pianist on that occasion was Schubert himself as "merely a tradition". It is a pity when it might so easily have been true, but perhaps it would be too pat for the good of one's historical conscience.

In any case, five years later Schubert set Grillparzer's gayest occasional poem to music for a female quartet and alto solo—the Serenade *Zögernd leise*, Op. 135. Both composer and poet had been commandeered by the mastermind of the Fröhlich sisters, Anna, who needed a serenade as a surprise for a young girl on her birthday. Anna's pupils sang the four-part passages, her sister Josephine the solo. The all-female party was taken from the city to the villa in the Döbling suburb (a house in which Beethoven had once lodged for a short spell) by three carriages, and the piano was magicked into the garden from the house after dark. The text, playful for Grillparzer, starts with the singers' soft-footed arrival, calls upon the "dear girl" not to go on sleeping when tenderness and friendship are knocking on the window, but then advises her that sleep is better than all she may "know and be" —so the singers depart softly, as softly as they have come.

To put another link into this Biedermeier chain: the young girl so serenaded was to marry Leopold Sonnleithner, Schubert's devoted partisan and Grillparzer's cousin. And she happened to be the daughter of a wholesaler from northern Germany who had settled in Vienna after abandoning his Jewish faith and becoming a Lutheran. None of this raised a barrier against him and his family among well-educated Viennese—then.

Any picture of "Schubert and his times" would be misleadingly sunny and harmonious without the contrasting or even clashing colours and the shadows which naturally belong to it.

seven and she sixty-eight—the students came to cheer him because of his anti-clerical stand in the First Chamber—and never forgot her "dear, fresh, matronly face framed by a pleated cap and still preserving a trace of young-girl enchantment".

The circle of intimate friends, and their friends, in which he moved was remarkable in its aesthetic range and intellectual vitality. If Hermann Bahr could usurp the name *Jung-Wien*, "Young Vienna", for the young writers of the 'nineties, this looser group of the eighteen-twenties might have claimed the same title, even though its strongest common bond was not literature but music, personified in Schubert and his songs. For a time, the liveliest minds of the young generation gravitated towards it, and newcomers from the provinces were easily drawn into the orbit. Schubert himself was the only creative musician in the inner circle. But painting was well represented, best of all by Moritz von Schwind who rebelled against the ruling academic taste, which was classicist, and became the representative Romantic designer. There were poets such as the melancholy Mayr-hofer, who loved freedom so much that he tried to commit suicide after the fall of revolutionary Warsaw in 1831, and feared an ugly death so much that he did commit suicide during the cholera epidemic five years afterwards—but nearly all those young men wrote verses, many of which caught Schubert's fancy. There was the witty, voluble playwright and rhymester Bauernfeld, then at the beginning of a career which was to bring him close to real achievement in the comedy of manners. There was the brilliant exhibitionist and all-rounder Franz von Schober with whom Schubert roomed more often than with anyone else, and who was most creative vicariously, as a stimulator. Others, critical and receptive, were equally important to keep the balance. The one person who, besides Bauernfeld, brought a political note into the group, fell victim to the witch-hunt instituted by the Vienna police after 1819. This was Johann Senn, a young poet from Tirol, Schubert's schoolfellow and later his occasional companion, who was arrested as an active member of a students' association after the suspect German pattern, kept under detention for fourteen months, and then deported to Tirol. When the police came to arrest him and search his place, Schubert was one of the friends present, but was not molested any further.

Schubert's nonconformism—music apart—assumed a different shape. Like the majority of his friends at this stage of their development, and like a great number of Viennese altogether, he was anti-clerical, that is to say, he disliked the hierarchy of the Roman Catholic Church in Austria. This sort of popular Viennese anti-clericalism is not in-compatible either with an inbred attachment to the Church or with strong religious feelings. Franz Schubert was spontaneously religious after his fashion, which was not that of his strictly orthodox father, nor that of romantic pietists or converts. In Mozart's generation people who felt similarly tended to join the Freemasons. In Schubert's generation, Goethe's pantheism, Romantic poetry, and the newfound delight in nature—"The Creation"—opened other channels. The undercurrents make themselves felt in his church music. One of O. E. Deutsch's notes (*op. cit.*, p. 59) says that "Schubert did omit the words 'Credo in unam sanctam catholicam et apostolicam ecclesiam' from his Masses, but of course not the *Credo* proper"—this as comment on the jocular passage in a letter to Schubert that he, Schubert, did "of course" not believe in the words of the *Credo*. And in the year of his death Schubert set the 92nd Psalm for the synagogue in the city. It was at once a piece of slightly disingenuous special pleading and an intrinsically true statement when Schubert seized upon his *Ave Maria* to explain to his father:

My new songs from Walter Scott's "Lady of the Lake" especially had much success. [This was in a private circle in the Upper Austrian town Gmunden.] They also wondered greatly at my piety, which I expressed in a hymn to the Holy Virgin and which, it appears, grips every soul and turns it to devotion. I think this is due to the fact that I have never forced devotion in myself and never compose hymns or prayers of that kind unless it overcomes me unawares; but then it is usually the right and true devotion. (Deutsch, *op. cit.*, p. 415.)

The other side to this was most clearly expressed in an exchange of letters between Schubert and his eldest brother Ignaz, an obstinate freethinker who resented the *Bonzen*, as he always called priests in his letters. In 1818 Schubert was piano teacher in the family of Count Esterházy of Galanta, at his summer residence in western Hungary. Ignaz wrote to him complaining about the vicissitudes in the lives of "scholastic beasts of burden", in particular their humiliating subjection to "fat-headed bonzes". Franz would be surprised to hear that at their school things had come to such a pass that "they no longer even dare to laugh when I tell them a funny yarn about supersitition in the Scripture class". He, Ignaz, was often seized by a secret anger and knew liberty only by name.... The postscript to this letter, however, warned brother Franz not to touch upon any religious matter if he happened to write to him and their father at the same time. Schubert replied in a letter addressed to his two brothers and Ignaz's wife jointly, and said: "You, Ignaz, are still quite the old man of iron. Your implacable hatred of the whole tribe of bonzes does you credit. But you have no conception what a gang the priesthood is here. . . ."

The attitude of the Schubert brothers was no doubt in some part a reaction against their father, and in Ignaz's case exacerbated by his experiences with the school authorities, but it was widespread even at a time when new Catholic societies and religious orders were making intense efforts at an inner mission, at a revival of dedicated piety. Moritz von Schwind, for instance, had been educated at the *Schotten* grammar school, by Benedictine teachers; he was deeply influenced by the German Romantics many of whom sought a way back to the experience of faith; in his house Schubert saw one of his first Christmas trees; but he was, in the Viennese way, an anti-clerical. The orthodox tenets of his fiancée led to quarrels, first manageable, later serious, and it was this difference which was at the root of their final estrangement. Both the light-heartedness of Schwind's retort to his girl that she should go and fall in love with the Pope (as he wrote to Bauernfeld, much to the latter's delight, since he introduced the remark into a comedy of his), and the hearty gruffness of Schubert's comments to his brother, are deceptive. With all this superficial *Gemütlichkeit*, Young Vienna took problems of the mind seriously—just as there was an undertow of seriousness in the primitive popular jokes which were creeping into farces on the suburban stage, as digs against the Order of Redemptorists, hub of the Catholic revival movement.

In his unobtrusive, self-effacing manner, Schubert had great intellectual curiosity and stamina. A letter from one of his friends and hosts at Linz to Josef von Spaun epitomises the amazement his rare self-revelations caused even among those who thought they knew him: "I was more and more amazed at such a mind, of which it has been said that its artistic achievement is so unconscious, hardly revealed to and understood by himself, and so on. Yet how simple was all this! —I cannot tell you of the extent and the unity of his convictions. . . ." This was in 1825 when Schubert had come through the great ordeal of an illness of which, in the words of Professor O. E. Deutsch, "there is no doubt that it was venereal, probably syphilis". He had doubted whether he would ever recover, and it changed, inevitably, his outlook on life. In 1824 he wrote to the painter Kupelwieser, then in Rome:

Imagine a man whose health will never be right again, and who in sheer despair over this ever makes things worse, instead of better; imagine a man, I say, whose most brilliant hopes have perished, to whom the felicity of love and friendship have nothing to offer but pain, at best, whom enthusiasm (at least of the stimulating kind) for all things beautiful threatens to forsake . . . each night, on retiring to bed, I hope I may not wake again, and each morning but recalls yesterday's grief . . . (Deutsch, *op. cit.*, p. 339).

But he was courageous. He did not throw himself into a whirl of loud gaiety, though he went again to dances, to coffee-houses and taverns with his friends, and only became a little more curt with mere beer-drinkers and sausage-eaters who broke up the high seriousness of the friends' reading circle. In March 1824, he began to write the String Quartet in D Minor, known as *Death and the Maiden* because of the variations in the slow movement on the theme of the song so entitled —which he had set in 1817. It was finished in 1826, and was no great hit. Even his admiring friends gave scant support to his chamber work, perhaps because they cast him exclusively in the rôle of the great *Lied* composer. And his next song cycle, *Die Winterreise*, startled them by its sombre, desperate strength; it was finished by October 1827. Beethoven, whom Schubert had never known to speak to, had died in March.

1828 was a creative year. Schubert wrote the songs posthumously published as the collection *Swan-Song*, three piano sonatas, the so-called Great Symphony in C Major, a Mass in E Flat Major, and the wonderful String Quintet in C Major. The number of his published works had noticeably increased but was still a fraction of his output; far more was stowed away in his own and his friends' music closets, where it was sometimes doomed to stay for many years, or to disappear without trace. He spent the summer of 1828 in the company of his friends, as usual, and lodged with Franz von Schober. But he did not feel well, and moved from the airless city to the Wieden suburb, into his brother Ferdinand's small flat. There he went down with abdominal typhus: the water was bad. His closest friends and relatives rallied round, unafraid of the infection, except for Schober to whom he wrote his last note, asking for the loan of some novels by Fenimore Cooper. On 19 November 1828 he died, in his thirty-second year. Schwind, by then in Munich, wrote to Schober: "Schubert is dead, and with him all that we had of the brightest and fairest."

He was given a second-class funeral, paid for by his father, and was buried not in the cemetery to which the Wieden parish properly belonged, but in an outer suburb on the far side of Vienna, because his brother Ferdinand believed that such had been his wish: in the Währing

Cemetery, three graves away from Beethoven. In what is now a public park, the two empty monuments—the remains were transferred to "tombs of honour" at the new Central Cemetery in 1888—still stand there, backed by a wall, facing grubby seats, and shadowed by trees loud with birds. Beethoven's is topped by a truncated obelisk. Schubert's is simpler, two small columns flanking a portrait bust, and the flat architrave under the plain triangular pediment bearing the inscription worded by Grillparzer:

DIE TONKUNST BEGRUB HIER EINEN REICHEN BESITZ
ABER NOCH VIEL SCHÖNERE HOFFNUNGEN
FRANZ SCHUBERT LIEGT HIER
GEBOREN AM XXXI JANUAR MDCCXCVII
GESTORBEN AM XIX NOVEMBER MDCCCXXVIII
XXXI JAHRE ALT

The art of music here interred a rich possession
But hopes far fairer still
Franz Schubert lies here
Born on 31 January 1797
Died on 19 November 1828
31 years old

The Archives of the City of Vienna include a file on Franz Schubert that starts with the sequestration act and among other documents contains the receipted bill of Balthasar Ausim, undertaker. The difference between Schubert's funeral rites, second class, and those of Mozart, third class, shows in the amounts paid to the clergy: the tax paid to the parish where Schubert died, and in whose church the funeral Mass was celebrated, is item 5 on the bill, 20 florins 27 kreuzer, the largest single amount on the list; the fee paid to the parish priest of St. Stephen for the last rites on Mozart was 8 florins 56 kreuzer. This could not have provided for singing or for organ-playing. To Schubert's father the ritual of the Church, and the decencies, were supremely important. To Schubert's brothers it was important to honour him. The undertaker Ausim put on his bill 15 florins 30 kreuzer for wreath-binders' work, and all the other figures were insignificant: a painted coffin, which meant cheap deal, not polished hardwood; a "fine" shroud; 4 lb wax for candles, 150 printed announcements of the death; knocking up the neighbours with the news (very cheap, less than a florin); a beautiful pall; two mourning cloaks; crape; a Cross; washing and laying out the body; praying in vigil; tips, and so forth. The total amounted to 84 florins 45 kreuzer.

At the Währing Cemetery there were additional expenses. The individual grave alone cost 30 florins, paid to the local priest. (One does not know what, if anything, had to be paid to the priest at St. Marx Cemetery where Mozart was put into the narrow grave shared by a dozen strangers for ten years.) Schubert's last recorded fee, for the Pianoforte Trio in E Flat Major, was 60 florins. After his death, his brother Ferdinand was offered 70 florins each for the last three sonatas by the music publisher Haslinger.

Schubert had always been on the verge of poverty, and had never seemed to mind it as much as his friends did on his behalf. When he wanted to go to Graz where he was invited and eagerly expected, he had to make a special effort to try to raise the money. He never complained about failures and disappointments, such as his ill-starred operatic ventures, and his attempts to get his works into print were anything but energetic. Nobody could care less about the outer trappings of fame. He was so free of vanity that he went to the première of a play by Grillparzer on an evening when, a relatively rare event, one of his works was on the programme of a public concert. He refused to cultivate such aristocratic patrons as were left, to the point of neglecting useful contacts if there was more congenial company elsewhere. On the other hand he did not share his brother's naïve pleasure when the musical clock at the Hungarian Crown Inn ran cylinders with his waltzes; he would have preferred Ferdinand to be excited about his chamber music.

Such a man, essentially clear-headed and certain of his purpose, was likely neither to accumulate riches nor to get into serious debt. When Franz Schubert fell ill at his brother's flat he had the sum of 118 florins on him, which went towards the expenses during his sickness. He had been paying a small sum to his brother for room and board, but was in arrears with similar payments he owed to Schober who was going through one of his financial crises. There were outstanding bills to two tailors, a shoemaker and a pianoforte-maker who had done repairs for him, presumably on Schober's piano which he had been using of late, not having any of his own. All these debts were punctiliously paid by the Schuberts; the father, who was a little better off as head of a primary school and owner of a house, advanced money, while Ferdinand acted as treasurer. He was able to give his father a detailed

account which showed that within six months of the composer's death
the debts had been more than covered by the fees coming in from
publishers. In November 1829 Ferdinand made an agreement with
Diabelli in Vienna, which assigned to this firm the songs for one voice,
all piano pieces, the "music for string instruments", but nothing else,
for a payment of 2,400 florins. (By way of comparison, the sum which
Beethoven left to his nephew Karl was 9,000 florins.)

On Schubert's death, the local government machinery designed for
this purpose began to function. The sequestration official came to
Ferdinand's house to make an inventory of all the deceased's belongings, to assess their value, and to pronounce the official sequestration of
the estate until the last will and/or last obligations had been duly examined by the authorities. The findings were entered on a printed form,
and the whole was called *Sperrsrelation*, Sequestration Report. It was
signed by the official in charge, the valuer, and the nearest relatives of the
deceased, and deposited at the municipal office, the *Magistrat* of the
City of Vienna—even the Wieden suburb, like the others, came under
the jurisdiction of the city in such matters.

The procedure had not varied since Mozart's death, except for a
significant detail which had to do with police surveillance, hence not
with a municipal but with a government body: at the foot of the
relevant page was a sentence asking whether "there were books among
the property, and whether a report about them had been made to the
K.K. Book Revision Office immediately after sequestration". There
were no books in Schubert's case (either Ferdinand had taken them,
or he had left them at Schober's). The sequestration was purely
formal, since the estate was "insignificant", and its value far below
the sum which the father could demand according to the receipts
in his possession for expenses due to illness and death. These
expenses were 269 florins 19 kreuzer. The total estimated value of
Schubert's assets was 63 florins. The sum consisted of the following
items:

3 cloth dress coats, 3 frock coats, 10 pairs of trousers, 9 waistcoats	37 fl.
1 hat, 5 pairs of shoes, 2 pairs of boots	2 fl.
4 shirts, 9 neck- and hand-kerchiefs, 13 pairs of socks, 1 sheet, 2 blanket-cases	8 fl.
1 mattress, 1 pillow, 1 blanket	6 fl.
Apart from some old music material valued at	10 fl.
there is nothing else belonging to the deceased.	

Schubert's friends and supporters belonged by birth or upbringing to the upper reaches of the middle class. His own family did not. Self-respecting, and raised to modest security by their teaching jobs, they remained on the fringe of the suburban lower middle class and shared its daily worries.

Franz Schubert died of typhus, as his mother had done before him. Typhus was endemic in Vienna. In 1806 there had been an acute epidemic of "nervous fever" as it was called, at the peak of which "up to 60 people" died every day. Schubert's father had fourteen children from his first two marriages (he married three times); five survived. His brother Ferdinand married twice and had twenty-five children; twelve survived.

Infant mortality and the death rate from typhus, dysentery and pulmonary tuberculosis were so high that up to 1815, and then again between 1831 and 1835, there was a population deficit of 8–10 per cent in Vienna. In 1831, nearly half of the Viennese who died (28·2 per cent) were less than twenty years old.* If the city was in fact slowly increasing in population, this was entirely due to the influx of workers from the Austrian dominions, and of foreigners. It was bound to affect the structure of Old Vienna as time went on.

The Emperor Franz I and his police ministers were preoccupied with the rise in the number of proletarians, who were considered unreliable, and indeed potential revolutionaries after the pattern of Paris—whence the terms proletariat and proletarians had been taken over into German. For years, ever since the beginning of Franz I's reign, there had been unrest among the lower orders. In 1792 a group of weavers had accosted him, obsequiously enough, because they were out of work; it amounted to a demonstration in the eyes of the authorities. During the next few years—until the trial of the Austrian Jacobins, so called—small groups of sympathisers with egalitarian ideals of the French Revolution subsisted among officials and even officers; the leaders were executed, although the expression of their ideas had been harmless. Open criticism ceased, but the police (Joseph II had created the system mainly as a check on the new bureaucracy, and his nephew increased its scope) kept a close watch on public opinion, particularly on signs of

---

* The statistical facts and economic details in this connexion are taken from G. Otruba and L. S. Rutschka: *Die Herkunft der Wiener Bevölkerung in den letzten hundertfünfzig Jahren, Jahrbuch des Vereines für Geschichte der Stadt Wien*, 1956/58, and Josef Karl Mayr: *Wien im Zeitalter Napoleons*, Vienna, 1940.

discontent. In 1802 unskilled workers in a village on the outskirts of
Vienna went on strike; the leaders were flogged and sentenced to hard
labour in irons. In 1805 the resentment of the workers against rising
prices and racketeering tradesmen exploded in a series of riots. The
bakers were the immediate targets, and in several suburbs their shops
were smashed. One of the demonstrators allegedly shouted at Baron
Kübeck: "We haven't eaten and won't wait any longer for you high-
ups to do your stuff—we'll take what's ours by right." Cavalry
suppressed the riots: ten dead and hundreds of injured. The following
years were marked only by small outbreaks of looting, but in 1811 as
many as 1,500 shoemaker-journeymen demonstrated in the streets
until they were dispersed by the fire-watch and cavalry units. Even
after the end of the wars, in 1816, a sudden rise in the price of tallow
candles (wax candles being a privilege of the better-off) was enough to
cause mass unrest in four suburbs.

In between there had been a certain amount of sympathy with the
French during the two occupations of 1805 and 1809. Napoleon's
administration was cleverly designed to expose, by contrast, the weaknesses of the Austrian system. The fact that there had been collaborators,
commonly called "the Blue-Tinged" because French uniforms were
blue, came out here or there in wry jokes of some popular farce that
survived, or in the broadsheets called *Eipeldauer Letters*, but on the
whole only the version of a uniformly patriotic behaviour was passed
on. Everything else was driven underground, partly by necessity and
partly by the change of mood during the final War of Liberation.

The incontrovertible fact remained, however, that there existed real
misery bordering on starvation, not only among the poorest workers
but also among the lowest paid clerks in the public services, who were
virtually driven to petty corruption and tried, pathetically, to get relief
by sending petitions to the Emperor. The rise and fall of small tradesmen, too, became a hackneyed story. The boom during the Congress of
1814–15 did not last, and in the years immediately afterwards the
tensions worsened again, not far below the surface. The police had to
record an exceptionally high number of suicides in 1819.

Franz I, who evolved a technique of dismissing petitioners so that
they believed in his active sympathy with their claims, but who in fact
never made a positive decision on the spot, preferring to settle problems
by "letting them lie", believed in preventive measures. After the bread
riots of 1805 he kept a strong garrison in Vienna as a domestic safeguard.

Steps taken to halt the entry into the suburbs of people looking for work (the dreaded "proletarians") had far-reaching consequences. For years the building of new houses was restricted; this helped the landlords, but failed to stop the drift from countryside to town. Casual workers had to obtain special marriage permits from the police; this did not prevent the procreation of children in insanitary slums. For a time the establishment of new factories or workshops was prohibited in city and suburb; this affected the industrial development of Vienna as well as the investment of capital, and distorted the shape and rhythm of the industrial revolution at the centre of the Habsburg empire.

On the other hand the Emperor, who had his own brand of toughness, ignored confidential reports that his popularity had suffered badly during the two occupations. The deep distrust he felt towards the populace was always covered by a façade of fatherly kindness, and he appeared to take the enthusiastic receptions given him on both his returns after defeat at their face value. In the end the publicity machine —from Gentz to the journalist who wrote official propaganda disguised as satire in the cosy vernacular of the *Eipeldauer Letters*—proved effective. It would not have been so effective if it had not answered a need, whether that of wretched newcomers drifting through the streets and gratefully responding to the illusion of a dream town, or that of "old" Viennese who, discovering themselves in a succession of gay characters in dialect comedy, co-operated in the creation of a legend. Even the most inveterate grumbler liked the extension of the collective ego implicit in the praise of the *Kaiserstadt*, the Imperial City, when it was launched from Vienna's suburban stage.

The Austrian police ministers and their commissioners had never underrated the value of the theatre as a safety valve, least of all in the tense years after the bread riots of 1805, when the Police Department of the court had prevented the closing of the Theater an der Wien:

The people are accustomed to theatrical shows.... In times like these, when the character of individuals is affected by so many sufferings, the Police are more than ever obliged to co-operate in the diversion of the citizens by every moral means. The most dangerous hours of the day are the evening hours. They cannot be filled more innocently than in the theatre....

In 1822, Adolf Bäuerle, the same who had invented the umbrella-maker Staberl, and who in the meantime had become the all-powerful and not altogether incorruptible editor of the *Theaterzeitung*, staged at the Leopoldstädter Theater a new fairy-tale comedy with music by Wenzel Müller. It was called *Aline oder Wien in einem anderen Weltteil* (*Aline, or Vienna in Another Continent*), and was an immediate hit. Everybody went to see it, including Schubert. The song that conquered Vienna had the refrain: "Ja nur eine Kaiserstadt, ja nur ein Wien"—Only one Emperor's Town, only one Wien. The Viennese were glad to be told so and glad to believe it.

The story of Aline was unimportant. It was a good sample of the fairy-tale parodies which were beloved by Viennese audiences trained in the tradition of baroque stage settings, with endless transformations and no boundary between magic illusion and the nearest approach to reality that was still tolerable. More important was the comic couple, speaking and breathing the Viennese idiom, and in this production played by the two best popular actors, each of them a strong personality, and each an epitome of the epoch in its brightest and darkest aspects. They were Ferdinand Raimund and Therese Krones.

Raimund, as already mentioned, was born in 1790. He was the son of a cabinet-maker who came to Vienna from Prague, and married a Viennese girl; both died of tuberculosis, the father when Ferdinand Raimund was fourteen. He was apprenticed to a confectioner, which put an end to his school education, and sold pastries in the gallery of the old court theatre, the Burgtheater. It fired him with the longing to be a tragic actor himself, but after years of travelling with a small troupe in provincial towns he was taken on as a comic at the third, and smallest, of Vienna's three suburban theatres. By 1818 he was established as a comedian of a new kind, one who played characters with a subtlety and gentleness unique on the popular stage.

He was candid, passionate and serious, and a poet. All these qualities contributed to the involvements which bedevilled his private life. He fell in love with the daughter of a coffee-house proprietor near the theatre, and she with him, but her parents were too narrowly *bürgerlich*, middle-class, in their ideas of respectability to accept the bohemian suitor. He was rejected. In his distress he had a brief encounter, not even what is called an affair, with an actress who happened to be the daughter of his director and protector. Though he repented of it in the act, he was forced into marrying her almost at the point of a shot-gun. It was no true marriage, and his beloved Toni forgave him generously, but the inevitable divorce from his promiscuous wife-in-name did not set him free to marry again. He was a Catholic, and he, for one, was deeply religious even if he made little external show of it. In 1821 he took Toni to a small image of the Virgin, set up on a pillar in a vineyard near the Wienerwald village Neustift, and there they two swore marriage vows to each other in the face of God. They suffered atrociously during the years that followed, she because her milieu made her equivocal position hateful and painful, he because he needed to live with her in peace. It took nine years of austere self-discipline on his side, and bitter loyalty on hers, till her parents agreed to let them live together in a room of their house; but by then much between them had withered. His letters—Toni's were destroyed—tell a haunting tale of mutual torment and self-torment. He had developed a tragic sense of life at war with his faith, at war, too, with the optimism that was demanded and expected of him as the most popular playwright (which he had become in the years after 1823). When he committed suicide in 1836, because he thought he had been bitten by a mad dog, he was in truth the victim of that inner war.*

When Raimund wanted a good part for himself at his benefit performance in 1823, he wrote a fairy-tale farce à la Bäuerle round the figure of a barometer-maker transplanted to a magic island—topically enough, a ruined artisan. His second comedy, *Der Diamant des Geisterkönigs* (*The Fairy King's Diamond*), had more originality, and some of the song numbers set by himself have survived as folk-songs, at least in snatches the source of which few people know. His third and fourth plays were acclaimed as works with a streak of genius, even by Grillparzer who was then the great author of tragedies on the "higher" stage of the court theatre. The play that marked Raimund's break-through was called *Das Mädchen aus der Feenwelt oder Der Bauer als Millionär* (roughly: *The Girl from Fairyland, or The Peasant Turned Millionaire*). Both titles are characteristic, each of a different aspect of the play. Once again, the plot, with its romantic and baroque conventions, matters little—it transfers a rough peasant-farmer to town, to Vienna, by the simple trick of letting him find a fairy treasure, and makes this a test of character. There is no hint at the rise to riches of some farmers

---

* Except where I have based my interpretation on the plays and on documents directly, the material on the popular Viennese theatre and its dramatists is derived from the following: for the Theater an der Wien, Anton Bauer, *op. cit.*; for Raimund, the critical edition by Castle and Brukner, Vienna, 1925–34. For the overall history, countless details, and stimulating opinions, the authoritative work by my old teacher, Otto Rommel: *Die Alt-Wiener Volksbühne*, Vienna, 1952.

during the times of food shortage and speculation, no whiff of social criticism; but the peasant's clumsy behaviour as an upstart must have rung not a single bell but a whole peal. What gave to the play an enchantment that still works on the Viennese stage was the melancholy wisdom underlying it, and its most famous scene, in which the slow development of years is condensed to the allegory of Youth departing and Old Age taking over in a flash. Raimund played the peasant Fortunatus Wurzel, who changes from rough, selfish manhood to bent senility as the *Aschenmann*, the poor dustman who collects wood-ash and sings a rueful song with the refrain: All ashes, all ashes. But first there was that exquisite moment when Youth came to sing its farewell song, Youth in white breeches tied with rose-red ribbons, a white satin waistcoat with rosebuds on the collar and silver buttons, a short rose-red tail-coat, and a rose-red ribbon on the white satin hat with curling brim: Therese Krones. This was how Moritz von Schwind drew her, making her plumper than by all accounts she had been, but radiantly young; and the society lithographer of Biedermeier Vienna, Kriehuber, turned the drawing into a much reproduced engraving (Plate 8). In this guise Therese Krones appeared on cups and saucers, ribbons and cushions, and on prints for children to cut out. Since a comedy must have a happy ending, Raimund's play ended with everybody proclaiming the blessings of modest contentment and self-restraint, and even the dustman's song had a last conciliatory verse finishing on the faintly optimistic line: No ashes, no ashes. Thus it was the pink-and-white image of Youth that stayed triumphantly in people's minds, and came to stand for Biedermeier gaiety, with the piquant face of Therese Krones smiling under the curve of the silk hat.

Therese Krones, daughter of a stage-struck Silesian artisan, was a child when she began to tour the Austrian backwoods with her family —like Dickens's Crummles family—as a member of miserably poor theatrical companies. At the Leopoldstädter Theater in Vienna she became a star, playing Viennese girls with a racy charm that could not have been more "native" had she been born within sight of St. Stephen's. (In this, she was neither the first nor the last.) Contemporaries described her as thin, dark, almost wild, electrifying, and graceful even if she said something shockingly coarse in her husky voice. When her chance of fame, riches and passion came, she seized it avidly. It did not last. She spent herself recklessly. She was twenty-seven when she wrote her last will, a holograph of 18 August 1828, and died two years later, on 28 September 1830, after long, hopeless suffering. Her carefully penned testament betrays anxious piety, and a desire for respectable orderliness. Her disease (its exact nature is not clear from the documents in the official file which I examined at the City Archive) must have frightened her. She begins: "Since experience warns me that we are often overcome by a rapid illness and have no time . . ." Then she lists her last requests and bequests, obviously in the belief that she was a woman of means: eighteen Masses for her soul, a grave of her own (shades of Mozart!), and once this is paid, monthly allowances to father and brother, a lump sum to each of her brother's three children, and her personal belongings, with dresses, chemisettes and silk stockings specified, to her sister-in-law, the remainder to her friend Rohrer, a businessman with whom she seems to have been living at the time. After her death her estate was valued at 288 florins in the sequestration document. The most valuable item was a set of upholstered furniture, a sofa, six chairs, and two armchairs. All her money, and she had earned a great deal, was eaten up by her illness; even so her friend Rohrer had had to pay considerable sums out of his own pocket, a total of 546 florins 4 kreuzer for expenses during her illness and in connection with her death. He also paid for the Masses (12 florins) and her single grave (14 florins 5 kreuzer), but on probate was relieved from the obligation of paying out the bequests to her family. All he had inherited from Therese Krones was ashes, ashes, and—one imagines— a memory of the fierce flame of her life before it burnt itself out.

The sequestration form had changed in the two years since Schubert's death in one significant detail: the query about books was now more explicit, and ran:

Whether books and other objects of censorship exist, of which kind, and whether a report on them was made immediately after sequestration to the K.K. Book Revision Office, also whether among them there are prohibited works, as far as this can be established.

Once again the screws of censorship and police vigilance had been tightened, and there were strong reasons for it. In July 1830, two days of fighting on the barricades of Paris had driven the Bourbon, Charles X, into exile, and enthroned the "bourgeois king", Louis Philippe of Orleans, in his place. Metternich's whole continental system, built on the principle of legitimacy and absolutism, was shaken, and the tremors were halted neither by the Austrian frontier posts, nor by the officially inspired versions in the Viennese press. "The French have driven out their king", Grillparzer wrote in his journal, "who tried . . . to break the constitution and turn them into a sort of—Austrians, which, civically and politically, seems to be the worst that can happen to anyone. I wish I were in France. . . . It is still better [i.e. the danger inherent in democracy is still better] than to have the spirit defeated and the noblest human needs sacrificed to an abominable system of stability. . . ." And Bauernfeld, younger, more superficial and more optimistic, wrote in his diary: "If liberalism wins in France it cannot fail to affect Austria as well. To this we must cling, for this we must hope."

In 1831, a slim volume of anonymous poems printed in Hamburg by a progressive publisher—by Hoffmann & Campe who published the two dangerous rebels, Heine and Börne—and entitled *Spaziergänge eines Wiener Poeten* (*Rambles of a Viennese Poet*) made a stir among German-speaking intellectuals everywhere. It was immediately outlawed in Austria, but copies were soon circulating in Vienna. These ballads were a confession of political faith, and a politely pointed attack on Vienna's reactionary rulers, from Metternich down to the anonymous censors and political clergy. The author was quickly known to the police—and among his friends. He was a young aristocrat, Anton Alexander Count Auersperg, who had already published poems in the ballad style of the later German Romantics under the pen name of Anastasius Grün, and was at home in the Viennese circle of writers— Grillparzer, Raimund, Bauernfeld, and the lyrical poet Lenau—when he was not looking after his country estate. Not an easy target for the police!

Anastasius Grün (as a poet he never used his real name and title) had not written the first German political poem by any means, but his cycle of *Rambles* was the first group of political poems to come out in the German language, particularly impressive as it came from becalmed Vienna. The long, rolling lines and declamatory rhythms were in the fashion; now a familiar metre was put to a new use, always fluently, and sometimes with great pungency. The "Viennese poet" leaves the town to gain the freedom of the Wienerwald hills. Looking down from the Cobenzl, he asks for light and truth to be let into the council-chambers of the rulers. "Three hundred thousand of our brothers down there dream the dream of life. . . ." But it is time to fight the sly, gaunt priests who are creeping in everywhere, just as our forefathers under Joseph II had fought the fat, greedy ones; in fact it would be wise to call back the fat priests so as to get rid of the new breed. He soliloquises in front of the statue of Joseph II, who had been a despot, yes, but "a despot like the day". The "spirit"—intellect—crosses the frontiers with the smugglers of books: why not throw the black and yellow toll barriers wide open? The most miserable sinner and blasphemer of all is the censor; let him go hence and become a human being. The ubiquitous police informer poisons gay, innocent thought. A nightmare: the city in darkness, ruled by owl and bat, the street lamps prohibited because "people can find the way to their mouths even in the dark"; and a Redemptorist monk the only being to profit from the murk. A little man watches the antics of the authorities, and asks continually: Why? They decree that this wicked question deserves no answer, since their doings must remain sacrosanct—the mannikin asks: Why? The poet sings a hymn to freedom, "the great watchword that resounds through all the world", and then defends himself against those who want him to stay "with his flowers", rather than disturb the harmless joys of others by reminding them of their chains. Yet he does it because amid so much beauty and gaiety the rattle of chains is doubly hateful. The Greek freedom fighter Alexander Ypsilanti had sought asylum in Austria, was sent to the Hungarian fortress Munkács for seven years, and died soon after his release: "I fancy it was of our freedom he died." The last of the ballads—there are many more—addresses the Emperor himself: "Sire, free the prisoners, free Thought and Word."

The best-known poem, "Salonszene" (Drawing-Room Scene), can be read as epilogue to the romantic play called Viennese Biedermeier, or as curtain-raiser to the drama of Biedermeier's disintegration. Without mentioning any name, it describes Prince Metternich at a great reception. The man who steers the Ship of State and acts for sovereigns is so bland a courtier that it must be gratifying to be sent to Elba or the Munkács dungeons by him. He wears his decorations with nonchalance and smiles gently, whether he plucks a rose from a lovely bosom or tears kingdoms to shreds like wilted flowers. As he happens to be in good humour, would he not see a needy client waiting outside the door, anxious to be made happy by a gracious nod? No reason to be afraid of him. He is courteous and sage, carries no knife hidden in his shabby coat. It is the Austrian people, well-mannered, discreet, asking quite modestly:

> ... Dürft' ich wohl so frei sein, frei zu sein?
>
> May I make so free as to be free?

3. TOWARDS THE IDES OF MARCH

Books on Vienna were multiplying. The home-grown variety was, with rare exceptions, about as reliable as heavily re-touched publicity photographs are in our days. Local journalists cultivated the local legend. Life in the raw was relegated to the asides of popular comedy and impromptu farce, to street songs, and to diaries not meant to be published—and even in those, the writers would leave blanks, for the censorship did much work by its mere existence.

Abroad, Vienna had remained on the map (the edge of the map) ever since the great Congress. The picture of gay crowds and sparkling festivities, all of it drenched in good temper and good music, had caught people's fancy through travellers' tales and reportage. (Comte de la Garde-Chambonas's famous chronicle revived and embellished the tales—twenty-five years after the event. *Fêtes et souvenirs du congrès de Vienne* appeared first in 1843: not a good source!) On the other hand, liberal opinion had been roused to sharp antagonism by Metternich's foreign policy in the decade after the Congress, and by reports on the practice of Franz I's administration at home. The alliance between Austria, Russia and Prussia, Metternich's support of every reactionary régime in Europe, the sufferings of the Italian radical poet Silvio Pellico and the Greek leader Ypsilanti in Austrian gaols, and not least the blunders of the Viennese censors, were by-words. It was impossible for travellers coming to Vienna in the late 'twenties and the 'thirties to be unbiassed, to have the innocent eye, even if they came on a purely musical pilgrimage. They had heard too much. This was not a question of politics: nobody with declared opinions opposed to the official doctrine was likely to get the necessary visa anyway, so that visitors tended to be either non-political or staunchly conservative. But they all had read about the Viennese character, and about the sights to see and record. No one had any reason to concentrate his curiosity on the slums. Hardly any had an opportunity to see the inside of a poor household. They would see the dance hall where Johann Strauss the Elder fiddled like a man possessed, or St. Brigitta's Fair with its unaggressive exuberance, or the Prater filled with a friendly bucolic crowd. They would find what they expected to find.

Visitors from northern Germany in particular, while noting the lack of intellectual ferment, liked to stress and over-stress the happy-go-lucky enjoyment of naïve pleasures by the Viennese. Sometimes seriously, sometimes sentimentally, sometimes patronisingly, they would confirm the beneficial results of the tutelage which kept the Viennese artisan, shopkeeper, worker and domestic servant from any contagion by unsettling thoughts.

English observers took a similar line. In 1836, Mrs. Frances Trollope, Anthony Trollope's mother, came to Vienna with the illustrator Hervieu in tow. Her books of reportage, *Paris and the Parisians* and *Domestic Manners of the Americans*, gave her a standing which recommended her to Metternich, more so as she was a Tory and could be relied upon to be a useful propagandist. She was given access to circles of the high aristocracy that normally were closed to all but members of the self-styled *crême de la crême*. The outcome was a travel book which could not have been more flattering to Metternich personally, the Austrian governmental system, and the state of docile happiness conferred by it on the Viennese population. Everything she was told about the goodness of the late Franz I, or about the sad mistakes made by that rash reformer, Joseph II, was set down religiously. But however tinted her spectacles, she had sharp eyes for concrete detail: the simplicity of the furniture in her expensive lodgings ("chintz-coloured calicoes" only for sofa and chair upholstery, draperies but no curtains for the windows), the exorbitant rents, the excellent taste of the accessories (since the days of Lady Mary Wortley Montagu the Viennese novelty industry had made rapid strides forward), the rigid seclusion of the highest aristocracy, the rise of a stock-exchange nobility including some Jewish families, the bizarre diversity of the throng in the streets, the supreme acting of Shakespeare at the Burgtheater, the temporary eclipse of serious music, the absence of intellectuals, whether scholars, writers or painters, from the aristocratic gatherings, which were just a little monotonous for that reason. Nobody she met was able to tell Frances Trollope that there existed such a thing as a circle of Austrian writers and poets of more than local significance; she mentioned an official bard, with a few good ballads to his credit, as the outstanding poet, but not Grillparzer. And yet Byron had said many years before that the world would be forced to remember the outlandish name; though Grillparzer himself, who hated it, had put a caustic question mark to Bryon's dictum in his secret diary.

In short, Mrs. Trollope noted much that was interesting, not **always** correctly when she had it second-hand, and came to a general conclusion which reinforced the accepted view:

. . . This singularly strong national *besoin* of amusement and music, and the manner in which it is not only unchecked, but cherished by the authorities furnishes, in my belief, one of the principal keys to the mystery of the superior tranquillity and contentment of the populace of this country over that of every other.

The book in which Mrs. Trollope set down impressions and opinions, with the avowed intention of dispelling false prejudices against the Austrian system, was called *Vienna and the Austrians*, published in two volumes with many of Hervieu's engravings (see Plate 6) by Richard Bentley, New Burlington Street, London, 1838. It was immediately translated by an "Austrian patriot", of course.

Another book of a similar tendency was published in 1840 by John Murray. It was a work in two volumes entitled *Austria*, with a single chapter specifically dealing with Vienna, though the Austrian capital naturally comes in repeatedly; its author was Peter Evan Turnbull, F.R.S., who seems to have gone to Vienna immediately after Mrs. Trollope, and to have read her book, not entirely with approval, before he finished his. He used no journalistic trimmings and far less local colour than she, and he was no writer, but his information was more substantial, and substantiated, where possible, by a modicum of research. This did not save him from occasional blunders or rash judgements—one unfortunate excursion into the dreary plain to the north of the Danube was enough for him to dismiss the environs of Vienna as unattractive.

Turnbull noted the dark, damp, narrow streets inside the walled city, and the small dark shops whose exterior belied the excellence of their wares. He thought that the striking contrast between Viennese and German ways derived from "a greater infusion of the Italian character" in Vienna. He saw no appearance of poverty and no beggars. Master-tradesmen whom he interviewed told him that "their work people and apprentices expended very little in [*sic*] their food, in order that they might be able, in respectability of appearance, to be equal to their superiors. Tractable, sober, industrious, they were ever willing to work . . . a most happy and enjoyable people. . . ." He discovered no excessive gaiety in Vienna, except during Carnival and for a few weeks after Easter, and thought the "middling classes" austerely simple in their habits. All along, however, he felt some doubts about the reasons underlying so much good behaviour; in his view it came from inbred attitudes, not from stern, upright principles.

He had illuminating things to say about the ban on foreign books. There were three different types of book which booksellers could import under police sanction: "purely innocent ones", which they were entitled to exhibit in their windows; more doubtful works, not to be seen in the windows "lest the good Austrians of the common ranks be led into temptation—but may be kept in the shops to meet the eyes of those more literary persons who frequent them"; and a third group, still more objectionable, to be kept in separate store-rooms for "persons who actually applied for them out of their own mere will and previous knowledge" . . . for instance, Byron's works.

On the whole, Turnbull found the ill-famed police quite unob- trusive. He had more qualms about the censorship. Although he recognised that it was part and parcel of the administrative system which "sought to preserve tranquillity, by the exclusion of whatsoever might excite doubt or discontent, discussion or comparison", he thought that it weighed oppressively on native talent. The twelve censors installed in Vienna, and their colleagues in the provinces, all of them "imbued with the genius of the government", were applying a "jealous and mischievous system" even to scientific literature:

. . . The result of the whole is that, save more practical works on the arts and sciences, philosophy and theology, statistical treatises and history sobered down to the mere recital of facts, very few are the publications that emanate from the Austrian press. The wings of imagination are pretty closely clipped by educa- tion and early habit; but should they ever by chance expand and soar aloft, they usually take flight across the Austrian frontier. . . .

Holding that Austrian education produced loyal subjects but also an excess of mutual tolerance and laxity in matters of religious faith, Turnbull wavered between praise and criticism. His scientific bent led him to analyse "morality" from the statistical side as well, and he came up with the fact that in 1834 there were in Vienna (worse, in this respect, than any provincial capital except Graz) ten illegitimate births to every twelve legitimate. He blamed it largely on the legal impedi- ments to marriage: a priest could celebrate a marriage only if the parties were armed with certificates of "education" and "morality", and evidence that they would be able to provide for a family. (This

was, though Turnbull did not know it, one of the safeguards Franz I
had introduced, a generation earlier, against the increase of a suburban
proletariat in his capital.) And yet, having examined and recorded this
set of problems, Turnbull was still capable of saying, and obviously
believing, that: "frugal, cheerful, and contented, they [the Viennese
working people] seek no alteration in their conditions; they know little
of their government but its mild and paternal influence; and they
dread change of any kind as fraught with evil".

In March, May and October 1848, less than ten years after the
publication of Turnbull's book, crowds of those cheerfully contented
workers poured from their rat-holes near the Line Wall on to the
barricades, to shout, fight, kill, and be killed.

If foreigners with preconceived notions saw nothing but a well-
behaved "populace" afraid of any change, theirs was a venial sin
compared to the smug blindness and deafness of nearly all Viennese
commentators during the years which Austrian historians, by hind-
sight, call the *Vormärz*, pre-March. To borrow a simile from a famous
popular comedy, those upstairs were taking no notice of the happen-
ings in the basement of the social edifice.

In 1810, the population of Vienna (including the suburbs) had been
about 225,000; by 1840 it had risen to roughly 330,000. The mortality
rate continued to be higher than the birth rate, and at that time this
was not due to family planning. Even from the irregular statistical
data issued it was evident that the increase came mainly from the mass
of workers flocking into the suburbs—and from their children, legitimate or illegitimate. The industry which absorbed most of them was
that supplying the fashion trade from small and medium-sized factories, particularly exposed to the effects of boom and slump. Workers
outside the protective order of company or guild, who were not
natives of Vienna, were liable to be sent back to their home parish
if the police and city authorities considered them undesirable or
expendable; thus they were the most defenceless group of all. When
factories closed and even journeymen were laid off during the cholera
epidemic of 1831, these authorities launched public works for unemployed born in Vienna, but transported "great numbers" of those
from outside to their home parishes. (The legal basis was the legislation
corresponding to the Poor Law, which laid the care for people without means, as well as for morality so called, upon the parish where they
were born.) Naturally they drifted back to Vienna if they had their

family there, trying to find one of the jobs considered relatively easy
—with working hours from 5 a.m. to 8 p.m. during the week, but
only from 5 a.m. till noon on Sundays.

The workday was long not only for industrial workers. Young
Obermayer, Rosa Mayreder's father, came to Vienna from a small
Upper Austrian market town. An orphan, he started to work as an
apprentice waiter at a suburban inn kept by his elder brother. He
slept up in the loft where snow drifted on to his bed in winter. When
his brother took over a better-class tavern in the city itself, he slept,
like the other apprentices and waiters, in the taproom. He bedded
down in the hollow of a bench fashioned as a chest to hold bedclothes
in the day and serve as a bed at night. He thought it a great advance in
comfort: it was warm. On top of his interminable duties as an apprentice he had to look after his brother's collection of caged nightingales,
sometimes nearly a hundred of them. If other fanciers came, he would
cover each cage with a cloth, and start passing a brush along a sheet of
paper for hours, amid utter silence. Sometimes the rustling sound
induced the birds to sing. The boy found it merely torment. He
had no leisure time at all. As an adult man he was dour, taciturn, heavy-
handed, a domestic tyrant in both his marriages, childlike in his respect
for the culture and learning which were out of his reach, and ultra-
conservative in his style of living. But he threw himself, not by action
but in passionate partisanship, into the freedom movement of 1848, and
never recanted, though he came to be a wealthy citizen as owner of a
famous beer-house in the centre of the old town. The stamp of his
austere youth—but it belonged to the Biedermeier era, too!—and of
the pre-March years was indelibly upon him.

Johann Strauss the Elder seems to stand at the other extreme of the
Viennese scale, not only because of his European waltz-king fame and
creative gift, but even more because of his spell-binding ebullience.
All the same he burst out from a childhood and a milieu as drab and
crabbed as Obermayer's, with the difference that Strauss was born and
bred in Vienna. His father kept an inn in the Leopoldstadt suburb, on the
lowest fringe of the respectable middle class. Johann was apprenticed
to a book-binder. The story was told that as a small boy he ran away
with his fiddle, dimly intending to walk to the Kahlenberg, of all
places; when he got tired he sat down at the foot of a sloping vineyard, and was picked up by a friend of the family who happened to
come past.

There was no holding Johann Strauss. He joined a small dance band
as a viola player; Joseph Lanner was the first violinist. When Lanner
broke away with two others to form his own trio, young Strauss, then
fifteen, followed him. Their quartet—two violins, viola and guitar—
was enlarged to a quintet by a 'cello, and remained unchanged until
1824, when Lanner was twenty-three, Strauss twenty, and between
them they reigned, in the words of Mosco Carner, "as undisputed
kings of light music". Played by a small string band as they were
played in those years, Lanner's dance tunes and the earlier waltzes of
Strauss sound delicately gay rather than intoxicating, and this was—
for a limited time—as much a true image of popular moods and needs
as Raimund's earlier plays. At the same time, the waltz tunes channelled and shaped those moods, at least superficially. Indeed, the fair-
haired Lanner, son of a Viennese glovemaker, came very close to the
mirror-vision of Biedermeier in his modest charm, melodic poetry and
unforced sentiment. It fitted into the picture that he played with his
band to "the people" under the tall trees of the Prater. But times were
changing, and the proverbial winds of change are no gentle zephyrs
once they start to blow.

Lanner's string band grew to a full-scale orchestra in step with the
expansion of Vienna and the increase of a public which demanded a
stronger stimulus, a headier entertainment than that offered in family
circles or at private dance parties to the sad-and-gay, sedate strains of
Schubert's and Lanner's waltzes collected in printed albums. Lanner
ceded to the demand, split his swollen orchestra into two, and put the
second half under his friend—and already rival—Johann Strauss. This
started the years of competition which in the mid-'thirties gave the
spectacular victory to Strauss, with his greater showmanship and
fiercer temperament, dividing the Viennese *aficionados* into two camps
of fans as enthusiastically partisan as the supporters of two Spanish
matadors with contrasting styles in the bull-ring. In the end Lanner and
Strauss parted ways, and even their musical patterns slid apart. For a
time Lanner was musical director of the Court Balls, but was dismissed, allegedly for being rude to Archduchess Sophie. He continued
to conduct his own orchestra with his bow, and to pour out a stream of
waltzes, polkas, marches and so forth, deepening his mastery of rhythm
and orchestral shading, but staying within a Viennese tradition that
made him akin to Schubert. He died in 1842, of typhus.

Johann Strauss, "the Moor" with olive skin and black locks, was of tougher fibre, the Demon King of popular fancy at a time when high excitement, not serene pleasure, was sought for as the great escape route. From 1830 onwards he was tied by contract, though not by exclusive contract, to the great amusement palace of Sperl in the Leopoldstadt. There he led his inflated orchestra and mesmerised a devoted public, oddly mixed of staid middle-class families who would drink and eat, in spring on the terrace outside under trees in bloom, and of young people from every layer of the working population, who would wait for the moment of blissful surrender to the swaying rhythm, the fulfilment of the Sunday dreams.

Every visiting German journalist had to write purple passages about the Viennese spinning bacchantically to the irresistible fiddle of Johann Strauss.

"The violence with which music took hold of people in this era is the outstanding, if not the only, characteristic of Viennese culture in the pre-March years": thus the summing-up in Otto Rommel's huge monograph (*op. cit.*, p. 613). The causes of such violence lay outside music. That it was transferred to music, and that this music reached every cranny of society, down to the cheapest wine-garden where a street musician would play the harp and sing the pop songs of the day, shows not only the living strength of Viennese musical tradition, but also the quick absorption of newcomers into the town. The thousands who were arriving annually from Bohemia, Moravia and Silesia— the largest contingent of immigrants—brought with them their own musical traditions, not least an addiction to, and inborn talent for, the violin. Johann Strauss, himself driven by violent impulses, was the right man, and his music had the right lilt, to sweep the others along. By comparison, his success on his tours through western Europe, including England in the Coronation year, 1838, was shallow. And even in Vienna his musical dictatorship did not outlast the year 1848. Relatively few of his waltzes and polkas, and only one of his marches, the *Radetzky March*, which is another story, have genuinely survived. In his monograph *The Waltz* (London, Max Parrish, 1945), Mosco Carner analyses the differences between the waltzes of Lanner and the elder Strauss, and comes to the conclusion that "posterity has given judgment to Lanner".

As a private person Strauss hardly fitted the public image of charm and bonhomie. He tried to force his three sons into professional careers and prevent them from becoming musicians. All three were musicians, and became professionals in their domain of music—which the father regarded as his prerogative. His attitude may be explained, and excused, as true to lower-middle-class Biedermeier form with its cult of respectability, and to the despotic position of the *paterfamilias*, corresponding to that of the Emperor as the father of his people. Yet Strauss was also resentfully jealous of his eldest son, Johann, who quietly showed that he was an infinitely more resourceful and more accomplished composer, with a temperament no less compelling than his father's as leader of an orchestra. Johann Strauss the Elder left his wife and family, to share a household with his mistress, by whom he had five children. In 1844 he obtained his divorce. In 1844, also, Johann Strauss the Younger opened the autumn season at Dommeyer's elegant casino near the gates of Schönbrunn Castle with his own orchestra and his own waltzes. This was rebellion. Worse, the rebellion was succcessful. In March 1848, the son was to be in the ranks of the revolutionaries, the father an ardent supporter of the collapsing paternalist régime.

In the early 'thirties, when the changes on the surface of Viennese public life looked trivial, a mere matter of taste or fashion on the lines of the cult of the virtuoso, the rivalry between Lanner and Strauss had a peculiar parallel in another field of popular art. This was the rivalry between two actor-playwrights of genius, Ferdinand Raimund and Johann Nestroy. Starting from a different style of acting—Raimund's gently humorous identification with each part as opposed to Nestroy's uncomfortably ruthless caricature of reality—it developed into a contrast between a declining and a rising attitude to art and life, to ideas and to social facts. Both men belonged to Vienna, root and branch, and both created an image of their Vienna in their plays.

Up to his death in 1836 Raimund was the acknowledged master of the fairy-tale play, which in his hands fused the elements of Viennese baroque comedy, romantic poetry, and the local character farce, as Bäuerle together with his lesser rivals had evolved it. Three times Raimund attempted ambitious philosophical allegories, tragic in conception but relieved by scenes and character of an unashamedly Viennese comic strain; he had to accept defeat. His public insisted on the accustomed fare, on fairy kings who could safely parody contemporary rulers (some of those Raimund invented were good-natured caricatures of the paternal absolute monarch and the system of letting-things-slide), and on numbers destined to become folk-songs in the

settings by Raimund himself or by a theatre composer like old Wenzel
Müller. Even in Vienna, the baroque tradition had too far receded into
limbo to make strange Greek divinities, furies and demons bearable as
vehicles for a tragic conflict between the universal laws and human
insufficiency. Raimund had to find other means of expression, and
he did, in his last play which was called *Der Verschwender* (*The Spendthrift*), and had its première in the smallest of the three suburban
theatres, the Josefstädter Theater, whose Biedermeier façade still
exists.

Raimund described this play as a tale of magic, a *Zaubermärchen*. But
the magic of the fairy Cheristane, who loves the hero Flottwell, is
powerless in face of the supreme law that man alone can bring blessing
or disaster upon himself. In spite of its allegorical and poetical devices,
this is a tragedy of character. Its three acts are spaced over twenty-three
years. The young spendthrift who in the first act chucks his money
about, without thought of other people even in his acts of generosity,
ends as a broken man who has brought death to his wife and children,
and ruin to himself, by sheer irresponsibility. Cheristane's magic can
do no more than spare him the humiliation of a beggar's existence and
its alternative, suicide in despair; sums he has given to a beggar—
her helper in human disguise—are restored to him, but they do not
amount to much. When a theatre director clamoured for a friendlier
ending—couldn't Flottwell be reunited with the daughter he believes
to have died in a shipwreck?—Raimund flatly refused to tamper with
his work.

It was not realism. Only in the first and second acts are there a few
touches referring to everyday problems, as for instance a builder's
explanation of his shoddy methods—a house is to be strutted two years
after its construction because landlords want to let rooms in quantity
and reduce walls to the thickness of paper. But though there existed
many examples of financial ruin caused by a young heir's extravagance
(the banker Geymüller's nephew and heir was even then careening
towards bankruptcy), Raimund saw the tragedy of self-waste in a
wider context. Possibly Flottwell was to some extent a transmutation
of Raimund's own dark experiences at an earlier stage, when his reckless surrender to passion devastated other lives as well as his. In his play,
however, the part he wrote and took for himself was that of a vastly
different character, a simple artisan incapable of hurting anyone and
incapable of excessive passion. Valentin, the carpenter, is in the first

act one of the spendthrift's lackeys, a little too soft, naïve and easy-going for that corrupt milieu; but when his sharp-tongued fiancée is insulted by the all-powerful valet, he throws up his job, deals with the man, goes back to his trade, and marries her. In the third act, as a hen-pecked husband and harassed father, he wants to help his impoverished former master by taking him into their household, imposes his will on his shrewish wife, and so gives Flottwell his one experience of human warmth. The best beloved of all Raimund's songs is Valentin's last number, sung at the carpenter's bench: the "Hobellied", the song of the plane. It expresses, very simply, cheerful resignation and the acceptance of whatever life—and death—may bring; and its sentiment verges on sentimentality.

The good fairy in *The Spendthrift* has the power, magically, to save the wastrel from the suicide he is pondering. Raimund's despair at the human condition was deeply embedded underneath his allegories. Two years later, he committed suicide "while his mind was disturbed". But even if it is possible that he was a helpless rebel against the world in which he found himself, there is no trace of rebellion against things-as-they-were in his last play, or indeed in any of his work.

It is on this point that the rival actor and dramatist struck a discordant note almost from his beginning.

Johann Nepomuk Eduard Ambrosius Nestroy was born in Vienna in 1801, the son of a lawyer in straitened circumstances. He went to a grammar school and to the university; before he finished his studies—jurisprudence—the court opera engaged him as a bass-baritone. His first great success was as Sarastro in *The Magic Flute*. A rash early marriage (which ended in disaster a few years later when his wife left him, and their small son, for an aristocratic lover) induced Nestroy to go to Amsterdam, where he could earn a better salary at the German Theatre, and afterwards to enter into a series of engagements in Austrian provincial capitals. He accumulated a vast all-round repertoire, not only in opera but increasingly, whether from inclination or because he had overtaxed his singing voice, as a comedian. By the time he achieved his ambition, a good contract in Vienna, he had switched over to burlesque and character parts, startled critics and public by his uncanny vitality, and began to specialise in those popular Viennese comedies which were successful outside Vienna in spite of their local settings, thanks to the lingua franca quality of the Viennese dialect in a slightly stylised version. In the meantime he had also found a solution to his vexed private problems. In Graz he had met a singer who became his life's companion and his wife in all but the name (though he got his divorce, he was barred from remarriage, being technically a Catholic), a good mother to his son and the two children she had by him and whom he adopted, and the shrewd manager of his theatrical business. Both were strong personalities, so that they enforced respect for a union which was no hole-and-corner affair.

Nestroy began his conquest of the Viennese public in 1831 at the Theater an der Wien. All three suburban theatres were in a state of financial and managerial crisis then; entrepreneurs were taking over from the older and old-fashioned directors who, themselves actors and often authors for the stage, had relied too much on improvisation. There were signs of fatigue in the programmes with their repetition of stale stage tricks and their adaptation of foreign comedies thinly coated with local colour. Raimund was a lonely figure, and in any case he no longer appeared regularly on the stage. Some of the best comic actors had died. Therese Krones was dead. When Nestroy first appeared he caused a sensation that was by no means entirely favourable. Here was no mildly comforting humour and familiar good fun, but relentless exposure of human weaknesses: a comedian who could be wildly funny and yet strike the spectators as sinister and somehow diabolical. It was a new voice and a new tone.

Inevitably Raimund's admirers accused the new star of exaggeration and cold, grotesque distortion of the human reality. Raimund himself kept Nestroy away from parts in his own plays, as though afraid that his characters would be dehumanised. The contrast between Raimund and Nestroy was too patent not to become a topic of discussion in the coffee-houses of Vienna; at least one diary, that of Raimund's close friend, the court-theatre actor Costenoble, recorded this. Inevitably, too, Raimund was cast in the part of the fair-haired champion of noble dreams (and the good old times), while Nestroy was the dark spirit of disillusion. Within a few years, a whole legend of their irreducible enmity had sprung up, which modern scholarship has disproved, without destroying it—the story is too good not to be repeated in popularising accounts—and also without impairing its symptomatic interest. The critics were divided, the ordinary theatre-goers mainly on Nestroy's side, though there were some first-night rows. Grillparzer, in his hopeless quest for inner harmony, struck at Nestroy in a poem of 1833 which contrasts the kindly humour of a comedian whom he had admired in his childhood and youth, with the up-to-date joke that "laughs with a grin, as desperation laughs". At least Grillparzer blamed it not on an individual but on the sombre, confused times—the same times which to others, looking back on them, seemed so bright, friendly and transparent.

In 1833, Nestroy, who had started to write plays as vehicles for his acting, put on his fairy-tale farce *Lumpazivagabundus oder Das liederliche Kleeblatt* (*Lumpazivagabundus* or *The Dissolute Trio*). Its traditional frame of good and bad genii, caricatured in the usual manner, the hackneyed plot, the stereotyped minor figures, did nothing to soften the impact of the trio of journeymen whom Nestroy had lifted out of real life without tidying them up too much. They are what they are: one, the carpenter, a kind, clumsy fellow longing for the smug and decent home he finally gets; the second, a tailor, a volatile drifter out for a good time; the third, a shoemaker, a compulsive drinker who cannot bear to be orderly and settle in a groove. Each one is human, a mixture of good and bad, true to himself even if this means being true to squalor, and no object for humane improvement. As a sop to Cerberus the final tableau forecasts a friendlier future, when the two incurable good-for-nothings are tamed by wedded love. It carries no conviction.

In description and in reading, the play seems harmless enough, including the character played by Nestroy himself, the drunken shoe-maker Knieriem. It must have jolted a considerable part of the Viennese public in 1833. At that time, the good citizens of Vienna were accus-tomed to see a flattering, or at worst a gently teasing, image of them-selves on the stage in comedies which followed Bäuerle's pattern. In Raimund's mature plays, on the other hand, they felt the warm glow of poetry, saw misguided people grope towards something higher, and heard the gospel of moderation from the lips of guileless, simple men and women. Now Nestroy confronted them with individuals stripped of every shred of pretence (especially when he acted the part), but did it so wittily that the theatre-addicts had to laugh against their will and come back for more punishment. If the phrase existed in German no doubt someone would have complained that Nestroy was too clever by half. And some did in fact complain, as time went on, that he was a grave-digger of Old Vienna with his disintegrating, negative wit to which nothing was hallowed.

However, the tradition that demanded undisturbed laughter was

stronger and older than the smug Biedermeier attitude to which
Nestroy refused to conform. He was too good an actor not to hanker
after applause, so he tried to write—though not to act—according to
accepted formulas and on the model of French or English popular hits.
Most of the plays he churned out were written for the day and forgotten with the day; but since he had integrity, there came now and
again those flashes which shocked the public out of its complacency,
flashes in his acting or in the implacable realism of a small scene. It
was still in the eighteen-thirties, that is to say, before the political
unrest became vocal and Nestroy one of its mocking voices, that he
scored his second great success with the comedy *Zu ebener Erde und
erster Stock* (*Ground Floor and First Floor*). It has a happy end, with
every Jack getting his Jill and virtue its reward, and the social order
restored to stability after having been rocked for a moment by the
move of the poor family from the bleak ground floor (in English terms
it would be a basement flat) to the first floor. Yet it has once again those
new, uncompromising notes which Nestroy had sounded four years
before in his fairy-tale farce of the dissolute trio. The poor family is
bitterly poor, but seen through no rosy spectacles. The children are
snotty. Not everyone is resigned to his station. To be an old-clothes
man corrupts the heart and sometimes it corrupts honesty. If there has
been no sale and everything that could be pawned is gone, there is only
bread for the children; when there is a small windfall, they get potatoes,
perhaps even sausage; and when they really strike it lucky, father—not
a good example of thrift—takes his whole family on an eating spree to
the nearest inn. They eat fried chicken, but the gourmet among them
plans to have soufflé fritters and french bean salad as well, and the men
get a little tight. Leftover chicken wings are wrapped up and taken
home.

Nestroy's realistic scenes are among the few examples of social
reportage of the period, and they are limited in scope. His setting is
nearly always suburban, the cast shopkeepers and their assistants,
modest tradesmen, artisans or journeymen, and people in fringe
occupations, but hardly ever industrial workers, who, even for him,
had not yet emerged as individuals. For the poorer among his characters, the landlord, and not the employer, is the most important man
on earth. (There is nothing like Dickens's scenes of backyard squalor,
not only because Vienna was a small metropolis with no vast slummy
areas, but also because local comedy has other laws than a novel. And

there had never been a good contemporary novel of Old Vienna to compete with, and enlarge on, Nestroy's snatches of unvarnished realism.) Tiny details of behaviour are sharply observed, as long as Nestroy does not slide into grotesque caricature. If he supplies his family of old-clothes dealers with a menu, it is more reliable than the exaggerated presentation of a millionaire's party on the first floor. The scene in *Ground Floor and First Floor* is also one of the few Biedermeier passages to mention the chicken fried in breadcrumbs, the *Backhendl*, which according to legend—Bauernfeld helped to popularise the term, but he did so in later years—was so much the common fare of the Viennese then that it has provided the tag of the *Backhendlzeit*, the Fried Chicken Era. In fact it was, among ordinary people, a dish for special occasions; most of them could not afford it so very often. Equally, another delicacy for which Old Vienna was famous, and accused of gross gluttony, the confectioners' artefacts in marzipan, candied fruit and the sugar mixture called *Tragant* (sugar worked to a pliable mass with the aid of tragacanth), were special treats for most Viennese, a sort of edible valentine. The moderation which Raimund had preached out of the mouths of his most likable characters existed not only as an ideal, but also as everyday reality—a virtue born from necessity. Nestroy showed its reverse whenever he let hunger and greed flash through a brief scene.

He also preserved in his dialogue the subtler shades of a specific form of Viennese snobbery: the use of the ennobling particle *von* as an arbitrary addition to a commoner's name, and the motives behind this usage, from mere courtesy to abject flattery—or, when it was suddenly dropped, to deliberate rudeness. The habit had started at the end of the eighteenth century. Early *Eipeldauer Letters* mention it as something practised by foolish vulgarians. Naturally people who wished to be addressed in this way returned the compliment to others in a similar position. In the decades of the rise of a numerous sub-nobility consisting of officers, civil servants, professional men and prosperous business men, those in the strata just below, pushing upwards but not yet lifted up, tended to overrate the magic of the particle, and help themselves to it by mutual consent. It was common enough but never a general custom. In an older local comedy, a self-respecting Viennese housewife praises a visitor because he, unlike many others, does not try to flatter her by calling her *Frau von*. The letters of the Schubert circle show no signs of the habit. On the contrary, one or the other would write to a friend who belonged to the titled gentry, like the Spauns, without the proper address. These men, however, had no sense of social insecurity or inferiority.

It was in other sectors of the middle and lower middle classes that snobbery was rampant, together with its inverted form, servility. Nestroy tilted at both with neat, quick thrusts in many plays. The daughter of a millionaire who has inherited his *von* together with his million confers the title on their landlord when she wants to let him down lightly as a suitor. An ingenious sponger tries to climb back into favour with the young man he has betrayed while believing him poor and friendless, by calling him on a rising scale *Herr von*, *Herr Baron*, and *Herr Graf* (Count). In a farce, all male characters endowed with money—listed as a rentier, a "rich man of private means", a capitalist and a former manufacturer—are given plebeian names and vulgar manners, but also, to a man, the *von*, self-styled or not. In a comedy of 1841, a grocer and another shopkeeper begin their conversation by addressing each other as *Herr von* So-and-so; in the list of characters, neither of them is called *von*, of course. And so it goes on.

In other words, within little more than a generation the spurious use of *von* had become as ubiquitous and as meaningless in Vienna, as the use of the stately address *Don* had become in Spain by the end of the nineteenth century: though never a title of nobility, *Don* had been the designation for gentlemen, indicating a status above those who lived on their trade or by the work of their hands, and it ended as a courtesy form applied to virtually anyone who was not a manual worker or peasant.

The cult of the particle *von* did not die with the Biedermeier. It grew while the flow of titles of nobility continued to raise successful business men above their colleagues. My maternal grandmother, who had the right to use it, would have felt churlish if she had not addressed women of good old Viennese *Bürger* stock as *Frau von*; it must have become as difficult to draw the line as it is for the English today over "Esquire". The usage degenerated to a courtesy in doubtful taste when democratic ideas impinged seriously on the public attitude to an aristocratic hierarchy. Though some of it lingered on until the First World War, and among the elder generation beyond it, it was by then scarcely more than a joke played by those in search of tips on those who liked to have their vanity tickled. Fiacre coachmen and waiters evolved an intricate game with titles, graduated to a nicety—and often taken only too seriously, as a regrettable Viennese trait, by earnest foreign observers.

At the time, however, when Nestroy made his satirical sallies, this make-believe practice had not yet reached its peak. It was only one of the symptoms of a structural change then in its beginnings. What he really captured in his dramatic snippets of reportage was the insecure, equivocal position of rising tradesmen and businessmen who found themselves in a no-man's-land of society: a good if easy target for the satirist.

Friedrich von Gentz, who had a patent of nobility but was too clever not to realise that the older aristocracy looked down on him in spite of Metternich's patronage, saw the cult of the *von* in a different light, from a different place in society. In 1830, when the young dancer Fanny Elssler, the woman who warmed his brittle old age, was fêted in Berlin, he wanted his two unmarried sisters who lived there to make friends with her. In the postscript to a letter he explained to them:

I suppose you know that in Vienna every distinguished woman is addressed as *Frau von,* and every well-bred, cultured girl as *Fräulein.* Therefore a person like Fanny is generally called *Fräulein.* Ladies of a standing as high as yours, being the sisters of a high personage like myself, with my 9 or 90 decorations, are at the very least *comtesses.* All this is extremely ridiculous, but it is the custom of the country.

As usual Gentz was disingenuous. He exaggerated grossly so as to flatter his sisters and persuade them that the accomplished dancer was also well-bred and socially acceptable. He obviously wanted his Fanny to be addressed as *Fräulein,* which corresponded to the *Frau von* granted to married women, because, however much he mocked at it, he could not but approve of a local custom that implicitly paid tribute to the feudal pyramid. Behind his arch boastfulness and condescension ("a person like Fanny") there stands an observation worthy of note: at least in his milieu, the upper middle class rubbing shoulders with the aristocracy, it was *Bildung*—a cultivated mind—which secured accept-ance and respect. The small fact that popular stage artists could be included in the gratuitous ennoblement-by-usage—a fact confirmed by pre-March concert bills in which female singers increasingly often figured not as Demoiselle, the title used in court theatre bills until the Revolution of 1848, but as *Fräulein*—was in itself a sign of change. Within a few years it was to be so general as to pass unnoticed: below the fossilised high aristocracy, caste boundaries were getting blurred. This process began in Vienna later than in London or Paris, so that its side-issues and subsidiary effects were noticeable in the life of the city for a long time to come.

Gentz himself died in 1832, when the Emperor Franz I was still alive, and the collapse of the system which Metternich strove to perpetuate was as yet no more than a spectre dimly perceived by a few. One of those who saw it coming was Gentz, who wrote: ". . . if the destinies of States should once again favour the cause which I have served loyally for so many years, although this is highly improbable . . ." A year before his death, after the fall of insurgent Warsaw, he even published a sensational article which culminated in a gospel of coexistence between "the system of orderly progress" and "the system of con-servation", in a resigned acknowledgment of the strength of the new forces.

It was to these new forces which Gentz sensed and feared that his beloved Fanny Elssler owed her mass public. This was paradoxical, for in person she seemed, and in many ways was, a true incarnation of Biedermeier ideals: graceful rather than beautiful, with a quiet oval face under glossy dark hair, natural and simple in manner, "modest to the point of shyness" in Gentz's words, but utterly ravishing when she danced one of her fiery folk dances, such as the Cachucha, or a romantic ballet invention. Her grandfather had played the violin at the side of Haydn in Esterházy's orchestra, her father had been Haydn's copyist and valet, she grew up in a Viennese home steeped in music but frugal in its habits. As a child, she, like two of her sisters, was trained at the ballet school of the Vienna court opera, where the technique of Noverre, the revolutioniser of baroque ballet in Gluck's time, reigned supreme; then she went to Naples, where she learnt a novel freedom of mimic expression, and her rise began. When she was twenty, already a star of the Vienna ballet going on international tours, Gentz said that there was nothing glamorous or extraordinary about her except "her dear face and lovely figure"; that his affair with her, an open secret, was not disapproved of by his high-born friends; and that her unselfish devotion gave him the greatest happiness he had ever known.

Fanny had two children, the first in Naples when she was half a child herself; she never married, was a devout Catholic, and conducted her emotional life with impeccable decorum. At forty-one she withdrew

from dancing—this was in 1851, so that her professional career barely
outlasted the pre-March and Old Vienna—and in 1884 she died of
cancer, a living legend. As a public figure, however, she belonged less
to the Biedermeier world than to the era of virtuosos and of a mass
public. For one thing, she was the first Viennese artist to embark on an
international career. She even made a conquest of the New World.
In Paris she was acclaimed as the only equal to Marie Taglioni, though
Fanny was no innovator as was Taglioni with her ballet *La Sylphide*
and the technique *sur les pointes*. Théophile Gautier characterised the
rivals in two famous tags: Taglioni was the Christian, Elssler the pagan
dancer—Taglioni's dancing was air, Elssler's fire and earth. She
brought to foreign spectators precisely that image of Viennese charm
which they wanted, and her personality, charm incarnate, helped to
spread the legend. Her peculiar blend of romance and earthiness
dissolved in poetic beauty had its roots in Vienna, where she danced
less often than elsewhere during her great years. They were the same
roots, *mutatis mutandis*, as those of the *Magic Flute* libretto and of
Raimund's best plays, so that at home her art could be understood, or
at least felt, as something familiar bursting into flower. Seen in
retrospect she had another importance for Vienna as well. Fanny Elssler
was one of the artists who attracted a public different from that of the
suburban theatres, but also distinct from the still powerful aristocratic
patrons in the boxes; a public in which the old Viennese *Bürgertum*
and the new rising bourgeoisie began to merge.

For this public the most important stage was not, however, that of
opera or ballet, but of drama: the Burgtheater. The Burgtheater was to
keep its influence, and even to increase it, for several generations; it was
to remain a focus of Viennese civilisation; but its structure was evolved
in the Biedermeier years, its social function established in the pre-
March decades.

The Hofburgtheater, to give it its full name for once, was the smaller
of the two court theatres. Lower in its construction and darker than the
Kärntnertor-Theater which housed the opera, it had been converted
from the court hall for ball games, and given an unobtrusively pleasant
front in 1760. It had its name of Burgtheater because it was virtually
stuck on to the imperial palace, the Hofburg or Burg for short. Joseph
II decreed in 1776 that it should be exclusively devoted to German
drama—previously its repertoire had largely been French—and become
a "National Theatre". It did rise to the position of the leading German

stage in the years between 1815 and 1830, under the leadership of an artistic director of near-genius, Joseph Schreyvogel, who left his mark not only on the court theatre but on Vienna.

Schreyvogel, born in 1768 as the son of a prosperous Viennese tradesman, took the ideals of the Enlightenment with him into the nineteenth century. He was, a rare thing in Vienna, a Kantian imbued with ethical and aesthetical purpose, but he was also an exceedingly practical man of the theatre. In the teeth of a top-heavy, clumsy, parsimonious administration by high court officials of varying insight— he himself, as a commoner, was never given the formal position of a director—and in constant guerrilla warfare with a censorship acting on arbitrary instructions from above, Schreyvogel succeeded to an astonishing degree in putting his ideas into practice. Slowly he broke down the resistance to the dramas of Schiller and Goethe, though at the price of bowdlerising cuts and changes. (*Wilhelm Tell*, *Don Carlos* and *Götz von Berlichingen* all contained explosive thoughts and lines, and situations which Franz I and his entourage could not stomach.) With a team of distinguished actors he created unified performances based on sensitive rehearsing, far ahead of his time. Since he conceived the task of the Burgtheater as humanising and universal, his great concern was to create a repertory which would embrace not only good entertainment and effective theatre in the fashion of the day, but above all the noblest dramatic works of world literature. When he was done, the enduring stock of the Burgtheater, as he called it, included Lessing, Schiller, Goethe, Kleist and Grillparzer, Spanish classics, some in his own skilful translations, Corneille, Racine and Molière, and above all Shakespeare: *Romeo and Juliet*, *King Lear*, *Hamlet*, *Othello*. . . .

There exists a record of the impact which *King Lear*—with Heinrich Anschütz as Lear—made on Biedermeier Vienna, in a few pages of Stifter's novel *Der Nachsommer*. It is no reportage. Stifter always filtered and stylised his impressions, and when he wrote the book, his student days in Vienna had receded into a beautifying distance. In this case, however, he described his own reactions together with those of the civic élite he most admired. The hero's father belongs to the Viennese merchant patriciate and observes strict rules:

When we [he and his younger sister] were more mature . . . we were on rare occasions permitted a visit to the court theatre. Our father chose for those visits plays which he thought appropriate for us and beneficial for our development.

We were never allowed to go to the opera, let alone the ballet, nor to a suburban theatre. . . .

King Lear played by Anschütz was said to be "the highest that a human being can achieve in the sphere of art", and the court theatre "had the reputation of being a model for all Germany". So young Heinrich goes to a performance of *King Lear* and notes that

the ordinary seats as well as the boxes were crowded with people in festive dress, as was the custom, and on that day a much more numerous and mixed multitude poured into the rooms . . . probably attracted by the fame of the play and the actor. Men standing next to me pointed this out, and indeed there was in the attendance many a figure which must have come from the most distant parts of the suburbs. . . .

A condensed account of the tragedy follows, as it would strike some-one who had never read it. When Lear kneels down in front of Cordelia, Heinrich records:

My heart felt as though crushed, I could scarcely contain my grief. I had never imagined anything like it; this was no longer a spectacle, what I saw was the most real reality. The favourable end superimposed on performances of the play in those times, to mitigate the terrible feelings which this event roused, had no effect on me, my heart told me that it was impossible . . . I saw that all faces were still turned to the stage, as if riveted to the scene by a powerful emotion.

In a Viennese existence which was, in Bauernfeld's definition, "a Dutch still-life where no noise of the outer world, no ray of daylight, could penetrate", this was an irruption of elemental force, comparable only to that of Beethoven's last works.

Schreyvogel, the man who had opened doors of communication with the "outer world" at least of drama, stumbled over an intrigue of the court bureaucracy and was pensioned off. He died two months later, during the cholera epidemic of 1832. Bauernfeld, who believed that Schreyvogel had been too competent not to provoke the animosity of a mediocre aristocratic chief, wrote in his memoirs: "He died of cholera, so they said—in reality of heartache, of the K.K. Court Chamberlain's Office, and of the Austrian System." His achievements in sixteen years as secretary to the theatre were so solidly built that not even inept immediate successors were able to destroy them. The ensemble of the Burgtheater remained, and there remained a public that had become accustomed to intellectual stimulus—at least now and then, in between entertainments. Also, Schreyvogel had been midwife to the first successful plays of two Austrian playwrights, one on the high road and one on the low road: Grillparzer and Bauernfeld.

He had fought diplomatic skirmishes for Grillparzer in the early years of the Biedermeier, when after the first sensational hit, *Die Ahnfrau*, came a succession of dramas—*Sappho, Das goldene Vliess* (Medea), *König Ottokar, Ein treuer Diener seines Herrn, Des Meeres und der Liebe Wellen* (Hero and Leander)—which fascinated audiences by their poetic force, yet increasingly bewildered them by psychological depths, unfamiliar thoughts, and a scarcely veiled personal immediacy of problems. Here was the first great creative writer born and bred in Austria since the Middle Ages, the greatest dramatist in the German language since Goethe and Schiller (with the possible exception of Kleist), and as such he was widely acknowledged. It would, however, be untrue to pretend that those plays either expressed or influenced the intellectual mood of Grillparzer's Viennese public. His poems, prose pieces, letters and diaries are all of inexhaustible value for the comprehension of Vienna and Austria in the first half of the nineteenth century. Even the way in which the Austrian System fitted, at the same time as it deepened and distorted, his peculiar introvert loneliness is part of the evidence. His plays transcend the frame. Only their theatrical history and public reception properly belong in this sketch of Viennese civilisation.

Schreyvogel's death was a blow to Grillparzer, who lost in him a sympathetic producer, loyal champion, and congenial friend. Within a few years Grillparzer was out of favour with the new masters of the Burgtheater, who had little liking for plays outside the stream of fashion and demand as his were. When *Weh dem, der lügt* (literally: *Woe to Him Who Lies*), his only dramatic attempt in a ligher mode, had its first performance in 1838, it was so insensitively produced and so badly miscast that it was a complete failure with a first-night public that otherwise might—just might—have given it a chilly but respectful reception. A play about an ethical problem, labelled *Lustspiel* (comedy), only because it fitted into no other category, a play which was witty and wise but not funny, was staged as a farce. A high-born barbarian who should have been played straight, as a man of uncouth strength, was played as a ridiculous moron; this seems to have offended the aristocratic habitués of the Burgtheater who took it for a parody of their own caste, and it twisted the meaning of Grillparzer's whole plot. But even if a cleverer production had avoided this pitfall, shuttered minds would still have resented the defeat of Count Galomir, the Teutonic barbarian, and Atalus, the cultured French nobleman, by the resourceful hero, a mere scullion. After all, Grillparzer's most literate friends had been doubtful when he read the manuscript to them; and in the Burgtheater, not only the box public but the majority of fairly cultivated theatre-goers failed to perceive the delicately poised, double-edged meaning of story and dialogue, or even the filtered simplicity of the verse lines. They did not know what to make of the summing-up by the saintly bishop, Gregory of Tours, who exclaimed that "all of them tell the truth, are proud of it—and yet she [the heroine Edrita] lies to herself and him, he [the hero, Leon the scullion] lies to me and her, the other lies because he has been lied to—and even so all of them tell the truth, all of them, all", because truth is many-sided, and this world of deception is such that one has to be content if corn grows over the ineradicable weeds.

The première came close to a theatre scandal, and the author took the rebuff badly. It was the reason, or the excuse, for Grillparzer to with-draw into silence, to sulk like Achilles in his tent in demonstrative isolation, sheltering behind his daily bureaucratic round in the Treasury Archive, and doubting himself more than ever because, as he justly felt, not so much a bad production as lack of communication between him and his public had defeated him.

It was left to modern Austrian scholars to decide that *Weh dem, der lügt* was the most "Viennese" of Grillparzer's plays, invisibly linked with the old baroque drama in which the metaphysical and the real worlds met, and with the fairy-tale plays of popular tradition. (Not for nothing had the libretto of *The Magic Flute*, read aloud by a nurse-maid, been Grillparzer's first dramatic impression.) Hero and heroine, too, are undeniably Viennese, of a breed favoured by Grillparzer who even in private life turned to women of sturdy character and mother wit: Leon and Edrita are shapely, natural, warm-hearted, full of common sense, and honest, but also gaily prepared to use, and misuse, truth and untruth at the dictates of immediate necessity or of the higher needs of deep feeling. It was this ambivalence, this yes-and-no to the ethical principle, which a public steeped in a laxer kind of ambivalence refused to grasp.

The Burgtheater public of 1838 reacted, more sharply than the majority of another audience might have done at another time and place, against a work that exposed ambiguities in individual motivation and action, without offering the comfortable reprieve of a clear-cut decision at the end. Just then the air of Vienna was saturated with ambiguity and indecision. Three years after the death of Franz I, the sense of stability which in spite of everything his rule had instilled—largely, as it turned out, through the Emperor's own pettifogging but consistent and ubiquitous interference—was vanishing fast. In its stead, a feeling of stagnation in the public sector was rapidly coming to the surface. The new sovereign, Ferdinand I, was mentally backward, feeble-minded if kindly, and his condition was no secret. The Regency Council consisted of three old men and one who was younger but insignificant: two lay-figures, the archdukes Franz Karl and Ludwig, and two ministers, Prince Metternich for Foreign Affairs and Count Kolowrat for Home Affairs, who were adversaries, intrigued against each other, and immobilised one another efficiently. The State had an administration, but no government capable of governing.

On the other hand, the new bourgeoisie and the new professional classes were gaining in economic and social influence as well as in numbers. The finances of the empire were in bad shape, dependent on loans from the house of Rothschild. The first of the Viennese Rothschilds was made a Baron (this, unless it was a very much older feudal title, meant less in the aristocratic hierarchy of Austria—or Germany—than in that of Britain), and, more significant as being a breach of existing laws, a citizen of Vienna in spite of his Jewish faith. This was a reward for his services to the ailing exchequer and for his enterprise in financing the first great Austrian railway, which linked Vienna with Moravia and later Bohemia. The number of textile factories supplying the market for fashion goods increased in and around Vienna; they drew immigrants from the countryside to the capital. Joint-stock companies and new banks to finance new trades began to play an ever-growing rôle, while the old privileges of merchant companies and guilds were reduced to mere obstacles in the way of a development that represented progress—a timid start of the Industrial Revolution. Since the Austrian dominions together with the Hungarian realm were a vast inner market with considerable resources of raw materials, foreign trade was comparatively weak. All the same, the notions of the age, connected with the economic changes abroad, seeped through the Austrian customs barriers in defiance of every isolationist device. From Germany, France and England came ideas which coagulated into "isms": liberalism, socialism, and what was then called communism, although the time had yet to come for Marx to write that a spectre was abroad in Europe, and that this spectre was called communism.

In the intellectual field, the handicaps imposed by the system were still in force. (These were the years in which Turnbull observed the pernicious effects of the Austrian censorship on scientific publications.) However, the narrow channel of exact research ran deep. Scientists were trained in meticulous observation; kept off theoretical flights, they tended towards a critical and agnostic empiricism which found its way into textbooks. Contemporary German philosophy barely trickled through. Herbart's ideas about the interaction of forces which constituted the human mind influenced young nonconformists. But the greatest single philosophical influence among Viennese intellectuals was probably that of Goethe, and his was no closed system. Altogether Vienna had, and retained for several decades, a mental climate in which neither speculative theorems nor pure science thrived, while pragmatic research and technology developed powerfully and fruitfully. By the end of the eighteen-thirties, schools of geography and geology had sprung up (Metternich himself was pleased to patronise the geographer Simony who in his turn deeply impressed and stimulated the poet Adalbert Stifter) and the foundations of the Viennese school of medicine were laid. When I. P. Semmelweis—the luckless Hungarian who discovered the causes of puerperal fever in a Viennese maternity ward and came up against the conservatism of obstetricians all over Europe—started his studies in Vienna, he was inspired by two pioneers of modern medical science, Rokitansky, the founder of pathological anatomy, and Skoda, the great diagnostician. Semmelweis's experiences with the Viennese medical authorities and pundits of the 'forties were ugly, but when he was hopelessly floundering, both Rokitansky and Skoda fought his battles for him against their colleagues in Vienna and abroad.*

The mould in which Viennese academic medicine and medical research had set in the pre-March years was still predominant when

---

* The French novelist L.-F. Céline, himself a doctor, wrote an imaginative account of Semmelweis, which is fairly careful in its factual detail though less reliable in descriptions and generalisations. It appeared in an English translation by Robert Allerton Parker, Allen & Unwin, 1937, together with another prose piece, under the title: Mea culpa and The Life and Work of Semmelweis.

Sigmund Freud began his grammar school studies in 1873, and it was still discernible some twenty years later—beneath a layer of personal idiosyncrasies and jealousies—when Freud clashed with the medical establishment. The textbooks which first reached him in his adolescence, the tradition of the medical school, the outlook of his older Viennese teachers, in particular of Theodor Meynert—all carried the imprint of the period in which this establishment had been established. Thus Metternich's governmental principles, and the peculiar twist their pressure had given to academic life and scholarly research before 1848, contributed to the form, though not to the deeper causes, of Freud's oscillation between exact research and a bold reach for the illuminating hypothesis in his early years, and even to the course of his later conflicts in Vienna.

Here I must admit that I have used Freud as a stalking-horse to lead to a recognition of the importance which an apparently remote era of the past has for a much later stage of Vienna's cultural history. But the context is wider. Out of the pre-March years burst the Revolution of 1848, another of the half forgotten, much misinterpreted events which shaped the collective life of Vienna, and if this Revolution was virtually leaderless, the explanation can only be found in the social growth that came before it. It was in these pre-March years that the new bourgeoisie and the liberal professions began to emerge, chafing under the restrictions of a decaying régime, impatiently conscious of the time-lag which made them, whether industrialists or intellectuals, feel out of step with western Europe. From the end of the 'thirties onward the pace of economic development quickened even in Austria, while the political stagnation became more evident and irksome by contrast.

In this period Eduard von Bauernfeld constituted himself the mouthpiece of an evolving bourgeois society. He wrote plays which amused and titillated the liberals by asides and undertones, but kept prudently within limits still acceptable to the Burgtheater authorities and the upper crust. Those slight conversation pieces were mildly topical, they lent themselves well to the acting of the Burgtheater team, and their tinge of Viennese dialect was no stronger than was natural in any upper-class salon—slighter, perhaps, than the Viennese inflections which the Emperor Franz I had affected, according to all extant accounts of audiences or interviews. Newcomers to Vienna, and social climbers too, were able to absorb fashionable mannerisms and idioms while being entertained. If it was all a little synthetic, it was widely enough

imitated to be converted into reality. It also helped that in plays such as
Bürgerlich und Romantisch (*The Bourgeois and the Romantics*) Bauernfeld tipped the scales in favour of the sensible, agreeably humorous
representative of the middle class, against a romantic sentimentalism
which was already a little outdated.

In the sharper atmosphere of the 'forties, when Bauernfeld—who had
courage and integrity even though his first wish was to please—was
among the most active propagandists for the freedom of the printed
word, his plays began to change their tune. The feeble little comedy
Zwei Familien (*Two Families*), first performed in 1838 and printed in
1840, still had no more than one faint whiff of opposition, the civic
pride of the hero's father, a merchant who refuses to get himself
ennobled, in strict contrast to the shabby parasitic existence of a titled
family. A few years later, the pattern was different. The hero of
Industrie und Herz (*Industry and Heart*) is not an old-fashioned Viennese
merchant but a modern industrialist, the villain is a share-pusher who
"palms off shares on shoemakers, tailors, innkeepers, tinkers—it's up
to them to see where they get their dividends from!" An aristocrat is
invited to become the figure-head president of a new joint-stock
company, refuses, and prefers to emigrate to America, there to retrieve
his self-respect, and his fortunes, by hard work. This play, bad enough
in all conscience, appeared in print in 1847. In the same year, Bauernfeld wrote a comedy which was a satire on Metternich's system, under
the title *Grossjährig* (*Of Age*). And, incredible though it sounds, it was
staged at the Burgtheater, ran to full houses and gales of appreciative
laughter until February 1848, a month before the Revolution which put
an end to the derided system.

The central figure in *Of Age* is Herr Blase (the name means literally:
bladder), aged guardian of the juvenile hero Hermann. Blase has reared
Hermann in utter dependence on him, so that he is incapable of decision
or action, to all appearances a slow-witted, amiable child in spite of his
young manhood. Of course it is Blase who administers, and mis-
manages, Hermann's estates. Wanting to bind the young man even
more closely he decides to marry him to a penniless niece of his, and
for this purpose declares him—belatedly—of age. The theatrical plot
is obvious: the girl is spirited, she has audacious and even revolutionary ideas; Hermann falls in love with her, and is inspired to rebel.
The curtain falls on Blase's defeat and the prospect of an ending that
will be happy in every way.

To the pre-March audience it became evident who was meant by
Blase, as soon as he said, in the very first scene:

... You may think what you like, thoughts don't concern me. Thoughts are
among the licensed goods insofar as they're produced at home—in a brain. But
as soon as they're spoken or written, and pass the frontier, and are smuggled
abroad, that is, into another head, then the customs guards intervene and treat
them as contraband.

In the second scene it is rubbed in, when the bailiff mentions the
danger of the schoolhouse roof collapsing any day, and Blase answers:
"Let's wait and see . . . wait and see . . . that's the main secret of good
administration. The poor boy isn't capable of administering his
estates himself, he isn't ripe for it. He never will be. ..." At the bailiff's
warning that the young man is showing signs of "free ideas", Blase
bursts out: "What, in my house? How ever have they got in? Where
does he take them from?" The answer is that they are "in the air".
The bailiff himself is portrayed as a lickspittle. Every inclination to
speak his mind has been squeezed out of him when, in his youth, he was
expelled from university as being "suspected of leanings towards
tendencies approaching liberal ideas". Even the convinced Liberal, a
friend of the family, cuts no heroic figure; he spouts set phrases and
stammers in between, but at least he is honestly convinced of the
need for an opposition and progressive change. Blase, certain that God
Almighty is conservative and the universe built on the principle of
stability, decides to sit it out, wait and see, even when his ward has
broken away from his tutelage: no doubt his signature will still be
needed. ...

How was it possible that so blatant a satire was accepted by the
Burgtheater and passed by the censorship, which was by no means
withering away? Bauernfeld tells his version of the story in his
memoirs. He claims that he had long intended to attack the Austrian
System as such in the outwardly innocuous form of an ordinary
"middle-class comedy". He had re-written the play four times, and
shown it in its final form to his friend Alexander Baumann (one of
the small boys in Paumgartten's Biedermeier water-colours!), who
worked in Count Kolowrat's department and was a favourite with his
chief. Invited as a house guest to Kolowrat's summer residence, Baumann had there staged the play with amateur actors, himself playing
the comic Liberal. Kolowrat had been delighted, probably because he

thought that it was directed exclusively against Metternich-Blase, and failed to realise that the target was the whole system of which he himself was part. Out of malice against his great rival, Kolowrat had seen to it that the comedy was passed for performance, and not even its reception by the public had shaken his complacency. He told Bauernfeld that some days after the première Archduke Ludwig—not quite such a nonentity as his nephew Franz Karl, the other archducal member of the Regency Council and father of the future Emperor Franz Joseph—had mentioned to him a rumour according to which he, the Archduke, figured in the play. Kolowrat had assured him that the harmless middle-class scenes were free of innuendoes. A couple of days later the Archduke had accosted him again and said: "Yesterday I saw that play—I'm in it after all, and so are you, really." Yet *Of Age* was repeated on the Burgtheater until the eve of the Revolution.

Some of this tolerance or indifference, so strange in a police state, may be held to be a sample of Metternich-Blase's Wait-and-See policy: laughter at Bauernfeld's cues could still be a useful dispersion of a potentially dangerous mood. The "ward", to speak in the allegory of the play, was not ripe for action and never would be. Such complacency doubtless betrayed an unbelievable ignorance of the real situation. At bottom, however, a corresponding ignorance inspired Bauernfeld's blithely optimistic faith in a peaceful happy end. As the Ides of March—it was truly to be the date of the Roman Ides, with the 13th and 15th of March 1848 as the decisive days—were going to demonstrate, Bauernfeld was the representative of his social group on the stage and off stage, not least in his muddle-headed ignorance.

Grillparzer represented no one but himself, or rather, his various selves, but he too changed with the times, more than his later essays in self-explanation cared to admit. His withdrawal from the Burg-theater stage made it easy for him to keep outside the circles and, during the last years before 1848, the political discussion and action groups of the new progressives. It was even difficult to get his signature on something he had much at heart, a petition of the writers demanding freedom from censorship, and he took a dislike to his former friend Bauernfeld, who was busy in all such matters. Grillparzer professed contempt for so much facility and thoughtless, cheerful activism; this contempt was not unmixed with envy. The poet's own eternal yes-and-no, which precluded public action, was an unhappy and tormented condition of the mind. At the same time it never blunted his sharp analysis. In 1839, when Metternich was gravely ill, it was rumoured because of shocking reverses in his foreign policy, Grillparzer wrote the poem *Der kranke Feldherr* (*The Sick Commander*). Nothing could have been more implacable than this indictment of the "champion of the powers of darkness", the gifted leader who has become a hollow man, monstrously inhuman in his *hubris*. The last lines give a dry order: lift him up, nurse him, care for him; if not, bury him, because "though not yet dead, he is no more alive".

In the nine years that passed between this incident and the Revolution, Grillparzer was agonisingly aware of the deadness and disintegration which a system that had outlived itself was spreading over his beloved country. When the liberals in the Lower Austrian Estates showed some signs of life, he was clear-sighted enough to discover the vagueness and superficiality of much of their talk. The old Josephinian sensed the coming catastrophe, feared it, and was unable to understand it in new terms. In January 1848, one month before the outbreak of the Revolution in Paris, the Government sponsored, as an answer to the pressing demands for intellectual freedom, a reactionary pamphlet on censorship by one of its camp-followers. This sign of incurable blindness worried and exasperated Grillparzer. It was then that he wrote one of the political poems meant for his own eyes only; it was called *Vorzeichen* (*Omen*), and was uncanny in its prophetic gravity. "I know a country that lay so motionless it scarcely moved its limbs, like a worm; day after day it dragged its loops to the meal; time was no more than the clock striking from the tower." The highest share the degradation of the lowest. Then a fever, an evil shudder, shakes the country, the waves break the dams and smash the old ties of custom. Even then, dull wits seek an explanation afar, failing to see the heart of the matter at home, in past sins. Cowardly palliatives are attempted, uselessly. This is madness—the guardians have gone mad, which means the end. Where there is no power of resistance, disaster approaches and everything collapses. The poet weeps, because this is his own country.

Grillparzer recognised the sickness without knowing or attempting to know a cure. This, too, was abdication. When the people of Vienna took to the streets, he was not surprised, but he was an onlooker. In his mind many of the doubts of the older Viennese during the revolutionary months were prefigured, and many of their inner contradictions.

Old Vienna did not "die" on the barricades of 1848, and this not merely because the Old Viennese survived the various ordeals, by fire, by bullets, by muddle, by the coalition of students and workers that frightened them. Yet the petrified shell of Biedermeier Vienna was soon engulfed by buildings of vastly different patterns. Its style of living was soon enshrouded in self-indulgent nostalgic legends. And the new beginnings, the growing points it had contained, became starting positions not for the victors, but for the temporary losers of the Viennese Revolution of 1848.

IV

Revolution and Counter-Revolution

THE REVOLUTIONARY year of 1848 was the culmination of a period of unrest throughout Europe. The portents had been there for everyone to see. Nowhere had they been more assiduously recorded than in the files of the Viennese police department, where reports accumulated, not only about actual disturbances within the Habsburg empire, but also about suspect persons and potentially dangerous groups abroad. While some of these reports were sober appraisals of conditions or ideas, the majority gave details which permitted a close control of everything remotely smacking of conspiracy. It was an obsession with reactionary statesmen—Gentz had called it Metternich's besetting sin —to see the hidden hand of conspirators behind every disquieting symptom; this was the most comfortable explanation, since conspirators could be arrested, conspiracies suppressed by force of arms, whereas deeper-seated causes would have demanded positive (and mostly unpalatable) measures.

In those pre-March years, when the pauperisation of industrial workers and their rapid numerical increase were equally indisputable facts, any rise of embryonic working-class associations could not but arouse the greatest fears. Austria as a whole, and Vienna in particular, were kept free of them; every journeyman who had been in touch with socialist circles in France or Switzerland was tracked down and arrested almost as soon as he crossed the frontier. From the check and counter-check of police agents it was evident that foreign subversive ideas had at worst tainted a few intellectuals. Even so, trouble broke out sporadically in factories and slum areas.

The greatest threat to the rickety structure of the Habsburg realm came from the Polish and Italian provinces under Habsburg rule, where nationalist movements against foreign domination were growing, and conspiratorial groups did exist. The Viennese régime was forced to keep troops there, while it still believed that in Hungary the great aristocrats in the seat of power would be able to dominate the Diet, forming a dam against the rising liberal tide.

Ever since the defeat of the great Polish insurrection against Russia in 1831, the Austrian part of Poland, Galicia, had been shaken by risings. In 1846, the Free City of Cracow was occupied by an Austrian general and subjected to military rule. In the same year, Polish landowners in the western part of the province rose in revolt. They attempted to carry their peasantry with them by promising the abolition of servitude, but a savage peasant war broke out and turned against the overlords. This *jacquerie* played into the hands of the Austrian district commissioners, who were not loath to employ the scythemen for their ends, earning the horrified contempt of liberals everywhere. The insurrection was suppressed, and the dark roots of the lynchings remained hidden, not least by the legend that the peasants had been set in motion by Austrian officials.

In Lombardy there was no single great outburst before 1848, so that the nationalist forces were left to develop. However, small-scale friction was the order of the day; independent Piedmont under the House of Savoy was next door, a constant challenge; and the young generation was fired by the ideals of Mazzini's republicanism. A multinational Austrian army was kept garrisoned in the fortresses of the strategic quadrangle known as the Quadrilateral. But in Milan, the Austrian officials and officers were increasingly shunned by members of good society: gone were the days of Stendhal's consular service when he could comment on the virtues of Austrian rule in northern Italy, and observe that the Italians were quite content with it. There may be something to the contention of a few historians that resentment was provoked in the Italian cities, centres of trade, by a customs warfare which had started between Piedmont and Austria: Piedmont had banned the import of salt from what was then the Austrian province of Venetia, and in retaliation the Viennese Treasury had more than doubled the customs duties on Piedmontese wines. Yet on the whole economic motives did not rise to the surface of the Italian nationalist movement—an apparent freedom from social issues which may well have helped to engage sympathisers abroad. (It was only later, when—after the outbreak of the Revolution in Vienna—Venice rose to proclaim an independent Republic, that submerged tensions exploded: on 22 March 1848, workers of the arsenal stormed the building and lynched its director who had ill-treated them for years.)

By way of contrast, there were as yet few signs of a national move-ment in the Czech regions, but there were many of deep industrial unrest. In 1844, factory workers rioted in Prague and in northern textile industry districts. It was the old Luddite story: introduction of labour-saving machinery, dimissals, lower wages, starvation sharpened by prices rising in the wake of a bad harvest, demands for the scrapping of the machines, refusal by the mill-owners, assault on the mills, destruction of the machines—and bullets. The government set up a commission authorised to hunt ringleaders and then to investigate the causes of the workers' distress. The commission duly meted out punish-ment, and sat down to its studies. No conclusion, and of course no action. Two years later, a similar chain of riots swept Bohemian factory towns. And another two years later, in 1848, when the revolu-tion in Prague took the shape of pressure for a limited home rule through a Diet, and of a more militant nationalism in the first All-Slav Congress, national and social currents crossed as much as they mingled. In June 1848, clashes between workers and soldiers, which the historian Heinrich Friedjung was to call "the most confused of all the risings in the revolutionary year" (*Österreich von 1848-1860*, vol. I, p. 57), gave Prince Windischgrätz a welcome opportunity to shell and occupy the city, establish martial law—and let Czech conservatives attempt to find a federal solution by negotiations with the court, against the liberal German bourgeoisie and against the rebellious Czech proletarians.

Vienna, centre and hub of the Habsburg universe, stayed quieter than the other Austrian cities even during the years of economic crisis leading up to 1848. Only the prices rose, together with the numbers of unemployed, bankrupt tradesmen, beggars, prostitutes, juvenile delinquents, and symptoms of naked misery. Outbreaks of looting, mainly directed against butchers and bakers, were confined to the outer suburbs and quickly squashed. Soup kitchens for the poorest of the poor were established in 1847, that was all. One has to turn to confidential memoranda and reports in the archives, and to memoirs written years after the final explosion, to find facts about the swift deterioration of the standard of living among the middle and working classes of Vienna. The scanty statistics of the time contradict the often repeated statement that the Viennese Carnival season on the eve of the Revolution was particularly gay and brilliant; the unexciting truth is that even the entertainment industry was hit by the economic

depression. On the other hand the great balls and small dances did take
place. The surface of Viennese life was untroubled. Except for the
slums—but who would ever have taken them into account when
speaking of Viennese life? No doubt all this helped to keep the ruling
set, from Metternich down to his Police Minister Sedlnitzky, suspended in the belief that a wait-and-see policy adorned with a few
minor concessions would meet the situation in the capital. They
continued to think so, and let the official press say it in so many words,
even when the Republic had been proclaimed on the barricades of
Paris, on 24 February 1848.

The French February Revolution set off a chain of revolutionary
risings over half the European continent. It set a pattern, demonstrated
the power of the street, and inspired liberals with the hope that the
advisers of crowned heads would hasten to come to terms with them
rather than risk the democratic convulsions racking Paris. Nor were
their hopes unfounded.* By all accounts it took the world by surprise
that the second great upheaval came in Metternich's own citadel, in
Vienna.

On the morning of 13 March, university students in romantic
uniform, staid gentlemen in frock-coat and top hat, and workers in
cap and blouse (as the year's lithographers drew them) assembled at
the Ständehaus, the building where the session of the Lower Austrian
Estates was to open. The demonstration was expected. Two liberal
centres, one an association of business men and manufacturers, the
other a club of intellectuals and civil servants, had prepared a petition
to the emperor, to be submitted by the Estates with whose progressive
wing it had been concerted. Another petition, demanding freedom of
science, teaching and study, as well as civic freedoms, had been voted
the evening before by a meeting of university professors and students.
The main demands were: freedom of the press, public accounting of
the exchequer, ministerial responsibility, a municipal charter, and a
central Diet with participation of the middle class. A moderate programme indeed, not even mentioning the word Constitution. But

---

* Britain was outside the stream. The Chartist movement was disintegrating,
its mass demonstration of 10 April 1848 an anticlimax. In his *Short History of the
British Working Class Movement 1789-1927*, G. D. H. Cole ends his few pages on
the "year of revolutions" with the flat statement: "The revolutions and counter-
revolutions which convulsed Europe in 1848 and the following years found no
further echo in Great Britain."

1. VIENNA

The walled city on the eve of the Turkish siege of 1683

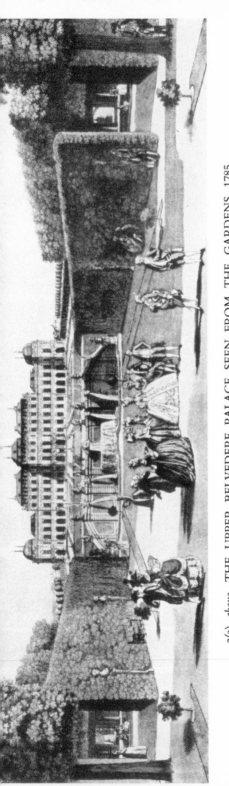

2(a) *above*. THE UPPER BELVEDERE PALACE SEEN FROM THE GARDENS, 1785

(b) *below*. THE FREIHAUS AND THE WIEDEN SUBURB SEEN FROM THE CITY, 1780

3(a) *above*. SCHÖNBRUNN CASTLE TOWARDS THE PARK, 1780
(b) *below*. A SHOPPING CENTRE IN THE CITY, 1786
(young Haydn lived in an attic of the house on the right)

4(a) *above left*. EMPEROR JOSEPH II
(b) *above right*. EMPEROR FRANZ I WITH HIS FOURTH WIFE,
CAROLINA AUGUSTA, *c.* 1830
(c) *below*. SCHUBERT WITH HIS FRIENDS JENGER AND ANSELM
HÜTTENBRENNER, *c.* 1826

5. TWO AMATEUR WATER-COLOURS, *c.* 1820, OF BIEDERMEIER
SCENES
(a) *above*. Christmas—the first pictorial documentation of a Christmas tree in
Vienna
(b) *below*. A meal at home

6. MARKET DAY IN THE HOHER MARKET SQUARE, IN THE
CENTRE OF VIENNA, 1837

7 *right*. ST. CHARLES BORROMEE CHURCH
AND A VIEW OF VIENNA IN 1820

8(a) *above left*. JOSEPH LANNER
(b) *above right*. JOHANN STRAUSS (father) as a youth
(c) *below*. JOHANN STRAUSS (son), in 1850

9(a) *above left*. THERESE KRONES, ACTRESS, as Youth in Raimund's play *Das Mädchen aus der Feenwelt oder Der Bauer als Millionär*, first staged in 1827
(b) *above right*. FANNY ELSSLER, DANCER
(c) *below left*. FERDINAND RAIMUND, ACTOR-DRAMATIST
(d) *below right*. JOHANN NESTROY, ACTOR-DRAMATIST

10(a) *above*. FRANZ GRILLPARZER, 1841
(b) *below*. GRILLPARZER'S "ETERNAL FIANCÉE",
KATHI FRÖHLICH

11 *right*. 1848: THE OUTBREAK O
13 MARCH

13. HANS MAKART

Riding at the head of the festival procession which he designed to celebrate
the silver wedding of Franz Joseph and Elisabeth in 1879

12(a) *left above*. 1848: THE CLIMAX
The Students' barricade on 18 May

(b) *left below*. 1848: THE END
Croat troops storming the main barricade in the
Leopoldstadt suburb on 28 October

14(a) *above.* "MAKART" ARCHITECTURE
The pavilion and stand erected on the Ringstrasse to the guests of honour at
the silver wedding celebrations, 1879
(b) *below.* RINGSTRASSE: THE NEW TOWN HALL OF VIENNA
WITH THE RATHAUSPARK AS PROJECTED IN 1870

15(a) *above*. DR. KARL LUEGER
Mayor of Vienna, 1897–1910
(b) *below*. VICTOR ADLER
Leader of the Social-Democratic Party

16(a) *above*. KARL KRAUS
by Oscar Kokoschka, about 1909
(b) *below*. EGON SCHIELE
Self-portrait, 1911

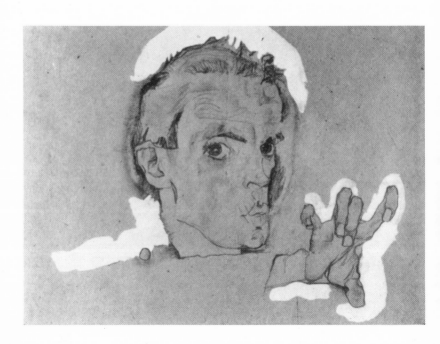

what the slogans chalked overnight on walls (even on the door of Metternich's son-in-law), what the voices in the street and the first improvising speakers demanded, was the resignation of Metternich as an earnest of constitutional freedom.

At one o'clock soldiers fired a volley at the crowd. The first to fall were students. The tumult turned into a mass rising. The students broke into the city armoury and formed their Academic Legion. Outside the city gates, which had been closed against crowds of excited workers, excise sheds were smashed, machines destroyed, and factories set on fire. City guards and soldiers both went into action against the suburbs that were in revolt. Among thirty dead listed for the date of 13 March, the majority were artisans and labourers. And yet it was the unexpected support of the "barefooted districts" which had given irresistible strength to timid demands. For a brief spell, class differences were submerged in a common purpose, in spite of the misgivings of those who "had not thought of the workers" and of whom "few were strong enough not to feel disturbed when seeing them outside the Ständehaus", as the radical chronicler E. V. Zenker* put it. Late in the evening, Metternich ceded to the clamour of the revolutionaries, and perhaps even more to the pleas of a helpless, terrified court. He resigned. The next night he left Vienna and went abroad.

In Budapest, Milan, Venice and, outside the Habsburg frontiers, in Berlin, the news from Vienna sparked off revolts: if the Viennese had driven out Metternich, everything was possible except the survival of absolutism.

Among the Viennese themselves, triumphant elation followed the wave of collective anger. Not even sceptical onlookers kept cool. Friedrich Hebbel, always critical of Vienna, by conviction an enlightened north-German conservative who believed that the "paving stones of society" should be left untouched, wrote in a letter two years later:

In March I should have been willing, at a pinch, to go along on to the barricades; also, one of the first victims outside the Ständehaus fell next to me and spattered me with blood. . . . Then I had an attack of berserk fury, and did all sorts of things I do not care to remember, because it happened in mental unfreedom and was like a discharge of electric matter.

* In *Die Wiener Revolution von 1848 in ihren sozialen Voraussetzungen und Beziehungen*, Vienna, Hartleben, 1897, p. 106.

Grillparzer, also writing two years later, and obviously editing his reminiscences, said that the students facing three ranks of grenadiers with their muskets up had struck him as "heroic children". Grudgingly he had to admire their readiness to lay down their lives when the promise of a Constitution was withheld for a day—under the increased popular pressure it was proclaimed on 15 March. His opinions had "condemned him to passivity", yet he wanted to give his countrymen their due: "in the early stages they behaved so lovably that one felt like kissing every one of them. I myself began to distrust my own apprehensions." He added the rider: "Incidentally, it was the gayest revolution imaginable. Favoured by the most beautiful spring weather, the whole population filled the streets all day long."

It was an illusion. Victory was not won. But while it lasted, it had a powerful impact. It speaks through a poem by Gottfried Keller, then a young man living in Germany and no revolutionary, though a sturdy Swiss democrat. He addresses Vienna—"city of pleasure, city of music, morning-happy, proud Vienna"—to make an apology: We have sinned when resenting your gaiety and your apparent self-indulgence. It is true, you floated on the waves of your dances and pretended luxurious ease even while the storms were gathering. But as icy grey, dead guardians kept watch outside your tune-filled house, you sent noble fighters out into the rosy dawn, singing. This, the poet hints, gives Vienna the right to lead a German emperor through the German countries for a last time. Then the dream of a German *Reich* will fade into the distance like other myths, and "young emperors" will lie in a thousand cradles, free sons of free mothers. . . . So much for a poetic response to Vienna's March Revolution.

The second revolt swept Vienna in May 1848, after Emperor and court had fled the city and a *coup d'état* against the organs of the Revolution had been attempted. Sixty barricades—some sources say 160—rose in a single afternoon; the workers came into the centre of the town to protect their allies, the students—but the press drawings of those days no longer show frock-coated, top-hatted men on the parapets. A new cabinet, the fourth in rapid succession, proclaimed a democratic Constitution, with a single Chamber based on universal suffrage. (This Reichstag was to meet in July—opening in Fischer von Erlach's magnificent Winter Riding School—pass a bill to abolish the peasant servitudes, and produce the seeds of a bewildering, conflicting mass of fertile ideas.) Some days later, a Viennese daily published another poem saluting Vienna. This "Greeting from Saxony" was signed by Richard Wagner, then *Kapellmeister* at the Dresden court. It was bad poetry, but full of excitement at the courage of the Viennese who had "drawn the sword", and it promised that, rather than submit to new bondage, the Saxons would follow the example: "Wir machen's wie die Wiener!" Wagner hoped too much for himself from the new rulers of Vienna; when he went there shortly after his poem had appeared, to propound the merger of all the city's theatres in a single national institution, his project went adrift on somebody's desk. But he was a witness to the rôle of Vienna in the imagination of German radicals. Indeed, by the early autumn of 1848, Vienna had become the strongest hope of all those wanting to push on with the revolution in Germany, which had come to a halt—to paraphrase the words of a modern historian, Golo Mann, in *Deutsche Geschichte des neunzehnten und zwanzigsten Jahrhunderts*.

The court, with poor Emperor Ferdinand as a willing hostage, was back in the capital; its ruling clique, the camarilla, was intensely busy with intrigues and counter-revolutionary manœuvres, by-passing the liberal Government and relying on aristocratic soldier-statesmen for action against the Hungarian rebels. But Vienna was no longer the Emperor's City. Even in the mixed-manned Parliament which sat in a barnlike building outside one of the western gates the Hungarians had democratic defenders, the German-Austrian democrats. They were backed and driven by the Viennese revolutionary committees. Though something like a fifth column was developing among the well-to-do; though the number of people tired of economic and social unrest was growing; though the concessions granted to workers in the first flush of the rising crumbled away, the alliance of students and proletarians endured. And these groups realised that their own hopes of freedom were bound up with Hungary's.

Torn by internal strife, menaced by an Imperial army, insurgent Vienna kept faith with insurgent Hungary—forgetting the capital's own interest, as Austrian history-writers were to say afterwards, reproachfully. Against the facile interpretation that the Viennese revolutionaries were self-centred German nationalists, hostile to the movements in other Austrian dominions, the fact has to be set that it was a mass rising to stop the dispatch of troops against Kossuth's army which introduced the last and darkest chapter of the year 1848 in Vienna.

In the first days of October, War Minister Latour—always suspected of reactionary contacts by the Left camp—decided to send detachments of the Viennese garrison as reinforcements to the Croat army of Banus Jellačić, the Croat nationalist who was at the same time the fiercest enemy of Hungarian self-rule and a staunch supporter of an absolutist régime. Jellačić was at that moment operating between Bratislava and Vienna, so far against the Hungarians, but as Imperial commander of all troops on Hungarian soil. The first battalion to leave Vienna consisted of Italians who may not have welcomed their orders, but showed no sign of insubordination. The next to be posted, however, was a German-Austrian grenadier battalion whose barracks were in one of the radical suburbs, and whose NCOs had been instructors to the Academic Legion. When they were marched to the railway terminus on 6 October, they were escorted not only by cavalry, but also by a vast crowd and by National Guard units of the "democratic" wing. The terminus was occupied by revolutionaries; the rails were torn up; the alternative route across the Danube was blocked. The soldiers refused to force their march through, and fraternised with the crowds. When other military units attempted to enforce the departure of the grenadiers, they were defeated in a skirmish, and a triumphant mass of people, flushed with victory, drunk with successful violence and with bitterness, flooded back into the city. Near the centre of the town there was more fighting, this time between anti-revolutionary sections of the National Guard—Black-and-Yellows, as the partisans of an authoritarian monarchy were called—and radical sections. Again the military intervened, again they were defeated, but this time there were more victims, and all passions were let loose. The War Ministry was stormed, Latour was lynched. On the following day the court fled (as foreseen) to the Moravian town of Olomouc, and the powerless Government followed quickly. Windischgrätz as Imperial general-issimo, and Jellačić as the nearest commander in the field, began to move against Vienna.

The Viennese revolutionaries, such as they were, prepared their defence. By that time, all but the most determined groups—a still considerable part of the students, the workers organised in a Mobile Guard after the French pattern, and the impoverished artisans and tradesmen of the suburbs—had abandoned a cause obscured by in-fighting, incurable anarchic muddle, and vagueness of aims. In fact, though not by name and deliberate action, their committees were pushing towards a republican solution. Here and there, workers' associations attempted to devise programmes and self-help. Yet the leap from the unpolitical subservience of pre-March days to unguided responsibility led to failure—often to noble failure. In the meantime, thousands who had turned against the Revolution left the city to wait for the success of armed force. Many inside the walls were pressing for negotiation and surrender. But there was to be no easy surrender.

During those days, Freiligrath expressed in rhyme the helplessness of the German revolutionaries:

> Wenn wir noch knien könnten,
> Wir lägen auf den Knien,
> Wenn wir noch beten könnten,
> Wir beteten für Wien . . .

"If we still could kneel, we'd lie on our knees—if we still could pray, we'd pray for Vienna. . . ." But the poet told his German comrades that the only way to defeat Jellačić was for each one to defeat his own Jellačić—tenuous moral support, this, for an isolated Vienna that was soon besieged by an army of 40,000 to 50,000 regulars, taking the forces of Windischgrätz and Jellačić together. The men on the outer defences of the Line-Wall, the bastions, the barricades blocking the city gates, and the houses converted into flimsy outposts, were hoping for a Hungarian army: surely they would come to the rescue, out of solidarity, and out of self-interest. Then the city was shelled. Windischgrätz expected unconditional surrender. A deputation of the City Council tried to negotiate it, but "the street" refused to capitulate. Messenhauser, the commander who wavered in face of the odds, was replaced. Vienna went down fighting. There was fighting within the walls, too, between moderate and radical sections of the National and Mobile Guards. On the fourth day of the siege and bombardment, a Hungarian force was reported near. It came too late, was too weak, and suffered defeat within sight of Vienna. And still they fought on in the town, most stubbornly at the Burgtor, the gate by the Imperial Palace. It took Windischgrätz another day to break down resistance. On 31 October his army entered, and retribution began in Vienna.

The Viennese Revolution had lasted from 13 March till 31 October 1848, over seven-and-a-half months. It has had what might be called a bad press, at home and abroad.* In Austria, too many had gone from enthusiasm to disenchantment, from casual participation to righteous repudiation, out of a genuine change of mind, or out of the urge to be on the winning side, or because the dark underworld of their society had frightened them. Those who were most vocal, above all the early historians, had to explain things away to themselves and others. The lack of leaders and leading ideas furnished abundant matter for criticism. Petty instances of muddle, and the bathos often overlaying tragedy, made it easy to belittle and ridicule the extremists. The anonymous mass served as a collective scapegoat; "the mob" was not even distinguished by court martial and execution, as were some well-known intellectuals, like the musicians and journalists Jellinek and Becher, the delegate of the Frankfurt parliament Robert Blum, and the luckless Messenhauser, last-but-one commander of the National Guard. Nine persons were executed in November 1848, altogether twenty-five in the first year of martial law until November 1849; the number of those arrested is given as 2,375 by Alexander Bach, the most painstaking of the Austrian historians (*Geschichte der Wiener Revolution im Jahre 1848*, Vienna, 1898). But what about the "little men" killed by looting soldiery or shot without further ado in the city moat? I have found no reliable figure. An eyewitness report quoted by Bach (*op. cit.*, pp. 845 ff.) claims that in a single suburban street fifty-seven people were killed by Jellačić's soldiers, not in battle but in their house-to-house search. But once quiet was restored, decent citizens preferred not to think of the outer fringes of their society. Dead or alive, gaoled or free, the individuals lumped together as rabble were present, in many memoirs and historical works, as faceless and dangerous brutes. This made the order imposed by official brute force more palatable to liberals who refused to turn their coats completely.

Abroad, the Viennese Revolution was overshadowed by the national wars in Hungary and Italy, with their brilliant leaders and easily understandable slogans. The criss-cross of political and social conflicts that bedevilled the insurrections of Vienna were less apt to engage sympathies. Still later, the whole painful process was pictured as half-hearted, not really serious, and therefore "typically Viennese":

* A conservative Austrian historian, J. A. von Helfert, quoted the London *Times* in his important work, *Geschichte der österreichischen Revolution*, vol. 2, p. 27, as saying that in the days of March Vienna had a government "of idle schoolboys and workmen".

the gay image was retrieved. Indeed, this concept of the Revolution of Vienna contributed to one of the labels for the Viennese, the label of unprincipled fickleness.

There have always been other voices, of course. Thus Friedjung says (*op. cit.*, vol. 1, p. 89):

The resistance of the Viennese workers and petit-bourgeois, led by the students, was viewed with scepticism by the better-off section of the population, who in their hearts were on the side of the attackers. No wonder, then, that contradictions and slackness in command and execution were the result. Yet if one compares the conduct of Vienna with that of Berlin and Budapest, which surrendered noiselessly to the entry of Wrangel's, Windischgrätz's and Haynau's troops, it becomes impossible to dismiss that five days' fighting as contemptuously as has been done so often.

And a footnote adds:

It is an old experience that revolutionaries are never brave enough in the eyes of conservative historians, professors and *Geheimräte*. Springer, Helfert and Zwiedinek judge the Viennese Revolution in part ironically, in part disparagingly. Karl Marx, however, who after all had some knowledge of how to make a revolution ... sums up his opinion in the words: "... we would not wish to exchange all the glamorous victories and glorious battles of the Hungarian campaign, for the spontaneous, isolated rising and heroic resistance of the Viennese. ..."

Many twisted strands in the Viennese tradition—leaving the wider political implications for the whole of old Austria aside in this context—lead back to 1848. My own strong partisanship was tied in its childish origins to one of those strands. I was a small girl when my father, the greatest influence in my early life, told me that his grandmother had boasted of having taken food to students on the barricades, and that an old family governess claimed to have fought there as a girl, in man's clothes and acclaimed by the students as their lieutenant. I scrambled the two figures together (it was much later, reading my father's memoirs, that I was able to separate them), and put the adventurous girl in my secret pantheon together with Joan of Arc, dreaming of great deeds for myself. From this I proceeded, when I was a little older, to curious questions about barricades. It was marvellous to think that my father had known someone involved in the making of history; no cold water he poured on my fancies dislodged them. It was crystal-clear to me that he himself had been touched by

that girl's fiery past in his youth. (In fact, he said in his memoirs that his
grandmother's tales of students had awakened *his* partisanship for the
Revolution.) Still later, when we took modern history in the fourth
form of grammar school (I was then thirteen) I wanted to read something about the Viennese Revolution, being in the first flush of oppositional feelings. My father casually gave me a volume of Berthold
Auerbach; he was a minor German writer, often cloyingly sentimental,
but also the author of a vivid diary of Vienna in 1848. I didn't know
enough to read it critically; much of it left me cold. But there was a
description of 31 October, the last day of insurgent Vienna, at the
town centre: groups of wild, desperate men trying to rouse people to
arms—the empty square of St. Stephen's—guns thundering in the
distance—and a drummer in shirt-sleeves coming round a corner,
beating his drum in a ceaseless alarm roll. "Aber—niemand kam".
(But—no one came.) The sentence sank in and hurt. Then I read
another description, probably of the same incident but set in another
empty square at the centre. It spoke of an old proletarian beating his
drum, accompanied by a young boy holding a flag. I forgot the author,
tried in vain for years to identify the passage, and began to wonder
whether my imagination had not embroidered on Auerbach. Recently
I found it. It occurs in Moritz Hartmann's eyewitness account and is
indeed over-written. But it has one short sentence, almost identical
with Auerbach's, which I have never forgotten: "Sie kamen nicht"—
They did not come. When I first read it, I wished with all the passion of
my years that I would answer the call if it ever came to me.

In my first year at University, several socialist students' associations
jointly held a *Märzfeier*, a meeting in honour of the March Revolution
and its dead, in the small assembly hall. The Social-Democratic
leader Otto Bauer was speaking of the alliance between Viennese
students and workers forged in the March days of 1848, when members
of the nationalist students corps—forerunners of the Nazis—began
to interrupt him from the back of the hall with antisemitic slogans,
then, goaded by his mordant retorts, to push towards the platform.
Their wave threw me on to the dais just as they started to hurl chairs
at us, and I got a slight scratch on the back of my hand. Things looked
ugly. We were the prisoners of a howling multitude which filled the
immense entrance hall downstairs. Impossible to get through un-
scathed. But one student had slipped out and given the alarm. Suddenly
there was a commotion and shouts: "The workers have come!" It

was midday. Workers from nearby factories had marched to the University on hearing that Otto Bauer was in danger, and socialist students at the mercy of nationalist rowdies. After negotiations between delegates and the Dean of the Faculty of Jurisprudence—who had intervened for Bauer's personal safety—a lane was opened between the jeering ranks of Teutonic warriors. We had to walk through in single file, as though running the gauntlet in a nightmare. It was hard to keep one's temper. Before the wide open-air staircase of the University, between the bare trees of the Ringstrasse, workers were waiting until Bauer and "their" students had come out. They made no attempt to burst into the academic precinct which for disciplinary purposes was independent, inaccessible even to the police. Some had suggested an assault but, as a speaker proclaimed from the pillar at the ramp, the academic freedom which those others had dishonoured was one of the precious legacies of 1848.

Somehow the idea had survived, through the tenuous pipe-lines of tradition and the annual revival of memory ritualistically repeated. I do not believe that it survived the spring-tide of aggressive nationalism which swept the students in later years. But on that day I felt with romantic pride that a common fight for the dream of freedom, at a remove of seventy-three years or so, made it easier for workers and students of Vienna to belong to a single movement.

Mine is a late generation, possibly the last, to feel a breath of the storm of 1848. But those who lived through it carried the mark and the memory, not only of a common experience, but also of private decisions or indecisions, unswerving loyalties or changes of heart. These deeply felt reactions worked themselves out in the second half of the century, in a changing society; negatively or positively they shaped Vienna's political and cultural life, and its myths.

Take the case of the two Johann Strausses, father and son, each a popular figure, almost an idol.

The elder Johann Strauss had been band-leader of the First Regiment of the innocuous Citizens' Guard since 1843, while his son and rival Johann had held the same post in the Second Regiment since Lanner's death. When the city militia was absorbed in the National Guard after 13 March, old Strauss, hostile to the radicalism of his sons Johann and Joseph and by temperament an authoritarian, restricted himself to dance music, which he played in places of entertainment for the loyalist good society. In such a place he first presented the march which became part of Austrian folklore, and still has the power to thrill even those who dislike marching in rank and file: the *Radetzky March*. It was dedicated to old General Radetzky after his August victory against the insurgent democrats of Milan.

There was markedly less sympathy in Vienna, even in the radical camp, for the Italian national insurrection than for the Hungarian. Few among the workers had come from Italy in recent years. Italian music, and in particular Italian opera, was associated with the aristocratic upper class, as Eduard Hanslick once remarked to explain a popular outbreak against the Italian opera season in the spring of 1848.* Also, there were many Viennese conscripts in the field against the Italians, and last but not least, large sections of the public resented the fierce anti-Austrian attitude of the Italians, considering, unthinkingly, that the Italian provinces were a part of the Austrian patrimony. Thus the irresistible if unmartial rhythm of the patriotic *Radetzky March* won its own victory over Vienna.

At the same time, however, the political conduct of the elder Strauss was by no means passed over as an artist's whim. H. E. Jacob, on whose biographical work *Johann Strauss und das neunzehnte Jahrhundert* (Querido-Verlag, 1937) I have had to rely for nearly all details about the Strauss dynasty, says that after the occupation of Vienna by Windischgrätz and Jellačić, old Strauss received threatening letters. He minded the loss of his popularity, and the absence of the carnival mood on which he thrived, to such an extent that he escaped from Vienna to Prague, only to meet with worse rejection, and from there to German towns where students demonstrated against the representative of the Black-and-Yellows. Even in England—where he paid his respect to the distinguished refugee, Metternich—he was persecuted by letters which reminded him of the musicians Jellinek and Becher, shot by his friends in power. Back in Vienna he challenged unofficial opinion by composing a *Jellačić-March*, and went down with scarlet-fever and meningitis on the eve of a banquet in honour of Radetzky, at which he was to conduct the orchestra. He died on 25 September 1849. Eduard Bauernfeld wrote in his obituary verse that "today Old Vienna will be buried". Strauss had a funeral as he would have wished: official pomp and weeping women, and a spectacle in which the crowds were actors and audience in one.

* The passage is quoted at length in Henry Pleasants's introduction to Eduard Hanslick: *Musical Criticisms 1846-99*, Peregrine Books, 1963.

Johann Strauss the Younger had made no secret of his opposition to the old régime, and he became *Kapellmeister* (Principal Conductor) of the National Guard. He turned out a stream of marches and polkas with revolutionary titles: *Revolution March*, with an engraved cover showing students and National Guards romantically poised on a barricade of paving stones; *Liguorians' Sighs*, a "mock-polka" catching the popular mood at the expulsion of the Order of Redemptorists; *March of the Students' Legion*, *Freedom March*, *Songs of the Barricades*, etc. But he had to drill and be on duty like every other member of the National Guard. Jacob tells a story which may even be true, though it sounds almost too nice an anecdote: young Johann was on sentry duty on 22 August 1848, in very hot weather, when his comrades and he were sent off to alert their unit: a workers' riot had broken out in the Leopoldstadt suburb, and they would have to suppress it. Perhaps he cared as little about the Revolution and its problems as Jacob suggests, perhaps he, like most of the students, did not want to fight against rioting workers—in any case he simply went home to his mother, had a meal, and did a spot of composing.

However, he seems to have taken his musical duties very seriously. In the days of fighting, even in the October weeks when many others disappeared from the scene, he led his band to the barricades—where they played stirring tunes, from the *Marseillaise* to Strauss's own *Revolution March*. Jacob makes the point that "had he been killed then, he would scarcely have died for the Revolution, but rather for his own intoxication and for beautiful music". This is doubtful. By October, this kind of intoxication must have been hard to maintain, as civil war clashes have a cumulatively sobering effect; while not politically minded in any narrow sense, young Strauss cannot but have had strong convictions. He was certainly no turncoat. There exists a police record of an interrogation on 6 December 1848 (mentioned by Jacob, *op. cit.*, p. 188) which proves that Johann Strauss the Younger had the guts to play the *Marseillaise* in a crowded suburban inn at a time when Jellačić and his soldiers were the ruthless masters of Vienna. His defence was that he always played musical pieces according to their "essential value", not because of their political significance. He got away with it. Though Vienna was ruled by a military governor, the current of the Revolution had not yet petered out sufficiently to encourage the administrative authorities (not exclusively composed of reactionaries either) to aggravate the sullen mood of the public. Punishing Johann Strauss, on whom the mantle of his father had fallen in every sense but the political, would have been a foolish measure. Did he not show a laudable attitude to the young Emperor, Franz Joseph, crowned on 2 December 1848, and was he not willing to let his band play the *Radetzky March*, for its essential value and in spite of its associations?

However, even as a dutiful subject and the most successful of public performers, Johann Strauss the Younger never became subservient. His private life, with unconventional marriages and friendships, his conversion to Lutheranism so as to sidestep the Roman Catholic marriage laws, and his adoption of another nationality (to be able to marry his third wife at Koburg), show that he found no safe niche for himself in the new establishment. On a deeper level, his obsessive fear of death and its trappings speak of unresolved personal tensions— neurotic tensions. As for his operettas, and leaving out his unsuccessful essays in serious opera (which resemble the attempts of a brilliant comedian to conquer the part of Hamlet as being nearer to his idea of himself), they were never nostalgic pastiches of Old Vienna; only the self-plagiarising work of his last year, *Wiener Blut*, patched up from his old hits, tends that way. *Die Fledermaus* and *Der Zigeunerbaron*, his two best-loved operettas, have some curious under- and overtones: one carrying the gay disruption of all settled rules to the verge of parody, and then clothing the dream of human brotherhood in the glad rags of champagne drunkenness, as if sober reality could not sustain it; the other caricaturing the victors of a forgotten war (the comic hero Zsupan returns from Spain with watches dangling from his waist-belt), and concentrating all light and passion on the untamed Hungarian gypsies, on a love that is consecrated not by a priest in church, but by the portly bullfinch, the bird called in German *Dompfaff* (prelate). Even the *Blue Danube* waltz has that famous slow, almost heavy opening which originally corresponded to a sceptical text:

> "Wiener, seid froh!"
> "Oho! Wieso?"
> "Ein Schimmer des Lichts—"
> "Wir sehn noch nichts." . . .

Viennese, be glad. Oho, why so? A shimmer of light—We see nothing as yet. Carnival is here. Oh yes—well, then. . . . How do sadness and

regret help? Be merry and gay! These were, approximately, the words
of the hack-poet Weyl in 1867, which Johann Strauss set to music (for
a male choir), and dissolved in the dance.

I do not want to pretend that this dichotomy can be "explained"
by the effects of the Viennese Revolution on Johann Strauss, nineteen
years after the event. What I suggest is that his glittering career en-
closed an alienation from the very society which supported and spoiled
him, and that this alienation may, to a considerable and decisive
degree, have been fixed in the traumatic year.

The development of Johann's younger brother, Joseph, provides a
foil. Joseph had resisted his father's pressure to become an officer in the
regular army, out of convictions: "I do not want to kill human beings,
I do not want to be distinguished by a higher military rank for my
services in a man hunt, I want to be useful to humans as a human, and
to the State as a citizen." He enrolled at the Polytechnic, joined the
Academic Legion in March 1848, and fought in it to the end. After the
defeat he, like those of his colleagues who were able to do so, plunged
back into safe civilian obscurity. In his absence, five Polish soldiers—
those under Windischgrätz's command had a reputation for ruthlessness—came to look for him in his mother's flat. Whatever her private
leanings may have been—and she was not likely to side with the
Revolution, having taken refuge in a monastery during the bombardment of her suburb—she covered up for her son and got rid of the
soldiers for a few pieces of silver.

Two years later, she pushed Joseph into a conductor's career to
assist the overburdened Johann, the family bread-winner. Joseph left
his studies reluctantly; though a sensitive, highly gifted musician, he
saw his vocation elsewhere. He had the success Johann predicted for
him, never overcame his shyness, and never turned exhibitionist. In
his dance compositions, an astonishing output of 222 pieces within a
few years, there was a vein of poetic melancholy, and he died young.
The fatuously alliterative title of his popular waltz *Mein Lebenslauf ist
Lieb' und Lust* (*My Life's Course is Love and Joy*) contradicts both an
inner life full of nervous tension and high idealism, and an outward
life of quiet restraint.

The composer A. J. Becher, who had been executed in the city moat
on 22 November 1848, for his radical writings, had earned the citizenship of his adopted town in death, but his musical radicalism was
outside the Viennese tradition. He remained a solitary and intriguing

figure.* The Strausses, father and sons, were musical traditionalists
even when they widened, each in his way, the popular forms they had
chosen. They channelled the Viennese urge for patterned entertainment, the two Johanns before 1848, Johann Strauss the Younger and
Joseph—later helped by their cool, competent youngest brother,
Eduard—after the Restoration. They were all within the main stream
of Viennese life, and this makes it all the more legitimate to trace their
responses to the upheavals of 1848. Individual though they are, they
have more than individual significance.

The same is true of the writers, who had to show their true colours
because their medium was that of words, which could not be retracted
once they were published, though they could be, and sometimes were,
re-interpreted in retrospect.

A flood of daily papers, periodicals, pamphlets and broadsheets
poured forth as soon as the censorship was lifted; inevitably, their
quality was poor, more often than not dictated by the mood and
demand of the day. Baron J. A. von Helfert, one of the eminent conservative historians who described and assessed the Revolution, published a collection of verse written in Vienna in 1848. He called it,
somewhat pompously or else with ironic intent, *The Viennese Parnassus
of the Year 1848*: these were at best low foothills of Parnassus. Yet the
poems reflected all shades of opinion. There were the royalist and
loyalist voices; they chimed in with the lusty cheers of the Viennese
crowds for the Emperor Ferdinand—who was popular in his way
because everybody knew him to be a good-natured if disabled figure-
head. A non-ruler if ever there was one, and yet the symbol of an
ancient mystique. There were songs celebrating the students, such as
the poem L. A. Frankl, a journalist from Prague, wrote on guard duty
during the night from 14 to 15 March; the words "Die Universität"

---

* Alfred Julius Becher, by origin a Rhinelander, was born in Manchester, and
settled in Vienna as an adult musician. He made a name as a music critic, but failed
as a composer. As Ernest Newman notes (in his *Life of Richard Wagner*, vol. 2),
"the young Wagner was impressed by Becher's sharp intellect, Berlioz by his
harmonic audacity" and bold experiments with the quartet form. Hanslick says
in *Geschichte des Concertwesens* etc., p. 322, that Becher's "original but abstract
music, developing from the later Beethoven, pleased no one and at best interested
the experts". He had a few unsuccessful public concerts introducing his chamber
music, songs and symphonic compositions. Grillparzer ridiculed the new sounds
which appeared unmusical to him, and refused to accept Becher's qualifications
as a music critic. I have seen no modern appraisal of his work.

were title, last line of six stanzas, and guiding rhyme sound in one of the first leaflets to be printed uncensored. ". . . There comes to the bright sound of drums The University . . . The shackles of the free word, bound, fettered and mocked since Joseph's time, were smashed by the vanguard of The University . . . Look at the pallid victims fallen for Freedom, and see: the price of the first bodies was paid by The University." Frankl, a sincere, confused democrat, was no longer in the foreground when the social conflicts grew violent, but he remained a liberal who considered himself the repository of the true spirit of 1848, and is the source of many, not always reliable, stories about the Revolution.

There were few notes of social rebellion in those poems. Here or there they voiced the worries of a particular group, such as the low-paid public employees. But who was going to lend rhymes, however bad, to the needs of unmanageable unemployed workers? The alliance in battle between the young intellectuals and the proletarians was not born from common convictions, but from common hopes and fears. And if many of the budding democrats of 1848 turned against working-class aspirations in their later careers as lawyers or politicians, it was not so much a betrayal of earlier opinions, as a discovery of their class position, frankly admitted. The political poets of Germany, Herwegh and Freiligrath, were following different ideas, but then social and political thinking had developed much further there in public discussion before 1848. When Karl Marx visited Vienna in August 1848, he spoke in a newly formed Workers' Association—and nobody seems to have remotely understood his analysis of wage-labour and capital.

The one Viennese poet of talent who was a "man of the people", the bohemian Ferdinand Sauter, had no great interest in politics. Yet on the last day of 1848 he wrote an obituary for the bygone year:

> And streams of blood were flowing
> For freedom and for right.
> Proudly though they were given,
> Reward was always slight.
> The naked truth is outlawed,
> Unless it's naked lust,
> History's a fairy story,
> Life's face is masked with dust . . .
> I've taken the world's measure,
> My witness be you all.
> So with the last drop shatter
> Your glass against the wall.

About six years later he wrote an obituary for himself, which ends:

> And a man in his shroud
> Is a book that is closed.
> Therefore, wanderer, pass on—
> Putrefaction's no fun.

"Denn Verwesung stimmt nicht heiter". . . . It is difficult not to believe that, in the gloom of post-revolutionary Vienna, Sauter identified his inner decay with the smell of decay around him. He died in 1854 of tuberculosis, a drunkard and a pauper.

From this lonely outcast to the buoyant Bauernfeld is a far cry. Yet Bauernfeld, whom I have used extensively as an exponent of the pre-March middle class, stands for the other Vienna through his rôle and attitude before, during and after the Revolution. He wrote about it amply, if not very precisely, in *Erinnerungen aus Alt-Wien*.

Bauernfeld had never outgrown the romantic spirit of opposition he shared with most of his friends in the Schubert circle, not least the mild Moritz von Schwind who, in Munich, drew sharp political and anti-clerical caricatures for the weekly *Fliegende-Blätter* in 1847–48. As early as 1845 Bauernfeld had helped in preparing the petition against the censorship which was presented to Metternich by a committee of eminent intellectuals, and drew from him the comment that he did not know what a committee signified—in Austria. Not having been himself a member of the deputation, Bauernfeld thought that Metternich was right in principle: "Our petition, when there was no right to petition, was the first harbinger of the coming Revolution." In the tense months before March 1848 he stayed with Baron Doblhoff, once a member of the Schubert set, and long suspect with the police as a pupil of the unfortunate democrat Senn (see p. 142), now a leader of the progressive wing in the Lower Austrian Estates, and soon to be a minister in two successive constitutional cabinets without losing his integrity. Bauernfeld was busy as go-between of the liberal groups, clearly overrating his position and seeing himself as a favourite of public opinion and the court. His hour came on 15 March.

Early in the day unrest was rising because the expected promise of a Constitution had not come, while a delegation of the Hungarian Diet under Kossuth—Hungary had enjoyed a form of constitution before, but the democrats had pressed on successfully for more, and "Free Hungary" hoped for an alliance with a "Free Austria"—was expected within a few hours. Bauernfeld says he resented the idea that the Austrians would perhaps get their Constitution in the wake of the Hungarians. He also felt another form of pressure: walking through the dense crowds with his friend Count Auersperg (*alias* Anastasius Grün, who had been the poet to ask, in 1831, whether the Austrian people might "make so free as to be free") he heard a speaker "haranguing the people from a tub, in the face of the military and their guns", and winning enthusiastic cheers for his "hitherto unheard-of ideas of social democracy". This surprised and frightened him; he saw the spectre of anarchy looming. It also inspired him to force an entry into the ante-chamber of the court, to plead with generals, princes and archdukes for the grant of a Constitution which alone would prevent a catastrophe. Whatever his true share in the proceedings, there seems no doubt that his sheer fluency helped to overcome the limitless confusion of the ruling clique. After hours of to-ing and fro-ing an imperial proclamation was issued (there were ludicrous complications about its printing) which promised a central assembly "with an increased representation of the middle classes" and with the purpose of "establishing a Constitution". Bauernfeld's claim to have written the draft was denied by one of his colleagues, but he did bring the news to his friends, feeling he was the herald of history. The mere magical word *Constitution* released frenzied optimism and fraternising celebrations all over the town. When the printed manifesto appeared, a writer of popular (and bad) plays rode out to read it to the crowds. There were fireworks and singing, in a wave of feeling that emerges even from the soberest and most belated memoirs.

It speaks for Bauernfeld's political instinct that he worked himself into a fever of worry during the next two days, because the old gentlemen of the Regency Council were hanging on and no government was appointed. But it shows his abysmal political innocence (possibly also, as he puts forward in explanation, the beginning of a serious illness which broke out the following day) that he wrote, and printed at his own expense, a poster which deserves to be quoted:

Urgently needed!
Provisional Government!

Constitution is an empty word without a real Government, and in a constitutional country governing is impossible without a Cabinet. This Government and Cabinet can only be provisional, since the Constitution has been resolved but not yet drafted. The old System has fallen—but with it fall all the men who have been its real representatives, and the new men, to become members of the Provisional Cabinet, must be those who possess the confidence of the country. In any case there must be government, which does not exist at this moment. I have not noticed it during the first few days, because I was so Constitution-happy, but now things are getting too crazy, and I must ask for calm, so that I can work at last. Hence, for God's sake a real Government, and tomorrow at latest—it can no longer be delayed—or if possible today.

How pleasant it would be if tomorrow the regulars and the National Guard could march together hand in hand!

Long live the constitutional Emperor! But may he govern us fairly through his responsible Minister!

Now I shall stroll about again, constitutionally.

17 March 1848   Bauernfeld

These posters were never seen by the Viennese. Bauernfeld distributed copies to the members of the Estates, kept one for himself, and destroyed the rest. His story is that he had heard the printer murmur: "If you let this go up in the street it'll only make people crazier still." The text, with its unlikely mixture of cool statement and childish egomania, was reproduced in only one of the chronicles of 1848, and the author's *Memoirs* do not contain it. But the incident is "in character"—in Bauernfeld's, and in that cultivated before and after him by many Viennese who caught the limelight.

Bauernfeld himself had enough sense to keep out of politics after his recovery from illness, which he recognised to be a blessing in disguise. (From this distance, it is impossible to say to what extent it had been psychosomatic.) Of the rest of his reminiscences, the most interesting part is that which deals with the October weeks. He, to whom the proletarians had seemed Vienna's "cauchemar" (nightmare), now says that after the departure of nearly 20,000 Black-and-Yellows there was greater calm and unity in the town than before, that the men of the Mobile Guards were "recklessly brave" in attacking the Croats; that the dreaded workers "committed nothing bad at all" until mid-October; that the equally maligned "Aula" was the only authority which was listened to and fulfilled its task of maintaining order; that nothing but good could be said of the Viennese population as a whole. "Just try to leave Paris or London without government for some days —and what scenes would ensue! Well, Vienna was in that position for seven months . . . more or less ungoverned; but apart from the caterwauling mock serenades, nothing happened that could have dishonoured the city. The only evil deed, Latour's assassination, arranged and paid for by foreign emissaries [sic], can hardly be counted against the Viennese."

This, published about twenty years after the event, amounted in a mild way to a profession of faith. Bauernfeld dared not paint himself as a hero ("for a few days I was a local celebrity", he said), but recorded baldly that he left Vienna on 15 October because he did not feel like "being conquered by Croats". However, when the military government actually treated Vienna as a conquered town in 1849, he behaved with some dignity even while making the best of his connections in high places. His one-act sequel to the comedy *Of Age*, a feeble piece but innocent of any attempt at currying favour with the restored old régime, was rejected by the theatre for political reasons. Bauernfeld talked to the military governor Welden, defended the unruly Viennese, and criticised the weaknesses of Metternich's rule, eliciting the admission (or so he claimed) that "you're right, at bottom we'd all been silly bastards". The comedy *The New Man* was performed in April 1849. It caricatured the daunted liberals, satirised the reinstated authoritarians, and ended with a general reconciliation which only just tipped the scales in favour of the "new man", the emancipated one-time ward of Blase-Metternich. Even this weak brew provoked so much "radical noise" in the upper balconies that the Lord Chamberlain found it wiser to strike it from the repertoire.

For the remainder of his long coddled life Bauernfeld kept to his rôle as licensed entertainer of good society, though he tried from time to time to break a lance for free thought, indirectly in his few serious (and tedious) dramas, directly in his personal conduct. He dropped his old friendship with Alexander Bach, the most versatile politician coming from the Left, who had executed a complete turn and became the legalistic wizard of the aristocratic governments in the first years of counter-revolution, the Minister who ruthlessly manacled the press. Bauernfeld's poems and his book about the Viennese, both published in Germany, could not be publicly advertised in Vienna during the 'fifties. Bauernfeld disliked the new absolutism, especially when it was administered by an ex-liberal climber in the person of Alexander Bach. In 1858 he was invited to become a contributor to a new illustrated weekly. This seemed unacceptable to him at a time when, in his opinion, the official organ of the Roman Catholic Church alone had the freedom to write and attack. (This was after the Concordat of 1855 which particularly incensed the old Forty-Eighters, anti-clericals to a man.) Not without complacency he included in his *Reminiscences* a sarcastically highfalutin, politely aggressive letter he had written to the Editor: ". . . If I'm not supposed to write as I feel, I'd rather not write at all. . . . Old Vienna has outlived itself, the new one is, unfortunately, not yet completed. . . ."

Bauernfeld took care to republish *Erinnerungen aus Alt-und-Neu-Wien*, as he now entitled it, in volume XII of his Collected Works. Warts and all, the self-portrait is far from being a failure. And yet—this makes the memoirs not less but more suggestive—there is something spurious about the general picture. The edges are carefully blurred; the conciliatory summing-up of the Revolution is contrived; legends of Old Vienna are built round the kernels of truth; the snippets of valuable information are coated in creamy sentiment and/or well rehearsed self-mockery. In transmitting to prosperous bourgeois Vienna of the 'seventies his own, honestly held feelings about freedom and unfreedom, revolution and counter-revolution, Bauernfeld did keep a flag flying, but one he had trimmed and crimped to make it acceptable.

The best example is the way he treats the lynching of War Minister Latour. He deals with it in the throw-away line which I have quoted, putting the guilt on foreign money and "emissaries"—by which he accused the Hungarian party without mentioning them by name. Modern research has disproved the convenient rumour. Dr. Hermann Oberhummer, official historian of the Vienna Police, summarises his findings from the archives about the prosecution and execution of persons involved, or alleged to have been involved, in the murder of Latour; there is no evidence whatsoever of foreign machinations (*Die Wiener Polizei*, Vienna, 1937, vol. I, pp. 217–18). The most interesting point is that three workers, skilled men employed at the Southern Railway workshops, were hanged, one of them as the supposed fanatical leader. He had also threatened with hanging Minister Bach and Archduchess Sophie, who, together with Latour, were regarded as prime movers in the complicated manœuvres of the court camarilla, which to the radicals of Vienna were simple treason. Most railway workshops were strongholds of democratic radicalism; the Southern Railway workshops had kept in close touch with the revolutionary students. And since the end of August, when the "proletarians" had rioted and been beaten down by the middle-class units of the National Guard, a mood of violent desperation had built up. Whether those three workers tracked down and hanged had been the killers of Minister Latour or not, they certainly had been in the forefront of an outbreak of savage hatred: homegrown on Viennese soils, as were the underlying social tensions. Yet who could have been less ready to understand this than the author of pleasant drawing-room comedies, Bauernfeld? It would have shattered his, and his patrons', vision of fried-chicken cheerfulness in Old Vienna, as well as the refined, acceptable version of 1848 he was at pains to transmit.

The case of Franz Grillparzer is simpler than Bauernfeld's, because he did less in 1848, and wrote less about it, and at the same time more complicated, because of his incomparably more complex mind and character. Here was the greatest poet alive in Austria. He had been, as everyone knew, an implacable critic of Metternich, and a *frondeur* under the old régime, although he had kept morosely apart from the clubs and reunions of the liberals. What was he going to say?

On 1 April 1848 he published a poem entitled *Mein Vaterland* (*My Country*). It started with a salute to Austria "on her new road". What had been lacking so far, was now achieved, "half obtained by childlike, trusting entreaty, half enforced by challenge": freedom. Then came the warning not to follow the lure of false formulas, but to remain the country of old, in possession of the highest good there could be— natural common sense and right feeling. It expressed the apprehensions of many of his age group, good Josephinians like him, who none the less distrusted the mass movements, and found little pleasure in the German flag, black-red-yellow, which students had stuck into the bronze hand of Joseph II's equestrian statue on 15 March. Grillparzer believed in the Habsburg State—the State rather than the Habsburgs, who were its symbol to him—and in orderly central government, with the German language as the connecting link "joining together what, foolishly, feels sufficient in itself", as he had put it in his poem to Joseph II years before. Every form of aggressive nationalism was hateful to him, not least German nationalism, but he resented most anything that menaced the cohesion of "his" country such as the movements for self-rule, let alone independence, in hitherto Austrian dominions and in Hungary. This, rather than the early days of the Viennese Revolution, drove him into despairing silence.

A liberal journalist who was to become famous in the second half of the century, Friedrich Schlögl, wrote about the effect of Grillparzer's silence in one of his local chronicles (*Wienerisches*, Vienna/Teschen,

1883, pp. 388 ff.). Schlögl was an enthusiastic young free-lance writer when he was "so blessed by God as to witness the glorious days of March, and the insurrection of Vienna, and the fall of Metternich and Sedlnitzky"; a generation later, something of that happy excitement still infused his writing. (Characteristically, he used a line from Schiller's *Hymn to Joy*, which is the text of the choral movement in Beethoven's Ninth Symphony, to express the sense of fraternal love, all-embracing "except for the executioners of the spirit, who anyway had been sent packing".) He described how, with the abolition of censorship, everybody had something to say in print, however silly it may have been. Most well-known authors turned up in the free-for-all. "Only one was silent, one to whom all eyes were turning, for whose lowest whisper all were listening: Franz Grillparzer." Schlögl felt so strongly about it that he wrote a passionate rhymed harangue "To the One", imploring him to hallow the hour of liberation of the press by a single poem. To the author's profound, richly deserved embarrassment, the limping stanzas were published in Bäuerle's newspaper— incidentally, a rallying point for anti-revolutionaries in the later months of 1848, so that Bäuerle safely made the crossing to the other shore after the renewal of absolutism.

In June 1848 Grillparzer broke his silence with a single poem, which was anything but the song of freedom his young admirer had pleaded for. It was, in fact, his one political act: entitled *Feldmarschall Radetzky* and apostrophising the old general, it lifted him, and his army fighting against the Italian insurgents, to symbolic heights. "In your camp is Austria—we others are nothing but shards." There, in the army, is discipline and obedience, which is peace-in-war; there, no youth boasts of knowing better than the Marshal, or dares to dignify his dreams with the name of wisdom; there, nations and languages fuse into a commonweal.

The poem is more thoughtful, with its under-current of ideas far removed from the battlefields of Lombardy, than the summary can suggest. But at the moment when it appeared, its subtleties counted for nothing compared with its obvious message. It put Grillparzer into the Black-and-Yellow camp, more squarely than he liked. Later he complained to intimates that he felt sad at having his patriotically conceived stanzas misinterpreted, and often endowed with a "coarse" tendency which had been far from his mind. Schlögl, who recalls this, comments blandly that Grillparzer's strictures on insubordinate youth sounded unfriendly. Still, they continued to love him and to cram into performances of his dramas. What came to light after the poet's death was four drafts of open letters to his "friends and fellow citizens", all written between the end of March and the end of May; they start with appreciation of the early achievements, and work up to warnings which get more and more agitated. The last draft, written after the May revolt and explicitly addressed to the Academic Legion, pleads: "If peaceful burghers begin to think that our disorders are the result of freedom, the majority will soon regret the former conditions, happily discarded in the days of March, and in the end even wish for their return." He spoke partly, perhaps largely, for himself. He warned the students not to overrate their power: if the burghers—i.e. the middle class—and National Guards underwent a change of mind, which allies would the students call in then? He shuddered to think. So much he wrote, but did not say that he was thinking of the workers who had been the allies of the students in May, when the Academic Legion was threatened with disbandment. After a few more sentences, the draft broke off.

Grillparzer wanted to speak out, but doubted if he could achieve anything by doing so. Torn between the fear of "horrible consequences" if things continued to drift, and the fear of a fruitless intervention, he turned to the ideal of a unifying force in the service of order. It would not have occurred to him to think of the Church in this light; in this, if in little else, he was at one with the anti-clerical majority of Vienna, from the city centre to the outer suburbs. The only other institution that could serve as an embodiment of that ideal was the Imperial Army in the field; not the one under Windischgrätz, which was then investing Prague—and Windischgrätz, a grandee of grandees who was caste-conscious at least as much as he was an upholder of the absolutist monarchy, could not be turned into a father figure—but that under the old soldier, "Father" Radetzky. The poem for which Grillparzer was fêted and decorated by the conquerors of Vienna was not a militarist paean, but a disguised appeal to an idea which might rally those as much afraid of political disintegration and social chaos as he was.

A couple of months before the outbreak of the Viennese Revolution, Grillparzer's longest and most beautiful *novella* had been published, *Der arme Spielmann*, usually translated as *The Poor Musician*. It is a marvellously achieved transformation of Grillparzer's inner history, above all the conflict with his father, and an analysis of an artist's failure

—the poor musician hears perfect music in his mind, but produces only miserable sounds on his fiddle. The melody that haunts him was sung by a servant girl whom he, the inhibited, rejected son of an eminent father, had not dared to win for himself; now the strong-minded wife of a suburban butcher, she is still his only link with ordinary, healthy life, and on his death she hangs on to the violin for her son. Into this story Grillparzer introduced glimpses of the common people of Vienna as he saw them. At the beginning he shows the exuberant crowds at St. Brigitta's Fair, boisterous, happy—and harmless. To the butcher's wife he gives an independent common sense and secret softness which makes her akin to his own Katty Fröhlich. But then comes the description of the attic room in a gardener's cottage, which the old musician shares with other lodgers. A chalk line divides it into two worlds, one of cleanliness and order, the other of slovenly dirt. The dirty world is that of two journeymen-artisans; they and the poor musician have nothing in common except the door.

Indeed, Grillparzer was hopelessly separated from the suburban factory workers (unless they were in their Sunday best as at St. Brigitta's Fair), and even more from the sullen unemployed who were given expensive but to them meaningless occupation at municipal earthworks in the spring of 1848—the August riots sprang from their grievances, they were drafted into the Mobile Guard in autumn, they were the allies Grillparzer dreaded for the students. It was the story of the two worlds all over again. In common with other enlightened conservatives of the older generation, who had welcomed the fall of the old régime but refused to risk bolder changes, he sensed, yet failed to understand, the structural and human problems arising from the Industrial Revolution. They were alien to him, and, to an almost comic degree, he and people like him found a crumb of comfort in the thought that the most disturbing "anarchists" had come from outside Vienna, that most of the proletarians were immigrants with no right to the title of Viennese. But seven months of shared hopes, hates and dangers had given to those newcomers a stake in the town, although the citizens continued to think of it as their property, in which the decent lower middle class of the older suburbs were modest partners. Grillparzer unwittingly furnished a useful metaphor: he, and his group, had chalked up an invisible dividing line in their minds to keep their familiar, neat world inviolate. They were unable to cross it, or to accept that those on the other side had won the beginnings of a new tradition for themselves. To recapture the sense of stability when all group boundaries were shifting, the partisans of order bowed to a strong, authoritarian government as the lesser evil, at least for the time being, and nursed the embers of liberal notions in private. Grillparzer did so, uneasily.

Bauernfeld, always a valuable gauge through that very capacity for drifting with the stream which angered Grillparzer, says in his memoirs: ". . . the 'Reaction' period left a considerable measure of resentment among the middle classes, and above all among the lower orders. For some time it was impossible to enjoy life. We were the more ready to retire into an intimate circle of friends, the more uncomfortable the general mood of Vienna became during the long reactionary era. . . ." Oberhummer (*op. cit.*, vol. 1, p. 224) records some of the difficulties facing the Viennese police, reinforced though their ranks were by soldiers from Slav regiments—a suggestive detail this, because it hints at a cleavage of importance in later developments. Insults to police guards were so frequent that heavy sentences were imposed; students expressed their opposition, and their sympathy with German democracy, by wearing "Germanic" clothes, broad-brimmed hats, and their hair in long locks; this had to be suppressed—eighty students were detained in a single week of 1851. Under the new Police Director, who was soon as widely loathed as Sedlnitzky had been, a horde of self-appointed denouncers and informers—who always follow in the wake of a suppressed revolution—was systematically employed. A peculiar side-effect of this was, according to Schlögl, that people in coffee-houses and inns no longer joined unknown customers at a table, as before, but would prudently and sombrely sit alone.

It was in those bleak years of the Restoration that Grillparzer reviewed his own attitudes, justified them to himself without complete conviction, and found the official honours won by his Radetzky poem turn to dust and ashes in his mouth. In September 1849 he called on Marshal Radetzky, expecting to find him a warm and genuine person. He was disappointed. The old man struck him as foxy, "empty and cold in the middle", and interested in the famous poem only because it flattered him, and because it had served his ends. But, so the entry in Grillparzer's diary adds, other statesmen, too, had imagined they had merely to confer orders upon him, and enlist his vanity, to make him perform "like a blinded chaffinch", pouring out patriotic effusions; in fact, even in that poem Radetzky had been the occasion rather than the subject. However, Grillparzer did perform. He wrote an official poem to Jellačić, so feeble as poetry and as propaganda that the underlying dislike comes through. Though he agreed with the purpose of the military rule and the absolutist turn of government, he had no liking for the caste-proud soldiers and caste-proud aristocrats at the top, and refrained from examining their methods. In public he did what he was bound to do in his rôle as a consecrated apologist for monarchy, army and empire. He wrote the poems *de rigueur*, let himself be pushed on to committees, and accepted homage which sometimes embittered him because it was given not to the poet as such, but to the political partisan-poet he could not be in his heart of hearts. The rhymed epigrams of those years were more bilious than ever, which is saying a lot.

Grillparzer's epigrammatic verses frequently contradict one another. They mean as much, and as little, as the grimaces or grins one may try on in front of a looking-glass, to find momentary relief from the public mask by donning one of the masks from the secret store. In 1848 he had written scathing quatrains about the students, about the misuse of freedom, and about individual figures who roused his ire; out of some epigrams he had even evolved a whole poem parodying the high-flown songs dedicated to the Viennese students (like Frankl's poem)—a parody in which one stanza at least sounds serious and sympathetic. Now, in the years after 1848, while he found himself courted and cosseted by important people he half despised, his watchful self-criticism gained an outlet in highly unorthodox poetic snarls, which remained his secret. Prince Windischgrätz? But he is simply old Metternich, a rhymed epigram says, only with leggings (a symbol of military rigidity) instead of hose; one who combines aristocratic and barrack-yard arrogance, says another epigram. It may have been under the influence of his disappointing interview with Radetzky that Grillparzer wrote a bitter quatrain: field-marshal or sergeant-major, they esteem nothing but the sabre; if anything could recommend poetry to them, it would be its virtue as fire-water for the soul. And two years later, addressing the rulers—in effect the young Emperor Franz Joseph, since by then the last shreds of a Constitution had been discarded—he wrote: "I am loyal to you, as before, but the reason is new: once I was loyal from love, now, from loathing the opposite side." For a civil servant of long standing, and the poet laureate of a régime, it was the confession of another failure, coming painfully soon after the crisis of divided sympathies: the enlightened conservatism for which he had hoped was proving an illusion. In the silent decade between 1848 and 1859, a similar disillusionment pervaded the Viennese groups most important as pillars of the Restoration, the upper middle and professional classes. Old Grillparzer spoke for them even if he did not speak aloud; there were ears attuned to his lowest whisper, to use Schlögl's phrase.

What most exercised those frustrated liberals and frustrated conservatives of the Josephinian school was the growing influence of the high Roman Catholic clergy with court and government, through the Emperor's mother, Archduchess Sophie, and through the devoutly religious Minister of Education, Count Thun. Even then, Dr. Joseph Othmar von Rauscher, Archbishop of Vienna, an eminent theologian, fine diplomat, and former tutor of the Emperor, was preparing the Concordat which was to be concluded in 1855. By no means an ultramontane, as supporters of the Pope's absolute authority were called—at the Vatican Council of 1870 he belonged to the minority of Cardinals who voted against the dogma of the infallibility of the Pope in matters of faith—he restored to the Church an independence *vis-à-vis* the State such as it had not enjoyed under the Habsburgs since Maria Theresia. He campaigned, avowedly and successfully, against the last remnants of Josephinian attitudes in these matters. The Catholic associations which had sprung up during the Revolution, and were given preferential treatment by the authorities afterwards, were not yet influential, but they provided a basis as well as a single-minded editor for the *Wiener Kirchenzeitung*, the newspaper which Bauernfeld had attacked for having a monopoly on freedom from censorship. Political Catholicism thus possessed the rudiments of an organisation among the battered, bewildered shopkeepers and landlords of the suburbs, and direct access to the seat of power. In the stillness imposed on Vienna by the year-long state of siege, the voice of the Church sounded with novel authority. But it also woke the ingrained antagonism of the majority of cultured Viennese, from moderates to radicals. Many of the embittered battles of later generations stemmed from those post-revolutionary days when anti-clericalism, inactive but not impotent, was virtually the only channel left open to rebellious feeling.

For the third time in his poetic output, Grillparzer conjured up the ghost of Joseph II. It speaks with a tired, hopeless voice, unlike the earlier pronouncements (see p. 123). Scathing reference is made to the

usurpation by the Emperor, called Franz before his accession, of the
additional name of Joseph, and to his abolition, by Imperial Decree
on 20 August 1851, of the embryonic Constitution which he himself
had proclaimed only two and a half years earlier.

This poem of disgust is not often used in illustration of Grillparzer's
changing political moods and opinions. Indeed, other poems from the
same period are impeccably loyalist, one even movingly so. But the
third Kaiser Joseph poem cannot be dismissed as if it were an epigram
jotted down in haste and spite. It is a polished, careful piece of work.
Though it bears no date, it has been established that it was written
after the attempt on Franz Joseph's life in 1853 (on which Grillparzer
produced a short lyric addressed to the Emperor's mother), and after
his marriage with Elisabeth of Bavaria in 1854 (for which the poet
wrote an epithalamium, with some unconventional touches). In any
event, the fact that Grillparzer found himself driven to deny to the
young Emperor the right to bear the name of Joseph, at least "for the
time being", clearly because he had forfeited it in the poet's opinion,
pricks the balloon of a widely held legend about his unswerving
dynastic devotion. It is only right to stress that the decisive and most
aggravating factor in his eyes must have been the Concordat of 1855,
the "black magic". About that time Grillparzer wrote a couplet against
Count Thun, the Minister of Religion (*Kultus*) and Education, which
became famous by word of mouth long before it could be printed:
"Gentlemen, hear the notice of a suicide—the Minister of Religion has
killed off the Minister of Education." This, because the Concordat,
which Thun promoted, delivered the schools to ecclesiastic control
just when reform projects mapped out during the Revolution were
taking definite shape.

(To exemplify the vast gulf between Grillparzer's intellectual
dilemma combined with emotional revulsion, and the hostile mood of
the slums in those years: when the Hungarian tailor János Libényi
attacked the Emperor with a knife, but only grazed him, it did not
produce outbursts of jubilation in all quarters that the sovereign had
been spared. A caustic folk-song about it was still current in my early
youth, though with an emasculated, puzzling text. In exact translation
—from heavy Viennese dialect—it ran: "On Simmering Heath A
tailor's been blown away, And it served him quite right—Why's
his sewing so bad?" When I repeated this at home, I was told by my
father that it referred to the tailor who had tried to knife Franz Joseph,

and was hanged for it "on Simmering Heath", the unlovely waste land south of Vienna. And originally the key word of the last line had not been "sewing" but "sticking", *stechen*, which in German means stitching with a needle as well as sticking with a knife. The inference was inescapable: *vox populi* in its roughest pitch blamed Libényi not for trying to kill the Emperor, but for failing in his attempt. Young Franz Joseph had started his reign with executions and prosecutions; it took a long time before the responding hatred faded away—as the Emperor himself, and his military advisers, knew in spite of loyalist manifestations. But no one would have been more horrified than Grillparzer if that message from far beyond the dividing line had come to his ears.)

The last paragraph of Grillparzer's incomplete reminiscences of 1848, from which I have quoted before, starts: "This would be the place to justify myself for my lack of enthusiasm for freedom. Despotism has destroyed my life, at least my literary life, therefore I must be granted a feeling for freedom. But . . ." It ends: ". . . I was condemned to passivity, for, had I said: what you are doing is folly, nobody would have believed me. Above all I was old, and progress was credited only to youth."

In fact, he had condemned himself to passivity long before, for reasons far deeper than the political or social context. Bauernfeld had challenged him about it in the heyday of their intimacy, in the still-rosy Biedermeier atmosphere. His best friend during the pre-March years, Ernst von Feuchtersleben, a distinguished humanist, physician and poet, had criticised Grillparzer's olympian refusal to "stimulate a higher vision in the people". But the example of Feuchtersleben in the politics of 1848, when he worked himself to death—literally—as a reluctant if dedicated Minister of Education in one of the short-lived liberal governments, only served to confirm Grillparzer in his inaction. The counter-revolutionary years drove him still farther back into himself. And yet he preserved a peculiar balance, by those malicious epigrams which somehow (he turned a blind eye to it) became known in Viennese intellectual circles, as anti-toxins to conformism, and by small symbolic acts of self-liberation.

E. H. Gombrich tells about one of these in a short article (*German Life and Letters*, vol. 16, April–July, 1963); he had heard it from a granddaughter of the geologist Eduard Suess, who was a young civil servant when Grillparzer was about to retire in 1856—this is one of the chains of oral tradition linking four generations. The story is, briefly, that young Suess was in Grillparzer's office when a messenger came to ask the Director of the Treasury Archives about a file; Grillparzer said he hadn't got it. The messenger came back twice, because his superior was certain that it could only be there, and it was urgently needed. Grillparzer threw him out. Then he opened a drawer. " 'Here it is,' he said, 'but I won't be plagued.' " A childish gesture, yet, as Gombrich points out, a means of holding on to his self-respect: "He had avowed to himself that what he secretly desired was their hostility rather than their politeness." At the same time the incident is saddening, although it is given a humorous twist by the Viennese idiom, "sekkieren lass i mi net". If it had been known to the passionate young critics of Grillparzer among the generation of 1848, it would have enraged them—unjustly—as a further proof of his failure to be their leader in fight.

The plain truth is that there were no leaders, moderate or radical, either during or after the Revolution. If its half-baked ideas and chaotic events had immense influence on the evolution of modern Vienna, it was because it set social changes in motion which could not be reversed; because not even a military dictatorship could stamp out the notions of personal and sectional freedom which had germinated; and because—this has to be stressed over and over again—too many people, from the new Emperor downward, had been touched in the roots of their existence by it. They became transmitters, in semi-silence like Grillparzer, or in myth-building articles like the journalists who had burst into print after the March days, or in stories told to children and grandchildren. The decade of renewed and even tightened censorship made it impossible, at least inside Austria, to defend the defeated revolutionaries. Journalists who had remained undaunted partisans, men such as Friedrich Schlögl and Ferdinand Kürnberger, made detours into local history, with more or less of satire in them—which satire was watered down by imitators, and turned into a romanticised legend of Old Vienna as the asides against the old régime lost their point.

It was ironical that the picture of Merrie Old Vienna, a Biedermeier Paradise Lost, was painted in retrospect by writers who had chafed under the restrictive practices of the old régime and done their best to overthrow it, as for instance Bauernfeld and Schlögl. They were better at it than the professional defenders of paternalism. It was even more

ironical that the legend gained strength while, and because, any
discussion of the un-cosy reality was banned from the printed
page.

About the same time, another legend of implicitly oppositional
character revived, that of the Good Emperor Joseph. It became a folk-
myth, which, somewhat later, was further developed by popular
novels with a liberal slant. Rosa Mayreder records in her autobiography, *Das Haus in der Landskrongasse*, that the almost illiterate old
nursemaid who came into their family in 1858 told stories of Maria
Theresia and "the marvellous Emperor Joseph. . . . He walked among
his people in every kind of disguise, always on the spot where there
was trouble or oppression, punished the rogues and rewarded the just,
opening his homely grey coat to reveal the glitter of his Imperial
garb. Secretly, old Hanni was convinced that the Emperor Joseph had
never died but would return one day to set all things right." It was a
fairy-tale to the young Obermayers in the 'sixties, but their nursemaid
must have imbibed it long before, when it was pregnant with another
meaning—the popular counterpart to Grillparzer's Josephinian poems.
Certainly no Viennese child of an ordinary middle-class family will
have heard nursery stories about a Good Emperor Franz, or a Good
Emperor Ferdinand, though these would turn up in school readers.
So did the Emperor Joseph stories, once they had lost their reproachful
hidden edge. And then, nearer to our times, the Viennese invented the
gag: "You shall never learn my name—I'm the Emperor Joseph!"

Of all those who expressed the changing moods of 1848 and after, no
one was more independent, and at the same time closer to the ordinary
Viennese, than Johann Nestroy. He did no flag-waving at the outbreak of the Revolution. It would be difficult to imagine him in the
melodramatic pose of the "popular poet"—writer of sentimental
plays about the "people"—Friedrich Kaiser, who rode through the
city on 15 March as a herald to read the Imperial manifesto which
promised the Constitution. Nestroy, like other actors, joined the
company of the National Guard set up by his theatre director Carl,
with arms from the stock of props—a good publicity stunt, which duly
attracted and amused the public. There exists a caricature from those
early days, showing Nestroy, tall, gaunt and saturnine, in high top
hat, long frock-coat, and plaid stove-pipe trousers, holding a sabre in
his hands, and next to him the excellent comedian Wenzel Scholz, a
short, roly-poly figure in a roly-poly top-hat, tails, almost bursting out

of his light-coloured trousers, a sabre dangling between his legs and his arms crossed—both of them on sentry duty.

Nestroy was a whole-hearted partisan of the democratic movement. He was to make this quite clear when it was no longer the fashion. But he never lost his sharp, ironical wit and sense of humour about it, and this too he made clear, even at the height of mass excitement. On 1 July 1848 his *Freiheit in Krähwinkel* had its first performance in the former Leopoldstädter Theater, recently rebuilt and renamed Carl-Theater. Until the place closed down at the end of the month, it was played daily to over-full, enthusiastic houses. And this, although the influential critic Saphir (who had been a lick-spittle before, and was again to change his tune, abjectly, later in the year) accused the play of dragging the cause of freedom into the mire. Seen in perspective, Nestroy's impudent political farce is the most vital literary work to grow out of the Viennese Revolution. Its vitality still survives.

As so often, Nestroy borrowed the frame and used a hackneyed, tritely romantic plot with lovers and intrigues about a will. Only the frame is important. Krähwinkel had been invented by Kotzebue in 1803 (in *Die deutschen Kleinstädter*) as the prototype of a backward provincial town. Since then, the name, and the characters of the mayor, a small-town despot, his beadle, the local poet, etc., had been used over and over again for popular farces, with topical themes, in Vienna with unmistakable Viennese accent and allusions. By appropriating these familiar fictions Nestroy was able to do a double-take. Bringing Freedom to Krähwinkel enabled him to repeat, on the level of bur-lesque, the sequence of events in Vienna, from the first timid murmur-ings to the flight of the local tyrant; in the weaknesses of the Kräh-winklers he exposed weaknesses of the Viennese—especially of his own side. But because this was only Krähwinkel, while "freedom" was already won elsewhere and particularly in Austria, he could introduce echoes of greater problems, though always in satirical or farcical form. His hero, the radical journalist Ultra, has come to Krähwinkel from "freedom-bright" Austria. Only in Ultra's speeches and songs is there a hint of seriousness, but he is so much the gay swaggerer intoxicated with his own exuberant wit, that he embodies personal freedom even when preaching freedom with a capital F. It is Ultra, too, who holds the pet aversions of the public up to ridicule, by appearing disguised first as a Redemptorist friar, then as a Russian nobleman, and finally as Metternich.

The Mayor, on the other hand, provides an opportunity for popular propaganda "tableaux", as well as for a warning, by having convenient dreams. First he sees in a dream the courtyard of the Vienna Ständehaus on 13 March, with a vast crowd and a speaker calling for freedom-to-be-won—as it had been. He wakes terrified, but worse is to come when he falls asleep again. He sees the so-called storm petition of the Viennese on 15 May, in front of the Imperial Palace. (Here it should be recalled that the moderates of Vienna, not to speak of the Black-and-Yellow anti-revolutionaries, were no longer fellow-travellers of the democrats when Nestroy staged his comedy; they, unlike him, retreated at increasing speed after the events of May. This gave propaganda significance to the second tableau.) When the mayor complains about his nightmares to his factotum, he is given something to exorcise them—something Black-and-Yellow, in the shape of the copy of a Viennese right-wing paper, to pillow his head on. Promptly he dreams of the triumph of "Reaction", himself arm in arm with a Russian general, Cossacks in the background. It is notorious that some of the more zealous theatre-goers in broad-brimmed revolutionary hats became restive on the first night at this juncture, and were only soothed by the turn of the plot, in particular the guying of Metternich.

Freedom is won for Krähwinkel by a revolution in miniature, by workers, citizens, even civil servants shaking off their apprehensions, and—young women disguised as students appearing on the barricades, since there are no real students about, and their uniform is sufficient to frighten the reactionaries out of their wits. The mayor escapes to England: to Metternich. Ultra, flag in hand, gets his private happy end. His curtain lines are:

Reaction's a ghost, but you know that ghosts exist only for the frightened. So don't be afraid, and there won't be any Reaction.

Freedom in Krähwinkel is divided into two parts, "Revolution" and "Reaction", though Reaction ends with the true achievement of a revolution. From first to last it is studded with lines which, if it were possible to quote and explain them, would supply a mental vocabulary of the Viennese Revolution, and a running commentary in Nestroy's own voice that comes flashing through the barrage of words. (It was that voice which Karl Kraus, the greatest moralist of Vienna in the critical years before and after the First World War, tried to resurrect in one-man recitals of Nestroy plays, giving equal weight to the verbal

H

fireworks and the essential gravity.) In 1848, when people's ears were sharpened by years of censorship—always the best education for reading between lines and catching the slightest inflection—few barbed shafts missed their targets. It is another question how much of Nestroy's camouflaged warnings was absorbed. Some quips are obvious even now, as when Rummelpuff, the municipal commander, proclaims: "Human beings start from the baron upwards", a remark attributed in all seriousness to several Austrian grandees. When the local poet produces the same kind of ludicrous ode, first in praise of the knout, to please the saviour of the Old Order, Ultra disguised as a Russian prince, and later, when the revolution looks like being victorious, in praise of freedom, the audience was bound to think of more than one well-known name. The type in itself is timeless.

It seems less obvious now what is meant when Ultra, fantastically got up as European Commissioner for Liberty and Equality, comes riding on a white horse (à la Friedrich Kaiser on 15 March), and to the sound of trumpets reads a grotesque proclamation, every part of which is either stupidly redundant or self-contradictory. The final phrase, "to avoid all contiguous dissensions there will be no system at all", does the trick. The mayor faints, everybody cheers, and the second part, the intrigues of the old gang, can start, as in Vienna. The mock proclamation, invented by Ultra because the Krähwinklers are not yet ripe for action while he knows that the real struggle is still ahead, is nothing but a travesty of the contorted Imperial proclamation of 15 March, which had caused such euphoria. The barricades of 26 May had to rise in Vienna before the promise of a Constitution on a "broad" basis was redeemed; in Krähwinkel, Ultra announces: ". . . an immensely broad basis which will slowly lengthen"—the German word unmistakably means that it will be indefinitely postponed.

Towards the end of the comedy, the beadle is afraid for his house and his belongings: ". . . in a Viennese paper, I've read about a sort of magic formula that works better than lock and bolt." He chalks the sentence on his door: "Let property be sacred!" Ultra, dressed as a worker, a pickaxe in his hand, and "feeling that he looks like a decent person again" after his disguises, comes past. And for once Nestroy-Ultra lectures his audience: "Let property be sacred? If these words weren't written in the workers' hearts—what would all the scribbling on doors be worth?"

In one of Ultra's *chansons*, Nestroy goes so far as to define the terrible difficulty of "one freedom uniting Austria": to bring about a circle of nations attached to a centre. For this is how he sees the empire: not as a truncated pyramid, with the Germans on top and the "servant nations" (in Hebbel's words) at the base, but as a circle of equals. In the scintillating patter of his proverbially fast delivery, the great dream can hardly have been more than a spark.

The last performance of *Freedom in Krähwinkel* in revolutionary Vienna was on 4 October, the eve of the finale.

The next time the curtain rose on a farce by Nestroy was at the beginning of February 1849. It was called *Lady und Schneider (Lady and Tailor)*. The editor of Nestroy's works, Otto Rommel, says succinctly (*Gesammelte Werke*, vol. 5, p. 136): "In spite of an excellent reception, the play had only six performances. The reviews reflect the political excitement it caused."

Vienna was under martial law. The censorship was restored. Yet the Parliament was still plodding on in the Moravian town of Kremsier, at a safe distance from Vienna; some of the freedoms, and many of the habits of thought acquired in the revolutionary year, lingered on. The police pressure was severe, but the régime had not fully reverted to absolutism. Some of this ambiguity shows in *Lady and Tailor*. Not in the story, as fatuous an intrigue round a noble lady from England as any, but in the dialogue and characters of a couple of Viennese craftsmen. On the surface, there seems to be nothing to justify "political excitement."

Hyginus Heugeign, the part Nestroy wrote for himself, is a young, muddle-headed tailor who has been bitten by the bug of political ambition. As a prolific orator in the back-room of his tavern he has become swollen-headed. He is willing to believe that the lady, as a "High Tory", will employ him as an "agitator" for some obscure upheaval. "They'll have to put me at the head of something somewhere, it doesn't matter if it's a movement or a club, liberal, legitimist, conservative, radical, oligarchic, anarchic or non-anarchic, it's all the same to me—only, at the head of something!" Hyginus's endless speeches full of polysyllabic words amount to a caricature of a silly young boy from the suburban lower middle class, who does not know what to do with "freedom of the word". But he is at the same time a mask for Nestroy himself. Suddenly there is sense in his nonsense— and then it is mostly an attack on turncoats, couched in tolerant terms, but completely firm, and with a cold anger underneath which is

Nestroy's own. As Hyginus, Nestroy sings *chansons*. One of them speaks, with a plaintiveness that can only have pleased the censorship, of the things which have destroyed the old Viennese cosiness—women interested in politics, who first took frankfurters to the students on the barricades, and later flirted with the soldiers—equality at the expense of tradesmen—the bad temper, the sad carnival, the differences of opinion—and the barricades in the Leopoldstadt. But in commiserating with the suburb, the *chanson* not only mentions the barricades, it also speaks of shells and flames, without a single word in welcome of the restoration of order by force.

In the figure of Hyginus's prospective father-in-law, Nestroy creates a devastating caricature of the tradesman who is afraid of his own shadow and scents trouble in every unexpected noise because it might mean a riot, the portly suburban citizen who wants peace at any price; and again there is cold contempt somewhere behind the character designed for the jovial actor Scholz. In short, in *Lady and Tailor*, Nestroy lashed out against cowardice, vague selfishness, and the mental laziness of the "little man". The "excitement", surely, was aroused by his whole attitude, not by particular passages. The Reaction was here, but he was not afraid.

He put it to the test in three more comedies of 1849 and 1850. As acting, and writing the parts for himself as he needed them, were both his life and his living, Nestroy tried several forms of disguise. Only one was entirely successful, and will have to be described more fully. Of the two others, the farce *Höllenangst* (something like: *The Devil to Pay*) was performed five times at the end of 1849, and then buried together with its topical cargo. Once more this cargo seems not very heavy, on the face of it. All the same the play was successfully disinterred in 1948, with contemporary allusions and a monologue which Nestroy himself had suppressed (forestalling the censor), and opened the season of a new Viennese theatre (see a note by Rommel in his edition of Nestroy, *op. cit.*, vol. 5, p. 253).

Nestroy's vehicle is a young worker, Wendelin, who might be intelligent if he were not superstitious, and hag-ridden by his fear of the devil (hence the title). Wendelin is a less convincing mask for Nestroy than others. The discrepancy between his silliness and moments of shrewd insight is too great; after his childish reactions, the political vocabulary of his speeches and songs comes as a surprise. Also, if he speaks of himself as a proletarian, a former factory worker, there are no telling details to make this side of him come alive. When the phrase "our dream of freedom" turns up in a *chanson*, it is Nestroy himself speaking with bitter sarcasm through a rent in the mask; it is the same when the best verse of another song portrays the weathercocks who now wish to stamp out the very memory of 1848, crying for more censorship, while they had cried for terror against absolutism the year before. "Do they mean it now . . .? One can't help feeling some modest doubts." Here is Nestroy's voice again, using mild Viennese circumlocutions with deadly accuracy. But then he is also Wendelin, bemused and more muddle-headed than Hyginus the tailor, declaring that he refuses to be talked out of his superstition because it's good to believe in something.

Among the drafts for the suppressed monologue is a passage characteristic not of Wendelin, but of Nestroy's view of current slogans:

According to new-fangled ideas they call us proletarians, and tack other notions on to it—communist, rebel, danger to the State. It's really funny, the way they dress up the poor. It's true, a poor man is a born revolutionary, but there's nothing all that dangerous to the State about him. I know. I'm one myself. . . .

The last line of a song railing at destiny, to cap the monologue, claims that tyrannic destiny has one advantage over any ordinary tyrant; you can safely grumble about it. If it doesn't help, it's at least a relief to know that it won't land you in prison.

The most serious and mature of Nestroy's plays in the wake of the Revolution is not a farce, and scarcely a comedy in spite of comic interludes and some farcical characters. It calls itself simply a *Volksstück*, a popular play, or rather, a play for the people. The title is *Der alte Mann mit der jungen Frau* (*The Old Man with the Young Wife*). It was written in 1850, and never performed in Nestroy's lifetime.

If the conventional melodrama is disregarded, the heart of the plot is the escape of a political prisoner in 1850, and people's responses to it. Every character worked out on a level other than caricature helps him, and helps his wife before his escape. There is shooting in the background: the reactionaries are absurd, but no longer harmless. The hero, Nestroy's own part, is the "old man", a well-to-do manufacturer called Kern, who is all-tolerant until the moment when his integrity is at stake. Quite at the beginning he says:

Because of their short intoxication with freedom, political offenders are sentenced to ten or fifteen years in a fortress, but not one of them loses his honour for a quarter of an hour. The respect one gives to every man who sticks up for his opinion, risks his life for his faith—that respect is his for ever. . . .

When the young man, befriended by Kern after his escape, wants to explain himself, he is told calmly:

. . . What you did, was done by hundreds of thousands, by nearly everybody— no matter if it was by deed, word or thought. . . . Revolution was in the air, everyone breathed it in, and so, what he breathed out, had to be Revolution again. Nobody's got to give himself airs. It's just that one person or another attracted more attention. . . . Don't condemn your judges either. After a Revolution there's no such thing as a right measure of punishment. According to the law, hundreds of thousands deserve death—that's impossible, of course. So one man's shot "for life", the next gets fifteen years in gaol, this one gets six weeks, and another gets an order. And at bottom they've all done the same.

The Old Man with the Young Wife never passed the censorship, though Nestroy must have hoped for it, as he had already drawn up a list of the cast. But in 1850 all restrictions were tightened up, the new absolutism being safely in the saddle. The year—and the play with its saddened resignation—marked a change in Nestroy's work, a change towards greater tolerance and a gentler treatment of human weakness. He had lost his exuberance, and much of that aggressiveness which, far from being solidly misanthropic, had been rooted in the hope of a brave new world, within reach of his own kind if only . . . but hope had gone when he understood the defeat. Not that he ever became a conformist or ceased altogether to hit out, but he was tired, wrote less, and accepted more. His revolution was over.

Before he suffered this change, however, he wrote a one-act skit which was as impudent as *Freedom in Krähwinkel*, and as libertarian in spirit, but protected by the unassailable form of a literary parody: *Judith und Holofernes*. It was first performed exactly one year after the outbreak of the Viennese Revolution, on 13 March 1849, and was a triumph over every kind of censorship, official and unofficial. The literary historians label it Nestroy's parodistic masterpiece. In Austria, at least, it is read more, and certainly with greater appreciation, than Friedrich Hebbel's *Judith* which it travesties. Some of its gags have become part of the Viennese store of idioms. Yet I have to say at once that my conviction of its significance as a post-revolutionary act of rebellion is based exclusively on "internal evidence"; I have not found it treated as anything but a literary *tour de force* by the specialists; not even Otto Rommel mentions it in the essay "Nestroy als Politiker", (Nestroy as Politician; *Alt-Wiener Kalender*, 1922, pp. 34 ff.). I shall have to make out my own case, because it seems to me very important for three reasons. First, it shows another facet of the submerged resistance to the old-new order—provided I am right. Secondly, it is one of the key works of Nestroy, who is the most "Viennese" of my witnesses, and one of the least known abroad, and not only because of the difficulties arising from his use of dialect. The only historical work of modern scholarship in the English language to deal with the Viennese Revolution, R. John Rath's *The Viennese Revolution of 1848* (University of Texas Press, 1957), uses a vast apparatus, includes many obscure poems and pamphlets, but forgets to mention *Freedom in Krähwinkel*, and dismisses Nestroy in the list of Dramatis Personae—to be fair, the most defective part of the book—with the entry: "One of the most popular Viennese actors and opera stars of the 1840's, also wrote large numbers of librettos [*sic*] and plays." Thirdly, it seems to me of prime importance for my attempt to evoke that most elusive but enduring ingredient of Viennese cultural life, the capacity for cloaking deep convictions in mocking play.

The target of the parody was cleverly chosen. *Judith*, Hebbel's earliest great drama, verges on the ridiculous in the boastful speeches of Holofernes. During the revolutionary year, more of his tragedies had been given at the Burgtheater, once the bureaucratic straitjacket was loosened; if it cannot be said that his style of unalloyed gravity captured the Viennese public, he was at least well known to anyone interested in the stage—as were even the addicts of popular farce. The biblical story was, of course, familiar to all.

Nestroy built his parody round a Holofernes transmuted into the *non-plus-ultra* of a sly-stupid, kindly-brutal, and totally destructive general, played with disarming joviality by fat Wenzel Scholz. Holofernes is Viennese, so much that he once says *Wien* instead of Assyria, and speaks the cosiest dialect. His first short soliloquy on the march against Bethulia runs:

I'm the bright jewel of nature, I've never lost a battle, I'm the virgin among warlords. I'd like to set myself at myself one day, just to find out who's the strongest, me or me.

He conquers so many countries for his king Nebuchadnezzar that he might one day absent-mindedly "devastate a country and burn down a dozen towns", only to find out afterwards that they belonged to a prince who had peacefully surrendered. When Nebuchadnezzar sends him word that he wants to be adored as the one and only god, Holofernes comments that the king only says aloud now what he has been secretly imagining all the time. He tells a servant who pleads that he has "only been thinking . . .": "I'm the only one who thinks. Anybody who has the cheek to have thoughts commits burglary in my head." But he also kills when the spirit moves him. In front of Bethulia he uses his sword on three underlings, one after the other, and then gives the order, on hearing that Judith is coming: "But first get the tent cleaned up properly, there are dead bodies all over the place—I can't have a mess." (The Viennese word I have, inadequately, translated by "mess" is *Schlamperei*; this is one of the several sayings of Holofernes which have become part of the language, not always in exact quotation.)

Nestroy's Holofernes was a wicked take-off, in the first place of Hebbel's braggart generalissimo. But in 1849, when only too many Austrian generals were in action or had been, it was surely as difficult not to think of any of them when hearing Holofernes, as it was difficult not to think of Mussolini in the nineteen-twenties. One Austrian commander, Haynau, had not yet shown his full mettle as an executioner in Hungary when *Judith und Holofernes* was written, but less than a year before he had earned the title of the Hyena of Brescia; it was he whose Italian vocabulary was reputed to consist of the three words *canaglia*, *fucilare*, and *pagare*—rabble, execute by shooting, and pay.* And then there was Jellačić himself with his bluster and ruthlessness, too near not to be remembered even while Holofernes waddled across the stage exciting helpless laughter.

This was one side of the parody, the less subtle one. The other was the Jewish community of threatened Bethulia, which included Judith. In Hebbel's drama, Judith is a passionate woman who has to fight against Holofernes's sexual attraction. Nestroy switched the plot. Judith's brother Joab, "the handsome cadet", disguises himself as his sister, who is a famous beauty, counting on Holofernes's insatiable appetite for women; Holofernes is ready to fall for his visitor, but suspects treachery, and substitutes a dummy head for his own. This is the head which Joab-Judith—played by Nestroy—cuts off and exhibits to the Assyrian troops who immediately panic. When Holofernes

---

* Cf. Ferdinand Strobl von Rabelsberg's *Metternich und seine Zeit 1773–1859*, Vienna/Leipzig, 1907, vol. 2, p. 449. The author is not suspect of liberal bias.

shows himself it is too late, a commander who has lost his head is powerless, and he is dragged off in chains by the triumphant Jews. So much for the action.

Nestroy's device of disguising the Viennese as Jews was bold indeed. He used the speech of not fully assimilated Jewish immigrants as it could be heard in and around the Leopoldstadt; apart from a number of Yiddish idioms, the main trick was to change the order of words—the verbs placed after the subject even when compound, as in English or French, and not towards the end of the sentence as in German—and to use a surfeit of interrogatory phrases. Even Joab was given those inflections, except in the *chansons*, which are pure Viennese. Fundamentally, the method is the same as in *Freedom in Krähwinkel*: by holding a group of alleged non-Viennese up to laughter, Nestroy is able to expose Viennese weaknesses, hint at possible strength, and tilt at the enemy. But this time the camouflage has to serve a dual purpose, one towards the audience, another towards the watchdogs of the enemy now in power, whereas in Krähwinkel he was only manœuvring to recover his power. Aptly, the verbal disguise is double, a literary context and the Jewish accent. Its most curious aspect is the skill with which every line that sounds antisemitic turns into an attack on a Viennese target: poison used as counter-poison.

The people of Bethulia discuss the likely result of a siege by Holofernes, a black market, hoarding, rising prices, with the possibilities of profit and starvation: the people of Vienna had been through it all, actively or passively. The Bethulians dislike drilling in the Municipal Guard and grumble about their commanders: by what right do they give orders, when one Jew is no better than another? Translated into faintly different phrasing, this was the talk of reluctant camp-followers during the Revolution. (The graphic artist Anton Zampis drew them in a series of caricatures.) One Bethulian voices fears resembling those felt by many Viennese when Windischgrätz and Jellačić were at the gates and there was dissension about surrender or no surrender: "Our whole resistance is idiotic. Let's go and humbly open our gates to Holofernes, and say: Your Excellency, you are the benefactor of all Israel!" Only the name has to be changed. Possibly the audience could even think of a parallel to High Priest Jojakim, who fulfils his mission of bringing comfort to his people by eternally shouting: Woe, woe. If anyone were to miss the connexion between Vienna and Bethulia, there is Holofernes in person to explain: "What's being done with bayonets in modern times, we grey pre-historics do with swords." The gag had a sharp, if well concealed, edge.

It was not with bayonets alone that things were "being done" in the counter-revolutionary years, though the entourage of the young Emperor, bent on restoring him to the position of absolute lord and master by the Grace of God, relied on arms more than on adminis- trative measures. They distrusted the calm of Vienna. So did Franz Joseph himself. In 1850, when he was twenty, and had been reigning for nearly two years, he wrote to his mother:

Here [in Vienna] the spirit is getting worse every day, but the people are too cunning to let it come to an armed show-down. . . . On Sunday a great church parade on the Glacis, to show the dear Viennese that troops and guns still exist. . . . (Quoted in Jean de Bourgoing's introduction to the Emperor's letters to Frau Schratt, edited by him: *Briefe Kaiser Franz Josephs an Frau Katharina Schratt*, Vienna, Ullstein, 1949, p. 15.)

No set of documents, however, throws a sharper light on the attitude of the Emperor's military advisers, and at the same time on the am- biguous after-effects of the Viennese Revolution, than those which refer to the overdue razing of the old city walls, and the urgent extension of the town to include the suburbs.* As early as 1839, a consortium of the great bankers headed by Rothschild, Geymüller, Arnstein and Pereira, had adopted a project for the town's extension— an obvious necessity for any development of trade and industry, let alone for the adequate housing of a quickly growing population—and even the Imperial War Council was in favour of the idea. All they did was to make surveys of the terrain, which always started from the assumption that there had to be ramparts (in fact the bastions laid low by Napoleon in 1809 had to be restored), but that their ring should be widened so as to take in land for building. By 1848, the fortifications had not been shifted by an inch, however many blueprints and memoranda had been promulgated.

During the Revolution, the project was given an unexpected practical impetus when the Public Works Committee, set up in Vienna to create employment for the jobless workers, started not only con-

---

* Cf. Walter Wagner: *Die Stellungsnahme der Militärbehörden zur Wiener Stadterweiterung in den Jahren 1848-1857, Jahrbuch des Vereins für Geschichte der Stadt Wien*, vol. 17/18, pp. 216 ff.)

struction works for a dam in the Prater and for clearing the turbulent river Wien, but also earthworks in preparation for the new girdle of bastions. Liaison between the chairman of the committee, a distinguished bureaucrat, and the Viennese action committees was not undisturbed. Those emergency construction works became one of the thorniest financial and social problems to the moderates. They were interrupted by the events of October.

In October 1848, the fortifications round the old city had "made it possible for the insurgents to resist the regular troops longer", as the military experts emphasised. All the same, they first decided in favour of further strengthening those walls, thinking (I quote from W. Wagner's study) "primarily always of internal difficulties and not of an attack by an enemy from without". In the following month, November, a commission was formed to which Windischgrätz as Commander-in-Chief gave the task of protecting, above all, munitions from attack and looting in the course of popular risings. Such popular risings would come from the suburbs. What to do about the town? In the commission, the spokesmen of the army thought in terms of barracks placed on strategic points so that they could keep the centre and the periphery under fire. On the other hand the *Innere Stadt*, the old walled city, was inhabited by the "most prosperous and quietest subjects of the State". It would be a mistake to expose their houses, as well as State property, to destruction by guns of their own side. An insurrection of the non-property-owning part of the population, however, would be best crushed directly, with hand arms and grape-shot fire, not with heavy siege guns.

A highly interesting memorandum came from one of the archdukes, Maximilian d'Este.* He wanted to prevent the periodical social upheavals which he foresaw for Vienna, because the proletariat was no

---

* This Archduke failed by a hair's breadth to become the villain of 13 March 1848, but succeeded in creating a popular hero. In the evening of that day, two loaded cannons were facing a dense, excited crowd outside the gate of the Imperial Palace, when Archduke Maximilian d'Este arrived to inspect the situation, lost his head—there was shooting elsewhere—and ordered the guns to be fired. The master gunner, Pollet, first argued with him, since he had no military command, and then flatly refused to obey the order. This is the gist of reports which are contradictory in detail. The episode was romantically blown up, and Pollet given a dramatic line to speak, but even if this was invented, the fact remains. To stand up to an Archduke, even a minor one, was a courageous and a rare act. Pollet was not punished for insubordination, but made an officer.

longer reliable, having tasted blood. One of the dangers was that the soldiers would be subverted, too. Vienna was three things in one, a main trade centre through its geographical position at the crossroads, a market for buyers from the East, hence predestined to be an important industrial centre with factories and workshops, and the seat of the central administration, at times also of the court. The third function should be well separated from the first two, and rendered safe from outbreaks of the "brutal, licentious mixed trade and factory people". Vienna was even more dangerous than Paris, in the Archduke's opinion, because of its explosive mixture, in commerce and industry, of outcasts from all nations. The upshot of these views was that strong fortifications for use in the latent inner warfare were needed, and that the walls of Vienna should stand as a safe barrier between the upper and lower classes.

To begin with, the Emperor agreed with his military advisers. But on the commission, the civilians were making progress with their contentions. Behind them was the pressure of bankers, industrialists and high civil servants whom nobody could accuse of subversive ideas. There was not room enough in Vienna; the economic crisis could only be overcome by expansion; to pay a third of one's annual income for rent was bound to alienate even the most loyal citizens. Slowly the Emperor ceded ground, though for some years he still insisted on the principle that old fortifications could only be razed after the construction of their replacements. The most effective arguments against the diehards were put forward in 1852 by the *Ministerialrat* representing the Ministry of Public Works, Franz von Mayern. He argued that the force of public opinion, and its inherent danger, had once been underrated, but were now being overrated. A slow, systematic extension of Vienna was the right solution. He admitted that the hope held in 1850 "that special vigilance in the capital would soon be unnecessary" had proved an illusion. But insurrections rarely started from the property-owners; these were as a rule too cowardly to "hold down the proletariat" on their own initiative; the proletariat in its turn was not much hit by a destruction of houses . . . the inference was that bastions, ramparts and gun emplacements were no answer to any threat from below which the Revolution had left behind. A new Vienna might be a better answer.

In 1853, the year after Mayern's memorandum, Franz Joseph dropped the principle of replacing every old fortification by a new one. It looks as though he even ceased to consult the army bureaucracy about the projects for a modernisation of Vienna, for the final Imperial Decree came as a surprise to the Department of Engineers. The civilians had won.

On 20 December 1857, Alexander Baron von Bach, who had headed the Ministry under the absolute monarch since 1852, received an autograph communication from Emperor Franz Joseph I which began:

It is My Will that the extension of the inner city of Vienna with regard to its appropriate connection with the suburbs should be taken in hand as soon as possible, and that consideration should be given to the regulation and embellishment of My Residence and Capital at the same time. For this purpose I give My permission to abolish the circumvallation and fortifications of the Inner City, as well as the surrounding ditches.

The years of counter-revolution were coming to an end. The new bourgeois society of Vienna emerged from the upheavals as the winner, if not the victor. As they were fond of saying in the nineteenth century: the wheel of History cannot be reversed.

R. John Rath ends his book on the subject (*op. cit.*, p. 355) with the sentence: "In essence, the Viennese Revolution of 1848 was a liberal idea that failed."

It is extremely doubtful whether it is possible to sum up a revolution as "an idea", even "in essence". At any rate, the liberal and democratic ideas that had helped to release the Viennese Revolution, and those which were released by its convulsions, went on expanding and burrowing in the new Vienna. They were—to borrow from the most stirring of all German political poems, Freiligrath's "Die Toten an die Lebenden"—the victorious defeated.

V

Imperial City

I. THE NEW FACE OF VIENNA

IT WAS Karl Marx who once used the image of the "old age that is pregnant with a new one", and called violence—the violence of revolution—the midwife at the birth. The birth of the new Vienna was delayed, the midwife had not finished the job. Yet once the Emperor had decreed the disappearance of the old straitjacket, the fortifications round the town core, both demolition and construction followed quickly, even though the task was immense, and the capital needed proportionate.

The Imperial letter-patent to Bach was dated 20 December 1857. The first step was to set up a commission which would have authority for everything connected with the expansion and re-building of the city, finance included. On 31 January 1858, projects were invited, a competition thrown open to architects at which eighty-five blue-prints for the removal of the old and the planning of the new were sent in. On the three projects which were awarded prizes, the final proposal—by a civil servant—was based. It was accepted in September 1859. But eighteen months earlier, the ramparts facing the Danube Canal were razed, and a boulevard along the quay laid out. Other sections of the walls and bastions took longer; in many places they were too strong for the tools of demolition squads, and had to be torn up by explosives. The main parts were removed by 1864, the rest followed bit by bit. Only two short stretches of earthworks were spared, and they still stand. One of them faces the University. It carries the old, beetle-browed Pasqualati House in which Beethoven lived some years, in rooms from whose windows he could see the Wienerwald hills to the west—they are still visible, though the roofs in between have multiplied since his time. Once Prince de Ligne's rose-coloured little house stood on the bastion between taller neighbours; round the corner there is still a tiny eighteenth-century bandbox of a house, with stucco garlands above an oval window in its gable-wall. In 1683, this rampart had been the target of fierce attacks by the besieging Turks. However, neither historical nor aesthetic sentiment or sentimentality is likely to have saved the last remnant of the Mölkerbastei from demolition in the eighteen-sixties, but rather a surfeit of projects and the limitation of finance. Also, that corner of old Vienna was at the far end of the show sector on which architects, promoters and the authorities were concentrating.

The razing of broad ramparts, the filling in of moat and ditches, the final surrender of those parts of the Glacis that had been reserved for military drill and parades, together freed a large area for building. Beyond the Glacis began the old suburbs, now incorporated in Vienna; there were still some big estates with parkland which was sold in lots and built up; there, too, were countless small cottage-like houses that could be demolished more quickly and cheaply than the five-storeyed city houses of the Inner City with their thick walls and deep cellars. The suburbs were the place to build tenements for the growing industrial population. Nearer to or in the centre, the price of building sites was exorbitant. To exploit them profitably, new houses had to be built to order for the tastes of men of property. The most desirable site of all was at the crossing of the ancient road to the south and the new Ringstrasse. There the first of the palatial apartment houses, the Heinrichshof, was completed in 1863.

The Ringstrasse was the central feature of Vienna's reorganisation. It was, and is, a wide boulevard (mentioned in my first chapter) which followed the polygonal outline of the ramparts, in the shape of a horseshoe composed of straight sections, beginning and ending at the Danube Canal. In 1865 it was ready for use; Emperor and Empress drove along it on the First of May. From then on, public buildings rose in rapid succession, carefully planned for the middle stretch of the Ringstrasse, which bends round the bulk of the Hofburg—the Imperial Palace—with its vast outer courtyard and its gardens.

The first of the great new buildings to be completed was the Opera House. It stood close to the place where the old gateway to the south had been, on the inner side of the Ring, out of sight of the Hofburg, but connected with the town centre by that most important of arterial roads, the Kärntnerstrasse. The Opera had been planned before the city moat was filled in, designed to stand high and commanding. When the ground was levelled up, it looked sunken, low and squat. One of its

two architects, the hyper-sensitive van der Null, was so shaken by the
disappointment that he committed suicide. It was said that the Emperor
had made a disparaging remark; it was also said that its probable impact on the architect weighed so much on Franz Joseph's mind that
he decided to restrict himself to kind if empty words in the future—to
his proverbial phrase: "It has been very nice, I have been very pleased."

The Opera opened in 1869 with *Don Giovanni*. It is built in a lavishly
romanticised version of Renaissance motifs. Perhaps it is as near to a
confectioner's dream as to fairy-tale splendour. But few Viennese,
unless they are modern architects or strict self-disciplinarians, will
find it easy to be objective about the beloved building. When it was
rebuilt in exactly the same external shape, after having been burnt out
during the last days of fighting in 1945, it seemed the right vivifying
gesture.

Further along the Ring on the opposite side, the two "Court
Museums" for the History of Art—it housed the great Habsburg art
collections—and Natural History were built between 1872 and 1881.
They face each other in pretentious neo-Renaissance grandeur, with
identical cupolas and pillared façades, across a formal garden square
and the colossal monument of Maria Theresia. The original idea was to
connect them by a pair of triumphal arches across the Ring with a new
wing to the Hofburg—a wing of which only the middle part was ever
built, also in chilly neo-Renaissance, while the remaining space was
filled by a beautiful "English" garden not open to the public.

Facing the sober, dignified length of the old Hofburg, and set off by
an expanse of sanded square which reaches the Ringstrasse behind the
last surviving city gate, the low, classicist Burgtor, rose the new House
of Parliament in shining white, an exercise in severely marshalled
Greek forms. It was inaugurated in 1883, and replaced a barn-like
structure outside the city, which had been hastily raised for a far
smaller assembly of representatives. In sharp contrast to the museums,
in which the pomp of interior staircases and halls went at the expense
of their real purpose, the House of Parliament proved well suited to its
functions. Its creator, the Danish architect Theophil Hansen, adapted
styles of the past to functional proportions more boldly than any other
Ringstrasse architect. It was he who had built the Heinrichshof for a
wealthy industrialist and his wealthy tenants, using Renaissance designs
sparingly to emphasise height and width, and letting the best decorative
painters of the time paint frescoes on gold ground along the outside of

the top floor, as a distant gleam of rich colour. It was Hansen, too, who had used a restrained version of neo-Renaissance to build the concert hall of the *Musikverein* (in 1869), and the Stock Exchange (in 1877).

Since 1902, a fountain overshadowed by a statue of Pallas Athene has stood in front of Hansen's House of Parliament. When it was erected, it gave rise to a popular joke. A asks why Pallas Athene, of all things, had to be put there. B answers: Because she's the goddess of wisdom. A: So what? B: Well, you see, they've got to put her outside because you wouldn't find her inside.

A few minutes farther along the Ring, beyond a spacious public garden bisected by a very wide drive, stands the Rathaus, Vienna's new Town Hall, inaugurated in 1883 (to celebrate the bi-centenary of the second Turkish siege). Enormously long, in dark stone, with a central clock tower, arcades along its entire front and a gallery of ogival arches repeating the rhythm across the façade, it aims at an expression of newly recovered civic pride. It is not for nothing that the architect, Schmidt, found his inspiration in those Belgian town halls which were the homes of independent burgher administrators. This neo-Gothic edifice was meant to proclaim strength and self-confidence; it also proclaimed the romantic aspirations of the new generation of mayors, councillors and city officers, who were weighty citizens, and liberals. Vienna owed the restoration of its municipal autonomy to the year 1848. This was one of the revolutionary legacies which were respected and endorsed by the neo-absolutists.

Straight opposite the Rathaus, on the other side of the Ring and in an open space of its own, next to a public garden—the Volksgarten— which was partly laid out in the Biedermeier era on the site of a bastion destroyed by Napoleon, and extended on the razing of the other ramparts, lies the new Burgtheater. Its construction took longer than that of any other public building, from 1872 to 1888, when it opened with Grillparzer's fragment *Esther* and Schiller's *Wallensteins Lager*. Its principal architect, Hasenauer, gave it features similar to those of his museums: the pillared façade and the gala staircases of an ostentatious neo-Renaissance. Addicts of the simple old court theatre were to grumble about the new "Burg" for many years. But it did fit into the chain of representative new buildings along the Ring, which were designed to dazzle, and to convey the message that the Imperial City was once again secure in regained power and glory.

The new University building, which flanked the public garden in front of the Town Hall towards the right, had implicitly a different meaning. The old University in the heart of the town had always been too small, but its great assembly hall, the Aula, had been the centre of the academic world. In 1848, it had been the centre of the students' movement. As though to punish them, Prince Windischgrätz had put troops into the building, and there they stayed. For some years, even when lectures reverted to something like a normal pattern, students and teachers had to work with makeshift arrangements. The old University was cleared of troops in 1857, but turned over to the Academy of Science. The new University was built in the years from 1872 to 1884 after plans by Ferstel—still another neo-Renaissance shell. But it was truly a new academic body that moved into the new rooms. It was armed with legal guarantees of academic independence, freedom of teaching, and at least a modicum of protection against bureaucratic interference by the Ministry for Religion and Education, always a battleground for anti-clericals and bigots. In stages, those rights had been wrested from the various governments. It took a ministerial ordinance of 1873 to establish that "the right to academic honours would be independent of religious allegiance". But the basic principle, freedom of teaching and study, had been granted in March 1848, and not one of the men in power had ever dared openly to rescind it. In this, the new University and the new Town Hall had common ground.

Varieties of neo-Renaissance, varieties of neo-Gothic, all tinged with romanticism and at the same time with exhibitionism: indeed, the style of the Ringstrasse was—is—eclectic. And yet the rhythm of open space, the gardens, lilac in late April, lime-trees in June, tracery of branches against the snow, the spires of the old town in front and the ridge of the Wienerwald at the back, all help to give a quality of stately grace to the whole.

There is not a single building on the Ringstrasse which I can think of as beautiful. But one summer a couple of years ago, when I looked down from the top floor of the New Hofburg wing on to the Ring-strasse, and saw Parliament, Town Hall, University and Burgtheater linked by the great street's four rows of lime-trees, articulated by open spaces and gardens, and in the distance the line of blue hills shimmering in the dry air, the beauty of it caught me by the throat. It may have been simply because this was my town.

For the men who were shaping Vienna to suit their ideas, which were their time's, it was an electrifying experience. In 1883, Heinrich Ferstel (who had designed not only the new University, but also the severely Gothic *Votivkirche* with its graceful twin spires) wrote to Theophil Hansen, whose Parliament building was being completed even then:

You had come to Vienna as a young artist, though nearly a master already, at a time when architecture was in a state of deepest degradation. Architectural art was nothing but an expression of the bureaucratic system which dominated the State and the life of the people alike. It was only the year 1848 that released architectural art from the spell which had kept it in bonds until then. (Cf. K. E. Schimmer, *Alt und Neu Wien*, vol. 2, p. 534.)

What Ferstel meant was something definite and concrete. Between 1840 and 1848, all gifted young architects had chafed under the iron rule of the official architect-in-chief, head of the powerful Construction Department, Paul Sprenger. He imposed his own flat version of a classicist style; his public buildings—examples are still about—were not so much sober as uninteresting, without any trace of a personal touch, and leaden even if dignified.

An example of Sprenger's blighting influence, and of the releasing power of the March Revolution, is quoted by Austrian scholars who otherwise show little sympathy for radicals.* Sprenger apparently arrogated commissions to himself. Thus a new church for the suburban parish of Alt-Lerchenfeld was to be built according to his plans, along the conventional and outdated lines of a diluted "Jesuit Church" pattern. Against the opposition of younger men at the Academy, among them Siccardsburg and van der Nüll who were to build the new Opera later on, the work was started in 1847. The foundations were already laid when the Revolution broke out. Immediately, members of the recently formed Association of Engineers and Architects appealed to the new Ministry with a memorandum which called Sprenger's project "an architectural disaster". Work was stopped, and Minister Pillersdorf granted a fortnight's grace for the submission of new plans in a free competition. Out of eighty-five entries, the project of a young Swiss was accepted, and work resumed at once. The new design made use of round Renaissance arches, but its wealth of romantic detail was an innovation, a recoil from too much rational clarity. Müller, the Swiss architect, aimed at a coherent work of art, and when

* For instance, Richard Kralik in a history of Vienna published under the auspices of Archduke Franz Ferdinand: *Wien, Geschichte der Kaiserstadt und ihrer Kultur*, by R. Kralik and H. Schlitter, Vienna, 1912, p. 678.

he died prematurely, van der Nüll completed the profuse decoration. Führich, one of the Nazarene school of painters which was then preeminent, covered the walls with symbolist pictures. The result was a strange, isolated work, conceived as much out of rebellion against the enforced official cult of correctness, as out of that search for a childlike "mediaeval" faith, which is characteristic of German Romanticism; and—it was made possible by the Revolution.

In the orgy of decorative styles during the Ringstrasse era, opportunity and incentive were provided by the demand, the market. But the impulse came from the architects' own reaction to years of aesthetic uniformity. It does not affect the issue that the next generations turned with relief from the ornamental excesses of the "historical style", as it was called in a blithe euphemism, to the sobriety of late-eighteenth- and early-nineteenth-century fronts, including Sprenger's jejune designs, even before they hailed the uncluttered functional buildings of a new school of architects. (The spokesman of "Young Vienna", Hermann Bahr, is a case in point.) The fact remains that the mixture of inventive drive and petrified pride, of real and imitation marble, in the Ringstrasse architecture was appropriate as the official face of New Vienna. It was a contrived mask, but so are all official faces. Because of its bogus elements, not in spite of them, it was genuine in its way.

For behind the great Viennese building boom of those twenty-five years lies a story of economic speculation, disaster and recovery, of costly lost wars draining the exchequer—and public confidence—and of a spasmodic political development through internal conflicts, two steps forward, one and a half steps back. At no time could there be a sense of true stability and security in the capital of a State fighting for its coherence, and winning at best Pyrrhic victories. Vienna expanded and was, in the term of the Emperor's decree, embellished while the empire contracted; its social and cultural life was growing while the foundations of its importance as the centre of a multi-national State were assaulted and undermined. Those aware of it were a small minority, but the stresses were there. The pomp and circumstance of the Ringstrasse, the ostentatious façades and interior decorations of private dwellings which repeated the Ringstrasse patterns, often in vulgarised shapes, signified self-assertion and the illusion of permanence.

Within two decades, from 1849 to 1869, no less than eight Austrian constitutions were launched, retracted, revised, experimenting with federalism and centralism, indirect and direct franchise, authoritarian and representative government. Each unpopular war which ended with a reduction of Habsburg territory led to a constitutional change. The Crown was dependent on the material support of the bourgeoisie and the cities. The Italian campaign of 1859 lost Lombardy for Austria; it was followed by the "October Decree" of 1860, which instituted a Parliament limited to advisory powers, except for the privilege of authorising the budget and taxation, and counter-balanced this feeble house of representatives by the Emperor's prerogative and the provincial Diets. Since the Diets of the *Länder* were dominated by the conservative land-owning class—always tending towards federalism and anti-centralism in Austria, out of obvious class interests even when nationalist slogans were used—this solution incensed the liberals among the Germans and Czechs,* while the Hungarians resented the surrender of financial control to Parliament. The Government fell. The next Ministry was formed by one of the moderates of 1848, the "Old Liberal" Anton von Schmerling, who worked out the so-called February Constitution of 1861 on strictly centralist lines, with a Parliament of members elected by the Diets. Centralism meant reliance on the German-speaking bureaucracy controlled from Vienna, and on the German, or German-speaking, bourgeoisie of the industrial towns, the only social group ready to support a liberal administration which would favour its economic concerns. The franchise and the constituencies were therefore calculated to secure a predominant position in Parliament to the German upper middle class. (So, by the way, was the electoral system in Vienna at the time; the Town Council was nearly homogeneous.) Government, constitution and electoral procedure were violently opposed by gentry and aristocracy, and—from another angle—by Poles, Hungarians, Croats, Slovenes, the remaining Italians, and also by the Czechs, who had not boycotted the elections like others, but left the Parliament in 1863. The Schmerling Government tried to save its position by restoring Austria's

* The problems of the Slav groups in Austria were foreshadowed in 1848 at the Pan-Slavonic Congress of Prague, at which the burgeoning nationalist ideas blended with democratic demands. There, Bakunin, a dominating figure though not yet the great Anarchist leader, "proposed the unity and liberty of Slavs, at first to be realised outside Russia, through the community of the Austrian Empire. Bakunin drafted a constitution for this Slav federation of the future." I owe this summing-up to a private communication from Arthur Lehning, Amsterdam, the foremost scholar in this field and the editor of Bakunin's complete works.

influence in the German Confederation of States; Austrian participation, with Prussia, in the frontier war with Denmark over Schleswig-Holstein was a last attempt to prevent Russia from gaining supremacy. The calculation failed, the Government had to resign. Its successor, headed by an aristocrat, suspended the February Constitution and reverted to the old conservative method of combining the Emperor's authoritarian rule with federalism—the premier even planned seven Austrian regions represented by Diets. But another disastrous war overtook those plans.

In 1866 Austrian armies fought on two fronts, in the north against the Prussians, where they were devastatingly defeated at Sadowa, and in the south against the Italians, where they won sterile victories. The Peace of Prague gave Venetia to United Italy, and expelled Austria from the German Confederation. But before peace came, Vienna had faced the possibility of its occupation by the Prussians, whose troops had already crossed the border of Lower Austria and were trying to cross the Danube at Bratislava. A hastily fortified encampment on the left bank of the Danube, in sight of Vienna, looked as though it were meant as a defence position. Preparations were going on for the evacuation of State archives, treasury chests, and the gold reserves of the Bank. Evidently the highest quarters foresaw an invasion.

Rumours about the conduct of the Prussian campaign increased public distrust. General Benedek, made responsible for the débâcle at Sadowa, was said to have been the whipping-boy for a blundering archduke. The superior equipment of the Prussian infantry, above all their modern rifles, revealed the technical backwardness of the Austrian command. It was a sign of profound unrest in the capital when the mayor, Dr. Zelinka, together with a delegation of town councillors, sought an interview with the Emperor and told him of the people's apprehensions. Franz Joseph explained that Vienna was an open city and would be treated as such; he would leave town only with the last soldier, and only if and when military events made it imperative. He also assured the deputation that "only the constitutional course was envisaged for future developments" (Schimmer, *op. cit.*, vol. 2, p. 638). This was not sufficient for the mood of the population and for the Town Council, according to the chronicler. The Council voted an address which, with every expression of loyalty, made the current government under Belcredi responsible for the grave situation, and asked for its dismissal. The Emperor replied sharply. Loyal words would have to be confirmed by loyal deeds. He, too, shared the wish for a restoration of constitutional life, yet it was necessary to consider the needs not only of Vienna, but of the entire realm.

Some days later, while a truce was being negotiated, a state of siege was imposed on Vienna and Lower Austria. Officially it was explained by the presence of "many foreign elements in Vienna, which are prone to rioting". Unofficially it was explained as an act of revenge by the Government. And then peace came, overnight.

The discredited Belcredi Government hung on till 1867. Steps towards a "restoration of constitutional life" were slow and faltering. An extraordinary parliament was to meet and decide on a new constitution of the empire. This was by implication a revival of the discarded February Constitution; the polls for the Diets, from whose ranks the deputies to Parliament had to be elected, returned liberals in Vienna and in nearly all the other German constituencies, on a suffrage carefully restricted to the respectable tax-paying classes. At long last Belcredi resigned. The new Parliament passed constitutional laws which guaranteed human rights, the freedom of the individual, an impartial judiciary, and that freedom of belief and education which had been signed away under the Concordat of 1855. But it passed them only for the Austrian half of the Habsburg realm. Before the assembly met, the Emperor had himself negotiated a "compromise" with the Hungarian politicians, by which Hungary regained complete home rule, a responsible Ministry of its own on the basis of the laws of March 1848, and full authority over the non-Magyar nations within its frontiers. Only a joint Minister for Foreign Affairs and Minister of War (though the Hungarian army too was autonomous) under the common sovereign, as King of Hungary, were to link the two halves of the realm, together with a customs union and certain accounts subjected to revision every ten years. The Austrian Parliament was not asked to discuss, let alone amend, the agreement with Hungary, only to confirm it—and this at the request of the Hungarian leader, Count Andrássy, not by the initiative of the Emperor, who had still to learn the art of being constitutional. Henceforth the monarchy was no longer one empire, but the Dual Monarchy. Its Austrian half was not called Austria, *Österreich*, but had to carry the long, limping title of "The Kingdoms and Lands Represented in Parliament", although this sop to touchy nationalists in the old Habsburg dominions was a purely formal gesture. The name was too much of a mouthful.

Vienna, as seat of government and bureaucracy, was in future the capital of the Austrian half only, while remaining the capital of the Dual Monarchy for foreign diplomats by virtue of the Foreign Ministry on the Ballhausplatz, where Metternich had held court. It was no easy adjustment.

To quote Schimmer once more, as a typical Viennese chronicler:

Not because they grudged the Hungarians their constitutional rights, which they had won by their remarkable persistence, but because they saw in the re-constituted monarchy a reduction in the unity of the State, and a threat to Vienna's position, nearly all thoughtful people here observed this development with grave apprehension. However, they showed a sound instinct of self-restraint in accepting the situation, which spurred them to intense activity in order, by means of new institutions in all branches of local government, by economic measures, and by furthering education, to raise Vienna to a high level which would compensate for the loss of political significance. (*Op. cit.*, p. 639.)

For two years, the new Parliament sat in the shabby, half-timbered house which old Forty-Eighters like Rosa Mayreder's father would visit religiously to hear the liberal champions—and hammered out basic laws, some of them in force to this day. It established the Constitutional Court to deal with border conflicts affecting the limits of public and civic rights. When a Liberal cabinet headed by Prince Carlos Auersperg, but mainly composed of political experts who were commoners, took over as the first properly constitutional Ministry, it introduced legislation on the explosive issues of interdenominational marriages, civil marriage, the rights of denominations other than the Roman Catholic, and secular education. Each bill was an effective counter-stroke against the Concordat, and therefore roused strong opposition from the high clergy and their party. The bills were passed after impassioned debates in Parliament and outside, with an overwhelming majority in the Second Chamber, and a precariously small one in the First Chamber. In old Austria, the First Chamber was composed of hereditary peers, *ex officio* members including the archbishops, the archdukes, and a number of men eminent in public life who were appointed by the emperor, not as Life Peers with a title, but under their already sufficiently honoured names. The resistance to the "free thought" bills came mainly from great conservative aristocrats, apart of course from the prelates. Most eminent among Liberal speakers was Anton Count Auersperg, who had grown moderate since his young days as Anastasius Grün, in everything except his hatred of obscurantism.

On 21 March 1868, when the final vote was to be taken and all Vienna in a fever of excitement, Franz Grillparzer, seventy-seven years old, ailing and habitually a recluse, had himself driven to the Ständehaus where the session was held, and carried into the council chamber, to cast his vote "for Austria's spiritual and moral liberation". The words are not his but those of one of his editors, Alfred Klaar. (See a note to p. 140, which refers to his account in another context.) Klaar speaks of mass intoxication in the streets of Vienna when the result of the vote became known; of enthusiastic mobbing of the "citizen ministers" Giskra and Herbst; of a group of students, among them himself, marching to the statue of Joseph II and making speeches from the pedestal; and of their pilgrimage to Grillparzer's house in a quiet old street, to show him their gratitude. That night, Vienna was lit in a spontaneous festive illumination.

A distant echo of these discussions came to me through a little family anecdote. My maternal grandfather seems to have imbibed his firm anticlericalism while working for Dr. Cajetan Felder, the Mayor of Vienna who had fought and won the battles for the new Town Hall, and who regarded himself as the proud heir to the tradition of 1848.* Sometimes my grandfather would say, jokingly, of himself: "I, as a Christian-Catholic nobleman . . ." My mother repeatedly told me that this puzzled her, since her father, though brought up as a Roman Catholic, never used the term *Christ-Katholisch* otherwise, and certainly did not pretend to be a nobleman. But one day, reviewing her memories of him, it came back to her that the phrase had been

---

* The Archives of the City of Vienna conserve a vast manuscript of Dr. Felder's memoirs, entitled *Meine Erinnerungen*, of which the interesting parts have been extracted and edited by Dr. Felix Czeike. I was kindly given an opportunity to read the typescript. Meanwhile a shortened edition of the memoirs has appeared in print, but I have not seen it and do not know whether it includes the passages to which I want to refer. On p. 25 of the MS., Felder explains that in October 1848, he had stayed in Vienna while other town councillors had fled to the camp of the anti-revolutionaries. This fact had done him harm in the eyes of his colleagues and created professional difficulties for him. (He was a lawyer, as well as Town Councillor.) He continues: "Those who returned behind the bayonets of Windischgrätz and Jellačić regarded those who had stayed on as revolutionaries and accomplices". He calls the Viennese Town Charter of 1850 "that child prodigy born in the labours of the worst Reaction".

uttered with dramatic emphasis (as she was told) by one of the noble partisans of the Concordat in the First Chamber. It had become a standing joke, and was remembered when the immediate cause was forgotten.

It was during Dr. Felder's reign as Mayor (a mayor of Vienna is the elected chief executive, almost a small-scale head of government and anything but a purely ornamental figure) that the St. Salvator Chapel, in the gift of the Town Council, was handed over to the newly founded denominational group of the *Alt-Katholiken* (Old Catholics), a sect formed in protest against the decisions of the Vatican Council of 1870, in particular the dogma of the Infallibility of the Pope. (It still exists, mainly as a refuge for Catholics who do not accept the doctrine that marriage is indissoluble; this doctrine brings the deepest unhappiness not to practising Roman Catholics, but to people unable to believe in the doctrines of their Church, while forced to submit to Church-cum-State laws under the Concordat.)

The first Liberal Ministry was brought down by the attacks of clericals, conservative aristocrats, and dissatisfied Slav parties, but it was still able to introduce one important measure in 1869: compulsory education for all children between six and fourteen. This Act made local councils, from the smallest village to cities like Vienna, responsible for running the appropriate schools. Since earlier legislation had removed schools from control by the clergy, the range of influence of the local authorities was very much widened. At the same time, the field of political tension in local affairs was extended: at future elections, popular education would inevitably be an issue. In fact it was to be one of the reasons that made the ecclesiastic authorities in Vienna, and outside, back a party of their own. Yet education had been the object of a tug-of-war between the Church camp and the secular camp ever since two by no means radical ministers of 1848 had issued detailed proposals for a school reform which included new methods of teaching and new ideas for the training of teachers. Quietly, the liberals in the Council and administration of Vienna had been working along the lines traced by Grillparzer's friend, Feuchtersleben, backed by the powerful manufacturers who welcomed any spadework for the technological training needed to ensure a reservoir of potential skilled workers, as long as they did not have to pay for it except with advice and support. The liberal school reform of 1869 was essentially the work of the enlightened bourgeoisie of Vienna.

By 1870, when the industrial and building boom was nearing its peak, no more than 44·6 per cent of the people living in Vienna were Viennese in a legal sense. The rest were immigrants of some sort, the vast majority from rural districts. Adults working as labourers, of whom the building trade consumed great numbers in those years, could still be useful even with a rudimentary school education. But tomorrow, the new suburban factories which were springing up with improved railway communications would need more skilled men, mechanics, engineers, and technicians as well as semi-skilled workers.

The State, whose responsibility grammar school and university education still remained, was at this period setting up new colleges in Vienna, as well as putting into effect the blueprints of 1848. Care was taken not to let "two cultures" develop. Thus, the variant of grammar school called *Realschule* was designed for sons of the "industrial middle classes"; its school-leaving certificate entitled the student to enter the Polytechnic; but the teaching of natural sciences and technology was combined with a thorough grounding in history, geography, German language and literature, and in the higher grades French. For some years, before the boom collapsed, those schools were overcrowded. As a contributor to a memorial volume (*Wien 1848–1888*, published by the Town Council of Vienna, vol. 2, p. 86) puts it: "At a time when it was easy to acquire riches in the fields of commerce and industry, when men who entered the services of a railway or factory quickly earned high salaries, the value of general education sank, while that of a specialised professional education rose." *Realschulen* were, however, virtually closed to the sons of ordinary workers, not because of their accent but because they had to earn wages as soon as possible. For them there existed the municipal network of schools and institutes—a network which had to be improved at great speed, particularly the primary schools, to catch up with the influx of new inhabitants and the spread of tenement houses. Outside the old Wieden suburb there was a small huddle of houses, no more than five or six in 1850, when they were counted in with the suburban parish and borough. By 1870 they had been swallowed up in a densely populated district with its own parish church, and its own factories. It also had the largest colony of Czechs in all Vienna. And those factory workers of Favoriten, as the district came to be called, were the first group in town to establish a private Czech primary school for the benefit of their

children. I lived out there for some years, up to 1934, in one of the
blocks of small flats built for workers by a Social-Democratic Town
Council: nearly all my friends had Czech names, though few of them
could speak Czech any more, and it was still a factory district studded
with tenements built around 1870 and 1880, tall, sombre, insanitary,
the seamy side of the Ringstrasse era. But by then another new Vienna
was growing.

In 1862, Thomas Garrigue Masaryk—later to become Czechoslovakia's first President—came to Vienna to work as an apprentice,
twelve years old, with a Czech locksmith. He bolted back home, to the
estate where his father was bailiff. Seven years later he came again to
Vienna, this time as a private tutor, studied at a grammar school, went
to university and took his degree in philosophy there, became active
in a Czech academic association (the Česky akademicky spolek), taught
at a Viennese grammar school, and was a lecturer at Vienna University
before he took up his academic career in Prague. From 1869 to 1882
he was exposed to the conflicting influences of a city to which he never
surrendered. From 1891 to 1914 he was to be a member of Parliament
as a Czech nationalist—but never a chauvinist, always true to his
humanism—and to lead heated discussions in the new parliamentary
temple on the Ringstrasse. For better or worse, he learned about
the various shades of hollowed-out liberalism, confused socialism,
half-baked democracy, and bureaucratic "despotism mitigated by
muddle" (the famous phrase of Dr. Victor Adler, the founder and
leader of the Austrian Social-Democratic Party) in the Vienna of the
Ringstrasse era.

It sounds unjust to speak of hollowed-out liberalism, after recording
the solid achievements of the earliest Liberal Government and the good
work of the Liberals in the Town Hall of Vienna—which had many
other aspects, the most important being the construction of the great
aqueducts and water conduits for the supply of the city with pure
water from the limestone mountains, and the regulation of the Danube.
Both works, initiated and completed under Dr. Felder's leadership,
changed the everyday life of Vienna and went a long way towards
converting it into a modern metropolis. But liberalism as a current is
distinct from a Liberal Party; the party of the German and in particular
the Viennese Liberals was showing signs of fission. Transmuted liberal
ideas continued to fertilise the urban civilisation of Vienna, they went
into the making of a new democratic radicalism, and were absorbed by

the nascent working class movement. However, the Liberals with a capital L, who took office in successive governments up to 1878, when conservative combinations took over once more as they had done at intervals in between, were forced to show their mettle and colour under the stress of governing. Some emerged as true conservatives, like Schmerling or Giskra, though they retained their views on the political and cultural influence of the Church. Some proved excellent specialists—the Old Liberals had in their ranks a number of eminent jurists who did invaluable work on the codification of criminal and civil law, both as Ministers and in the First Chamber—but blinkered politicians. Some who had been enthusiastic members of the Academic Legion in 1848 veered towards a belief in German supremacy, from which the Josephinian gloss had faded. Others continued to be the cautious moderates they had already been during the Revolution, but now their moderation assumed a different tinge: they were moderate in face of the established order, not in their dealings with forces of the opposition against it. Those few who developed into democrats tended to leave their old circles. If Liberal leaders were accused of betraying their creed, the mistake was that of the accusers who had taken the shadow for the substance, and forgot that conditions had changed while the men merely remained their old selves. But for all Liberals in places of power the acid test was the "social question".

After a decade of financial stagnation, good times for promoters, financiers and share-pushers began as soon as the ground freed by the razing of the fortifications was released for purchase. A new law regulating trades and removing the antiquated privileges of craft guilds created better conditions for any manufacturer wanting to open a factory in or near Vienna; a new net of communication by road and rail began to take shape, as a first requirement for the growth of commerce. Textile trade and the textile industry were growing quickly. But there was no steady growth and prosperity even on the side of the manufacturers. Any external crisis of the State, in particular the Italian war of 1859, led to an economic setback, to foreclosures, bankruptcies—and mass unemployment. In 1862 so many spinning mills had to close and dismiss their workers that the Ministry of State called a conference in which the Mayor of Vienna and the Director of Police took part. The Mayor, Dr. Zelinka—a Liberal—"recognised that strict police surveillance of the unemployed, and the removal of harmful influence on them, were indicated, hence also the deportation [i.e. to their home parish] of those unemployed non-Viennese whose circumstances do not warrant special consideration. . . ."*

Working conditions had scarcely improved since 1848. The average working day was still twelve hours as a minimum—and was to stay so until the 'eighties. In the textile industry, more women than men were employed, as in other countries; and as in other countries in the early stages of the Industrial Revolution, child labour was employed as a matter of course. There existed a decree which banned children below twelve from factories, but exceptions were admitted, and were numerous. Even after the enactment of compulsory education for children from six to fourteen, it took many years before poor parents accepted it, and it was never wholly accepted by peasants in Austria. But among the groups of skilled workers in Vienna there began in the early 'sixties a movement for self-education which was a first political stirring. For five years, from 1862 to 1867, a few men tried again and again to obtain from the Government permission to start a workers' educational association. Liberal or conservative, the ministries always said no. Ludwig Brügel (*op. cit.*, vol. 1, p. 79) quotes an instruction from Anton von Schmerling—who was a Liberal-Conservative, the creator of the February Constitution—to the Governor of Lower Austria in which the rejection of the project to found such an association is explained as follows:

. . . In spite of the harmlessness of the stated purpose of this association, and although police investigations have not uncovered any positive objections to its foundation, a reference to experiences made in Germany outside Austria, particularly in Prussia, according to which similar workers' associations, if not alien to educational objectives from the start, always . . . pursue subversive tendencies in the political field at a later stage, rouses the serious apprehension that corresponding aberrations will also appear if a workers' association is formed in Vienna.

In Berlin, Ferdinand Lassalle had launched his "Workers' Programme" as the basis of a political mass movement for universal suffrage. Schmerling was not quite wrong when he argued that any working-class association would sooner or later go in the same direction. Two years later, in 1864, the first Workers' International Association was

* Ludwig Brügel, *Geschichte der österreichischen Sozialdemokratie*, Vienna, 1922, vol. 1, p. 734.

founded in London, with Karl Marx as its main inspirer. There was no
trade union, no working-class organisation in Vienna yet. Any strike
was a wild strike. Any movement was confused in its ideas, taking the
lead from Lassalle, or from a non-Socialist like Schulze-Delitzsch
who preached against "State-help" in favour of "self-help", or from
Bakunin, or from Karl Marx and Friedrich Engels. But the urge and the
need were there, and from Germany came workers who had finished
their political apprenticeship. In 1867, when the Ministry carried
through a liberal legislative programme, there were still no laws
granting freedom of association to the workers. It needed several
demonstrations in front of the Parliament to obtain a bill which,
hedged in by restrictive clauses, authorised meetings as well as the
founding of associations. The Workers' Educational Association of
Vienna was founded within a few weeks. This was the beginning.

It was followed by a period of aggressive enthusiasm. The manifesto
drawn up by one of the first workers' mass meetings demanded
universal suffrage, complete political democracy, and the systematic
"emancipation of the working class from capital"; it rejected all
religious and national prejudices, and appealed to workers of every
nationality in Austria to co-operate for freedom. A deputation took the
manifesto to Minister Giskra, who discussed it in detail with the men.
He told them that universal suffrage was wrong for Austria, then and at
all times. The "social question" was a slogan, bandied about but not
understood. (One of the workers answered: "A lot of people may not
know what that is, the social question, but everybody feels it.")
When another member of the deputation criticised the army practice
by which soldiers were ordered to go to confession, Giskra explained
that for a soldier religion was part of discipline. The interview, reported in the press, did much to estrange the politically minded section
of the Viennese workers—and to make them feel a radical distrust of
the Government.

In 1869, when the "government of citizens" had been replaced by a
conservative Ministry under Edward Count Taaffe (a man of Irish
origin), the economic situation had improved, the workers felt
stronger, their organisation, though still small, commanded wide
sympathies, and an open-air meeting of many thousands was held on a
part of the Glacis which was not yet built up. The purpose of the
meeting was to lend emphasis to a petition demanding the "right of
coalition", that is, the right to free association, above all in trade

unions. Karl Höger, who was present as a young man and became the leader of the typographers' union, says in his memoirs that building workers came in masses from the nearby sites along the Ringstrasse. Three workers, one of them the best speaker of the movement (but— a Berliner), took the petition to Count Taaffe, who called the whole procedure subversive. Next day a draft bill incorporating the points demanded was put before Parliament, and passed. But the mood of the meeting had not been tame. People had cheered Social Democracy, for which in Austria no party had yet come into being. Ten days later the ten workers who had signed the petition were indicted for high treason—Hartung, the Berliner, escaped in time—and given heavy prison sentences in a trial which shook the country.

The wind changed again. In 1873, the so-called Black Friday of the Viennese Stock Exchange crash finished off the boom, and started a chain of private financial disasters. Too many shares had been issued for too many unsound enterprises; when their value was wiped out or sadly reduced, money was scarce. Credits for building were stopped. Building in the private sector stopped. It was then that the State intervened, in the guise of an Imperial decree, to rescue the situation by large-scale public building. In this sense, the official show places along the Ringstrasse owe their existence to the collapse of the free market. The operation was successful: the patient did not die.

The slump, combined with renewed pressure by the police, split the new Socialist movement into a radical and a moderate group. The radicals drifted in the direction of Anarchism. The quarrels between the two groups grew violent. At a time when politics at parliamentary level seemed to hold out very little hope of fair play and assistance to the workers, the radical group with its programme of direct action appeared to offer far more than the moderates. Moreover, news from abroad was discouraging. The Communards of Paris had been crushed by a coalition of the victorious Prussians and the defeated French Army, turned Republican but not for that reason progressive. In prussianised Germany Bismarck's anti-socialist legislation did not destroy, but did hold down the Social Democrats. If Pope Pius IX had thrown an encyclical thunderbolt against liberalism, Leo XIII denounced in the Encyclical *Quod apostolici numeris* the "criminal league" of Socialists, Communists or Nihilists. In Austria herself, the Government of the day played one nationalist group against another, always securing the support of one or the other set of upper-class representatives. No

wonder that in a divided, bewildered, disorganised movement, a
council of despair seemed the only possible way: violence against
violence, as in Russia. A series of Anarchist attacks and a few assassina-
tions, proudly admitted, gave Count Taaffe an opportunity to declare
a state of emergency for Vienna and two provincial towns. This was in
1884, the year in which the new University was inaugurated, as the
last of the great Ringstrasse buildings except the Burgtheater.

From these depths rose the new, unified Social Democratic Party.
But its story begins in 1889, and belongs elsewhere.

Fifty years after the accession to the throne of Franz Joseph I, which
happens to be fifty years after the Revolution of 1848 as well, a Jubilee
Exhibition was organised in Vienna. It was, like all such exhibitions,
meant to demonstrate the qualities of Viennese products and help
export sales. A young architect, Adolf Loos, was commissioned to
write a series of articles about it for the most important Viennese daily,
the *Neue Freie Presse*. Loos, at that time twenty-eight years old, was an
iconoclast. After taking every collection of exhibits to pieces, as long
as it had anything to do with design, and not exclusively with technical
know-how, he turned against the vaunted façade of Vienna. In an
article entitled "Die Potemkinsche Stadt" (Potemkin's City),* he
first summarises the anecdote about Catherine of Russia's lover and
general, Potemkin, who rigged up villages in the Ukraine, with the
help of canvas and cardboard, to fake prosperity in a waste land for the
benefit of the empress. The term *Potemkinsche Dörfer*, Potemkin's
villages, is familiar in German. Then he attacks. Vienna is a Potemkin's
city. Every time he, Loos, walks along the Ring, he feels that a modern
Potemkin has tried to make Vienna look like a town populated by
noblemen. Everything that the Italian Renaissance conjured up as
palaces has been looted to give to "the plebs" the illusion of a new
Vienna. Even a simple man who lives on the top floor of such a
building, in a single room and cubicle, must have felt the thrill of
sharing in a feudal splendour, when looking at the façade.

Each front is "stuck on with nails". The ornamental details are
made of moulded cement so as to look like stucco or bronze or wood
or stone. The modern material is pressed into shapes that make it look
like something different. Everything is imitation. But this is typical

* Adolf Loos: *Ins Leere gesprochen* and *Trotzdem, Sämtliche Schriften*, vol. 1,
pp. 153 ff., Vienna, Herold, 1962.

of the last architectural period, the era of *parvenus*. The *parvenu* fondly believes that other people never notice the fake.

It is not shameful to be poor. We don't have to be ashamed of living as one tenant among many others, nor of the fact that some building materials are too expensive for us. Only if we accept that we are people of the nineteenth century (*sic*), not people who want to live in a house that pretends to belong to times past, will there be a genuine contemporary style. Nobody yet has found that style in Vienna, in our century.

Potemkin's spirit is hovering over nineteenth-century architecture in Vienna.

Thus Adolf Loos in 1898. Twelve years later he built the "house without eyebrows" in which there is no fake material, no pretence of past grandeur.

But as far as the Ringstrasse is concerned—and he speaks of the apartment houses which preceded and accompanied the public buildings, often anticipating their styles, however, since they were earlier efforts of the same architects—he is right and wrong in one. To chase at any price the "status symbol" and put, literally, a good front on it, was more than an aberration of taste or moral standards, and less than an attitude attributable to the whole city. It belonged to a definite situation and context: a social context in a given stretch of time. Behind Potemkin's façades there was waste land. Behind the Ringstrasse front there was a many-faced city. There were people in the painful transition stage between the old and the new, between mirage and reality. And they were found at every point on the social scale, from cotton-spinner to emperor.

2. THE RULERS

In the middle period of Franz Joseph's long reign, Viennese society still preserved intact the structure of a neatly stratified pyramid with the Emperor at its apex. He was no longer the absolute monarch *dei gratia*. His actions were limited and channelled by a constitution, his ministers responsible to Parliament. Yet in that Parliament, coalitions and configurations of parties constantly shifted. Governments would try to work through them, but simultaneously with and through the Emperor as the ultimate authority. Centrifugal forces tearing at the Austrian half of the Dual Monarchy made themselves unceasingly felt through various pressure gauges: the administrative machinery that had to function as if nothing were wrong, the parliamentary debates, and, on a different plane, the illuminating talk of soldiers who did their compulsory national service of three years in one of the regiments stationed at Vienna. There was no political stability, and people felt it. Thus the Emperor gained in importance at the very moment when his powers were constitutionally circumscribed, because he was the one and only fixed, unassailable figure: not a mere figurehead. It was indirect influence but all-pervading like radiation. This, then, is the point at which to consider the Emperor, his contemporary image and, as far as possible, the reality behind it.

In his great essay on Hofmannsthal and his times,* from which I shall have to draw contentious material more than once, Hermann Broch says:

Wilhelm I called himself the first soldier of his Empire, Edward VII was the first gentleman of Europe, Franz Joseph I was the abstract monarch as such.

And exactly this was the effect he had on his subjects, on archdukes no less than on the aristocracy and the middle class, and even on the workers. He, a man of very small calibre, a Habsburg in whom the hereditary characteristics of his race were not at all strongly marked, hence a man with little sense of political and social development, but also without immediate access to his fellow humans because he lacked any trace of humour, and in particular the Habsburg wit, in short, a rather blinkered, narrow, small-scale individual, was none the less able to become the epitome of majesty ... not because he carried a burden of personal misfortune almost as excessive as in a Greek tragedy, not because those misfortunes would have aroused reverence—reverential compassion is created from the stage, while in real life the mass is not an audience, and is therefore a stranger to compassion—but because he had come to be, perhaps through his very weaknesses, capable of taking upon himself the awe-inspiring dignity of absolute loneliness. ... Being the opposite of a people's emperor (*Volkskaiser*) he yet was "the" Emperor in the eyes of the people. (*Op. cit.*, pp. 74–75.)

It is necessary for Broch's vision of Viennese society or, as he calls it "Vienna's gay apocalypse around 1880", to see the Emperor in these terms. He describes how the idea of the State was hollowed out, "a rejected State" since 1848, a vacuum in which Franz Joseph identified the doom of the realm with his own, and turned himself into as abstract

* Hermann Broch, *Hofmannsthal und seine Zeit* (with a postscript by Hannah Arendt), Munich, Piper-Bücherei, 1964. This edition is a reprint from Broch's *Gesammelte Werke*, section *Dichten und Erkennen*, vol. I, Rhein-Verlag, 1955.

a figure as the State was an abstract concept; how the Emperor inevitably saw everybody, people, aristocracy and members of the House of
Habsburg, as destroyers driven by an urge for change, so that he alone
had to be immovable and unchangeable; how his own son's connexion
with ominous progressive forces was the "guiding trauma". Then
Broch explains that a "jelly-like democracy" existed in Vienna, in the
guise of a common language between the aristocracy and the people,
and a common flight into frivolity, with the image of the lonely
Emperor instilling a vague sense of the impending collapse of their
world. On the other hand, the machinery of the State was still functioning, even while its existence was in question; the only mystique, the
only "ethical and aesthetic" value to give meaning to the whole, was
the idea embodied in the solitary figure of the monarch. Of all the
social groups the one most firmly attached to the Emperor, de-
personalised though he was behind the "insulating layer", was the
Viennese middle and upper middle class. They found their own uncertain standards strutted and confirmed by the Emperor's conservative,
eclectic tastes which they eagerly tried to imitate, and were content to
be the public of court theatres, concerts and museums. The hallowing
seal was court approbation. And at the Burgtheater, at least, eclecticism was raised to the dignity of an original style with no other principle
than that of decorative entertainment: a non-aesthetic justification.
Less respectful strata might grumble, but the fires of revolt had died
down; the place of sharp popular satire had since Nestroy's death been
usurped by that frivolous travesty of the taste shared by court and
bourgeoisie, the operetta. It was pleasant and good-natured, *gemütlich*,
since nothing could be taken seriously in a state in which no one
believed. Vienna, the metropolis of *Kitsch*, becoming the metropolis
of the "value-vacuum" for the whole European era—this is how Broch
concludes the chapter.

I have given pride of place to Hermann Broch's argument about
Ringstrasse Vienna and the Emperor, although disagreeing with his
philosophical premises, his historical method, and several of his
interpretations, because his is by far the most distinguished version of a
judgement on that period and on Franz Joseph's character, which has
been expressed so often in various languages and generations that it
has to be taken seriously. Moreover, Broch's indictment, in explaining Hofmannsthal's lifelong quest for spiritual re-integration through
his recoil from the moral disintegration of late-nineteenth-century

Vienna, implicitly demonstrates the effect of the Ringstrasse culture on the rising generation. Hofmannsthal and Arnold Schönberg were born in Vienna in 1874; Karl Kraus, who was to become the implacable prosecutor of all that was rotten in the state of Austria and Vienna, was born in the same year in Bohemia, but grew to maturity in the capital. The second, "monumental" stage of the Ringstrasse building boom encompassed their formative years; they were adolescents on the threshold of a creative life when the era petered out around 1890, not with a bang and not with a whimper, but in shoddy pretentiousness, copying, pastiche. Hermann Broch, born in 1886, had not even childhood impressions of an exhilarating collective mood and gusto to temper his disgust, or if he had, he rejected them as spurious. And he, who was manager of a factory, knew the Viennese bourgeoisie only too well. But even to him there was still a sense of mysterious awe attached to the infinitely remote figure of the old Emperor, stiff with age and suppressed pain, but indomitably the defender of something that was going, going, and nearly gone.

Thus, Hermann Broch, writing in retrospect and from exile about the Vienna that had formed Hofmannsthal, but in truth about himself, the outsider, and his own mental world, is a witness with the kind of bias that obliquely illuminates the past. His portrait of Franz Joseph as the guardian of an impossible immutability of life, a man of "sparse humanity", indifferent to aesthetic values, a prisoner in his outsize "shell of solitude, in which he lived his uncannily bureaucratic, abstractly punctual life of a civil servant"—this portrait is, in its main features, the same that has been exhibited as life-like through three generations, from foreign observers of the 'eighties to Wickham Steed on the eve of the First World War, from the exasperated Austrian Josef Redlich's historical works and posthumously published "political diaries" to A. J. P. Taylor's *The Habsburg Monarchy*.

Rarely has the broad judgement on the disastrous function of a rigid monarchic system been so clearly endorsed from an unexpected quarter, and at the same time the public image of a monarch's personal character been so thoroughly overthrown, as by the publication of a significant part of Franz Joseph's private letters. But this was to come much later, from 1930 onward, under the first and second Austrian republics. In the early 'eighties, however, an old Russian ex-diplomat, writing in French under the name of Count Vasili* about that Viennese

* Comte Paul Vasili, *La société de Vienne*, 11th (enlarged) edition, Paris, 1885.

society whose top layers and top people he claimed to have known from within for many years, suavely contributed bleak details to the internationally accepted portrait of the Emperor.

He lived in Olympian isolation, Vasili said, not even mixing with the high aristocracy, but only with members of the Imperial house, the five-and-sixty archdukes and archduchesses who were numerous enough to make exclusiveness possible. If the Emperor ever descended from Olympus, for instance to show himself at an aristocratic ball, "it was not to live, be it for a fleeting moment, the life of a mere mortal, but to represent there the majesty of the sovereign"—for a short while, with a few gracious words. It was no different at other great balls, those given by important bourgeois corporations and associations, nor at the two ceremonial balls in the Hofburg, the Court Ball, to which not only the court but also civic dignitaries, army officers, and the wearers of Imperial decorations were invited together with their wives, and the Ball at Court, restricted to the Diplomatic Corps, officers on active service in Vienna (who made good dancing-partners for archduchesses), and the blue-blooded nobility.

Vasili, of course, recorded facts that were common knowledge, but no less characteristic for all that: the Emperor had only one relaxation, to go hunting in the mountains, stalking chamois or stag, or waiting patiently before sunrise for the moment when the black-cock, or the *Auerhahn*, the Alpine wood-grouse, would be deaf and blind in his mating-dance so that the hunter could come close enough to place a shot. Franz Joseph, though Vasili did not mention this, was not fond of battues, which so excited Kaiser Wilhelm II and Archduke Franz Ferdinand; he loved the lonelier and more skilful forms of hunting and shooting, perhaps because he had to prove to himself that in the end, when gamekeeper and stalker had officiously guided him, it was his own muscular co-ordination, steady hand and sharp eye which counted. This is a theme which was to turn up more than once, with rueful vanity, in his correspondence of later years.

But then Vasili touched on much the same points as Broch did two generations later, from the other extreme of the intellectual spectrum. He spoke of the way in which the Emperor in his early youth, under the impact of 1848, had been forced to subdue "all his tastes" to make public peace possible. Turning himself into a constitutional monarch "with an ease that has often been taken for lack of will", he renounced personal power. Everything he had wished of the future collapsed,

Vasili said. Instead of making traditional policy in the grand manner, as Maria Theresia's successor, he had to be satisfied with a muted rôle in a monarchy where the ministers carried the responsibility, to become "a kind of civil servant without initiative and without prominence. He accepted it simply, sadly, as a duty and discipline." Now he was signing papers put before him, starting at 5 a.m. and carrying on through lunchtime, with the help of a hasty meal taken at his desk. He would have discussions with his ministers, but without heat. (By all accounts, Vasili exaggerated the Emperor's coolness, though not his unflagging application to routine work.) He would read only a few papers, but study the press survey specially prepared for him as a cross-cut through public opinion. "He never oversteps the limits he has accepted. Only in hunting does he become himself again."

The new Dual Monarchy was full of contradictions. Many people would have liked a more personal, more representative monarch; on the other hand, the smaller nations would have resented any added pressure from the centre. The dynasty was the only connecting link, but since the Constitution was here to stay, there was no room left for a Caesar. If gratitude was owed to Franz Joseph for not having resisted "the modern current", it had also to be accepted that he withdrew himself into isolation, away from the masses. . . . For the past years he had only reflected the opinions predominating in his realm, so that he appeared in turn democratic and reactionary, clerical and liberal, centralist and federalist. This was the result of sublime self-effacement, the sign of a rare detachment. Vasili held that a remark attributed to the Emperor expressed his essence, whether it was true or invented. He was supposed to have said to Count Andrássy (who had been sentenced to death *in absentia* in 1849, had returned to Hungary after years in exile to become its constitutional premier, and was Imperial Foreign Minister between 1871 and 1878, as well as the confidant of the Empress): "I'm very happy those who were sentenced to death for high treason to me weren't all executed, because that way I could make them my premiers later on."

Count Vasili, then, was perceptive enough to credit Franz Joseph with self-irony and a dry sense of humour. It was, however, the more chilling part of the pen portrait—the punctual, frugal civil servant; the remoteness even from the high aristocracy; the lack of paternalism—which strengthened the prevalent foreign opinion. Vienna as a city was popular once again. The beautiful Empress was a living legend abroad, pitied for her unequal marriage with a dry stick. Viennese waltzes, and Viennese operettas by Johann Strauss, Millöcker and Suppé were acceptable exports. But neither the foreign policy of the Dual Monarchy, nor the Emperor who appeared elusive and unreliable as an ally, inspired much confidence among the makers of public opinion in other countries. A. J. P. Taylor quotes a dictum by Gladstone in the electoral campaign of 1880: "There is not a spot on the whole map where you can lay your finger and say: 'There Austria did good!'" (*The Struggle for Mastery in Europe, 1848–1918*, p. 284.) There can be little doubt that the figure which Franz Joseph had presented since his accession to the throne added to the distrust his many political blunders provoked; for it was one of the built-in dangers of his position that every mistake committed by a minister, whether he had shared actively in it or only let it happen, was laid at his door.

Even the half-hidden disasters of the Emperor's private life increased the chill that emanated from him in those years. It was a public secret that his marriage with Elisabeth had turned into failure and unhappiness: she made it more than obvious, she forced it upon people's consciousness, by staying away from her husband, the court, Vienna, and frequently Austria for many months. And it was not always an escape through illness, or rather into illness and neurosis. Whenever she was on her own in Corfu or Hungary, fox-hunting in England or Ireland, she seemed to blossom. In times of acute crisis, such as the war of 1866, she deployed nervous energy and self-forgetful warmth —leading in 1866 to a temporary resumption of her marriage, of which her last and most beloved child, Valerie, was the fruit. Otherwise she did as she liked, and mostly she liked to get away, something the Emperor had to deny himself. The Viennese resented her absences for bad and for just reasons.

Originally, when it became known that the Emperor's lovely child-wife was on bad terms with her formidable mother-in-law and aunt, Sophie of Bavaria (and the double relationship must have given edge to Sophie's arrogation of authority), all sympathies were with the Empress. The Archduchess was disliked by Viennese liberals, then a majority in the city, because of her political activities and her close alliance with Cardinal-Archbishop Rauscher. Since the Emperor was clearly devoted to his young wife, he profited from the wave of sentimental partisanship on the principle that all the world loves a lover. Yet as soon as the grapevine that connects even an insulated court with the outside world passed news of Sophie's victories—her insistence on an etiquette which would compensate her for having in 1848 renounced her own legitimate claim to be Empress, her management of the upbringing of the Emperor's two elder daughters, her continued influence on the Emperor himself, and Elisabeth's withdrawal from the rights and duties of her position—public opinion swung round. As far as it is possible to penetrate the fog of loyalist pretence and romantic legend (the stories about "Sisi" are of later date), it seems that the estrangement of the Imperial couple made people grumble equally at Archduchess Sophie's domineering, interfering ways, at the Emperor's weak-kneed subservience to his mother, and at the Empress's refusal to live up to a responsibility she had once chosen to accept. For the Viennese, it was added provocation that Elisabeth made a display of her love for Hungary and the Hungarians. They would flock to every pageant and public appearance of royalty, and cheer quite sincerely; but cheering is too infectious to be a yardstick of enthusiasm on such an occasion, and it is impossible to assess exactly what part of the city "they" represented. The private memoirs of the times, as distinct from descriptions calculated for publicity, show scant evidence of dynastic fervour. Still, the Viennese have always liked to look at any colourful spectacle.

Elisabeth herself was bitterly aware of her unpopularity in Vienna; it comes out in extracts from diaries of her ladies-in-waiting, published in Egon Conte Corti's biography of the Empress. And even a courtier like Vasili observed: ". . . in democratic Austria [i.e. in contrast to the chivalrous nobility and gentry of Hungary] the princess and the people are strangers to each other."

The anomalous situation of the Empress affected the court, by delivering it to the rule of Archduchess Sophie as long as her influence with her son lasted, and to the routine of the four chief officials. It was a lustreless court, inevitably. To quote Vasili again: "It is difficult to imagine a court entirely separated from the Emperor and meeting him only on very rare occasions, yet this is more or less what happens. . . ." Franz Joseph was too immersed in duties and worries to care. He could only be grateful to his mother who took over where his wife left off. The princes and counts who occupied the posts of Grand Master of the Household, Grand Chamberlain, Chief Marshal, and Master of the Horse, had to keep a vast machine turning for its own sake. It meant that some of the stiff old ceremonial crept back. True Spanish etiquette had died with Charles VI, as Maria Theresia's most faithful servant and Grand Master of the Household, Prince Johann Joseph Kheven-hüller-Metsch, sadly recorded in his diaries.* Joseph II had impatiently introduced further modern reforms, and Franz I had given a Bieder-meier air of domestic contentment and simplicity to his household almost to the point of middle-class cosiness, except on great occasions. Franz Joseph himself had called his governess *Amie* and was called by her by his pet name, Franzi. At that time, his mother Sophie had protected his gaiety, and with success, as his teasing letters to his brothers show. But now, with Franz Joseph chained to his endless working day, and the Empress abdicating her responsibilities, there was a void at court which the high-born officials filled with ritual. It insulated and isolated the Emperor even more. It may also (this is guesswork) have affected the highly-strung heir to the throne and pushed him into experiments with freedom.

Crown Prince Rudolph ended a suicide. Born in 1858, he was precocious, gifted and unstable. He had a surfeit of imagination and suffered from more than the customary occupational diseases of crown princes, the diseases of non-occupation and love-hatred for the sovereign parent. In him, the sense of guilt was obsessive; it took many forms, such as a desperate pessimism about the future of the realm he would inherit—it is trite but inescapable to think of a submerged wish for his father's death. The Empress, wanting him to have a rich, un-fettered life of the mind, loaded him with too many teachers on too many subjects. But his father, too, had been grossly overtaxed as a growing boy: Archduchess Sophie, aware that her feeble husband would never make an emperor, and investing her ambitions—in-

---

* *Aus der Zeit Maria Theresias. Tagebuch des Fürsten Johann Joseph Khevenhüller-Metsch, Kaiserlicher Obersthofmeister 1742–1776,* 3 vols., Leipzig, 1907. Kheven-hüller was on the side of the grand manners of the older generation, and upset by Maria Theresia's nonchalance, her readiness to introduce innovations, and by small symbolic changes such as the banning of the black Spanish court dress. In Vol. 2, p. 219, he complains that less trouble was taken to cover up a love intrigue than would have been "under the previous, very strict régime". On the following page he criticises, sharply for a courtier, the fact that at the memorial service for Charles VI, court ladies residing at Schönbrunn were permitted to turn up in "*sacs* or *robes de chambre*" instead of court or "apartment" dresses. His diaries record the gradual breakdown of the Spanish court ceremonial—and he did his best to delay it.

cluding her ambitions for a reunited Germany under a Habsburg—in her son, planned his education with a single mind but not always a good eye for the quality of his educators. (All this goes far to explain her possessiveness and Franz Joseph's addiction to her and her judgement, in spite of all, because it was she who had made him. Elisabeth, on the other hand, transferring her frustrated emotional and intellectual ambitions to Rudolph, sent him away, away from his father but also from herself.)

Between six and eighteen, Franz Joseph had learned French, Italian, Hungarian and Czech, had studied—meticulously—all that might be of use to a future ruler, from natural sciences and technology, as far as it made industrial development comprehensible, to ecclesiastical, criminal, common and constitutional law, and had been exposed to the influence of two powerful tutors, Metternich in politics, and Prelate Rauscher in philosophy. At eighteen, when he was crowned, he had emerged from that forcing process with his excellent memory trained, his capacity for absorbing facts developed, his curiosity blunted and his innate ebullience dimmed, but in no visible way a neurotic. His son Rudolph, however, had an entirely different potential. No amount of study or teaching could have turned Franz Joseph into an intellectual or a man of artistic sensibility. But Rudolph showed the makings of an intellectual at an early stage. He also lived—the overworked tag applies —in a state of emotional insecurity which he was at pains to hide from his father, and from the court he despised. By way of compensation Rudolph sought popularity, public approval, and friends. Soon he was very popular indeed; the democratic wing of the Viennese bourgeoisie adopted the Crown Prince as its white hope.

Crown Prince Rudolph travelled, and wrote two travel books, well-illustrated, fluent in style, best in their observations on birds and animals. Or so I seem to remember: I never read these tomes properly from end to end, they belonged on occasional tables in self-respecting salons of our grandparents' generation, together with other gilt-edged works, too heavy to hold comfortably, more steel engravings than texts, on the Khedive's Egypt, or on customs of the Bavarian Alps. But Rudolph's travel books were serious in their purpose and, above all, in their meaning for him. They made him free of self-doubt, one may assume, when he met Viennese intellectuals. The newspaper-owner and journalist with whom Rudolph became intimate, Moritz Szeps of the *Neue Wiener Tagblatt*, was clever, though not in the highest category of his profession; he launched his journal in 1867, in competition with the leading organ of the bourgeoisie, the *Neue Freie Presse*, stressed its democratic character, and was out to capture the cultured but not exactly wealthy middle class. In his many letters to Szeps, the Crown Prince was rashly communicative. One, which is often quoted, spoke of inevitable social upheavals to come. In a similar mood, Rudolph had written to his ex-tutor Latour as an adolescent, when he called the Habsburg empire a mighty ruin and predicted its total collapse at the next gale.

It cannot be said that Szeps abused the confidence shown to him, but he, and others like him in Vienna, could not but see themselves as powers next to the throne in a not too distant future. By his character and attitude, Rudolph created hopes and illusions among those who, vaguely progressive and modernistic, were not capable of forming a radical party with a clear programme. The government in power, at that time of the 'eighties one under Count Taaffe, kept a watchful eye on Rudolph and his circle, as well as on his far more doubtful private exploits. His marriage to a young Belgian princess, Stephanie, did little to domesticate him. Viennese gossip blamed Stephanie, who was considered a ninny. Rudolph, in any case, ran wild with friends, young aristocrats and occasionally bohemians, had abortive affairs with society women, and regularly stayed with a notorious woman of the *demi-monde* who was handled by a procuress (she, in her turn, kept the police informed to be on the safe side). He also contracted bad debts. Once, about two years before his suicide, he was treated for a "serious illness" that shattered his nerves, caused him anxiety for the future, and altogether sounded, in spite of circumlocutions, like syphilis. On two points, however, he was careful and precise. He zealously attended to his duties in the Army, not merely because the emperor would never have forgiven neglect but also because he loved army life as much as his father did; and he managed to cover up the dubious side of his private existence from everybody except his valet, his pet fiacre cabbie Bratfisch, and a couple of intimates.

Rudolph was getting more and more entangled with Hungarian politics, less harmlessly so than with the Viennese progressives. His friend, Stefan Count Károlyi, who belonged to the opposition, came to Vienna for a conference with him. If the Emperor learned about it (and Rudolph himself had a superstitious belief in Franz Joseph's omniscience) it must have cut him to the quick. Rudolph's biographer

Oskar von Mitis has adduced evidence that the file about Károlyi's visit to the Crown Prince in connection with a pending Defence Bill had been removed from the Court and State Archives; presumably it would have compromised Rudolph too badly. Another historian who must be counted among the monarchist sympathisers, Jean de Bourgoing, editor of the Emperor's letters to Frau Katharina Schratt, admits that Rudolph may have intended to be crowned King of Hungary in his father's lifetime, and that the whole Hungarian complex may have been cause and subject of a "fateful discussion" between father and son a few days before the suicide. Nobody knows, unless there is some record guarded from profane eyes in one of the family archives, what exactly happened. Perhaps several latent conflicts were brought up. Stephanie had talked to the Emperor about Rudolph's strangely changed behaviour. And Franz Joseph may also have heard of Rudolph's intention or attempt to have his marriage dissolved; the Head of Police, for one, accepted it as a fact that the Crown Prince had taken steps in this direction, either with the Papal Nunzio or the Pope himself, and put it down in his secret memorandum after the catastrophe. If the Emperor knew, what would have been his reaction? Divorce was impossible for a Habsburg sovereign or sovereign-to-be. Even Elisabeth had only taken herself away.

There was also evidence, before the final act, that Rudolph's mind was taking strange turns. He talked much of death and suicide. He had even asked one of his casual bedfellows to enter into a suicide pact with him, but she had run to the police in fright. Details accumulated in files that were known to *Polizeipräsident* Baron Krauss, the Head of Police, his deputy, and certainly to the Prime Minister Count Taaffe as well. Taaffe had too much political tightrope-walking to do not to be careful; he knew that Rudolph loathed his illiberal policies and himself. In any case, a network of agents and informers reported on the Crown Prince's movements, his conversations, his drinking and wenching. The reports were explosive matter. They were kept confidential —the Emperor could not possibly have countenanced this police procedure—and held in reserve.

Finally, least important but of some interest all the same, there was the story which first excited sensation-mongers and still feeds films about the "Drama of Mayerling": Rudolph's love affair with Mary Vetsera. Marie von Vetsera, usually called Mary by her friends, was seventeen, fresh out of convent, pretty, naïve, and deeply in love with

Rudolph. The two used to meet in the apartment of a Bavarian niece of
Empress Elisabeth's, the Countess Larisch-Wallersee, whom, in a later
interview with the Head of Police, the procuress connected with
Rudolph's *demi-monde* friend accused, with a professional's indignation,
of having acted as go-between. It is hard to say whether Rudolph was at
that stage capable of an outgoing emotion that could be called love,
but the young girl touched him, and she gave him a last companion-
ship. He had always been afraid of loneliness.

On the night of 29 January 1889, Crown Prince Rudolph shot first
Mary Vetsera and then himself in the bedroom, on the bed, of his small
hunting lodge at Mayerling, deep in the Wienerwald. They were discovered in the morning. The Empress was told about it, and she told
the Emperor. In the meantime, the Chief of Police and the Prime
Minister had been informed as well. They went into action, some of it
hasty, inept and, in retrospect, futile, like the fatuous attempt to
remove the worst stigma of scandal by a furtive burial of Mary
Vetsera. The first special edition in the streets of Vienna said that the
Crown Prince had died of heart failure. Then the Emperor himself,
and Dr. Widerhofer, the physician, insisted, against the resistance of the
court, on telling the essential truth to the people. The fiction of heart
failure was dropped. As a suicide, who had taken his life while of
unsound mind, Rudolph was entombed in the Habsburg vault below
the *Kapuzinerkirche*, with the shattering, humbling severity of the
ancient ritual of his house. It took longer for the part of the story concerning the unhappy girl Mary to leak out. She had been buried out of
sight. Her mother, however, talked, and newspaper men from all over
Europe were on the track.

Because it is a footnote to Viennese society in those years, Mary
Vetsera's family deserves an explanation. Her mother, Baroness Helene
Vetsera, was a luscious woman whom the Emperor had once shrewdly
suspected of designs on his son. Married to a diplomat, she came from a
Levantine family of bankers, the Baltazzis, who had been taken up at
Istanbul by some Austrian aristocrats, and had gone to Vienna, where
they flourished. They flourished by banking, inter-marriage with blue
blood, and horse-racing. Through racing, one of the brothers came in
touch with the Empress, and later, because he kept a stable, also with
the Emperor's friend, Katharina Schratt. Vasili mentions the Baltazzis
somewhat cynically: "That marriage [between Aristide Baltazzi and a
countess] is accepted because the Baltazzis are of those *roturiers* whom

the great world adopts and absorbs . . . the horse, as one knows, is an aristocratic animal that ennobles. . . ." The Emperor alone had his reservations. In a letter to Frau Schratt of 7 June 1888, he lightly warns her against Hector (Aristide) Baltazzi and his horses. Also,

though I speak with him myself from time to time, and the Empress was friendly with him and his wife in earlier years, he has not an altogether correct reputation in matters of racing and finance, so that some considerable time back he was warned off the turf in England. I don't know the ins and outs, and don't want to do him any harm, therefore I beg you most earnestly in no case to make use of my remarks. After all, I couldn't give him satisfaction [i.e. in a duel] in the Prater meadows, not even in the half-dark of dawn . . . (*Briefe Kaiser Franz Josephs an Frau Katharina Schratt*, edited by Jean de Bourgoing, Vienna, 1949.)

Two years later, when the Baltazzi-Vetsera clan had been crushed by their involvement in the Mayerling affair—during that inhuman night drive in the rain to hurry Mary Vetsera's body away, it had been the two brothers Baltazzi who had held their dead niece upright between them in the carriage—the Emperor wrote again to Katharina Schratt about one of them, this time Alexander Baltazzi. Obviously Frau Schratt had apologised for her continued friendly contact with him. Franz Joseph said, most characteristically:

I have never made any objection to your relationship with Alexander Baltazzi, because it would have been nonsense; on the contrary, I was grateful that through it I could learn much from you, at a difficult time, which it was important for me to know. That it was under his auspices you undertook the ascension in the balloon [an adventure of Katharina Schratt's which upset the Emperor as involving a silly risk, and a publicity scoop for others] doesn't matter a hoot to me, on my honour, but in the eyes of the wicked world this fact, which has been emphasised in the press, will be damaging for you, since the Baltazzi family is not well regarded in some circles after our misfortune.

It is not astonishing that Franz Joseph, with a faint dislike and contempt for those brash upstarts at the back of his mind, was at first convinced of a sequence of events which would have meant tragedy and death but not destruction of all his beliefs: he jumped to the conclusion that Mary Vetsera had poisoned his son, out of whatever passionate madness, and then taken poison herself. (On the first discovery, nobody had examined the bodies, and Count Hoyos had reported a glass on the night table.) It was very difficult for him to accept as truth what his trusted physician told him. Even now, when the external facts are sufficiently documented to sweep away the melodramatic fantasies which have accrued—now, when we have become accustomed to face rather than obliterate signs of mental sickness—there is a residue of enigma in the suicide and murder-by-consent committed by Rudolph of Habsburg. For Franz Joseph, there must have been behind it a spectre he had to exorcise from his mind at any price, if he was to go on, that of his wife's melancholia. And Elisabeth had to defend herself for the rest of her life against a conviction that she had passed on to her son a fatal streak of madness, of the Wittelsbach madness.*

There exists a record of the decisive days, written in longhand by the Chief of Police, Baron Krauss, as a secret *aide-mémoire*, accessible only to his deputy. It sounds like an attempt at justifying his inaction as well as his actions, is confused, has gaps and contradictions, but is supplemented by many reports of police officers, agents and outside informants, in all 248 registration numbers and about 500 pages. As nothing else could do, except, if it ever existed, an equally frank account by Count Taaffe, it reflects the attitudes of the highest executives and the wild confusion that spread from them downward through Vienna. In 1955, the documents were published in facsimile under the title *Das Mayerling-Original, Offizieller Akt des K.K. Polizeipräsidiums.*

Krauss starts with the day before the suicide, when Mary Vetsera had already left her home, having alarmed her family and friends with dark hints, and Countess Larisch came to appeal to Krauss to take action in Mayerling, where Mary was assumed to stay with Rudolph, before her mother went to the Emperor in her desperation. (Helene Vetsera did in fact go to the Empress the next day, and was told of her

* Edward Crankshaw, in *The Fall of the House of Habsburg*, Longmans, 1962, gives an excellent, comprehensive analysis of the characters of Archduchess Sophie, Empress Elisabeth, Franz Joseph I and Rudolph, their interrelationship, and the Mayerling story. Dealing with Austria's political history he uses a much wider canvas. To the best of my knowledge, his is the only account based on all the documents, letters, etc., published in recent years, which has appeared in English, so that it is a much needed corrective to earlier, inevitably lopsided works. I read it when the semi-final version of this book was written, and found myself in nearly complete agreement with his psychological appraisals; I also found that I had often picked the same passages for my purpose, which he quotes for his. I have not tried to change this systematically, because Mr. Crankshaw and I obviously have had to use the same sources—and sometimes the same conclusions seem to have been reached.

daughter's end by Rudolph's mother.) Krauss prevaricated. Mayerling was outside his police district so that he could do nothing; in any case it was Rudolph's private property, and investigations there were as much out of the question as in the Hofburg itself. Baroness Vetsera should lodge a formal complaint about her daughter's disappearance, but under no conditions could he "connect the name of the Crown Prince with the affair".

Marie Larisch was clearly frightened about possible repercussions for herself. Krauss, however, was worried neither about Marie Larisch nor about Mary Vetsera, but about complications for himself and his chief, Taaffe, should Mary's mother really have an interview with the Emperor. He hurried to speak to Taaffe and prepare him for all events. Taaffe lightly dismissed the problem with remarks about Baroness Vetsera, that old sinner, who probably had herself played procuress for her daughter in this case. But more should be found out. When Krauss called on Taaffe in the new Parliament a second time that evening of 19 January, just as the electric lighting was being tested, Baroness Vetsera had already been to see the Premier. Taaffe insinuated that another man might be responsible for the girl's absence; there had been gossip about Heinrich Prince Liechtenstein, and in any case the Crown Prince would not have had a first night with Mary. No *prima nox*, Krauss records: their minds were concentrating on means to avert from the Crown Prince the blame of having seduced a minor. But Taaffe had news, more concrete than Krauss's vague information through agents, that Rudolph had inexplicably stayed away from the family dinner in the Hofburg, where the Emperor had kept the table laid for him to the last, hoping against hope. Krauss and Taaffe seem to have believed in a row between father and son two days before because of a letter from the Vatican about Rudolph's divorce plans.

Before the day ended, before the final blow, Krauss arranged for his agents in the Hofburg to keep him informed of comings and goings— always that obsession with Baroness Vetsera!—and he also tried to find out whether Rudolph really had cooled off in his intermittent liaison with Mitzi Kaspar, a dancer, operetta *soubrette*, and mistress of a lawyer with whom Krauss was in touch via the procuress looking after Mitzi's interests. (As his record makes plain, Krauss had watched over Rudolph's "security" by surrounding him with a web of spies who reported on all his political and private escapades.) Perhaps he hoped

that the affair with Mary Vetsera could be played down if the Crown
Prince was shown to be otherwise engaged. Now he called in the
lawyer who paid for Mitzi Kaspar's apartment. He learned that
Rudolph had spent the night of 27 January, following the day on which
he was supposed to have quarrelled with the Emperor, drinking
champagne with Mitzi, but also making the sign of the cross, and
talking, as he often did, of death as an obligation imposed by honour.
It was all irrelevant, and at the same time tragically relevant, if Krauss
had been able to understand. He probably understood better that
Rudolph had been harassed by a debt, rumoured to be about 300,000
florins, to the international banker Hirsch; it was a rumour which he
reported to Taaffe, and in which Taaffe believed.

When 30 January was over, and at Taaffe's order Krauss had done his
worst with Mary Vetsera, spiriting away her body to the abbey of
Heiligenkreuz with the help of the Baltazzi brothers, reports came in
about Vienna's reaction to the news. According to the agents, the
favourite explanation of the inexplicable suicide was, among the
court circles, the hopelessness of Rudolph's passion for Aglaia Princess
Auersperg. The oddest popular rumour they reported was that a jealous
gamekeeper had castrated the Crown Prince who then had killed
himself out of unbearable pain.

The stereotyped version of Viennese chronicles is that the hours of
mourning which united Emperor and people on the death of the
Crown Prince, so sincerely beloved, forged a new bond between the
ruler and the ruled. A more discriminating historian, who however
belonged to the camp of the man who became heir presumptive,
Archduke Franz Ferdinand, says ambiguously:

For Vienna, Viennese society, and the intellectual currents in the capital, the
death of Crown Prince Rudolph in 1889 was of shattering importance. . . .
Archduke Rudolph was representative of that most interesting cultural period,
with all its spiritual ambitions and conflicts. His greatness fell victim to a fate
that was stronger. (Richard Kralik, *op. cit.*, p. 730.)

To this day, there are old gentlemen and ladies in Vienna, mostly
about eighty years old, who will speak of Crown Prince Rudolph as the
man who might have prevented the collapse of the Austro-Hungarian
Monarchy if he had lived to be Emperor. (He would have been fifty-
eight in 1916, when Franz Joseph died, and it would be futile to conjecture his psychological development without a catastrophe.) One

such old lady said to me in 1963: "The Crown Prince was so gifted and so modern-minded, quite a freethinker, he would have been the right leader for us." When I objected that she could not have been more than three at the time of his suicide, she answered simply: "But that's what my papa and his friends always used to say." For her, as for many with monarchist leanings in present-day Austria, the might-have-been of Rudolph was linked to nostalgic childhood memories. To her father, no doubt, his premature death was the loss of a potential leader who would have offered hopes of a social renewal without party battle—just what the non-political but vaguely democratic Viennese middle class longed for. Their utopia was killed on the day Rudolph committed suicide.

In reality, the beginnings of Republican convictions among the Viennese—and I have to confine myself to Vienna—go back to that day which brought it home to not a few that a hereditary system exposes the body politic to personal accidents with the widest, most disastrous consequences for the whole. The Emperor was getting old. His new heir was distrusted. Army and Civil Service might clamp the disrupted parts together in the name of the Supreme Commander-in-Chief, to whom they had sworn loyalty, but the feeling gained ground that Franz Joseph's death would be the end of the monarchy. The Empress herself felt it. She told her daughter Valerie, as Corti mentions in his book *Elisabeth, die seltsame Frau*, on the strength of Valerie's diary, that she and her husband should leave the country as soon as the Emperor was dead, because it was clear what would happen afterwards. And Norah Wydenbruck, daughter and granddaughter of princes and counts of the realm, says in her autobiography (*My Two Worlds*, London, 1956) that, ever since she could remember, everybody had been saying: "It will be the end of Austria when the Old Gentleman closes his eyes."

Franz Joseph had become *der alte Herr*, the Old Gentleman. (But people who wanted to make a joke about him without getting into trouble called him Old Prochaska, using a very common surname of Czech origin as camouflage.) He retired deeper into his official shell. But—in direct contradiction to Hermann Broch's portrait of him— his vein of humorous self-irony and his warmth did not dry up. They were reserved for the smallest possible circle, his wife and daughters, his trusted entourage, and his friend Katharina Schratt. It took Corti's books with their quotations from archducal archives, from the diaries

of the Empress Elisabeth's ladies, and from Franz Joseph's letters to his
wife and his daughter Valerie, and even more it took Jean de Bourgoing's edition of the Emperor's letters to Katharina Schratt from 1886
to 1916, to prove how different the public face in public places was
from the private face in private places.

Bit by bit another Franz Joseph stood revealed, one capable of giving
and receiving tenderness, and of making jokes against himself, a man
who would have been happy and successful as C.O. of an infantry
regiment, not a blimp, but scarcely with a marshal's baton in his trim
breast pocket either, and predestined to retire to a modest country
seat with good shooting attached. No small-scale individual of "sparse
humanity", as Hermann Broch believed the Emperor to be, even
though limited in his responses and ideas; nobody is "of very small
calibre" if he has the complete integrity and devotion Franz Joseph
gave to the smallest personal matter. But very vulnerable, a fusser
because he believed in the cussedness of people and things, a shrewd
judge of men as long as they were not out of the ordinary, and aware
that he was a bit of a bore.

There was Franz Joseph comparing himself in his Imperial rôle to a
turkey-cock, and cheerfully submitting to being called *póka* which is
Hungarian for turkey, by his wife hereafter; signing himself in his
letters to Elisabeth (it may set one's teeth on edge, but it was candid and
sincere) "Your Mannikin" or "Your Little One"; writing bluntly that
he was getting older and stupider (*blöder*) and that was all there was to
it. Again and again, to Elisabeth and Frau Schratt, he wrote, speaking
of some crowded gala function, that he had had only one wish: "I
want to get out." This, in Viennese dialect "Aussi möcht i", became a
formula with him. The "nimbus" as a wry word for the halo of
remote majesty he had to exhibit when on public show, seems to have
been another self-mocking formula he used, perhaps after having been
told by Frau Schratt that the nimbus surrounding him had awed her;
there was an occasion when the Emperor told Frau Schratt in a letter
that he would have dashed up to her in an exhibition hall as soon as he
saw her, if "that nasty nimbus" had not kept him back.

The letters to Katharina Schratt, written in a mixture of formal style
and Viennese turns of speech, not without the grammatic quirks of
Viennese dialect, are full of such small things. From Budapest he sends
her seven photos of her "brotherly friend" (this refers to a ticklish
conversation they had had) which would make her laugh; notably the

picture that "shows the great statesman musing at his desk", another in which "the commander-in-chief gives orders to his *aides-de-camp*", and then, "the incredible number of orders decking out the gala uniform". Her comments on the photographs had made him laugh a lot, he says in a following letter. He likes to poke fun at his own shortcomings as a public orator ("I spoke without getting stuck, and that without a prompter"), and to pat himself on the back whenever he had been particularly *aimable*—always the French adjective—at a reception or ball without being in the right mood for it. The emptiness of his speeches and official conversations is obvious to him: ". . . as usual, I said nothing intelligent . . ." His asides on people with whom he had conversed in his most *aimable* manner are sometimes a little malicious. Of course he spoke first with Baron Königswarter—one of the most important bankers in Vienna—on getting to the hotel in Gastein; the man had, after all, not only ceded him the use of a salon there, but also boasted everywhere about his largesse. The Queen of Rumania, Carmen Sylva, was very nice, almost too nice, and occasionally a little hard to take because of her exaltation. On the other hand there is an immediate, most human reaction to sorrow, other people's and his own. It occurs in a most peculiar form in a letter written after the death of Franz Joseph's personal valet. At first it sounds revoltingly callous. "I don't know what I shall do now, especially on journeys when I have to take along civilian clothes which are so difficult to wear and select properly." Franz Joseph says that Pachmayer had been "a gentleman through and through" (using the English term), but follows this up with the epithets ingenious, willing, indefatigable, clever. It still sounds cold, as though spoken from the top of the feudal pyramid—as it was, in its way. But then Franz Joseph tells his friend that even his adjutant-general Paar had had tears in his eyes. "Not I, because I have become too blunted by now (this was five years after Rudolph's suicide, in 1894, when the Emperor was sixty-four), but it has hit me most painfully all the same."

Katharina Schratt was a popular young actress at the Burgtheater when the Emperor first took notice of her. He went nearly every evening to "his" theatre, till 1888 to the old building next to the Hofburg and later to the less beloved new one, to find relaxation. On the whole he preferred French salon comedies or thriller-plays to grand tragedy. They were for him what crime stories or, for that matter, television may be to tired politicians in our days: a kind of drug, a stimulant-cum-sedative. Katharina Schratt had started as a comedienne with more than a dash of the tomboy; comedy and naïve parts remained her forte, although she fancied herself in dramatic rôles as well. Kate in *The Taming of the Shrew* was one of her successes, but she was best liked for her modern rôles, either in French plays like the dramatisation of Ohnet's *Maître de forges* and Pailleron's *Le monde où l'on s'ennuie* (still played with a brilliant conversational technique at the Burgtheater during the First World War!); or in custom-tailored comedies by Austrian playwrights who took over where Bauernfeld had left off (he died in 1890, at the age of eighty-eight), filling their plays with dashing officers and debutantes; or in pseudo-rural comedies in which she would play a wilful country girl, dirndl costume and all. On the outer curtain of the new Burgtheater which was opened in 1888, Katharina Schratt is painted as Thalia, the muse of light comedy, though rather too solid in flesh for the rôle, like most other women in that theatrical Olympus. I believe it was in connection with the Burgtheater curtain that I once asked several older people, very many years ago, whether "die Schratt" had been a good actress; on the whole they answered vaguely, not because of a belated and misplaced loyalty to the Emperor's taste, but because they had to admit that they had retained an impression of a personality rather than an actress. Katharina Schratt had been alive on the stage, it seemed.

She was extremely attractive, lively, strong-willed, very natural, and not at all beautiful. Her prettiness was much to the taste of Vienna: expressive eyes, strongly marked brows, vivid colouring, wavy hair between blonde and brown, and a well proportioned but buxom figure. Franz Joseph—like many other men—found her enchanting, fell in love with her, was for ever grateful to the Empress who had, in a bold psychological stroke, manœuvred their meeting in 1886, and discovered in Katharina Schratt the only gaiety, happiness and friendship of his bleak later years. The actress, thirty-three years old at the time and separated from her husband, an eccentric Hungarian nobleman, was wise enough to understand what Franz Joseph needed most. She chatted to him without restraint, told him theatre gossip which he lapped up (the comparison between the two olympian sets must have been amusing for him), and made him feel that she was utterly sincere and frank. She also gave him a taste of domestic bliss. She invited people for him with careful discrimination, had good meals ready, and adjusted her private, though not her professional, life so that she could fit into his exacting time-table (he kept inhuman hours, and would often call on her at 7 a.m.) joint breakfasts in her little villa at Hietzing, or her villa at the mountain spa of Ischl, and joint walks in the park of Schönbrunn or along the paths of Salzkammergut hills. But she did not give up either her independent life, her friends, or her career, and he respected this, even when he was a little jealous.

Because he loved her, he had once, in the early months of their friendship, broken his strict rule never to interfere with programme or cast at the Burgtheater, "because it's there for the public and not for me, and I don't consider myself a good judge of such matters". She, feeling badly treated by a new Director and finding her complaints useless, had asked the Emperor to do something about it. He had hesitated, from principle, and also because he feared to damage her reputation, but in the end he said "a few words to the *General-Intendant*". Afterwards he thought that his intervention had made little difference. "A minister has more influence. . . ." A minister had fewer inhibitions about pulling strings. Twelve years later, Franz Joseph did nothing at all when Frau Schratt had a conflict with the controller of the court theatres, the new Grand Master of the Household. It nearly cost him her friendship.

Nobody who reads the Emperor's letters to Katharina Schratt can doubt that they were never lovers in the accepted sense, nor that there was a time when self-restraint was difficult. It is somewhat odd to find Franz Joseph putting dashes for kisses, just as an arch schoolgirl might put crosses, or say it in words like: "I send you as many dashes (*Stricherln*) as you deign to accept." But his consideration for her, his contained tenderness, and his pathetic need of affection shine through it all. Most moving, perhaps, is his unselfconscious humility, in these letters even more than in those he wrote to his wife and of which we know fewer. He was aware of his own limitations, his pedestrian mind which could irritate quicker spirits, and was secretly prepared for new hurts. There is in the letters not the slightest hint that he, as the Emperor, had for that reason any special rights in private. There is only gratitude, mixed with shy apprehension, that he is allowed entry into another human being's life. He lost that entry in the end. The friendship with Katharina Schratt did not finish, but she withdrew it from him, temporarily, yet in the last analysis for good in all he valued most, after the death of the Empress. She had many complex reasons; a great deal can be explained by the fact that she felt her position to have become more equivocal, and that she had to contend with the antagonism of Franz Joseph's daughter Valerie. Also, both he and she had grown older, though her life was not yet nearing its end.

Elisabeth's rôle in all this was remarkable. She had acted on her conviction that her marriage had been a dismal failure for herself, and could be retrieved for him only if she were to sacrifice her finer needs to his endless devotion. She was not willing to do this. But she had a bad conscience on leaving her husband to his profound loneliness, from which he cried out to her in a stream of letters, saved from maudlin self-pity by their flat honesty of statement. (The same is true of his letters to Katharina Schratt after she, too, had left him alone.) Elisabeth not only engineered Franz Joseph's meeting with Frau Schratt when he was plainly infatuated with her, she also made a friend of the actress in the face of all the world as well as in private; the two even dieted together, and made the poor Emperor sigh at their joint craze. It may be suspected that the Empress realised that her support of the friendship between Franz Joseph and Katharina Schratt was, given his character, the most effective barrier she could have set up. Still, she had some attacks of envy or jealousy, to judge from Corti's quotations. Once she told Valerie that she wished to be dead because she only came between the Emperor and Frau Schratt: again, this was the best way to turn her devoted daughter against the relationship. (As will be noted, I feel somewhat suspicious about the psychological drives of Elisabeth, but they would require a more serious study; on the face of it, I tend to believe that she was an *allumeuse* and a prisoner of her narcissism.) Her death only raised the barrier higher.

When Elisabeth was stabbed to death in Territet by the lone-wolf anarchist Lucheni, in 1898, Franz Joseph was hurt beyond repair. He had never ceased to love her as the unattainable, almost incomprehensible ideal woman, and this love endured. But he needed, if not the reality, at least the possibility of human nearness. After Elisabeth's death, Katharina Schratt alone could give him that solace. She took herself away from him, and he submitted to it in helpless pain. Only the grandchildren were left; he could play with them and say to himself that his second childhood was here, as he wrote to Katharina. Everything else was duty borne without hope. "I am thinking much of the sad, hopeless future. . . ." It was then the Old Gentleman turned stubborn in defence of his tenets.

As Grillparzer had written in his notebook about an earlier

Habsburg, when planning his play around Rudolf II: "The tragic thing would be that he realises the advent of a new era . . . and senses that all action only serves to accelerate its advent."

3. NEW BOURGEOISIE AND OLD MIDDLE CLASS

During the baroque building boom, when the grandees of the Habsburg realm built great town houses in the narrow streets of the walled city, and palatial villas outside the ring of fortifications, their buildings were far fewer than the houses of commoners, but it was their style, their façades, which gave its face to eighteenth-century Vienna. They were the ruling class. During the building boom in private houses which started about 1860, with the razing of the first bastions and the sale of the new-won ground, it was the new bourgeoisie of bankers and rich industrialists which selected from the architects' blue-prints a style suitable for a ruling class, and invited painters to embellish it as though for Florentine merchant princes. The first houses that rose along and near the Ringstrasse even before the boulevard was finished were built, with a few exceptions commissioned by wealthy aristocrats, for *noveaux riches*. They alone could pay the exorbitant prices for the sites, money paid into a fund and administered by a commission which had to provide for communal ventures, the new roads, squares and parks, and some of the public buildings when the private boom came to an abrupt end.

The Heinrichshof opposite the Opera, three apartment buildings designed to look like a single great Renaissance palace, was built for Heinrich Drasche, heir to the man who had modernised the brick works outside Vienna and converted them into a limited company; the money for this building, the most striking and modern of its kind, came out of the building boom itself. Not far away on the other side of the Ringstrasse, a *palais*—a house was called a *palais*, in French, if it was wholly or mainly destined for occupation by the owner, and had a sufficiently grandiose front—was built for the banker and industrialist Nikolaus Dumba, who had come from Macedonia, but had taken root in Vienna and wielded considerable influence. His fortune was based on trade with the Near East. But Dumba also belonged to the group of the "Old Liberals", and was a patron of the arts. In later years he was in touch with the Crown Prince—and with Frau Schratt.

She stood on the balcony of Dumba's *palais* to watch the State carriages with the German Emperor, Wilhelm II, and her own Emperor drive past in 1890, to curtsey deeply, and be noticed with glee by Franz Joseph, who, however, called it simply "Dumba's house" in his letter.

At a point near the Opera where the Ring bends sharply north-east in the direction of the Danube Canal—this had been the site of a particularly strong corner bastion—a wide square opens up towards the suburbs, with the baroque front of Fischer von Erlach's Schwarzenberg Palace at the far end, beyond ramps and gardens, and nowadays half hidden by the Soviet War Memorial. This square was an ambitious piece of town-planning. It started with two pairs of symmetrical palace-like buildings, and the equestrian statue of Field-Marshal Prince Schwarzenberg in the centre of the space between them. One of these buildings was the palace of Archduke Ludwig Viktor, later taken over by the Army Casino; the other was the *palais* of Franz Wertheim, inventor and producer of internationally successful strong boxes. The architect was Ferstel, he who built the University and the Votivkirche; but those two palatial buildings came first. They were finished by 1863.

Almost the first *palais* to be built was that of a very wealthy banker, Eduard Todesco, later Baron Todesco. This house came too early, in 1861, to be fitted into the frontage of the Ringstrasse; it had a less ostentatious, if equally select situation, on the corner of the Kärntner-strasse beside the Opera which was yet to be constructed. Two years later, another banker-baron, Friedrich Schey, built a discreet *palais* in the street on the other side of the Opera-to-be. Both men belonged to the élite of Jewish financiers, the *haute juiverie*, and had come to Vienna from provincial towns, burdened by memories of ghettoes. Both were to make their houses centres of political, intellectual and artistic life.

One and all, those buildings were trial runs of the Ringstrasse architects, invariably in a neo-Renaissance style. The pattern was fixed before the great slump of 1873 switched building from the private to the public sector. If the occupant was not born into the "right station", the style of his house had to give him standing—to borrow a distinction which Miss Mitford made in *Our Town* more than 130 years ago.

Even leading members of the new bourgeoisie knew that, in spite of their economic power, they had to fight their way into the inner circles of Society—if this seemed important to them. It did, to most of them.

There were sharp class distinctions at the top in Austria, even though there was no longer a single ruling class in politics. Also, it was easier for a commoner, be he of Jewish origin, to become a minister (it had happened several times) than to attain certain posts in the diplomatic service or the administration which were still the preserve of aristocrats. It was after the turn of the century that an eminent professor of (I think) common law at the University of Vienna ploughed a student of ancient lineage during the decisive examination qualifying for the higher Civil Service, with the remark: "I know I won't prevent your being made governor of Upper Austria, Count, but at least I can delay it for a year." The title of nobility continued to be a useful passport although it was no longer taken as seriously as two generations before. Hence the most coveted of orders was that of the Iron Crown which automatically conferred such a title—conferred it on so many, in fact, that it became absurd, and the order was shorn of its ennobling magic. Before this happened, however, and before very much higher donations to charity were required of anyone who hoped to be made a baron, virtually all prominent bankers, industrialists and exporters in Vienna had at least achieved a modest *von*, and many the title of baron. But not one became a count.

The barons of finance were generous in their patronage to artists who added lustre to their houses. It was a good time for some of the painters. Not for all, though. The greatest painter of the older generation, Ferdinand Waldmüller, had been in advance of his time before 1848. He had developed a luminous realism of his own, in constant battle with the two schools reigning at the Vienna Academy of Fine Arts, on the one hand, the Romantics and Nazarenes (the German-Austrian version of pre-Raphaelites), on the other the classicists; he had argued against "chewing the cud of things handed down", and for the unlimited study of nature, the human body, and contemporary life. He argued himself out of his temporary post at the Academy, and later, by publishing a memorandum on reforms needed in the teaching of art, he brought upon himself a disciplinary suspension and was pensioned off from his post as curator, because he had neglected the proper channels. It was in the dark 'fifties when Waldmüller wrote: "Only that tuition can form artists which is kept free of all scholastic constraint, all pedantry of form, all surveillance and all tutelage from the State."* His biographer Grimschitz remarks that Waldmüller belongs

* Cf. Bruno Grimschitz, *Ferdinand Georg Waldmüller*, Salzburg, 1957.

"in the forefront of bourgeois realistic art", and compares his gemlike clarity with the art of Adalbert Stifter, who was not only a great writer but also a painter of air and light before his time. But this historical appraisal in general terms has little to do with Waldmüller's impact on the men of the middle class to whom he wanted to show —and to sell—his pictures. Before 1848 this impact was considerable, though stronger through paintings of genre scenes than through his nature paintings that tell no story. When he died in 1865, his works fetched no prices at all. They were too small in scale, too sharp in outline, too clear in colour, to fit in with velvet hangings such as had become the fashion. Even among his pupils—he had set up a private school when he quarrelled with the Academy—Hans Canon, who was a good draughtsman, able to paint heavy brocade in draped folds and to produce historical pastiches, was much more successful than the brilliant impressionist Romako, who painted a victorious admiral in an unbeautiful stance instead of a dramatic pose. The owners of the new *palais* had little taste for a Waldmüller, and scarcely more for a Romako.

Waldmüller's contemporary Carl Rahl fared better for a time, in the 'sixties. He was a classicist of great vigour, with an individual use of colour, so that the architects—as Hansen for the Heinrichshof—courted his collaboration. He painted frescoes for Todesco's house and for the new Opera. Rahl, too, had a story of rebellion behind him. He had been on the losing side in 1848 and had evaded unpleasantness by going to Munich for a couple of years. But he went back to his native Vienna at the end of 1850. The Academy took him on as a temporary teacher on probation, and he soon had a great following. This, as much as his known anticlerical opinions, led to his dismissal after a short period. He set up a private school, like Waldmüller, and his students followed him in an exodus, because he seems to have been an inspired and inspiring teacher. A devoted pupil of his most eminent antagonist, the Nazarene painter and pious Catholic Joseph Führich, gave glimpses of conflicts in his memoirs:

Between the pupils of the respective masters, a certain contact from colleague to colleague was further maintained, but more cordial friendships could not develop owing to the fundamentally opposed philosophies of the two groups. In any case, after a fairly short time Rahl, who had been the victim of petty political apprehensions and personal intrigues, was glorified and pushed into the foreground by the so-called liberals and freethinkers, whose influence was slowly growing again, and who considered him one of their men, although his qualities and convictions as an artist corresponded as little to the taste of the incipient economic "upsurge" as did those of the Nazarene, Führich. (W. O. Noltsch: *Bilder aus Wien,Erinnerungen eines Wiener Künstlers*, Stuttgart/Vienna, 1901, vol. I, pp. 114-15.)

This was essentially true. The severity of outline which underlay Rahl's most colourful frescoes was not quite to the "taste of the incipient economic upsurge". Interior decoration is a matter, and a part, of fashion; paintings taken as elements of the decoration of a room rather than independent works of art have above all to fit the frame. This frame had been changing, slowly at first, then rapidly, ever since 1849. Furniture had undergone several stages, from an adaptation of Biedermeier simplicity to curlier outlines and floral fabrics, to the "second Rococo", so called by the experts, and on to a third, more florid Rococo. Then the historical copies came in, excellent workmanship, select woods and *intarsio*, inlaid work in ivory or mother-of-pearl, or heavy carved oak—Spanish, Renaissance, seventeenth-century German, often beautifully finished copies like those described lovingly, over many pages, by Adalbert Stifter in *Der Nachsommer*. Of course the copies were copied again, more cheaply and crudely, for the consumption of not-so-rich middle-class families. But the heavy pieces darkened the rooms; they demanded heavier fabrics, coloured glass windows to diffuse the light, and figured tapestries on the walls, oriental rugs, or deep-toned wallpaper, anything but the clear, plain shades of earlier years. They also demanded the right sort of paintings to go with them, either copies of late Renaissance masters, or large still lifes, or pastiches on those lines, or a new form of darkly glowing decorative art, distinct from the Pompeian wall paintings which inspired Rahl.

These are not merely generalised impressions drawn from wanderings through Viennese museums, and from the furniture, or the tastes, surviving here or there deep into the twentieth century. The photographs, memoirs, letters and inventories of the Ringstrasse years are hard and fast evidence. In an introduction to the correspondence between Johannes Brahms and Theodor Billroth (the greatest surgeon in Vienna), the latter's son-in-law, Otto Gottlieb-Billroth, describes the great reception- or music-room in Billroth's eighteenth-century house (at one time owned by another famous physician who had received Beethoven as his guest there): "Here Billroth had the urge,

admitted by himself, to be transported into the realm of fantasy. This was the place where he accused himself of 'enjoying decoration'.
. . . The real adornments of the large room were good large-scale copies of old paintings, Bonifazio—Correggio and Caravaggio—Rubens; and in the spaces between, copies of antique bronze busts on columns." And Billroth, who belonged to the intellectual, but also the social élite of bourgeois Vienna, wrote in 1893, in one of his last letters to Brahms:*

After all, you admit yourself that pieces in a minor key are more easily absorbed by us, the moderns. I suppose this can be considered a parallel to the fact that we find muted, gentler colours on the whole more agreeable in our immediate surroundings than more dazzling ones. (It was different in our youth.) Modern people do not like dazzling light in their rooms either. The modern predilection for painted windows! . . .

The new decorative painter who suited the requirements of the new Viennese society so perfectly that his name is used as a label for a style of living, and a brief era, was Hans Makart. He was born at Salzburg in 1840 and came to Vienna for good in 1879. The first of the Ringstrasse tycoons to give him a commission was Nikolaus Dumba. Makart painted a frieze for the dining-room of his *palais* on the Parkring, after having gone to Venice at the expense of his patron to study the appropriate styles. His biographer, Emil Pirchan, describes the result, which I have never seen so that I must rely on a second-hand description:

With allegory upon allegory of Art and Science, Labour and Industry, Agriculture, Astronomy, Chemistry, and so forth, Makart covered the walls in the style of the old Venetians. Like a dark-glowing transparent tapestry, which at the same time shimmers and glitters in every colour, the *chiaroscuro* of the painting encompasses the entire room, which has come to be a monument of the Viennese style of grand display. (*Hans Makart*, Vienna, Bergland Verlag, 1954, p. 29.)

The Dumba frieze was completed just before "Black Friday" which, incidentally, did not ruin Dumba himself. But the first large-scale historical picture Makart painted, *Venice pays homage to Catarina Cornaro*—groups in velvet or brocade posing in theatrical abandon on the steps of the *Palazzo Ducale*—was exhibited at the ill-fated World

* *Billroth und Brahms im Briefwechsel*, edited and introduced by Otto Gottlieb-Billroth, Vienna, 1935, p. 480.

Exhibition of 1873, bought by an enraptured industrialist at a sensational price, and sold on his subsequent bankruptcy (not a result of his love for Makart's form of art, but of the crisis of private credits) to the Berlin National Gallery at scarcely more than half the price of purchase. The slump did not, however, affect Makart's commissions; the solid banking houses had not been involved in the share-pushing, and had withdrawn in good time from the bullish market on the stock exchange. And in those years from 1873 to 1880 Makart painted one show piece after the other, among them *The Triumph of Ariadne*, *The Five Senses* in long panels matching the long if opulently swelling legs of his models, and *Charles V Entering Antwerp*, with women, naked or decorously enfolded, throwing flowers to the young Flemish Habsburg.

Just as a rattlesnake announces itself, I ought to proclaim my life-long prejudice against Makart. It began at the same stage of my childhood, in the same old "Modern Gallery" housed in the Lower Belvedere, in which I fell in love with Waldmüller for good. I was never able to free myself from the first impression of vapid similarity between all those women, though I expressed it differently and more rudely then. It is with conscientious analysis that I have come to see the significance of so much luxuriant exhibitionism, the exuberant talent that Makart must once have had, the romantic evasion behind the display of splendour. But there it is: Makart was "the wizard" of Ringstrasse Vienna, the master of a supreme *trompe l'œil*, a visual trick that turned a non-style (as Hermann Broch called it) into the reality of patrician wealth. When the City of Vienna had to organise a procession in "historical costumes" to celebrate the silver wedding of Franz Joseph and Elisabeth in 1879, Makart drew up the plans, supervised the production of every Renaissance costume and the distribution of extras on the float of every single guild, and rode at the head of the civic pageant himself, on a white charger that nearly threw him, and in a Rubens costume with plumes on his wide-brimmed hat. And 'twas a famous victory.

Viennese gossip was constantly dissecting Makart's alleged love affairs, and it seems to have been a favourite game among smart people to point out in his pictures which noble lady had lent her body, which beautiful society girl her face, to this or that ambiguous figure. He also painted portraits, rigging out the sitter in period costume to obtain the colour effects which alone interested him. But when he painted Charlotte Wolter, the leading tragic actress of the Burgtheater, her eagle profile and statuesque pose as Messalina or Cleopatra became revealingly suited to his decorative manner: it revealed him as a theatrical illusionist, and her as a marvellous stage property.

In his famous studio, tucked away in a small eighteenth-century building which the Emperor had assigned to him when he first came to Vienna, Makart threw costly parties, studio fêtes in period costumes that were too unwieldy to make probable the rumoured nameless orgies. From this studio, many times painted, drawn and etched by contemporary artists, Makart's influence on interior decoration spread through Vienna, from the Empress Elisabeth's new-built Hermes Villa in the Imperial game preserve outside the suburban zone, to the parlours of modest newly-weds. It is this pervading influence, not the paintings, which justifies the labels of a Makart-age and Makart-style for the decade which ended with his death in 1884. Indeed, the Makart style survived him, while his fame as a painter did not. It consisted of a profusion of "picturesque" objects, curios, potted palms and ferns, arrangements of peacock feathers, Japanese fans, gleaming shells and dried flowers or reed stalks, everything screened by heavy dark curtains, and bathed in a soft golden light: this, of course, in its most developed form, with noble fabrics and genuine antiques, in the salons of those who could afford it. But the Makart bouquet, a few thistles or bulrushes combined with a paper fan and a peacock feather, was not beyond the reach of a small purse; even cheaper were imitation palm fronds, quickly put on the market when the craze started. As a matter of fact, some of the arrangements of artificial flowers in our 'sixties are fatally reminiscent of Makart bouquets. They have, after all, a similar make-believe quality to excuse their sheer ugly shoddiness. And they do last, as the housewives of Vienna used to say about Makart bouquets.

Makart died of cerebral paralysis. The usual formula is that he burned himself out. The funeral was a popular pageant of mourning. When his magpie collection of *objets d'art* and his paintings were auctioned, they found hardly any buyers. A revulsion had set in, had perhaps begun before his death and was now merely coming to the surface. His greatest pride, the soft colouring of his pictures, quickly dimmed; they turned greyish, because he had used ingredients which were meant to speed up drying, and put anilin colours on wet cement ground, so that unforeseen chemical changes destroyed many of his works. But some of his decorator's passion had gone into the Burgtheater productions under Dingelstedt, a Director who had been Makart's friend, and even Richard Wagner had learnt some stage effects from him—his wife Cosima at least was deeply impressed by Makart.

The taste of a whole generation of Vienna's upper middle class had been shaped by Makart, or by the struggle against his influence. Gustav Klimt, the most important painter of the rising generation, had to free himself from Makart and the Ringstrasse patrons before he found his own style—and yet it was always strongly decorative. The young leaders of intellectual opinion, who dominated Vienna in the 'nineties, broke with everything Makart stood for. Nobody slashed him more viciously than Hermann Bahr, the mouthpiece of the group. In the drawing-rooms of apartments behind a façade in Ringstrasse style, or in the French variation that followed it, a Makart spirit still lingered, and it was impossible for the young critics to have patience with it.

In one such apartment, on the second floor of one such pretentious corner house, I saw as a child a living-room and a dining-room which could have been transferred into any museum as samples of Makart *Kitsch*, kept unchanged since the early 'eighties. The house belonged to an old lady who had been a friend of my grandmother's and who, in her person, combined the tastes of the Viennese bourgeoisie, that is, the *nouveaux riches* of the 'seventies, with a much older but submerged and suppressed tradition. She was the widow of a builder who had become rich at the time of the boom, being also the owner of lime kilns and manufacturer of building material. Her house in the Wienerwald, near the kilns, was still furnished as it had been in mid-century, when her parents-in-law lived there. It had those clear-coloured, plain walls, those windows not darkened by their light curtains, and those few smoothly polished pieces of furniture in cherry- or pear-wood, chest of drawers, chiffonière, round tables, slightly upholstered, slightly curving sofa and armchairs, which—as I realised much later—belonged to the afterglow of Biedermeier. But in Vienna, her two reception rooms were so cluttered and shadowy that I was always afraid of bumping into a stuffed animal or overstuffed armchair, knocking a Turkish rug from an occasional table, or brushing against the bronze maiden in fluttering draperies who held a torch aloft that could be switched on to shed a red glow. Wonder of wonders, this house did not have gas light, as most others I knew, but electric light!

K

My adopted great-aunt Ludmilla, whose married name sounded Czech and whose maiden name was Italian, which made her most truly Viennese, would sit in her bow window, among many cushions and shawls, and recite ballads—romantic and exotic ones, by Uhland or Chamisso, Freiligrath or Fontane—which were nearly all sad and made her cry. But she explained to me, when I cannot have been more than seven, that it was good to cry like this, over noble sentiments and beautiful poems. I was less moved to sympathy when she spoke of her son who had died as a small boy, because she called him "my little angel", something I disliked. Then I would stare at the great fans of peacock feathers behind the looking-glass, or at the bulrushes in their tall Japanese vase; and I can see them now, when I have long since understood that the unreal trappings of the room, the Makart décor, helped the lonely old woman by making her feel safely sheltered in a dream word.

She, however, had been driven by her private experiences to contract out of life, so that she had never altered an interior decoration which had belonged to days of content. It was different for others of her class who went with the fashion, keeping up with the pace-setters, changing with their own changing circumstances—though the Makart room in Dumba's house was famous enough to last. It was different, too, for people from the old Viennese middle class, the *Bürgertum*, the social group Aunt Ludmilla thought to have left behind her. They had, as a group if not in each individual case, a security of civic status which kept them aloof from the Ringstrasse-Makart atmosphere, though not as a rule from Makart bouquets.

There was—there is—Lobmeyr. Josef Lobmeyr senior, coming from Upper Austria to Vienna as a simple glazier, had opened a shop with borrowed money in a side street off the Kärntnerstrasse as early as 1822. He was helped by his wife, who came from Moravia, and soon had a few journeymen as well. His son Ludwig would recall that the shop opened at 7 a.m. and closed at 8 p.m. The journeymen, who seem to have lodged with their master, were given a "simple break-fast", mid-day meal and supper in his parents' house, and had Sunday meals together with the family and the children's tutor; these patri-archal conditions—Stifter described similar ones for his Viennese merchant family in *Der Nachsommer*—lasted till the 'sixties.*

After obtaining his master glass-maker's certificate, old Lobmeyr

* Stefan Rath, *Lobmeyr—Vom Adel des Handwerks*, Vienna, Herold, 1962.

moved into a better shop in the Kärntnerstrasse itself, which was called *Zum Fürsten Metternich* until Metternich's fall in 1848. Under his two sons, who succeeded him, the firm became J. & L. Lobmeyr, K. and K· Court Glass-Makers and Court Glass-Ware Dealers. (The English "Purveyors to the Court" would be more correct, but would leave out the characteristic K. & K. They had run glass-works in Slavonia and, above all, Bohemia at an early stage, so that they had the best available workers, blowers, engravers and cutters at their disposal. But the designs came from Vienna. They were on the whole conventional, in current styles, either fine plain glass or coloured glass, decorated with engraving, gilding, enamel, or else cut crystal combined with engraving. But in 1856 Ludwig Lobmeyr designed a set of decanter and assorted wine glasses so austerely simple in line, and in the use of a clear, thin glass called "muslin" glass, that it could as well have come from a Scandinavian workshop of our days. According to Stefan Rath, the nephew who took over from Ludwig Lobmeyr, this set has remained a best-seller over a hundred years. He also says that the firm became the exclusive purveyor to the court in fact as well as in name, and enjoyed the support of "the Emperor, the archdukes, the aristocracy and the *Bürgertum*", which in this case must be translated as upper middle class.

Ludwig Lobmeyr collaborated closely with the two outstanding Ringstrasse architects, Schmidt and Hansen. From "classical" designs by Hansen, the firm produced table sets, magnificent vases and centre pieces for the table. And then there were crystal chandeliers, copies of mid-eighteenth-century models under the first Lobmeyr, new rococo shapes, under his son Ludwig, for export to the Viceroy of Egypt, and to Bavaria for Ludwig II's many castles, as well as modern solutions for electric light, fashioned for the ballrooms at the Hofburg, and the big conference room of Friedrich Schmidt's new gothic Town Hall. To this extent, Lobmeyr went along with the Ringstrasse style, but always abiding by the rules which his beloved material, glass, imposed. His collection of paintings was remarkable, being particularly strong in contemporary artists who were neglected by current fashion, like Rudolf von Alt, Romako and Pettenkofen.

During the Vienna season, he would "two or three times a week gather about thirty guests at his table, merchants, industrialists, artists— architects, painters, graphic artists, actors, musicians, writers—university professors, officers, ministers, civil servants, and diplomats". In politics he was a moderate, an old-fashioned liberal; even when he might have adopted a title of nobility after being appointed to the First Chamber, he preferred to remain a commoner. He was given the Freedom of the City of Vienna.

Stefan Rath, his successor, a small modest man, was himself an eminent designer, and as passionate a student of his material as his uncle. In the second wave of modernism in applied art (a term Rath rejected as synthetic), he was co-founder of the *Werkbund*, of which it might be said that it developed out of *art nouveau* in its Austrian version, but went beyond it. Rath felt that "the strength of Lobmeyr had never consisted in conserving tradition, but rather in taking the lead". Later, from 1910 onward, he was to bring in great architects of the new school to design for the firm, above all Josef Hoffmann, but once even the difficult Adolf Loos. And in the text of the small monograph which was published in 1962, two years after his death, to celebrate the 140th anniversary of Lobmeyr's, Rath proudly said that he was not an artist, but merely "the leader of an exemplary craft enterprise", which had created "a small crystal world".

If reduced to essentials, this is not a story of bold innovators, but of master craftsmen moving at the head of the current of which they were part, and belonging, by the very nature of the firm's commerce, to whatever establishment there was. Yet it also illustrates the cultural and civic poise of the "old" Viennese upper middle class at its best: it was a poise that excluded the need for exhibition and a hankering after high society. In the last quarter of the nineteenth century, this was getting rare among business men, though there would be a list of knotty individualists to quote, headed by the maker of pianos Ludwig Bösendorfer, a legendary figure on the Ringstrasse promenade in his narrow-brimmed top-hat and chequered stove-pipe trousers.

Old Bösendorfer had inherited from his father the world-famous piano factory—founded in 1828—but even when he was a very rich man he continued, with a loyalty to the craft as great as Lobmeyr's to his, to have special pianos for individual artists built under his super-vision. He discovered the ideal acoustic qualities of Prince Liechten-stein's riding school, an undistinguished eighteenth-century building in the Herrengasse, while he was watching horses being put through their paces; he rented it, and in 1872 opened it as a concert hall. It was a far more intimate and congenial hall, or so everybody said, than the huge gilt-pilastered one in Hansen's new *Musikverein* building; Liszt,

Rubinstein, Hellmesberger, Bülow—and others, great virtuosos, great singers, great conductors—were happy to perform in it. It is part of Vienna's musical history that the supporters of Wagner fought and won their partisan battles first of all in the *Bösendorfersaal*. When it was demolished in 1913, those who had sat and listened in it shed tears (much as the enthusiasts of the old Burgtheater had done when they had to transfer their allegiance to the sumptuous new building on the Ringstrasse), and swore that there had never been, and never would be, such a shell for pure music. (I remember people discussing it in the street while the walls were being torn down, because my primary school, temporarily lodged in a house almost opposite, was due to move into the tall modern office block rising on the site, so that we would linger and watch demolition and construction work with a proprietary interest.) Just as Ludwig Lobmeyr collected painters and paintings, Ludwig Bösendorfer collected musicians and masterly performances in his concert hall. Like Lobmeyr, too, Bösendorfer remained a commoner although he could have had the Order of the Iron Crown, with the *Ritter von* attached to it, ten times over. But he remained Old Bösendorfer, and not even the Emperor could have improved on that.

Though a number of artistic, musical and intellectual centres were thriving in those decades, the most interesting literary salon was that of Josephine von Wertheimstein. In its patrician assurance, it suggested the spirit of a Lobmeyr rather than that of a typical Ringstrasse *palais*-owner: it certainly had nothing of the *nouveau riche* about it, and yet it did not quite belong to the old upper middle class either. Josephine's husband, Leopold von Wertheimstein, was the first clerk of the house of Rothschild in Vienna, which made him a diplomat or high civil servant of finance. He was much older than his wife—it had been a *mariage de convenance*—and usually stayed in his town house, coming on daily visits to see his family. Josephine, in her turn, came from the distinguished Gomperz family of Brünn (Brno) that dominated the Moravian textile industry. Both were Jewish, both were born into rich "assimilated" families; neither had had to fight for social recognition and neither had felt the shadow of a ghetto. In short, they were of the Jewish aristocracy, even though economically they belonged to the rich bourgeoisie.

The villa in which Josephine and her only daughter Franziska, or Franzi, queened it over a court of friends, was as far removed from the

Ringstrasse as could be, both in distance—it lay in the outlying north-
westerly suburb of Döbling—and in style. It had originally belonged
to the outstanding industrialist of pre-March Vienna, the silk manufacturer Arthaber, a patron of painters, a moderate liberal, and in 1848
one of the well-meaning unsuccessful ministers. Built in the 'thirties, it
had a classicist portico and graceful fanlights over the windows.
Schwind had painted romantic-antique frescoes in the well of the
staircase. The simple, spacious proportions of the house and the rooms
demanded, and received, a lighter treatment than the Makart vogue
allowed elsewhere, although Makart himself did visit Josephine von
Wertheimstein, like everybody in Vienna's Who's Who during those
years. Josephine, a fascinating woman to the last, and Franzi, a lovely
fine-drawn girl, had the art of making people talk about themselves
and their work, and keeping them as friends, with every conflict
well sublimated.

Among the intimates were excellent singers, and music was a natural
part of Sunday afternoons, but an entertainment rather than the cult it
was with Billroth, who would organise special evenings—followed by
very special suppers—for "Brahmans" worthy of hearing Brahms
himself. The only composer among Josephine's collection of regulars
was a minor one, Dessauer, who composed the music for popular songs
written in a pseudo-dialect by another member of the circle, Alexander
Baumann, Bauernfeld's old friend, and one of the two small boys in
Paumgartten's Biedermeier album. But sometimes Anton Rubinstein
came to play at the villa, and then "half Vienna" was invited to the
feast. However, in this circle the emphasis was on literature and intellectual debate.

For many years, Bauernfeld was the lion of Josephine's salon, the
wittiest performer, and incidentally her most faithful admirer. He
retained his ability to read scenes from his own plays with a Burgtheater star's elegance up to the eve of his death. A few days after one
such recital under the trees he died in the cream-washed cottage on the
other side of the Wertheimstein park, which had become his home. In
the salon he was succeeded by Ferdinand von Saar, the most eminent
of the older writers since Grillparzer's death, a former officer who was
in his prose a melancholy realist, in his life a lonely self-torturer. He
was profoundly devoted to Franzi. When he felt unable to bear his
physical pains any longer, he waited until she was absent from Vienna
before he shot himself: he wished to spare her the crudity of an im-

mediate shock. For Bauernfeld and Saar, the Wertheimstein Villa was
the ultimate refuge.

It was a first refuge for the adolescent prodigy Hugo von Hofmannsthal. During the last few years before Josephine's death in 1894,
he went there to read his poems. His essays and verse were just beginning to make a stir in *avant-garde* magazines. He wrote under the pseudonym "Loris"; as a grammar school pupil he was not allowed
to publish anything under his own name. For his fastidious taste,
the house and its mistresses were deeply satisfying. He conceived an
intense friendship for Josephine. Whenever a glimpse of Franzi's
nervous, overbred beauty and her strange withdrawal from commit-
ment to life is given in a posthumous homage, written by her
friend Emilie Exner under a pseudonym (*Zwei Frauen-Bildnisse—zur
Erinnerung*, by Felicie Ewart, private edition, Vienna, 1907), the
breathless words evoke the mood of Hugo Hofmannsthal's early
poem, "Ballade des äusseren Lebens" (Ballad of Outward Life).

> Und Kinder wachsen auf mit tiefen Augen,
> Die von nichts wissen, wachsen auf und sterben,
> Und alle Menschen gehen ihre Wege.
>
> Und süsse Früchte werden aus den herben
> Und fallen nachts wie tote Vögel nieder
> Und liegen wenig Tage und verderben.
>
> Und immer weht der Wind und immer wieder
> Vernehmen wir und reden viele Worte
> Und spüren Lust und Müdigkeit der Glieder.
>
> Und Strassen laufen durch das Gras, und Orte
> Sind da und dort, voll Fackeln, Bäumen, Teichen,
> Und drohende, und totenhaft verdorrte . . .
>
> Wozu sind diese aufgebaut? und gleichen
> Einander nie? und sind unzählig viele?
> Was wechselt Lachen, Weinen und Erbleichen?
>
> Was frommt das alles uns und diese Spiele,
> Die wir doch gross und ewig einsam sind
> Und wandernd nimmer suchen irgend Ziele?
>
> Was frommts, dergleichen viel gesehen haben?
> Und dennoch sagt der viel, der "Abend" sagt,
> Ein Wort, daraus Tiefsinn und Trauer rinnt
>
> Wie schwerer Honig aus den hohlen Waben.

And children grow with deep and secret eyes
That know of nothing, they grow up and die,
And every man is following his road.

And acid fruits turn ripe and sweet, and lie
Like dead birds in the grass when they are shed
During the night, and soon they rot and dry.

And wind is always blowing overhead,
And there are many words we say and hear,
And we desire, and our limbs turn dead.

And roads run through the fields, and far and near
Are places, tree and torchlight, pond and grange,
And some loom threatening, some are dead and sere.

Why are they built, why all unlike and strange,
And why so many, more than one can name?
Why do tears, laughter, pallor interchange?

What good is all of this to us, this game,
If we are great and lonely evermore
And wander endlessly without an aim?

What good, to have seen many things like those?
And yet he does say much who 'evening' says,
A word from which meaning and sadness pour

As from the hollow comb thick honey flows.

It is customary to describe the irruption of Hugo von Hofmannsthal
into the literary world of Vienna, at an age when he was still wearing
knee-breeches, on the lines of Stefan Zweig in *The World of Yesterday.*
Zweig, younger than Hofmannsthal but under his spell since grammar
school days, based his account on Hermann Bahr's description of his
first encounter with the unknown author of an essay he had admiringly
accepted for his little review—the boy's shy entry into the old Café
Griensteidl where the littérateurs met—and on one by Arthur Schnitzler, who had invited the unknown schoolboy, almost condescendingly,
to read a short play in verse to him and a few friends. "I had the feeling," Schnitzler said to Zweig, "of having encountered a born genius
for the first time in my life, and never again during my entire lifetime was I so overwhelmed." (Zweig, *op. cit.*, London, Cassell, 1943,
p. 47.)

Neither Bahr nor Schnitzler had expected to meet anyone like young Hofmannsthal, with all that perfection of art, knowledge of life before he had started to live, and magical intuition while he was still attending classes at school. He appeared an alien and a prodigy. He *was* an alien in the fusty café, and even in Schnitzler's bachelor rooms; he was, however, truly at home in Josephine von Wertheimstein's salon that gave an illusion of being outside time and remote from loud reality. His diary records that her death was the first experience of heavy sorrow. In *Fanny von Arnstein oder Die Emanzipation* (Frankfurt, S. Fischer, 1962, p. 492), which analyses the beginnings of Jewish emancipation and describes the intriguing figure of Fanny von Arnstein, Berlin-born wife of a Viennese banker, and one of the brilliant hostesses of the Great Congress, Hilde Spiel says that the liberal era made room for intellectual Jewish salons in Vienna, "in which no longer the aristocracy but an enlightened bourgeoisie mixed with poets and artists. Fanny's place was taken by Josephine von Wertheimstein.... In her house and that of her sister, Sophie von Todesco, ... young 'Loris', great-grandson of the pious silk merchant Hofmann, read his first poems. From this circle rose the figure in which the many-sided heritage of old Austria was embodied." This, I believe, is true, and says more about the background of Hofmannsthal than the anecdotes of his first appearance among the intellectuals.

There are, however, two sides to it, one psychological and one social or sociological. The modernist movement whose leaders acclaimed "Loris" was in Vienna, as elsewhere, a reaction against the solid respectability, the two-dimensional realism in writing, the conservative ideal in painting, the consequential discourse on empty power politics, all of which were regarded as characteristic of a prosperous bourgeoisie. And much of this applied to the Wertheimstein circle. But Hofmannsthal was never a rebel. Though he emerged as the greatest lyrical poet of Vienna before his school gave him the "certificate of maturity" after the last exams, he was never (as Broch pointed out) a writer of true juvenile lyricism. To go on quoting Broch: "Like the Jewish Biedermeier barons who dreamed that they were exotic princes, which in reality they were, he walked as an exotic prince without companions ... through a reality which, out of his loneliness, deepened and widened into a dream, and so became his fairy-tale solace in his loneliness." Nothing in the essential atmosphere of the Wertheimstein household would have forced young Hofmannsthal out of his dream-reality. Rather, he could discover a kinship with Franziska who, though not young any more, still carried the stamp of being "early ripened, sad and fragile", as Hofmannsthal was to say in a famous line of the verse prologue to Schnitzler's *Anatol*. (*Anatol* is a very clever social satire and psychologically subtle play, but it belongs to another world than Hofmannsthal's prologue, for which cf. p. 105.) Moreover, the effortless divorce from the fragmented world outside, and the restriction of the circle to a chosen few, an élite, fitted into the young poet's feeling—or longing—for hierarchy and ordered privilege:

> Manche freilich müssen drunten sterben,
> Wo die schweren Ruder der Schiffe streifen,
> Andre wohnen bei dem Steuer droben,
> Kennen Vogelflug und die Länder der Sterne.
>
> Some, it's true, must perish down below deck,
> Where the heavy oars of the ships are passing;
> Others high up by the helm are seated,
> Know the flight of birds and starry countries.

Around 1890, it was rare for any sensitive person in Vienna to reject all thought of social reform—or at least the consciousness of mass indignity inflicted by the existing conditions, if the concept of another order was unacceptable. The view of society that Hofmannsthal began to develop was opposed to everything around him, but it was abstract, static and utterly remote from everyday social reality. This, in parenthesis, distinguished him once again from the two leading modernists, Bahr and Schnitzler. At that stage of his development, Bahr was still in sympathy with socialist ideas and in friendly contact with the social-democratic leader, Dr. Victor Adler. Schnitzler was at no stage a socialist, but his criticism of society, more often implicit than explicit, was thoroughly realistic. Josephine and Franziska von Wertheimstein, on the other hand, were set "so high by the favour of fate" (as their friend and apologist Emilie Exner explains, *op. cit.*, p. 78) that they had not the slightest understanding of any struggle (such as that for women's emancipation) in which grace and graciousness would be lost, and no sympathy for modern welfare work: "The mere contact with sickness or misery caused them psychological and physical pain." (This, to lower the key a little, recalls the old Viennese joke of a vintage well before the First World War—I could not say whether it was anti-

semitic in origin, or Jewish self-irony—about Rothschild, harassed by
the tale of woe of a poor petitioner, calling a flunkey and saying:
"Chuck him out, he breaks my heart!") Here, too, was a kinship
between the two women and young Hofmannsthal. And yet the ladies
Wertheimstein as well as Hofmannsthal had a high sense of responsibility, as long as it did not involve them in brushes with crude life.
Franziska's last will was to turn the whole estate over to the City of
Vienna, on condition that the villa should be used as a public library
and the park be open to all. Hofmannsthal, once his first lyrical flowering was over, and it lasted scarcely ten years, was to wrestle with a
poet's mission in his own time, the mission, as he saw it, of being
engaged, never in questions of the day, but always in revivifying
genuine values of the past and leading his public to universal ideas.

The sociological aspect of the temporary, but by no means accidental
link between the Wertheimsteins and Hofmannsthal hinges on the
Jewish question. Originally the Wertheims and Hofmanns, as they
had been called before being granted titles of nobility, had belonged to
much the same social layer of Vienna, though the Wertheims had
arrived, in both senses of the word, a century earlier. A Wertheim had
been confidential clerk to Samuel Oppenheimer, Leopold I's privileged
"court Jew" and banker round 1700. A Hofmann came to Vienna in
1788, and made a fortune in the silk trade. Franziska von Wertheimstein's grandfather, a banker, and Hugo von Hofmannsthal's great-
grandfather, the silk merchant, were both ennobled in Biedermeier
days by Franz I. But perhaps one century more on Viennese soil made
a difference in the family's outlook. The Wertheimsteins maintained
only a slight connexion with the Jewish community, but never became
converts. They melted, as it were, into Viennese society well before
the disgraceful laws discriminating against Jews were annulled by the
Revolution of 1848, and long before the influx of Jews from the eastern
provinces kindled a fear of commercial competition among tradesmen
—and re-kindled antisemitism, which had disappeared from the surface. Josephine's husband went to school with Bauernfeld—to the
Benedictine *Schotten* grammar school. The Wertheimsteins had no
cause or need to defend their patrician status, nor to develop a defensive
attitude about their Jewishness, as far as it went.

The founder of the Hofmannsthal fortunes, on the other hand, had
come from Prague, where the sense of religious identity and apartheid
was far livelier than in the sceptical, hence tolerantly lax, atmosphere of

Vienna. On being ennobled he chose for his coat of arms a mulberry leaf, symbol of the silk industry, for one field, and the tablets of the law for the other. Yet while the Wertheimsteins remained Jews, at least legally and formally, old Hofmannsthal's son married an Italian and turned Roman Catholic; his grandson, the poet's father, married an Austrian from peasant stock. Thus Hugo grew up as a Catholic, knowing that he was not Jewish, yet conscious of that Jewish strain in him, since his strong feeling for tradition and past-in-the-present made him sensitive to the whole gamut of his heritage: "Weariness of long forgotten races/I cannot brush off my eyelids."

At the time of Hugo von Hofmannsthal's adolescence, two different brands of political antisemitism had emerged in Vienna. One group was launched and led by a provincial squire, Georg von Schönerer. At the start in the early 'eighties his German nationalism had been anti-Slav, and apparently directed above all against the clerical reactionaries in the Czech dominions, who used their national claims to fight against a progressive lay education—which was part of the German centralist tendency. This identification of German culture with anti-feudalist and liberalising ideas—stemming from 1848—had led several Jewish idealists, notably Dr. Victor Adler who was soon to become an active Socialist, to join Schönerer for a short time as fellow-travellers. Since then, Schönerer had graduated to the most poisonous "Germanic" and antisemitic racialism. In Vienna he had little support outside the notorious "students' corps", the uniformed fraternities, but he was entrenched in the provincial towns, in particular among the half-baked intelligentsia, from where a steady trickle came to the capital to feed his movement. The other organisation was, for the time being, exclusively Viennese; it fed on the bitterness caused by the aftermath of the great slump of 1873 and the identification of share-pushers, stock-exchange jobbers and ruthless profiteers with well-known Jewish capitalists, and swept the suburban lower middle class along for the starkest economic reasons. It was fast becoming a powerful political factor, but cultured Viennese tended to despise and underrate it as mere rabble-rousing, even when it found allies in the clerical and conservative-aristocratic parties.

The salon of Josephine and Franzi Wertheimstein was in the widest sense liberal, and Josephine herself retained from pre-March days contacts and friendships with several important "old" Liberals, by then turned conservatives in everything except cultural and educational

matters. But the great attraction of this circle was that it was cosmopolitan, non-denominational, completely un-race-conscious, let alone
un-racialist, and non-political in its function as a clearing house—or
hot-house—of ideas. It is a mere assumption, but it does seem likely to
me that young Hugo Hofmannsthal, in spite of his astounding, mature
detachment, was not altogether impervious to the ugly slogans of
Schönerer, such as: "Jew or Christian, it's all the same, the nastiness lies
in the race." If the young boy shrank from it, that is, if he was conscious
of it at all as he was almost bound to be, the Wertheimstein circle
would have offered a relief from all tension, because it was patrician
through intrinsic quality, and gave the lie to the louts in the street and
the aula of the University. To the élite of Viennese intellectuals in those
generations it would have been worse than bad manners, it would have
been spiritual vulgarism, even to mention whether someone was of
Jewish blood or not. The sharpest adversaries of any such tendency
would have been the distinguished gentiles (but they would have hated
the label) who flocked to the Wertheimstein villa.

It seems to me important to stress all this because a rather different
picture of Viennese intellectual life in the last quarter of the nineteenth
century has come to be widely accepted, through a superficial acquaintance with Freud's struggles for recognition during that period. The
general impression is that the reason why Freud had to wait for twelve
years after his appointment as university lecturer (*Privatdozent*) before
he was made professor *extraordinarius*, and then by title only, was a
mixture of antisemitism and personal intrigue, or, in other words, that
the real reason for the delay was a combination of distrust of the revolutionary thinker and dislike of the Jew.

Personal antagonism and intrigues there were, there always are in
academic circles even when no Freud is involved, though the stature of
the leading men of the faculty of medicine, Nothnagel, Meynert and
Krafft-Ebing, is greater than those squabbles imply. Antisemitism was
mounting in the 'eighties and 'nineties; but it had not yet—not yet!—
infested the intelligentsia: the ominous antics of the *Korpsstudenten*, the
members of the nationalist students' associations, took place on the
fringe—again one should say, as yet. Freud's Jewish pupils and later
collaborators were bound to feel the pressure during their student days.
When Ernest Jones included their impressions in his biography of
Freud, they could not but tint his portrayal of an earlier period. And
it is also true that the firm belief of the liberal élite that antisemitism

was "not done" among the likes of them, that progressive education would be an antidote to it among the outer barbarians, was an illusion. It is highly probable that even then a carefully suppressed, but none the less potentially dangerous antisemitic resentment was beginning to develop in the minds of several of the younger medical luminaries—I am thinking, for instance, of Wagner-Jauregg—particularly as the number of eminent professors of medicine, heads of clinics, and famous specialists, of Jewish extraction, was strikingly high. This fact makes nonsense of the notion that Freud, for the mere reason of his being a Jew, did not stand a good chance of an academic career, but it also contains the germ of ugly future developments, parallel to the crassly materialistic, i.e. economic, motives that were even then, in the late 'eighties and 'nineties, driving suburban tradesmen into Karl Lueger's antisemitic mass movement.

The situation in the bureaucracy was different. It would be ridiculous to pretend that there was no subterranean antisemitism at all among the Viennese civil servants. Though acting as a State within the State (the "despotism mitigated by muddle", *Despotismus gemildert durch die Schlamperei*, of Victor Adler's formula, was not a despotism of the Crown, but of the executive-governmental practice as carried through by the administrative machine), the Civil Service was after all recruited from the whole Austrian half of the Dual Monarchy and sieved through the universities, hence in communication with every social and national group, by no means only with the cultural or social élite. The influence of antisemitic tendencies in the administration, however, waxed and waned with the political power of the clerical-antisemitic parties, and was at all times counterbalanced by a still surviving, indeed, still powerful Josephinian tradition in liberal disguise among the higher civil servants. The Ministry of Religion and Education, which had to confirm or reject proposals by the professional college of a faculty, was an old battleground of liberalism versus clericalism, and was to remain so until the end of the monarchy. This made itself felt in appointments and decisions, as also in the reports on new text books for schools, which had to be submitted for official approbation before a State school could use them, and were always given to two *rapporteurs* of opposite tendencies. The Minister himself was, of course, an eminently political appointment, and one which the clerical party regularly tried to capture or influence, though not always successfully. Not the slightest whiff of antisemitism came from the

Emperor. In his public behaviour as much as in his private letters he showed that he had a distaste for antisemitic politicians, and no more prejudice against a Jewish financier than against any other; in fact, he used a Jewish banker, who was a friend of Frau Schratt's, as his own go-between in a very delicate negotiation concerning a book on the Mayerling affair, which he thought scurrilous and whose circulation abroad he wished to prevent. This, then, was the general situation in which, from the point of view of the bureaucrats, a certain Dr. Sigmund Freud was an unimportant figure.

The documents of the case have been published in a monograph* which contains some very peculiar, unwarrantable remarks, conjectures and inferences in its commentary, but supplies the relevant confidential papers, from the archives of the University and the Ministry, in full text. Several legends are exploded. The professorial college and its sub-committee never ceased to renew their proposal that Freud should be made professor extraordinary, or at least, when this was ruled out, for him and a few others on technical and budgetary grounds, be given the title though not the salary. Their decisions were not unanimous, and the enthusiasm not exactly marked as time went on. With most of them it was far less partisanship for Freud, than pursuit of a principle in a long-drawn-out campaign against ministerial decisions and ordinances which in their opinion infringed on academic autonomy. On the whole the conflict was between the official interest in the training of medical students—a direct inheritance from Metternich's pragmatic, anti-theoretical principles for university education—and the academic interest in research: the Ministry insisted that a main condition for the appointment of a professor extraordinary should be that the lecturer had been a diligent teacher, while the medical college of the University defended its right to have professors whose work as a whole would benefit the faculty and science. Freud seems to have been blithely unaware of the rules and regulations governing his lecturership and future academic career; he certainly did not make it easy for his champions when he exhibited his lack of interest in teaching. In explaining the delays by favouritism, as he did, he merely conformed to a good old Viennese tradition, though it would have shocked him to become aware of it.

The medical college of professors at the University of Vienna

* Professor Dr. Joseph und Renée Gickelhorn, *Sigmund Freuds akademische Laufbahn im Lichte der Dokumente*, Vienna, Urban & Schwarzenberg, 1960.

decided on 12 June 1897, by twenty-two votes against ten, to propose to the Ministry that Dr. Sigmund Freud, lecturer, should be appointed professor *extraordinarius*—a salaried, not a titular appointment, hence one which would have given him a seat on the college itself. The vote was taken on a report by Professor Krafft-Ebing, since 1880 holder of the chair of psychiatry, author of *Psychopathia Sexualis*, a report which included the following paragraphs on Freud's contentious research:

The guiding thought of these studies was to gain a deeper insight into the mechanism of neurotic processes, through a new psycho-therapeutic method for which Dr. Breuer had given the idea; they also entailed the hope of finding ways for the cure of such neuroses. In pursuing this laborious clinical path, Freud came to surprising results of great importance to aetiology. He proved that a principal factor in the genesis of hysterical and neurasthenic conditions which hitherto had been unexplained in their causes (aetiologically), consisted in anomalies and occurrences within the field of sex life, and that only their discovery and elimination could help in individual cases, a fact demonstrated in particular as regards so-called compulsive ideas and phobias.

The novel character of these researches, and the difficulty of checking them, prevent as yet a definite judgment on their significance. It is possible that Freud is overrating them, and goes too far in generalising the results he has obtained. In any event, his researches in this field prove an extraordinary gift and capacity for guiding scientific investigation into new channels. (*Op. cit.*, p. 96.)

Considering that at that time Freud had not yet published his psycho-analytical findings nor had they reached a conclusive stage, but that the *Studien über Hysterie*, the result of his collaboration with Dr. Breuer, had appeared already in 1895, this is a balanced, sympathetic, and in no way niggling appraisal. However, Freud was quite justified when he wrote to his friend Fliess in Berlin, on 8 February 1897, after having learnt that Professors Nothnagel and Krafft-Ebing would propose him, that "we all realise how unlikely it is that the Minister should act upon the proposal". It took five years of chessboard warfare between the Faculty and the Ministry, with Freud no more than one of the pawns, and also a change of government, to obtain the title for Freud.

The point is, all the same, that Freud was at no time as isolated, underrated and misunderstood in Vienna as legend makes out. That he disliked Vienna for complex reasons—though he made no serious effort to get away—is an established fact. He was emotionally involved, and his reaction to antisemitism was above all emotional, an anticipation of hurt based on the repeated experience of hurts. As the son of im-

migrants who had both come from Galicia he was far more on the
defensive, and far more vulnerable, than Vienna-born Jews of that
generation. But even when all these factors are taken into account,
they still do not invalidate the facts of Freud's initial career: he did find
early allies and helpers, champions and protectors among his teachers
and colleagues. Some were Jews and some were not. They recognised
that "extraordinary gift" in him of which Krafft-Ebing spoke in his
report. Freud's experiences with Viennese antisemitism had little to do
with his early academic exploits. They went deeper.

To understand what would happen to a sensitive Jewish boy not
sheltered by great wealth and gracious living, I have only to read in my
father's memoirs. My father was born in 1871. His was the third
generation in Vienna on his mother's side; his father, a wine merchant,
was a kind of peasant figure, and it was the mother's family that
counted. Her father was a wealthy man, with a villa and a big garden
in one of the outer suburbs, almost a village still, and a house nearer the
centre in an old inner suburb. This did not protect my father when he
went to grammar school:

In my early youth it was still only dumb hate . . . not accepted by good society,
but we felt it badly. . . . The street urchins waged war against Jewish boys.
In nearly every road there was a young hooligan who attacked and tormented
the little Jew-boys he knew, and when we went home from our lessons in
religion, still given outside the regular school hours, we were often ambushed
by whole gangs. It was not so bad, it meant rarely more than some bumps,
and it was terribly bad: to meet a hatred we couldn't understand, and were
unable to combat, necessarily appeared to us the most violent injustice and
evil. . . .

In my father's case it led to a general nonconformism. Because he
rejected the "claustrophobic" atmosphere of a Jewish clan, he was
secretly glad, I think, when he was forced, by his marriage with my
mother, to become a Lutheran—to become a Roman Catholic would
have been unthinkable to him. My maternal grandfather welcomed
this marriage because he expected it to "bring intelligence into the
family"; my paternal grandmother, who had her private edition of the
Talmud, which permitted her to eat pork and ham, but only from
paper, not from a plate, accepted her gentile daughter-in-law with
naïve friendliness. To this extent, the liberal era worked in my father's
favour. But it did not save him from carrying the scars with him
through the years. They cannot have been as bad as Freud's. At least

the family of my grandmother believed that they belonged to Vienna. Her own mother, my great-grandmother, had taken food to the students on the barricades of 1848, after all. And my father noted in his memoirs that the assimilated Viennese Jews had a clannish aversion to newcomers, particularly to Polish Jews whom they thought plebeian, dirty, and unreliable.

It seems pathetically absurd now, all this, after the years of Hitler. But while it lasted, it was a part of reality. It conditioned those who had to grow up with this burden of pressures. Therefore it seems to me important to put antisemitism, as well as the temporary illusion that antisemitism was merely the "shouting of uneducated hooligans", into perspective at the juncture where the cross-currents touch the figure of Freud, in his early manhood and in Vienna.

At that time, Vienna was still gilded by the culture of a prosperous and not ungenerous bourgeoisie—not ungenerous, that is, outside the factories, workshops and brick kilns, and away from the tenement houses in the industrial suburbs. In the small, exquisite shell of the Wertheimstein villa, men came together who played a part in the life and career of young Freud. To look at them, singly, is to learn something about the background to his development and at the same time about Vienna's intellectual life. Also, there are some facts to be gleaned from Emilie Exner's unfactual but descriptive essay. True to her creed that women should keep out of the fray of debate so as to be able to make all combatants feel appeased in the end, she conveyed the manner rather than the matter of exciting discussions, but the men turn up: Theodor Gomperz, Franz Brentano, Ernst von Fleischl, Joseph Breuer, Theodor Meynert.

To start with one who had only marginal importance for Freud, though considerable intellectual importance in Vienna, there was Josephine von Wertheimstein's brother Theodor Gomperz, professor of philosophy and historian, and the author of a work on the history of Greek thought which was still required reading in my university days. As the editor of John Stuart Mill's complete works in German, he found himself in a quandary when one of the scheduled translators died, and on the recommendation of his fellow philosopher Franz Brentano "at a party" he entrusted the twelfth volume to Freud, a young student unknown to him personally. It not only provided some welcome cash, but also helped Freud "to cope with the boredom" of his year of military service (cf. Ernest Jones, *Sigmund Freud, Life and*

Work, vol. I, p. 61). Freud seems to have remembered no more about the incident, but the "party" surely was one of the evenings in the Wertheimstein villa, where Franz Brentano was a regular at that time. Also, the intended translator who had suddenly died was Dr. Wessel, Josephine's friend since 1849 and Franzi's much-beloved tutor—not exactly a young man in 1879, as Jones surmises, but one so highly esteemed by the family that the commissioning of Freud implies a very strong recommendation by Brentano. Gomperz's wife, Elise, was one of Freud's important patients twenty years later.

Franz Brentano, in turn, was a German philosopher and ex-priest who had thoroughly stirred the stagnant waters at the Faculty of Arts, and gained great influence on the young by his departure from current philosophical idealism, which took the form of a return to Aristotle. Most important, perhaps, was his work on psychology from an empirical point of view. Freud attended Brentano's lectures on Aristotle in his first year at University, and his seminars and courses for another year. In Josephine's salon he was a sparkling debater and had many discussions with Ernst von Plener, a witty conservative-liberal politician and at one time minister, across Josephine's round tea-table. (It was tea in the afternoon for the Viennese upper middle and professional classes, not coffee to which the less sophisticated petit-bourgeois remained loyal.) The fireworks started when the great Theodor Meynert, "a tamed lion of the desert", as Emilie Exner called him, joined in with his rolling phrases and provocative paradoxes. But it seems to have been a much younger man who dared to contradict the great orators and "stress quite different interests": Freud's unhappy friend Ernst von Fleischl.

Fleischl "had the charming and amiable manners of old Viennese society, ever ready to discuss scientific and literary problems with a flow of challenging ideas", says Ernest Jones of him (*op. cit.*, vol. I, p. 49), and he quotes Freud as writing to his fiancée, at a time when Fleischl was already suffering from an infection contracted during his anatomical work, which killed him by inches over many pain-filled years: "I admire and love him with an intellectual passion, if you will allow such a phrase. His destruction will move me as the destruction of a sacred and famous temple would have affected an ancient Greek. I love him not so much as a human being, but as one of Creation's precious achievements." Elsewhere in Freud's letters there are glimpses of Fleischl, who was taking cocaine on Freud's recommendation, spending nights in a water-bed while talking "of all possible obscure things" to his friend; for he remained mentally stimulating even when in physical agony (*op. cit.*, vol. 1, p. 100). But in Emilie Exner's little book darkness had not yet fallen; Fleischl was still the gay, mischievous, irrepressible young scientist who "at a time when the whole world concerned itself with hypnosis, catalepsy and similar problems, would demonstrate the most convincing experiments with hens in trance and crayfish standing on their heads at a big *soirée*, and comment on them in his own manner which was so utterly free from any learned pedantry". In fact, Emilie Exner had been first introduced to Franzi von Wertheimstein by Fleischl, a friend of her future husband (a physiologist who, likewise, had a part to play in Freud's career, though there was little love lost between them), at a Friday evening in the only intellectual salon which in the 'seventies competed with Josephine's, that of Frau von Littrow-Bischoff, wife of the Chief Astronomer. The gatherings at the observatory seem to have been "a little formal and earnest", so that Fleischl's pranks brought light relief to the younger set, and a twinkle into the eyes of the dignified hostess. Fleischl betting that amidst the assembled guests in evening dress he would produce from his pocket the vulgar sort of salty rolls called *Salzstangel*, eat them, and get away with it; and Fleischl slowly dying, but for his parents' sake not killing himself—these scarcely seem what in fact they were, one and the same man. Is it blasphemy to suggest that Freud might have loved him "as a human being" also, if he had ever been able to grin at one of Fleischl's light-hearted, pointless jokes, and recognise the validity of that Viennese blend of play-acting and courage?

Fleischl disappeared from the Wertheimstein court, presumably as soon as he was noticeably ill. Dr. Joseph Breuer—the same Breuer who gave Freud a first impetus towards psycho-analytic studies, helped him for many years in practical ways, but in the end roused Freud's antagonism through his attitude of mental reservation—looked after Fleischl to the last. But Breuer was also the family doctor of the Wertheimsteins and Gomperzes, especially the adviser of Franzi in her later years. From the cautiously worded remarks of her admiring apologist, Emilie Exner, it would seem that Franzi was a neurotic who shrank from love and marriage, sometimes at the very last moment, at times hid away in her room, and yet suffered from her self-imposed loneliness, from which she would occasionally flee to the lively house of her aunt, Sophie von Todesco—the house, incidentally, in which Johann Strauss the Younger met his first wife, the singer Jetty Treffz, while she was living with Eduard Todesco's brother. The neurotic symptoms (a term which I use loosely, as a layman) among this group of Breuer's patients were no doubt connected with repressions and evasions one may guess at, but they were given a peculiar twist by a mode of life divorced from the world of poverty and profit, although that same world supplied its material foundations.

After the sudden death of her son—perhaps from infantile paralysis —Josephine von Wertheimstein, too, had gone through a period of mental illness, from which she recovered at least externally. Her medical adviser during that time had been Theodor Meynert, the psychiatrist and brain surgeon of whom Freud said that he recalled him "as the most brilliant genius he had ever encountered" (cf. Jones, *op. cit.*, vol. 1, p. 72) although his original veneration had long turned into animosity. Meynert became a personal friend of the Wertheimsteins and a fixture at Josephine's receptions, but his towering personality is best considered away from her tea-table, through the not uncritical eyes of his daughter Dora.

Dora Stockert-Meynert wrote a short book which, rightly sub-titled "A Contribution to Austria's Intellectual History in the Second Part of the Nineteenth Century",* leads straight into the heart of the educated Viennese middle class, to the stratum of professional men and civil servants who thought of themselves and their families as the "middle estate", the *Mittelstand.*

Theodor Meynert's father had come to Vienna from Dresden, had married a Viennese singer, the daughter of a police surgeon, and settled down as journalist and historian, with right-wing leanings. In 1848 the fifteen-year-old Theodor Meynert wanted to go and fight on the barricades, but his maternal grandfather made use of his police authority to have the boy taken into protective custody; Meynert never quite forgave him. His radical feelings lasted. Among the poems he wrote as a young man were ballads in honour of Marat and Robespierre. (Later he was to exchange poems with Billroth, another amateur poet.) And, like most of his generation, he rejected organised religion. He had a predilection for satire, for he liked Nestroy, and

---

* Dora Stockert-Meynert, *Theodor Meynert und seine Zeit. Zur Geistesgeschichte Österreichs in der zweiten Hälfte des 19. Jahrhunderts,* Vienna, Österreichischer Bundesverlag, 1930.

excepted Offenbach from his dislike of operettas. When he married and had a family, he would never allow his daughters to see other than classical plays in the Burgtheater. His house was filled with classical music, and his wife, who had good social connexions, got famous virtuosos to perform at her parties. But she was, in contrast to the Wertheimstein ladies with their "cult of beauty", something of a committee woman, in particular after 1873, when the middle class suffered the after-effects of the slump. The Meynert circle, too, was limited, but it was not isolated from ordinary life.

Theodor Meynert, who was head of the lunatic asylum as well as the founder of the psychiatric clinic, had strong views about the duties of a *Kliniker*, a physician in charge of a department. He thought, as his daughter explains, that it was wrong for such a man to have a private practice as well, because he should not become a business man. By no means all of his colleagues agreed with him. But since Meynert held all his views passionately, it can hardly have endeared Freud to him that he gave priority to his private practice, for however good a personal reason. His daughter, who says nothing on this point, hints at another difference of opinion with Freud. According to her, Meynert explained to his former pupil that "the number of criminals is almost exclusively related to the productive capacity of a country; as you know, I feel very strongly about the sorrow of mankind, the crime against the vast majority that arises from the social structure". This does not mean that Meynert was a socialist, but he may have been influenced by the ideas of Franz Brentano, by the "university socialism" of those years, and by his nagging social conscience. In any case, he seems to have been beset by dark moods. At least it was after one of his lectures on the subject of Delusion that Ferdinand von Saar wrote to him in 1885: "It is true, all mankind is dominated and directed by megalomania and persecution mania. . . ."

It is all the more remarkable that the tetchy old psychiatrist recognised a new moral force in a man whom most of his class regarded as the gravedigger of their culture, namely Victor Adler. Adler had been Meynert's pupil a few years before Freud, and he too had gone to Paris on a postgraduate grant. But though he had dropped psychiatry, first with the intention of becoming a factory inspector (because the fight against subhuman conditions in factories seemed to him an immediate task), then turning himself into a general practitioner among the poor, and finally concentrating all his energies on work for the unification and regeneration of the demoralised, badly split social-democratic movement, Meynert did not turn against him. Dora Stockert-Meynert says expressly that her father "had the greatest admiration for the spotless integrity and personal sacrifices which he [Adler] brought to the fight for his ideals". She mentions no date, but Meynert can only have referred to the series of prison sentences and police tribulations to which Adler was subjected at the end of the 'eighties and beginning of the 'nineties, when Taaffe used the emergency laws, officially directed against anarchist violence, with the aim of suppressing the social-democratic organisation in time. It was too late. Thanks to Victor Adler's infinite patience and undogmatic guidance, a new united party was born at the conference of Hainfeld, 30 December 1888 to 1 January 1889. And when the Socialist International—the "Second International"—decided to organise an international demonstration for an eight-hour day on the next First of May, which should be a workers' holiday, the party passed its first great test. On 1 May 1890, an endless procession of workers with their wives and children marched four deep along the great Prater avenue, carrying red flags and singing. It was the most successful First of May demonstration of any socialist party in Europe, and from then onward the Viennese workers have always held May Day in special affection. But as seen by the rest of Vienna, it was more than a successful workers' procession.

The whole machinery of the State was ready for action. There had been many strikes and many clashes between strikers and police or soldiers—Victor Adler had been sentenced to four months' imprisonment for his journalistic intervention in one of them, so that he was safely behind bars on the critical day—and the Government sat several times, with the Emperor presiding, to discuss the measures to be taken. Franz Joseph was in favour of strong action, sharper prison sentences, and a clear-cut attitude of the government to the workers' "illegal" demand for a day off.* On the morning of the day itself, the *Neue Freie Presse*, the ever grandiloquent organ of the liberal bourgeoisie, wrote in its leader:

Soldiers are standing by, the doors of houses are being closed, in people's apartments food supplies are prepared as though for an impending siege, the

* Ludwig Brügel, *Geschichte der österreichischen Sozialdemokratie*, vol. 4, Vienna, Wiener Volksbuchhandlung, 1923, p. 126, quotes an extract from the minutes of the cabinet meeting, which summarises the Emperor's statement in this sense in greater detail, though not textually.

shops are deserted, women and children dare not go out into the street, every-body's mind is weighed down by the pressure of grave worries.... This fear is humiliating, and it would never have arisen if the middle class had not sunk low, if it had not lost all confidence in its strength through the rifts in it. (Brügel, *op. cit.*, vol. 4, pp. 119-20.)

The panic must have run through every layer of the middle class. Stefan Zweig, whose account of his youth in *Die Welt von Gestern* (*The World of Yesterday*) clearly shows that his family was sheltered, rich and well-established, recalls early memories of that first May Day, when the merchants let down the iron shutters in front of their shops and his parents forbade their children to "go out in the street on this day of terror which might see Vienna in flames". Karl Renner, the future socialist leader and first President of the re-born Austrian Republic after 1946, was a poor student serving his year in the army, in touch through his sister and brother-in-law with the new middle class of recent Czech immigrants. In his autobiography *An der Wende zweier Zeiten* (Vienna, Danubia Verlag, 1946) he records that his sister's landlord put two steel bands round his strong box, stowed it away in the cellar, and left Vienna with his whole family to spend the dangerous day in the country. In barracks they were kept in a state of alert the whole day, talking about civil war, revolution and collective property, listening to every loud noise from outside; when their corporal dismissed them in the evening, saying that nothing had happened beyond a march to and from the Prater by an enormous mass of people, they found this no less puzzling than the previous scare. It left them with an unsolved question in their minds. Yet everyone, the adversaries of a new social order as much as its champions, agreed that "something new had entered history".

This "something new" made the weakness and disruption of the Viennese middle classes more patent. To this extent the *Neue Freie Presse* was right. Since about 1880, liberalism had been in decline as a political force, and no new ideology had taken its place. The aggressive German nationalism of Schönerer became widespread among students, but it had a strong whiff of the provinces about it: of young men who thought of their future careers as teachers, or judges, or doctors backed by the pre-eminence of their language group, among a less educated mass of peasants. In Vienna, it was constantly renewed at the University, and here and there among the middle class, but it lost its converts almost as soon as it made them, either to another antisemitic group without the Germanic megalomania (because it was difficult in Vienna to find enough people of pure German descent), or to an anti-capitalist movement free of racial prejudices. In any case, Schönerer and his men helped to break up the liberal era, but they did not move into the vacuum left by the shrinking of liberalism. Nor were the militant Roman Catholics able to do so. They, too, were on the increase; since 1848, the Church had gained much ground through lay associations, and as leaven there were small groups fighting for a new religious fervour. The Concordat, already full of holes, had been finally scrapped in 1870, but this eased rather than complicated the situation for those who demanded denominational schools: they could concentrate on local authorities, and in Vienna this meant once again attacking the liberals. As a central issue, however, this political Catholicism was restricted to a minority. It still left the vacuum unfilled.

No democratic party developed out of the liberal debris, although there were individual radicals and democrats who refused to join the workers' movement. The Liberals had been profiting from the unliberal and undemocratic electoral system far too long to change their attitude; it was still the same as that of Giskra, who had told the workers' delegation that universal suffrage was not for Austria, then or ever. At both parliamentary and local levels there were several electoral bodies, each based on the property status of the voters, and with the seats allotted so that the richest had automatically the strongest representation. It was a great concession when in 1885 the limit for the franchise was lowered to five florins annually paid in taxes—but those "five-florin men", more numerous than greater tax-payers, were at first disenfranchised by the tricks of what was called electoral geometry. In Vienna their vast majority consisted of small shopkeepers and tradesmen: nearly 7,600 out of 12,250, with clerical workers as the next strongest group. The Taaffe government attempted a change of policy in 1891, so as to gain new possibilities for manœuvring in Parliament. The emergency laws were lifted, a bill for universal—but not equal—suffrage prepared. It was voted down by German liberals, Polish landowners, and conservatives of all national groups. Taaffe fell. His successor, Badeni, introduced a far more modest electoral reform, which reduced the franchise level to four florins of annual tax-payment, and in addition set up a new electoral group on the basis of a general franchise, but with fewer seats than the three existing groups. It was in this "curia" that the first Social-Democrats were sent to Parliament.

But in the Town Council of Vienna, where the corresponding reform was not carried through until 1900, the lowering of the tax-limit for the franchise justified the apprehensions of the Liberals. They lost their majority to the party of the "little man", under the leadership of a great administrator and greater demagogue, Dr. Karl Lueger.

Adolf Hitler wrote extensively about Schönerer and Karl Lueger in *Mein Kampf*, and contrasted Schönerer's "failure to understand the importance of the lower strata of the population" with Lueger's "correct estimate of the various social forces". (I am quoting from the translation published by Hurst & Blackett in 1939, p. 95.) It is a surprisingly well-balanced judgement on a man from whom he admits to have learnt much:

He [Lueger] saw only too clearly that, in our epoch, the political fighting power of the upper classes is quite insignificant. . . . Thus he devoted the greatest part of his political activity to the task of winning over these sections of the population whose existence was in danger and fostering the militant spirit in them rather than attempting to paralyse it. He was also quick to adopt all available means for winning the support of long-established institutions, so as to be able to derive the greatest possible advantage for his movement from those old sources of power.

Thus it was that, first of all, he chose as the social basis of his new Party that middle class which was threatened with extinction. . . . His extremely wise attitude towards the Catholic Church rapidly won over the younger clergy in such large numbers that the old Clerical Party was forced to retire from the field of action or else, which was the wiser course, join the new Party. . . .

. . . He possessed the qualities of an able tactician and had the true genius of a great reformer; but all these were limited by his exact perception of the possibilities at hand and also of his own capabilities.

The aims which this really eminent man decided to pursue were intensely practical. He wished to conquer Vienna. . . .

What Hitler most admired in Lueger, in addition to his shrewd appraisal of possibilities, was the flair for propaganda: ". . . they were veritable virtuosos in working up the spiritual instincts of the broad masses of their adherents." And what he most regretted about Lueger and his party was a lack of seriousness and principle in their anti-semitism. It was not truly racial, it was in reality an anti-capitalist slogan meant to win over the Czechs, as a very strong group among small tradesmen, but a group that might be alienated by racialist, i.e. Pan-German attitudes.

Hitler on propaganda has to be taken seriously. His opinions on Lueger were not, of course, formed during his stay in Vienna as a very young man; it is enough to look at the account given in *Young Hitler, The Story of Our Friendship*, by August Kubiczek (London, Wingate, 1954), to realise that. Hitler was far too preoccupied with his need to assert himself, to keep his trousers well pressed even while they had to lodge in a bug-infested room, to discover and despise whores behind half-drawn curtains, to get angry when his name sounded softened in Viennese dialect, to admire the Ringstrasse buildings and have architectural fancies about tearing down the baroque stables—mere brick and plaster—of Fischer von Erlach so as to rebuild them in stone. Analysis can only have come later, when he was mulling over his defeat in and by Vienna, not only at the Academy, but among the workers on the building site who respected him so little that they wanted to force membership of their union upon him. But during those years in Vienna from 1908 to 1913, Hitler did meet, above all, the lower middle class, Lueger's staunch supporters. His assessment of the principles of the Mayor of Vienna, as being subordinated to his tactical needs, has the value of a practitioner's opinion on another practitioner.

Karl Lueger was born in 1844, the son of a beadle at the Polytechnic; after the father's death, his mother, as the widow of a war veteran, was granted the licence of a tobacco shop—tobacco being a K.K. monopoly, such licences were mainly reserved for army veterans, invalids, and their kin—in the old suburb of Landstrasse; and there Lueger grew up. The Landstrasse was a useful background for a politician to have. At that time it was dominated by a powerful Liberal "Citizens' Club", but had also a Catholic-Conservative casino as rallying point for aristocracy and clergy, and above all a vast reservoir of the lower middle class, from tradesmen who had risen to the exalted position of houseowners and landlords, down to small shopkeepers and artisans crushed by the competition of modern retail shops, and resentfully dependent on bank credit. There was also in the Landstrasse district a particularly strong colony of Czech immigrants; it was still so in my childhood— I grew up five minutes' walk from the street where Lueger's mother had had her tobacco shop—and some of it is true even now, because it was only in 1963 that a Viennese taxi-driver, discovering that I was born in the street where he lived, told me it was a preserve of "Slavs" (more Croats than Czechs nowadays). All this was to be relevant for Karl Lueger's political career. So, I think, was the peculiar structure of the borough: eighteenth-century palaces clustering near plain Bied-ermeier houses; Prince Metternich's former garden villa in Regency style not far from the new *palais* built for the Chancellor's grand-daughter, Princess Pauline Metternich-Sándor, on a Paris Second Empire pattern; tall apartment houses with pretentious fronts, but no bathrooms, for bourgeois tenants on the best floors and ill-paid public employees higher up; and farther away from the centre, the low, almost rural little houses of small tradesmen, next to tenements for workers.

The Liberal club of the Landstrasse sent Lueger into the Town Council, then ruled by Cajetan Felder who had risen from an even more modest corner of the lower middle class, and started, exactly like Lueger, as a practising lawyer, but had come to stand, in the eyes of the anti-liberal masses, for the régime of speculators and Jewish bankers. Moreover, he was an autocrat in the Town Hall, and suspected of large-scale favouritism. Lueger set himself up as a radical democrat, the watchdog of the common people, attacked Felder (who resigned over a public scandal, though his personal integrity was not impugned), and then began, in a united front with Schönerer's antisemites, to attack the liberals as well as the economic system. At the same time he established contact with the small but dedicated Christian-Socialist band led by Baron Vogelsang, from whom he derived ideas about a form of co-operative and corporate planning which would not touch the foundations of private property. And in addition, the Clerical Party under a Prince Liechtenstein approached Lueger. Out of all this he created the *Christlichsoziale Partei*, the Christian-Social Party, limited at first and for a long time to Vienna, and based, in spite of his other associations, on the huge suburban lower middle class. With this party he smashed the liberal majority in local elections. He was voted into Parliament by the "five-florin men" of Vienna. And he was three times elected Mayor by the Town Council, before Franz Joseph ratified the nomination. (The Emperor, as his letters to Katharina Schratt from that time show, disliked any touch of antisemitism, but he acted un-constitutionally, against an autonomous and legal vote of the Town Council, even if he was following the advice of his Government. Ironically, many of the men and groups who later saw their best defence against the working-class movement in Lueger's party, then feared chaotic and "anarchic" disturbances of the existing order.)

Thus the vacuum left by the collapse of political liberalism, and by the withdrawal of the cultured middle class to the gardens where they could cultivate civilised aesthetic pleasures, was filled. It was filled by a mass movement of suburban "little men" fighting for their survival in a modern society ("threatened by extinction", as Hitler was to say); by a shapeless medley of ideologies and programmes ranging from anti-capitalist municipal planning to rabid anti-socialism in the name of the old order, from political catholicism to virulent antisemitism; by a cult of Viennese insularity and a publicity image of Old Vienna; and by the persuasive half-genius of Lueger himself.

Karl Lueger was, there can be no doubt, a man of immense talent and charm. Much of the Lueger legend was clever propaganda in his lifetime, and the usual "good old times" mirage conjured up by his political successors after his death. But "handsome Karl", *der schöne Karl*, was a first-rate orator, a prudent and yet bold administrator, his own best public relations man, a shrewd operator in politics, and one who managed to appear all things to all men, at least to men who had the right to vote, and to their women. He was no fanatic. He, who exploited antisemitism and enlisted the support of the clergy, was neither a convinced antisemite nor a particularly devout Catholic. With all his personal integrity in financial and administrative matters, he was unscrupulous: he had no principles at all, except his love for Vienna, which is a feeling and not a principle, and his determination to stay in power. While he was Mayor of Vienna, from 1897 to his death in 1910, he moulded Vienna's official mask. On his death, his calibre was acknowledged by his implacable political adversaries of the Social-Democratic Party, whom he had kept out of the Town Hall (though he could not quite keep them out of the Council Chamber) by retaining the unfair and restricted franchise even when universal suffrage had been introduced for parliamentary elections in 1907. As Friedrich Austerlitz, editor-in-chief of the socialist *Arbeiterzeitung*, said in his obituary, Lueger was the first middle-class politician "to take the masses into account, to move masses, and to send the roots of his power deep into the soil".

It was no mean achievement, but it was curiously ephemeral. The reasons lie in the social group on which he based his party, and in his personality. Karl Lueger had personal dash and style. But when all the disarming, even endearing anecdotes are brushed aside, and his famous warm voice, pleasant humour and jovial manner are discounted, one is left—I, at least, am left—with a chill feeling. Where is the hard inner core of this protean man? Has he any such core? If he is the epitome of Viennese character, as many have claimed, it is that variant of Viennese character which has every kind of attractive virtue, but no strength of conviction and no inner substance. Nestroy would have neatly exposed it.

I have had to ask myself, before coming to this conclusion, whether I was not merely influenced by political prejudice. I do not think so. Others of Lueger's party, who were bitter enemies to everything I believed in—men such as Dr. Friedrich Funder or even Prelate Seipel—never struck me as being hollow. Nor has my Austrian Republicanism prevented me from thinking, once I had read the published private letters of Franz Joseph I, that I had misjudged his intimate character all my life, or from saying so in these pages. But Karl Lueger is a different case. Because it brings the story close to our own times, it seems important to me to criticise a myth that has unduly impressed many outside observers, and affected their picture of Vienna as a whole.

Yet more important than this very important man was the mass movement which Lueger launched, and harnessed through his party. With it, a social class came to administrative power in Vienna which had been excluded from it before. Theoretically it should have brought a new, productive ingredient into the mixture of Viennese civilisation, for better or worse, as the old middle class had done in the Biedermeier epoch, and the new bourgeoisie in the Ringstrasse-Makart era—the era that was petering out even as Lueger fought his battles against the Liberals in the Council Chamber of the Town Hall. But the suburban lower middle class—as elsewhere, a *petite bourgeoisie* without inner cohesion, held together by pressures from without ever since its defeat in 1848 (and then its revolutionary participation had sprung from retarded economic impulses)—had, with one significant exception of doubtful quality, no contribution of its own to offer. This exception was the last version of the myth of Old Vienna, revolving round the cult of mental cosiness, *Gemütlichkeit*.

A collective characteristic which existed, as a complex, many-sided product of centuries, was grossly simplified, turned into a virtue to cover a multitude of sins, and into a hallmark of the true Viennese as distinct from the outsider. Lueger himself, a cultured man with an intellectual's armoury at his disposal, made a display of *Gemütlichkeit*. It was a "cosier" version of the Nazi's blood-and-soil mystique, setting the genuine Viennese with his heart of gold and palate for good wine against the sharp-tongued foreigners—well, not those with a Czech accent, for in their way they were good Viennese too, but certain others, you know. . . . Anti-intellectualism was part of it. Lueger's henchman Bielohlawek became famous for a remark which anticipated the Nazi dramatist Johst's "When I hear the word culture I cock my pistol" in a less violent form. "When I see a book I want to puke." (The Viennese dialect, of which this is a very free translation, makes it sound sillier and funnier: "Wann i a Büachl siech, hab i's schon g'fressn", which is not the accent used even in Vienna by educated people, but that of the dark reaches of inspissated philistinism.)

Lueger's reign was the heyday of local chroniclers. The popular press was full of sketches telling the Viennese what Vienna had been and was like. Half of them evoked the old times before the fall of the bastions, well-known figures or types of beer-houses, wine-gardens, and cafés, and the outlying villages before they became suburbs, when people still kept to their Corpus Christi processions as local feasts. The other half described—and invented—Viennese types of the day, with names that became part of the language, for the suburban cock-of-the-walk or the gossip-monger, and with family sagas much like those of television or radio going on for years in a serial. Some sketches, more satirical than their readers guessed, tried to take the place of the defunct local farce. Friedrich Schlögl, true to his 1848 beliefs, caricatured the playboys and prosperous landlords of suburbia, with their confused political prejudices, and dared conjure up the ghosts of the Revolution on the memorial day of the "March Victims". But he wrote in the *Neue Wiener Tagblatt*, which belonged to Crown Prince Rudolph's friend Szeps, and addressed itself to the progressive middle class. His arrows were ignored by their targets.

Suburban bourgeois and little tradesmen alike would go to operettas or the *Heurigen*, listen to the sentimental, mock-nostalgic songs of which they were the best customers, and find themselves too good for balls of the low-income and low-status groups of their own class, such as the washerwomen's ball and even the more famous *Fiakerball*. These balls, once spontaneous gatherings of men and women who did the same work, spoke the same language, and enjoyed themselves with the same abandon, had lost their character since the 'sixties. They had become commercialised. They were invaded by "temporary million-aires", as Schlögl called them, occasionally by young men of the best society, and were organised by Fiaker-Milli, a very popular and temperamental tart, so that they looked for all the world like publicity posters on the theme of Viennese gaiety. (In the second act of the Strauss opera *Arabella*, Hofmannsthal—who intended his libretto to be what it is, a romantic pastiche almost in operetta style—put Fiaker-Milli and the *Fiakerball* on the stage; Schlögl, who had written about them realistically, must have revolved in his grave.) Popular songs went through a similar development. Their local colour was as truthful as the colouring of the chromo-lithographs of the time. They told the Viennese that they and their city were marvellous, unique, and extremely lovable. The illusions and habits of the lower middle class, shorn of the quirks that made them genuine, were given the inflated rôle of symbolising the Viennese spirit. And this was not ephemeral. The fiction of suburban *Gemütlichkeit* and what it stands for has triumphantly survived, the one permanent conquest of the Lueger era.

For four decades, from about 1870 to 1910, a comedian called Alexander Girardi paraded the image of the typical Viennese through the town, on and off the stage. (He died only in 1918, but performed rarely in the last years of his life, so that as a growing child I had no chance to see him, though I could not help hearing stories about him, and seeing people strike poses, or pronounce phrases, with the explanation that Girardi had done it like that.) He was the last in the great line of Raimund and Nestroy, a singer even when his voice gave out, an actor who was witty and funny, but above all a creator of human beings, and his delivery of songs in the Viennese dialect was inimitable. One of the most famous of those songs was the *Fiakerlied*, the song of the fiacre driver proud of his two smart horses and his skill, his handling of the whip and clacking of the tongue: "anyone can become a *Fiaker*, but only in Vienna do they know how to drive". The refrain there is that egregious flattery again—everything is explained, because the *Fiaker* is a true-born Viennese.

This song was popular far beyond the theatre-goers or any particular class. Horses, racing, and even more the trotting-course, created a brotherhood of fans drawn from all social strata. Girardi had a similar effect; he was admired and copied by elegant young officers and by cobbler's apprentices. His rôles were always immediately comprehensible. He played, for instance, the character parts in Johann Strauss operettas—the pig-breeder Zsupan in *The Gypsy Baron* was among his greatest, and most copied, triumphs—and those parts in Raimund plays which Raimund had written for himself, the simple, good men like Valentin the carpenter in *The Spendthrift*. Walking in the street he had his special outfit, a boater and a stick: the boater was hereafter called a *girardi* and became the fashion. His flattened pronunciation of the Viennese dialect influenced people's speech more generally, though they would make a joke of it, than the immaculate German spoken in classical repertory at the Burgtheater, which was the high school of elocution for those who wanted to get rid of an undesirable accent. In short, Girardi was a model, and a promoter, of that "jelly-like democracy" of which Hermann Broch spoke, and which throve on the Old-Vienna and *Gemütlichkeit* cult made to measure for the lower middle classes, even though it engulfed a great part of the upper class as well. That he was, as an actor, the choice of intellectuals and non-intellectuals alike, was his individual achievement. The image he projected sprang from a collective fiction, and lent reality to it.

Many years later, Girardi's son published a biography of his father. The career itself recalls that of Raimund in his beginnings, but Alexander Girardi was not born in Vienna. He was born in Graz, in Styria, had knocked about as locksmith and actor, and came to Vienna only at the age of twenty-one. As a mature man he was intrigued by the origin of his "genuine" Viennese-ness, and came to the conclusion that the "apparent external and internal adaptation" on which he built his innumerable rôles was the outcome of a consciously critical attitude. Remaining deeply rooted in his native region, he played a Viennese for the benefit of the Viennese; he would say: "The way I play a Viennese for them isn't what they are, it's just what they'd like to be. . . . If I'd been born a Viennese, I'd never manage it." The son adds that his father really looked the standard type of a Viennese at the turn of the century in his manner of dressing and moving. His faint swagger, evocative of gaiety, the wide sweeping gesture with which he raised his hat, his mobile face, "all this was genuine, convincing Viennese-ness (*Wienertum*) transfigured into its own essential idea".*

Girardi's explanation implies that "the Viennese"—but the general term never applies to more than the predominant groups, varying with each context—had a mirror image of themselves which they saw realised in him. It was the image of a gay, agile man-about-town, a sportsman and good sport, with all the time in the world to saunter along the Ringstrasse and salute pretty women. Obviously a style of living accessible only to a few (for Girardi himself it was part of his

* Anton Maria Girardi, *Das Schicksal setzt den Hobel an*, Vieweg Verlag, 1941, pp. 357-58.

L

work), though anyone could copy the mannerisms, and nearly all young people did.

In an article on Girardi's fiftieth birthday in 1900, Hermann Bahr—always a shrewd observer, though unreliable in his generalisations—said that "a soldier courting a cook" and a young man of so-called good society, "the son of a suburban landlord" and any young count, would all stick out their heads, move their fingers, shape their lips, and intone their words on Girardi's pattern. The soldiers to whom he casually referred were the many conscript soldiers on service in Vienna for three years (but young men who had passed their grammar school finals had the privilege of serving one year only, as *Einjährig-Freiwillige*, and ending as Lieutenants in the "Reserve"), who carried Viennese inflexions back to their various regions. But the "sons of suburban landlords" were, in fact, an important rising group in Lueger's reservoir of voters, the new middle-middle class.

In his autobiography, Karl Renner makes a special study of such a set-up (*op. cit.*, pp. 201–2). He takes as an example of the "new rich middling class", not quite assimilated into Vienna either in language or in customs, the Czech landlord in whose house his sister's husband worked as a porter. (There are porters or concierges in all Viennese houses, usually living in a dark basement.) This man had come to Vienna as a shoemaker's apprentice, married a cook with some savings, set up his own shop and workshop, exploited the boom after 1866 to build a tenement house further out, on a small down payment and high mortgages, paid back the loans out of a rising rent-roll, and in the course of the years had been able to buy more tenements. As the influx of workers continued, rents kept on rising; the man married for money a second time, and retired to his own house where he devoted himself to accumulating cash in his strong box—the same strong box which he was at pains to save from the "Red rabble" on May Day 1890.

His sons went to grammar school so that they finished their military service with the rank of officers, obtained minor posts in the civil or municipal service, learned to "maltreat violin and viola just as the daughter maltreated the piano", and in one way or the other absorbed a modicum of "typically Viennese" culture. Their existence was crowned by the acquisition of a small villa in the country, to the west of the city. "Apart from occasional visits to the Burgtheater, their higher needs were satisfied by the *Volkssänger*, the street singers in *Heurigen* taverns of the western suburbs, then greatly in favour." And, like all newcomers to a city before they are truly absorbed by it, they were great local patriots.

Patronage of arts and letters among a new bourgeoisie grown beyond the stage of gaudy exhibition—solid cultivation of classical music and literature among the old-established middle class—lively journalism without much bite, but with tit-bits for connoisseurs—the poise of ancient, undisturbed privilege among those aristocrats who gyrated within a closed world of their own—a second society gathered round the wilful Princess Pauline Metternich-Sándor, patroness of countless welfare campaigns, organiser of brilliant pageants, and called "Notre Dame de Zion" because of her predilection for Jewish journalists and bankers—the court in fossilised routine—politicians evolving the art of bypassing Parliament, but lacking a consistent policy—an officer caste creating the semblance of unity above the fissures cracking the Austrian empire—an agglomeration of lower-middle-class groups struggling for status, and exuding a gluey pseudo-tradition of Old Vienna revisited: all this was Vienna at the turn of the century. But it was not all of Vienna.

There was a phosphorescent glitter about it that came from the irrevocable decay of the foundations on which the capital rested—from the crumbling of international power and internal cohesion. Not everybody was conscious of it, of course. The nationalist passions, meeting and clashing at the centre, disguised a vast apathy among the middle classes, profound pessimism and fatigue in the higher Civil Service, and the frivolous mood of *après nous le déluge* among a great part of the upper class. But the more sensitive among the young, and the more perspicacious among the older intellectuals, were affected by that reek of decay.

In Robert Musil's novel *Der Mann ohne Eigenschaften* (*The Man without Qualities*) there is a characteristic passage which draws on the writer's experience of a city that was not his own, though he knew it well. His hero Ulrich, as a pupil at the distinguished grammar school of the *Theresianum*, Maria Theresia's foundation for the sons of noblemen, discovers that "the Austrians had admittedly won victories, too, in all wars of their history, but after most of these wars they had to cede some territory. Ulrich wrote in his essay on patriotism that a serious patriot should never regard his country as the best of all . . . and was nearly expelled from the school." This is an oblique way of describing how adolescent Austrians at school in the 'nineties—like Musil himself and his Viennese hero—came to lose their belief in the power and stability of their country, and therefore the comforting self-identification with it, with the "father-land". Not everybody thus afflicted was able to hold on to the abstract idea of the monarchy, as Broch described it in his essay on Hofmannsthal. Only a few turned to the quickly growing socialist movement: if it is impossible, as the saying has it, to jump over one's own shadow, it is exceedingly difficult to jump over the shadow of one's social conditioning. But the fear of emptiness, *horror vacui*, combined with a scornful impatience of conventional solutions, created the atmosphere, or prepared the ground, for a new art which dissolved the sham of solid surfaces, and converted disenchantment and nervous tension into creative values.

The "decadent" movement and so-called art of nerves in literature and music, late Impressionism and Post-Impressionism in painting, *art nouveau* in interior decoration and, for a short time, in architecture, were of course not peculiar to Vienna. But in each field the Viennese version carried the mark of a specific crisis, and grew out of the past, whether by rebellion or by renewal, even when influences from abroad were fertilising it.

In music, the young generation turned vehemently against the aesthetic rules laid down by Eduard Hanslick and even against the conservative intellectualism of Johannes Brahms. "The good, solid masters of our fathers' time . . . were as suspect as the rest of the world of security", is Stefan Zweig's summary in *The World of Yesterday*. And Hermann Broch, too, speaks of Brahms as severely conservative, bound by tradition in his symphonic work and his songs, while Bruckner and Hugo Wolf represented an anti-rationalist revolution. The public of the concert halls and the opera in Vienna was still rejecting the innovations of Debussy and early Schönberg, when the young students were already fighting for them; similarly resistance to Gustav Mahler's symphonies continued even after his breakthrough at the Opera, with new productions and decorations in a modern style.

The artistic upheaval was not always the work of young men. The first public building in Vienna constructed not from the external aspect, from the façade, but from its inner functional core, was built with new materials—concrete, steel, glass—by Otto Wagner in 1904, when he was about seventy. The first President of the *Sezession*, the association of artists, formed in 1898, which broke away from academic painting

and brought the first impressionist pictures to the Viennese public, was
Gustav Klimt who, born in 1862, was older than the rest of his circle.
He had developed from the decorative school, away from Makart,
but without going through an impressionist phase, and arrived at a
style completely his own, but in the anti-realistic, subjective stream of
contemporary aesthetics, fluid in line, very subtle in colour, and in his
later stages—I have never been able to like this part of his work—
laden with ornamental patterns. On this point I prefer to quote an art
historian, E. H. Buschbeck (*Austria*, p. 231):

Space, in which real things exist, is replaced by rhythmical movement in the
two-dimensional plane . . . sensitive emotions, suspended moods, vibrating
nerves, spiritual and erotic sensations; all this expressed by a subtle and poly-
phonic play of expressive lines supported first by a glitter of delicate tints and
later by an ornamentation of metal and bold colours. . . .

From Klimt, whose stylised forms and ornamentation link him with
the applied art patterns of the *Wiener Werkstätte*, a brain child of the
architect Joseph Hoffmann, a connecting thread leads to a younger and
stronger painter, to Egon Schiele who died in 1918 of the Spanish
influenza, only twenty-eight years old. I have never forgotten the great
exhibition of his paintings in the *Sezession* the year after his death; the
bodies in his oils, with nerves and muscles quivering in the un-glossy
skin, and the powerful life in the ugliness of those tuberculous tarts
and rachitic children, seemed to assault me. But that was in 1919, when
I was very young, and the old society had collapsed to release a new
one. For Schiele's impact before the First World War, here is Ernst
Buschbeck again:

A proletarian rebel (in the human, not the political sense), he drew and painted
. . . with a painful intensity, a frightening wildness and, occasionally, a blood-
curdling indecency.

Yet Schiele was already part of a second wave of the modernist
movement. He was its heir in dissolving the solid surface of an unreal
reality, but also its opponent in reacting against its aestheticism. Oskar
Kokoschka, four years older than Schiele, went his different way from
a similar starting point, breaking out of the close mesh of intellectual
cliques. Both belong in a true sense to the next chapter.

For the group of writers who came to be called "Young Vienna",
and who had little in common except that deep unease in a hollowed-
out bourgeois world, the starting point was Hermann Bahr, whom I

have quoted several times. Bahr, born at Linz in Upper Austria in 1863, had been to Paris and Berlin and brought exciting news of intellectual movements to Vienna, with the aid of a magazine in which he launched his provocative, scintillating essays. He was versatile to the point of being unstable, but a genuine stimulator, and a brilliant journalist. His plays and novels were much more conventional than his ideas; he helped to fight for Ibsen in Vienna—and to fight against Ibsen's rationalist plays afterwards; he waxed enthusiastic about Zola, but rejected Naturalism in his later phase when he turned first to mysticism and then to a traditional Catholicism. In his early years in Vienna, he was the intellectual intermediary for many ideas. As a journalist he supported the change at the Burgtheater under a new director, his friend Burckhard, from a declamatory style and Makart décor, to a swifter, more nervous and "modern" treatment and simplified settings. It was through the Burgheater, and interpreted by Bahr's clever theatrical reviews, that Arthur Schnitzler rose to fame, even though his first important dramatic work, *Anatol*, was too mischievously satirical to fit the court theatre.

Among the men of Young Vienna, Schnitzler stands alone. Always excepting Hofmannsthal, he was the only writer of lasting importance. He had a perturbing knack of getting under the skin of conventional situations and attitudes. On 8 June 1906, Freud wrote him a letter to explain that he had been long aware of the "far-reaching coincidence" between their respective psychological interpretations, but had only recently dared express it in so many words:

I have often asked myself, wonderingly, from where you were able to draw that secret knowledge which I have had to acquire through laborious investiga-tion of the subject, and in the end I have come to envy the poet whom I had only admired before. (Published with other letters of Freud to Schnitzler in *Die Neue Rundschau*, 1955/1, with notes by Heinrich Schnitzler, son of the writer.)

In his narrative prose, Schnitzler traced the subtlest half-conscious feelings and impulses, always in beautifully shaped, filtered sentences. His experiences as a medical man in general, and neurologist in particu-lar, had taught him a pessimist's rueful tolerance that came out even in those of his plays which are amusing and, on the surface, frivolous. Because erotic tangles were the core of most of those plays, they were misunderstood. *Reigen*, for instance, known through the film *La Ronde* in versions far removed from the original, is a shattering study of the sameness in the mating habits of all social groups. Schnitzler character-ised the different types by shades of the Viennese dialect which have a deadly accuracy, and by the corresponding vocabulary. Comedies and anti-comedies, timbered to be effective theatre, reflect the code of Viennese society; those young drifters or officers or pleasant minor aristocrats tend to play-act with charm, expect others to do the same, and are surprised when tragedy arises from the human depths of another kind of people. Much in Schnitzler's plays is social satire, camouflaged either by fashionable wit, or by fashionable sentimentality. The plays take a current myth, such as the sweet girl from the suburbs—a myth with a substantial core of truth, and a facile term, *das süsse Mädel*, afterwards launched in a pop song—who is just right for elegant young men not yet inclined to marry, and reveal the reality behind it in a flash, after which everything slides back to normal. Thus the "sweet girl" and her lover turn up in *Anatol*, with charming coquetry, in *Liebelei*, as the helpless victims of convention and their own characters, and in *Reigen*, shorn of all glamour. But smart society people loved the plays, and felt confirmed by them in their poses. Legend was, as so often, shaping the mask of reality, but only in the way in which women's fashions shape the bodies and proportions of a generation.

As the invisible disintegration and decadence of Viennese society progressed with the years, so that conflicts sharpened, Schnitzler's prose went deeper, though he often made use of romantic devices. He explored the social seam where aristocracy and bourgeoisie over-lapped, observed the self-contained world of the barracks in which a duel was still the obligatory answer to any insult to "honour"—the inviolable status of the officer—and analysed the variations of friction between Jews and gentiles, *Mischlinge* (the offspring of mixed marriages, of whom Vienna was full) and race-proud Jews, the older assimilated generation and the disillusioned, insecure sons.

Schnitzler's small masterpiece, the selective interior monologue *Leutnant Gustl*, was written in 1900 and appeared the following year. A little lieutenant has by a chain of misfortunes gone to the concert hall to listen to an oratorio (he wouldn't have minded *La Traviata* at the Opera, where the standing room behind the stalls was reserved for subalterns, just as in the Burgtheater), and had a brush with a casual acquaintance, a rich vulgarian, in the crowded cloakroom. This master baker dares to lay hands on Lieutenant Gustl's sword; Gustl ought to chastise him, if necessary cut him down on the spot, but he does not have sufficient presence of mind. So he has lost his honour; if the affair gets round to his colonel, he will have to quit the Army, or else a court of honour will condemn him. In either case his career is ruined, he cannot rely on the master baker's discretion. Hence he will have to shoot himself. The whole story consists of Lieutenant Gustl's shapeless thoughts after this shock, in the course of a sleepless night spent walking and sitting about in the Prater. Before going back to barracks and settling his affairs, he has breakfast at his accustomed café. The waiter tells him that the master baker died last evening from a stroke. Gustl is saved; his reaction is a rush of barbaric urges to hurt others and make love. The hollowness of his code of honour stands revealed; it had never been a matter of inner integrity.

The story cost Arthur Schnitzler his rank as an officer of the Reserve. It was too revealing. With all its satirical touches, *Leutnant Gustl* was flesh-and-bone reality—the reality from which Karl Kraus was to distil the inane lieutenants whose conversations at the corner of Ringstrasse and Kärntnerstrasse are one thread in the huge, intricate tapestry of *Die Letzten Tage der Menschheit*, the epic of the dissolution of Imperial Vienna.

A few years later, Schnitzler published his novel *Der Weg ins Freie* (*The Road into the Open*—compare the quotation from it about the Wienerwald, p. 32). It is by far the most illuminating work of realistic fiction on Viennese society immediately after the turn of the century, and in its time was considered to be a *roman à clef*. Even without the key to the identity of all its many characters, a sufficient number of them are recognisable, either as composites or as individuals. They are men and women who meet in what is clearly the Café Griensteidl (though it is never named), and in the houses of a few well-to-do families, Jewish and gentile; the social range extends from rich financier to struggling intellectual, but remains within the bourgeoisie and professional middle class, except for the two young aristocrats at the centre of the story. One of them, the hero Georg, most probably represents the brother of that Baron Franckenstein who became a British subject and Sir George Franckenstein after the Anschluss, because he would not serve Hitler as Austrian Minister; the identification is important in so far as the two Franckensteins were close friends of Hugo von Hofmannsthal. In Schnitzler's novel, both Georg and his beautifully self-contained brother Felician have the breeding and finish

which Hofmannsthal looked for in his dream-aristocracy, but Georg
also has Hofmannsthal's own sensitive responses. Georg finds it difficult,
as in real life did Sir George's brother, to attain recognition as a serious
professional musician, since people from their kind of ancient family are
dismissed as amateurs. (Even while snobs tried to cultivate aristocratic
contacts if they were able to get behind the barrier, and imitated aristocratic mannerisms, it was generally held that aristocrats were all but
morons. A mother might say to her daughter, as I have heard it said
myself: "You really could marry a count", meaning that she was
pretty or charming enough for it, and hastily add: "But he'd be too
stupid for you.")

Through their intellectual or musical interests, these two brothers are
very friendly with young Jewish intellectuals, above all with a sceptical
and extremely perceptive writer—possibly with some features of
Schnitzler himself—whose father had gone mad when his early political
work as a dedicated German-Liberal had ended in bitter failure. Every
shade of Jewish attitude in the face of the antisemitic tide is represented;
the tough old financier who does not care if his accent is uncouth, and
his son who changes his religion and manners to be accepted in society;
the successful composer who relies on the general liking for easy
music, and his smart son who is integrated enough to remain what he is,
and copes blandly with brutal antisemitic fellow-officers; the tough
young Zionist from Galicia, and the aggressive son of a mild liberal
doctor. This particular young man, inclined to be a doctrinaire, has
had a term in Parliament as a Social-Democrat. He tells an anecdote
which is fabricated out of true Lueger and Bielohlawek stories: the
loudest antisemite in the Chamber had insulted him as Yid, but afterwards offered him some refreshment. The comment is: "Here with us,
indignation is as little genuine as enthusiasm; only pleasure at the
misfortune of others, and hatred of talent, are genuine here." This
remark might have come straight from Hermann Bahr, who at about
that time published an essay called "Wien", in which he railed
brilliantly and with enormous gusto at the Viennese.

Schnitzler, however, was never crude himself even when he put
crude sayings into the mouth of a character. In this novel, he dares to
tackle the delicate question of a gentile's resentment of Jewish touchi-
ness. His Georg, who despises antisemitism, is irritated because he
meets, wherever he goes, either Jews ashamed of being Jews, or Jews
proud of it, but afraid that they might be thought to be ashamed.

"Why did they always have to start talking about it themselves?" He finds an easy, spontaneous confidence with his two best Jewish friends somewhat difficult, as they don't trust him completely, but also because he has an obscure sense of guilt. "In an atmosphere of foolishness, injustice and insincerity, a clean relationship cannot thrive even between people who are clean themselves." His friend Heinrich accepts the reality of that atmosphere. He has always, since childhood, felt ashamed for other Jews whenever they behaved badly. Jews are prisoners. There is no "road into the open" for them; such a road is never for groups, always for individuals only. Georg von Wergenthin gropes for it, he leaves Vienna and his tangled love problems behind, but he is not certain of the escape. As Heinrich Bermann says: "The only thing that matters is always how deep we can look into ourselves."

The sensation of being shut up, without escape from poisonous conflicts, is pervasive. There is also the wise civil servant, Hofrat Wilt, friend and adviser of many people, young and old. At times he seems to speak like an anarchist: nothing would change in Austria if they kept away from their offices for a year. About eight years later, Schnitzler was to make such a civil servant, defending himself with cynical talk, one of the characters in his drama *Professor Bernhardi*,* which hinges on the conflicts arising from the refusal of the Jewish physician-in-chief of a hospital to let a dying patient, who does not know her condition, be shocked into awareness by the Last Sacraments. A remark of the *Hofrat* at the ministry became famous: "A civil servant seems to have no choice but to be either an anarchist or an idiot." The civil servant Wilt in the earlier novel explained what someone in his position, with his insight into administrative policy, was bound to feel—unless he was an idiot. Austria was "an infinitely complicated instrument, which only a master could handle correctly, and which produces ugly sounds so often only because any bungler thinks he can play it. . . . They will go on bashing at it . . . until all strings crack, and the case as well."

Because all the roads seemed closed to the people for whom Schnitzler spoke, whom he knew and diagnosed, it was necessary to "look deep into oneself", and to accept the uncertainty, before going on with the business of life. Freud, in a letter written in 1922, when strings and case had long cracked, called the analytical part of Schnitzler's work his

* In May 1965 this play was revived by the Burgtheater team, and stirred the Viennese public profoundly by its uncanny foreshadowing of subsequent events.

"dissolution of all cultural-conventional certainties". The poetic part
was the transformation of uncertainty into a game on the stage, or into
the deceptively lucid discipline of narrative prose.

In a verse play, *Paracelsus*, Schnitzler uses the line:

> We all act parts, and wise is he who knows it.

In this knowledge of the masks of life, and in the graceful game with
the knowledge itself and the masks, Schnitzler joins one of the strongest
streams of Viennese cultural tradition. His people, however, those he
invented and those to whom he belonged in illusionless detachment,
were prisoners of a crumbling world. The future of Vienna was not
with them.

VI

The Builders of the Future

IN ROUND figures, the population of Vienna rose from 490,000 in 1859, the first year of a modern census, to 705,000 in 1880, 1,340,000 in 1890 (when the outlying suburbs and new industrial settlements were incorporated, with the exception of Floridsdorf on the left bank of the Danube which followed only in 1910), 1,675,000 in 1900, and 2,031,000 in 1910. Before the rapid rise of Berlin, Vienna had been the third largest of European capitals; later it ranged fourth, after London, Paris and Berlin.

During all that time, a little less than half the total were Viennese by birth, with slight variations of the percentage; also, there was always a contingent of between 20,000 and 30,000 soldiers doing their military service in the garrison, and going back home at the end of their three years in uniform. Of the newcomers who stayed on, the great majority of men, and a large proportion of women, went into workshops, factories, the building trade, home industries, shops and domestic service as workers or low-grade clerks. No reliable statistics exist, but such part-surveys as there are indicate that people not born in Vienna, and their descendants, dominated the working-class districts from the years of industrial expansion onward.

Like many other capitals, however, Vienna was never an industrial city. The central machinery of the State alone tied up a vast number of people, and so did other administrative headquarters, public and private. Small retail shops with a few assistants, and tiny workshops producing goods for the individual consumer, still absorbed, up to the eve of the First World War, an army of workers, men and women, some trained in their craft and some semi-skilled, but all cheap labour. The master-craftsmen with workshops as well as retail stores of their own were, however, forced by competition to compromise in one of two ways: either by switching from handicraft pure and simple to hand-machines, which made them financially dependent on loans and credit, or by working on commission for wholesalers and big modern shops, which made them dependent in their patterns and techniques as well as their social status. The weakest among them were absorbed into the proletariat. The survivors fought for their existence with redoubled acrimony on two fronts: politically—through Lueger's party—against the Liberals, as the advocates of free enterprise, and "the Jews" as their own main competitors and/or financial overlords;* and economically against their workers. They were a powerful lobby, and gradually obtained measures of protection for small crafts against the encroachments of modern industry, which to some extent reversed the earlier legislation against restrictive practices in craft-trades. A statistical survey of 1902 counted among 105,570 gainful establishments no less than 90,714 which employed from one to five persons only. Slightly less than half of this group, 44,758 establishments, belonged to the "productive" sector—the industrial, as distinct from the distributive, transport and commercial sector—and these midget workshops employed nearly a third of all wage-earners in the category, 115,505 out of a total of 373,424. Another third of the personnel employed in production worked in small to medium-sized factories, in establishments employing between 21 and 300 persons. The pre-eminence of midget enterprises, in other words, of the small tradesman, master-artisan or shopkeeper, was still overwhelming in 1902, and accounted for the political and social weight of this class in Vienna at the time.

The *Technical Guide* from which these statistics are culled follows them up with comment, and with concise surveys of the more important branches of industry and commerce. The guide points out, for instance, that the rapid development of the use of electricity after 1902, and also the impetus of the boom years 1906 and 1907, went far to alter the picture, adding to the number of medium-sized factories, but without diminishing the importance or even the number of workshops and shops of the smallest size. It also adds the detail that of the eight plants which employed more than 1,000 persons in 1902, seven belonged to the metal industry, and all eight were situated in the outlying districts that had been incorporated into Vienna in 1890, or (in

* Concrete examples of this attitude are contained in Sigmund Mayer, *Die Wiener Juden* (Vienna, Löwit, 1917), an idiosyncratic book crammed with information and data from the author's experience in the textile trade, as well as observations interesting through their particular slant. Chapter 5 describes the genesis and structure of the trade in ready-made clothing, and on these grounds explains the early affiliation of the Viennese Tailors' Company to the antisemitic movement.

the case of Floridsdorf on the left bank of the Danube) as late as 1910. The one enterprise with more than 1,000 employees in the commercial-distributive category was the Municipal Tramway.

It is worth while looking at the statistical table itself, because it reveals the bones of Vienna's economic structure:

ENTERPRISES IN VIENNA GROUPED ACCORDING TO NUMBERS EMPLOYED

	Productive (industrial) Sector		Commercial, Transport and Distributive Sector	
Employing	Number of establishments	Persons employed	Number of establishments	Persons employed
1–5	44,758	115,504	45,956	77,930
6–10	6,771	49,942	2,081	15,420
11–20	2,454	34,489	846	11,992
21–50	1,254	38,647	428	13,239
51–100	453	31,642	90	6,268
101–300	329	53,219	51	8,064
301–1,000	77	38,154	11	4,765
over 1,000	8	11,727	1	3,817
	56,104	373,324	49,464	141,495

(From the Industrial Census of 3 June 1902, as quoted in *Technischer Führer durch Wien*, published by the Austrian Association of Engineers and Architects, Vienna, 1910, p. 563.)

The fact that the Viennese manual workers were mainly employed, either in small workshops below factory level, which escaped factory inspection for this reason, or in small to medium enterprises lodged, as often as not, in old-fashioned, unsuitable buildings, affected their working conditions, their wages, and the development of their trade unions. It was also bound to influence the outlook of those who became members or supporters of the Social-Democratic Party after 1889. Labour legislation for maximum hours and minimum wages, safety measures, industrial health, etc., was even more urgent for workers in small, insanitary workshops, and for industries in which a strike was difficult to organise because of their structure, than it was for workers in the big new factories. But such legislation could only be expected if a universal and equal suffrage was to give the mass of the workers a strong vote in Parliament. The Viennese party organisation under its leader Franz Schuhmeier was always the first to press for "action", ranging from mass demonstrations to the threat of a general strike, in the long-drawn struggle for universal suffrage.

However, the socialist movement in the capital would never have achieved such a striking force, had it not succeeded in giving a new sense of community to workers of widely different national backgrounds, and often with a language other than German. And this was a vital question for the city as a whole. The cultural identity and future development of Vienna depended on the extent to which the mass of immigrant workers could be absorbed. For them, there were no such incentives as pushed the second generation of the better-off lower-middle-class newcomers into copying an already adulterated tradition, and into a facile local patriotism—as illustrated by the suburban landlord and his family described by Karl Renner. They were bound to feel exploited by employer and landlord, oppressed by the dismal town houses and the darkness of small rooms for which they had to pay perhaps a fifth of their earnings, and mocked by the songs about Viennese gaiety. If they were to share in a tradition of Vienna, it could only be one they helped to evolve.

The most densely populated working-class district of Vienna was Ottakring, the 16th District according to the new label. From 106,000 inhabitants in 1890, it grew to 148,600 in 1900, and around 178,000 in 1910. It represented almost 9 per cent of the population of Vienna. In 1910, over 10,000 people living in Ottakring stated on the census form that their native language and that which they normally spoke was Czech; far more must have been the children of Czech parents. The last census to give details of people's occupations was that of 1900. It showed that Ottakring was truly a workers' preserve. In round figures, out of 75,800 gainfully occupied persons, 52,700 were classified as workers and day-labourers, 44,900 of the "workers" were employed in industry, only 5,800 in transport and distributive trades; a quarter of the persons occupied in industry were women, particularly in the clothing industry—which implied home work or sweat shops. The largest number of men worked in metallurgical factories, at that time machine-tool and tool works of medium size, as well as many smaller foundries and engineering works which had succeeded older locksmiths' and wrought-iron workshops. The local industry third in importance was that producing furniture; it also produced the greatest number of deaths from tuberculosis, in a district which had the highest mortality rate by tuberculosis in Vienna.

This was a direct result of housing conditions. Rarely was there a case which exemplified the worsening of proletarian living conditions as unequivocally as this Viennese district between 1860 and 1890—in absolute terms, not merely in relation to wealthier parts of the city— while the improvement during the last decade of the nineteenth century can be epitomised in a single fact: in 1890, there had been 10,437 persons sleeping as lodgers, but without a room of their own, with only a bed to pay for; in 1900 the figure had fallen to 9,144. To let a bed to a stranger was one of the ways in which a poor family could secure the money needed for a rent far in excess of their means—an average of 20–30 per cent of the family income—and grotesquely out of proportion to the value of the rooms. Out of 30,700 dwellings, 19,860 consisted of two rooms. In Ottakring, 4 per cent of the population had a room of their own; in the Inner City, the 1st District, a third had flats of more than seven rooms. Half of the houses in Ottakring had no running water yet, although the extension of the Viennese water system was one of the positive achievements of Lueger's rule. Not even all the staircases of tenement houses had gaslight—1,266 out of 2,094, the rest being lit with petrol or oil lamps, or in eight cases with electric lights. Few tenants of the single-room-and-kitchen dwellings could afford gaslight; for gas, like electricity and the tramways, was "communalised" under the Christian-Social administration of Vienna, and the high price of gas served to cover an appreciable part of the budget as indirect taxation.

Most of the houses built in the decades after 1880 had three floors. On each floor, a corridor would run along the rear wall facing a small courtyard, and the doors of the individual dwellings (they could hardly be called flats) would give on to this corridor, directly from the kitchen or, as the case might be, the single room. None of the tenants had a water closet or privy of his own; ten or fourteen tenants with their families would share one, either in the passage or across the yard. If there was running water, the tap too was in the corridor. Otherwise there would be a pump in the yard.

Of course there were quite a few middle-class people and middle-class houses even in Ottakring, but they were a small section: 1,222 flats with four or more rooms out of around 30,700. The statistics for 1890 established that in the 1st District, the Inner City, 65·32 per cent of all flats housed domestic servants, in Ottakring 10·64 per cent. The mortality rate in the 1st District was 9·35 per 1,000 inhabitants, in

Ottakring 21·11—a figure surpassed only by the other working-class District, Favoriten. The worst destroyers in a poor district were tuberculosis, diphtheria and measles.

Where could people take refuge from those airless, lightless rooms? There was much drinking and drunkenness, particularly among the older men, and those who had no interests to help them out. Dr. Felix Czeike, the author of the sociological study on which I have drawn for nearly all the details about Ottakring (*Sozialgeschichte von Ottakring 1840–1910*, Wiener Schriften No. 2, Vienna, 1955) concludes that for the worker his dwelling was merely an indispensable shelter which had to be as cheap as possible, and offered him no space at all for developing an individual life. For this he had to search outside the home.

On weekday evenings, after a working day of ten or eleven hours, there was nothing but the nearest beer-house, held in terror by the wives on Saturdays. But on Sundays there were the traditional *Heurigen* places where one could go with the children, and sit under chestnut or walnut trees at a trestle table, listen to the *Heurigen* musicians, violin, viola, guitar and clarinet, or go to the gaudy stalls along the road. Or go higher up the hill. The *Heurigen* inns and taverns of Ottakring were scattered on the lowest slopes of the Wienerwald along a small valley called the Liebhartstal. The old village of Ottakring, on the other side of the ridge, engulfed but not wholly destroyed by the harsh new buildings, consisted of two rows of vintner houses, low and whitewashed. A few vineyards were left, and here or there a bunch of pine branches, hanging from a stick over the broad curve of the gate to the yard, would announce that the owner was selling last year's wine, the new wine, from his own land. Here it was only too easy to drift into a maudlin mood.

Josef Weinheber, a poet who was born and bred in old Ottakring and resented anything that changed it, wrote a poem called "Liebhartstal":

> Das bisschen Wein, das südwärts noch gedeiht,
> lockt manchmal kleine Leute in die Schenken.
> Gelächter, Kreischen, Schrammeln, Trunkenheit,
> Schaubudenlust, Lampions und Hüteschwenken.
>
> Ein Rest von Wienertum, verfälscht, gestreckt,
> so wie der Wein aus den verbliebnen Gärten.
> Dienstmädchenelend, festtäglich geschleckt,
> Familienzank, Geraunz von Knasterbärten.

Im Herbst jedoch, an einem Wochentag,
ist alles hier wie einst. Kastanien liegen
vom Baum geplatzt am Weg; der Amselschlag
müht sich umsonst, die Stille zu besiegen.

Melancholie streicht sanft durch die Alleen,
liegt als Musik auf den gelösten Lehnen,
Und steigst du höher, siehst du fern und schön
die heissgeliebte Stadt ins Blau sich dehnen.

———

The wine still grown in gardens to the south
Draws to the inns on Sundays modest people.
Giggling and shrieks, folk quartets, drunkenness,
Hat-waving, Chinese lanterns, puppet shows.

What's left of Viennese essence, watered down
Just like the wine from those remaining plots.
Misery of housemaids dressed in shiny rags,
Family rows, and grouses of old cranks.

Yet in the autumn on a working day
All is as it had been. The chestnuts lie
Along the path cleft open. Blackbirds flute
In vain attempts to overcome the quiet.

Melancholy drifts through the avenues
And flows as music down the soft hillside.
Climb higher. See, stretched far into the blue,
Distant and lovely the beloved town.

It is catching. It may even catch a Viennese by the throat. But it is only, on an infinitely higher plane, the dream Vienna which the *Heurigen* singers purveyed to the "modest people" on noisy Sundays: an escape from the hideous reality of some 2,000 grey houses, and some 170,000 grey lives, between the domestic hill of Ottakring and the distant city.

In July 1889, Franz Schuhmeier, born in another suburb in 1864 as the son of an unemployed ribbon-maker, with six years of primary school, much reading and much discussion of socialism, and a few detentions by the police behind him, opened the Workers' Educational Club "Apollo" in Ottakring. He ended his speech: "The workers have to slave six days, therefore they must make good use of the seventh for themselves." The club flourished beyond all expectations, although Schuhmeier made members pay a small contribution for a library (mainly history and social sciences), and although the first lecture was on—Roman History. The courses included Czech for Germans and German for Czechs, elementary education in the three Rs, natural sciences, book-keeping, and the cutting of clothes.* He himself began to speak at public meetings on the eight-hour day— "We want to study, that's why we insist on the demand for shorter working hours!"—and the ideas of the newly founded Social-Democratic Party which he joined immediately. In him Victor Adler, who believed that intellectuals of bourgeois origin like himself should serve rather than lead the movement, had found one of those born leaders from the ranks of the workers themselves for whom he was looking. Nobody had to train Schuhmeier in dedication, political instinct or fiery speech, but he knew himself that he had many gaps to fill. He would go to the small circles of socialist intellectuals, and sit at the feet of men younger than he to learn what they had to give; then he passed it on to his fellow-workers in his own words, without much theory, through the weekly of which he was the editor, the *Volks-tribüne*. In its columns he would wage his war against clericalism and militarism, against the class order of society and the class-conscious régime in the State and the city, but even more for positive things: for universal suffrage, first step to social liberation, and again and again for the workers' self-education, for *Bildung*, which means culture, knowledge, formation and education all in one. In his articles he would tell his own people about Giordano Bruno and Jan Hus in their fight against what he thought of as obscurantism, but also of Schiller and the other classics: he believed that the working class should absorb the best of the past so as to shape the future.

Some of the things he wrote sound sadly over-optimistic today, but he did transmit an astonishing amount of his beliefs, and he was the leader of a band of self-made intellectuals of working-class origin who were to give the socialist movement in Austria its character, and the city of Vienna new life after 1918, when Schuhmeier himself was dead.

Seen in retrospect, Ottakring was a laboratory for socialist political education. The Ottakring *Arbeiterheim*, the Workers' House, was more than the usual headquarters of labour organisations and a labour club.

* For details on Schuhmeier, I have drawn mainly on Helga Schmidt and Felix Czeike, *Franz Schuhmeier*, Vienna, Europa Verlag, 1964.

It was opened by Schuhmeier as a "future university of the working class", because it was also the centre of the party's vast educational activities. The *Volksheim*, a popular adult education centre, took over on a grand scale what Schuhmeier had once tried to do in his "Apollo" club; eminent university teachers and famous poets (even, for that matter, Josef Weinheber) considered it an honour to lecture there. But the pattern of the great district, and of its friendly rival Favoriten which was led by Schuhmeier's friend Jakob Reumann (the two had worked in the same paper factory before they both started their political careers in earnest), influenced the whole socialist organisation of Vienna. When the educational sections were centrally organised by the Party, it was under Schuhmeier's friend Dr. Wilhelm Ellenbogen, of all intellectuals the one closest to him and, after Schuhmeier's assassination by a muddle-headed murderer in 1913, the best man to keep the image of the "people's tribune" alive in its mixture of Viennese wit and single-minded idealism. It was again Schuhmeier, through the workers of Ottakring, who created a model for the whole party, when he levied a weekly contribution for his *Volkstribüne*, and had it collected by helpers who distributed the paper and at the same time acted as propagandists, informants, and organisers.

Schuhmeier had an independent mind, and sometimes his instinctive radicalism, his revolutionary impatience, clashed with the pragmatic approach of Victor Adler to the burning problem of universal suffrage. He was prone to overestimate the pace of development, and to have too much faith in the weapon of a political general strike; for even though the industrial strikes led to clashes with the police or with the troops, there was much sympathy with the workers among the conscript soldiers, so that he thought in terms of a great popular rising, while the majority of the party leaders under Victor Adler's guidance were in practice gradualists. Ever present, for men like Schuhmeier even more than for theoreticians, was the simplified teaching of Karl Marx that the movement of the working class was historically destined to win through and transform society because it was action by the majority of the people in the interests of a still vaster majority. Wilhelm Ellenbogen expressed the significance of this very much later, in an article entitled "Das Erlebnis des Marxismus" (Marxism as Experience), in the monthly of the new Socialist Party of Austria, *Die Zukunft*, of February 1948:

... the opening of a road, the goal of which could be reached within several generations ... an objective, sharply defined task—Life is given a palpable content and meaning—... An action by the greater majority that lifts humanity to a higher level, in full consciousness of the significance.... A higher step among the many which lead to inner freedom has been ascended....

In the 'nineties, this new-won self-confidence made Schuhmeier and many of his friends impatient when the promised electoral reform laws were withheld, and the final electoral reform law proved a mean concession. In Belgium, the workers had won universal suffrage for men by a general strike. A new verse was added to the text of the Austrian "Workers' Marseillaise", beginning: "Out in the street we'll win our rights, The way that Belgium's shown...."

When parliamentary elections took place in 1897, with a fifth electoral college on the basis of universal suffrage added to the four existing ones tied to position and privilege, Social-Democrats were sent to the Second Chamber from other constituencies, but not from Vienna. Only Ottakring had given Schuhmeier a majority, and this was invalidated by the results of other districts. It was a defeat for the Viennese Social-Democratic organisation, and a victory for Lueger who in that year was confirmed as Mayor by Franz Joseph. For Schuhmeier, it meant an intensification of his educational efforts among the workers, to make them conscious of the gulf between their interests and those of the bourgeoisie. But he rejected at the Party Conference of that year suggestions—from Engelbert Pernerstorfer, who never quite lost the traces of the German-nationalist beliefs of his youth when he was among Schönerer's strong supporters, though before anti-semitism was added to German nationalism—that the Social-Democratic movement should seek contact with the German-nationalist currents. Schuhmeier said quite soberly that a Social-Democrat would certainly be more successful by taking up a proletarian point of view than a German one.

The same Workers' Marseillaise already quoted has a verse which summed up Schuhmeier's crucial conviction: "The enemy we hate most deeply, Who black and dense encircles us, It is the ignorance of the masses Cleft only by the spirit's sword." Like nearly all texts of the early fighting songs of Austrian workers, this was atrocious doggerel, but sung by marching columns on May Day, or at the end of a meeting, it was profoundly stirring.

When Schuhmeier was elected to the Town Council by Ottakring in 1900, to represent alone with Reumann of Favoriten the proletarian opposition to Lueger, he was confirmed in his contempt for the Christian-Socials as a whole by their school policy—which penalised progressive teachers and maintained classes of enormous size—and by the gross anti-intellectualism of a Bielohlawek. The fight for school reform became, by no means only through Schuhmeier, but supported by his matchless energy, one of the most important planks in the Social-Democratic platform. At the next local elections in Vienna, one of the councillors elected was the young teacher Karl Seitz, who had worked his way up from the darkest proletariat and suffered a setback in his career because of his outspoken views. Seitz was later to be, until deposed by the Dollfuss *coup d'état* of 1934, Mayor of Vienna, leader of the Social-Democratic majority in the Council Chamber, and chairman of the national Party; following, in the first two rôles, Schuhmeier's friend Jakob Reumann, the first post-war Mayor. Both men were formed in the Schuhmeier era. The shape of Vienna after the First World War, whose ravages so dismayed foreign visitors in search of the fabled glamour of the past, was moulded in a spirit to which Ottakring and Favoriten, Schuhmeier and his generation, had given reality.

Schuhmeier was also returned to Parliament by Ottakring in 1901. He became the counterpart to Lueger in Viennese politics, equally true-bred in a narrow local sense, equally capable of quick repartee and good-natured jokes, equally irresistible, though very different in style, as a mass orator. Lueger took great care to show him friendliness, almost with a wink as though to say: After all, you and I, we're of the same breed. But unlike Lueger, Schuhmeier was a man of firmly held convictions. The workers trusted him because of his shining sincerity. He often spoke up for them in the councils of the Party, too. In 1905, Ellenbogen's report to a Party Congress on the current situation and the campaign for universal and equal suffrage was interrupted (this is a famous episode in Austrian history) by telegrams which reported that the Tsar had promised a democratic Duma, forced by the mass movement in the wake of the lost war against Japan. Schuhmeier spoke. He said: "Tonight we shall demonstrate outside the Parliament and the Hofburg. . . . Tomorrow we'll consider here the question of a general strike. And then no more sitting in council. Then we go to the people." That evening the workers marched to the Parliament building with their red flags. On the following day, the Party Congress voted in favour of a general strike at the right moment, if needed. The right

moment never came, because after an interlude in which the government hesitated, and then announced an electoral bill, it was, or so it
seemed, enough to go into the streets once more. On 28 November
1905, work stopped in all industrial towns. In Vienna the workers
marched to the Ringstrasse. Victor Adler himself had said in Congress:

I have always been against a discussion of mass strikes, and still am. But I do
think it necessary, once one has come to the conclusion that a mass strike is the
suitable weapon, not to discuss it, but to prepare for it. . . . We live through a
moment when it is necessary to achieve all by every means. . . . We need the
right to vote, so that we can be rid of the question. . . . We cannot speak about
it [the misery of militarism] because we have no universal vote. We cannot
speak of anything, we cannot do anything, without hitting against this, this
wall of Austrian idiocy, this wall of Austrian political crime. We must get over
the wall. It must go!

There were 200,000 Viennese workers in the procession. Those who
saw it spoke of it many years later with awe. Nothing had been so
impressive as those endless ranks of men and women, marching in
silence and complete discipline, with the seriousness of dedicated
purpose: so my father, who in those days was a progressive democrat
but not a socialist, used to tell. The march past lasted from 9.30 a.m. to
3 p.m. Among the groups were delegations of Czechs, Slovenes,
Croats and Ruthenes. By the time the spokesmen bearing the workers'
demands arrived at the Parliament, the Premier, Baron Gautsch, had
already, immediately after the opening of the session, told the House
that his Government was preparing a bill for universal suffrage.

It took two years, and required the threat of a three days' general
strike, before the bill was enacted, under another Premier, and not
without pressure from above. It is on record that Franz Joseph supported the move in the hope that a stream of new deputies with common interests would make the business of governing easier, by bridging
the national differences. This proved an illusion. But when the bill
became law, the Social-Democratic members of Parliament went to the
Hofburg for the first time to hear the speech from the Throne—which
in Austria, characteristically, was not read to the House. At the Social-
Democratic Party Congress soon after this, Schuhmeier, whom no one
could accuse of lack of radicalism, spoke to explain the step. (What he
could not say was that the Archduke Franz Ferdinand headed a camarilla opposed to any democratic concession, and that the respect paid
to the old Emperor had its tactical significance as well.) His speech

culminated in the sentence: "Today Austrian Social-Democracy is so strong that the door of the poorest cottage cannot be shut to it, and the gates of the Hofburg itself must be thrown open."

The Town Hall of Vienna, however, was still protected by the limited franchise, and from his point of view Lueger was right. Once the Town Council was elected on a universal and equal vote, the majority sent in by a workers' party—and there was only the Social-Democratic Party—could only be dislodged by force.

Schuhmeier was shot dead by the moronic brother of a Christian-Social politician, on 11 February 1913. The similarity between this killer and the anarchist Lucheni who stabbed the Empress Elisabeth to death is startling. Schuhmeier had a funeral "like a king". It started from the Workers' House in Ottakring. The crowds who walked in the procession were estimated at a quarter of a million. Wilhelm Ellenbogen said at the grave:

For us you were the embodiment of the proletarian spirit with its urge to rise higher, its pugnacity, and its thirst for knowledge, its drive forward, its desire to raise mankind to the loftiest heights. . . .

When due allowance has been made for the emotion of the moment, and the tradition of graveside speeches, his words were true, for Schuhmeier's spirit survived in the movement, in his collaborators, and was carried over into the other new Vienna by them. He had helped to give purpose and a sense of "belonging" to the social class from which he came—a creative achievement in a period of gradual disintegration.

What it meant to be absorbed into a great foreign city, and into a community of purpose, is the substance of a small book of reminiscences which I am summoning to confirm my point. It is called *Jugendgeschichte einer Arbeiterin* (*A Working Woman's Youth*), was published originally in 1909 with an introduction by the German socialist leader August Bebel, but without the name of the author, and was written by Adelheid Popp, the first leader of the women's section within the Austrian Social-Democratic Party. In her Foreword to the third edition she said that she had written it because she recognised in her own story that of hundreds of thousands like her, and "saw in what surrounded her, and caused her grave difficulties, the working of great social forces".

Adelheid was born in 1869. Her parents had moved from the Czech village which was their home parish to a factory town in the country, where the father, a weaver, did piece-work at home for a textile manufacturer. He was a harsh, unhappy man, drank much, particularly when money was scarce, and beat his wife when she nagged him for it. Adelheid had not a single bright memory of good words or gaiety from her childhood years, but only of ugly scenes and her terror at her parents' rows. After her father died of cancer, her mother took care of the five children and for a time worked twelve hours a day in a factory. She had never learnt to read or write, and did not believe in the new-fangled laws which would have kept her children at school for eight years. Adelheid's elder brothers started work when they were ten. She herself earned a few coppers even while she was still at school, sewing mother-of-pearl buttons on to strips of gold and silver paper, in the evenings and on free days. At that time the great dream of her mother and herself was that the Duchess who had a castle nearby might take an interest in them.

When Adelheid was ten years and five months old, her mother moved to Vienna with her because it would be easier to find work there. Because the mother was illiterate, the girl filled in the registration form for "foreigners" at the police station, but omitted her own name: she did not enter herself in the space for children, as she never thought of herself as a child, being a worker already; but she could not register as a worker either, being below the legal age. Thus for the authorities she did not exist. At first she and her mother shared a bed in a room in which an old couple slept in another bed—her autobiography does not say in which part of Vienna. Adelheid found work. She had to crochet shawls for twelve hours at the workshop, and took work home if she wanted to earn a few kreuzer more. She accepted it all as something natural. Her only wish was to be able for once to sleep as long as she wanted. But if she ever was so fortunate, the reason was illness or unemployment. Sometimes she crocheted in bed because it was too cold to stay up in the room.

After some time her mother, disliking the old woman from whom she rented the bed, because she would try to speak insinuatingly to Adelheid of rich men, rented a tiny room of her own; it had no window, its only light came through a transom, and four people slept in it, the two women in one bed, Adelheid's younger brother and a mate of his in the other. After a year, Adelheid started as an apprentice making trimmings for ladies' dresses: twelve hours a day bead- and lace-work, and at the height of the season, work to be taken home. The pay was irregular, because the rate for piece-work fluctuated. Out of her earnings, she indulged in the luxury of borrowing books at a cheap lending library. At that time (she was not yet twelve) the "fate of unhappy queens" and stories about bandits thrilled her so that she lived in a dream world; but she also began to tell those stories to her workmates, and even read aloud to her employer on Sunday evenings. She resented Sunday work, which was frequent, mainly because it kept her from the books.

At thirteen, Adelheid changed over to a factory producing bronze articles, and her pay improved. But her health suffered, she had a breakdown, and after a spell in hospital had to seek work elsewhere. A metal printing works—a cartridge factory—and then another spell of illness, with a hospital bed that was clean, with clean linen, and time to read books lent by a doctor, including Schiller and Alphonse Daudet: this was her happiest time so far, though spent at the psychiatric clinic—Theodor Meynert's clinic. Then the search for work started again, without much luck. She grew so weak, and so prone to dizzy spells, that she had to go back to hospital. This time a blow fell. Since she was considered permanently unfit for work, and the hospital could not keep her, she was transferred to the poorhouse where she spent a few nights cowering in a large dormitory, amid asthmatic old women. The food was poor even by her standards. The administrative officer told her that she would be sent home to her parish unless someone was there to look after her in Vienna. But her home parish was in Bohemia, she had never seen it, and did not speak Czech—it would have been a catastrophe to be expelled from the city where her mother was, and she, after all, had been keeping herself by dint of hard work for the last four years. The official was friendly; he had her fetched home by her mother—her mother who was working at a loom in a textile mill, and had festering sores on fingers and arms from poisonous wool dyes.

Adelheid's next lap of work was in the underwear industry. Her mother even paid a small sum to a woman running a small workshop so that the girl should serve a regular apprenticeship. But fashions changed, orders dropped, and the attempt failed. By then her eldest brother was at home, jobless and a burden on her mother, after three years in the army. She could not find work for some time. In despair, she was made to write begging letters on her mother's behalf, to the

Emperor, to "archdukes known for their charity", and to other bene-
factors of repute. They did receive five florins each from the Emperor,
one of the archdukes, and one of the rich men. In the end Adelheid
landed a job in a small factory making glass- and emery-paper. During
midday breaks she would stay in the work-room, eat soup or a vegetable fetched from a cook-shop, and read one of the hundred instalments of the novel *Der Raubritter und sein Kind* (*The Robber Knight and
his Child*). But the attentions of one of the firm's commercial travellers
frightened her away from the factory, and into hysterics—she was
fifteen by then. Her mother blamed it on her books and threw them
out into the passage. Adelheid rescued them, but dared not read that
evening, and for the next few days dared not tell her family that she
had left her job. She tried to find work elsewhere, failed, walked the
streets, and on Christmas Eve prayed in vain for the miracle which
would give her the two florins she needed to face her mother with
apparently normal earnings for half a week. When mother and brother
found out about her desertion they called her lazy. Writing it down
twenty-five years later, the bitterness breaks through:

The weight of this childhood pressed on my mind for many years and turned
me into a prematurely serious creature, disinclined to gaiety. Much had to
come, something great had to enter my life, to help me overcome it.

At long last Adelheid found a job in what she calls a "big factory",
a cork factory employing 300 women and 50 men. They worked from
7 a.m. to 7 p.m., with an hour's break at noon and half an hour in the
middle of the afternoon. The boss was a good and considerate employer, the wages were the best she had ever had, rising from four
florins at the start to six florins. But in her own eyes, she had gone down
a step by becoming a factory worker; as an apprentice she had heard
factory girls described as bad and sluttish. She decided to spend her
money on clothes so that nobody should recognise her as one when she
went to church on Sundays.

She found her new colleagues friendly and helpful. Many had to
support parents, or a child, or a husband out of work. Adelheid began
to understand the much-maligned factory girls' ways of enjoying
themselves. "Yes, they did go dancing, they did have love affairs;
others stood in a queue outside a theatre from three in the afternoon
till the evening, so as to be able to get a ticket at 30 kreuzer. In summer
they went on excursions and walked for hours to save a few kreuzers'

fare. Then they paid the price for a few breaths of country air, by having their feet ache for days. You can call it frivolity, if you want, or inordinate love of pleasure, or being loose, but who would have the face to do so?"

Slowly, Adelheid Dvořak (as her name then was) began to find life a little easier. If she still stinted herself during the week—"sometimes two of us would buy a piece of boiled meat for eight kreuzer"—she could look forward to a "marvellous Sunday dinner" for the family, twenty kreuzers' worth of meat. She even satisfied a secret ambition, bought herself an outfit of dress, shoes, a silk sunshade and a flower-decked hat, by instalments of course, and at the age of seventeen, which is very late for a Roman Catholic, was at last confirmed. Her mother, too, was able to stay at home and do some piece-work there. The two women and Adelheid's youngest brother now lived in a room with two windows; there was no lodger either to share the brother's bed. Adelheid was reading as much as ever, but her taste had changed to include Goethe and some of the Romantics. Her nightmare was another illness. She twice went on a pilgrimage—on foot—to a famous church with a miracle-working image of the Virgin Mary to rid herself of her fears, only to find that the noisy crowds, the drinking and roistering after church disgusted her.

Within a short time, the small improvements in the family's standard of living, and in Adelheid's working conditions, released her pent-up energies, once the difficult years of adolescence were over. Her reminiscences reflect the chaotic state of her insatiably curious mind. Even as an apprentice she had liked to buy a newspaper now and then. As a solid wage-earner, she bought a "strictly Catholic paper" three times a week, and imbibed its patriotic and religious teachings. She knew more about the doings of archdukes and foreign royalty than about matters directly concerning her orbit. She dreamed of heroic deeds of her brothers if a war were to break out, and would have liked to cast herself in the rôle of a heroine. But then the first religious doubts crept in. She read historical works about the French Revolution and the Viennese Revolution of 1848, and did not know what to think. An antisemitic pamphlet, which accused the Jews of wanting to rape the daughters of gentiles so as to spare their own wives and daughters, upset her so much that she stopped buying her clothes from a Jewish shop. But then came the emergency laws under Taaffe, trials of so-called anarchists in which Social-Democrats made speeches to expound their creed, and she was enthusiastically on their side. When there were clashes between demonstrating workers and soldiers, she "dashed to the theatre of events" as soon as the factory closed, and was not afraid of mounted soldiery or rifles.

The next stage came when she met men who worked in the same profession as one of her brothers. She began to read the periodical of their trade union. She listened to the most intelligent of the group, who was the first live Social-Democrat she ever saw, and heard him explain the difference between socialism and anarchism, monarchy and republic. Impulsively she decided that she was a Social-Democrat and a republican, even though she was to weep for days after Crown Prince Rudolph's suicide. Then she became a regular reader of the Social-Democratic weekly, finding theoretical articles too difficult to grasp, but everything about the hardships of workers an illumination of her own life. "I learned to understand that everything I had suffered was not divine dispensation, and my whole being craved for action." It was impossible to keep to herself what she had read; at home she would climb on a chair and make a speech as if she were at a meeting. One of her brother's mates brought her books from the library of his labour association—perhaps Schuhmeier's, which had the richest library—so that she worked her way through "nine volumes of world history". But it was *The Situation of the Working Classes in England* by Friedrich Engels which both shook and encouraged her most. Adelheid began to change. So far she had been shy and aloof, wrapped in her "melancholy sentimentality"; now she had a purpose, was filled with the conviction that all should share what she had learned; she dropped her reserve and spoke freely with the others, not of herself but about her new creed. It could have created difficulties for her in the factory, but she took care to be doubly conscientious at work: "if one wants to serve a great cause, one must do one's duty in small things too." In fact, Adelheid Dwořak stayed eight years with her employer, though she was promoted away from the manual workers to a clerical job, and left only when she took up a post in the socialist women's organisation.

First, however, she had to break into the male precincts. At the first Social-Democratic meeting to which she went in 1889, she was the only woman; at the second there were two apart from herself; at the third, for voters only, she had to hide in a far corner of the hall to listen to a swift destruction of her usual ideas about the army, militarism and dynastic wars. The new thoughts seemed only natural and inevitable to her. But she had a burning wish to be an active citizen of her new world. Whereas, before, she had kept away from company, now she liked to go out with her brothers, their wives and friends. She wanted to talk politics, which was easier with men than with women, though she found with surprise that she, the young girl without the right to vote, could teach many a man what an electoral fund was good for. And being an activist, she had to do things, not only to talk.

On the first May Day of all in the history of the Viennese workers, that of 1890, Adelheid did her best to make her fellow workers in the factory demand a day off, but she failed. They were too afraid of losing three days' pay as a penalty. All she could do was to turn up in her Sunday best at work on the great day. It gave her great pain all through the twelve hours from opening to closing, she said later. The wooden shutters of the factory windows were kept closed against stones which demonstrators might throw at them. Next pay day, every male worker found an additional two florins in his packet, every woman worker one florin, in reward for their "devotion to duty". Adelheid took hers to a fund for those penalised for their share in the demonstration of 1st May. The next year, her factory too closed down on May Day, and she knew that it was her doing. Shortly afterwards, she made her first public speech at a union branch meeting. It was an overwhelming success. At Whitsun that year, she was present at the Social-Democratic Party Congress as a guest, but demanded to speak, and—as she put it herself in an official booklet of the Austrian Social-Democratic Women's Organisation, published thirty-nine years later—from then on she was the centre of the working women's movement. After only a year of activity in the organisation, and with three years in a provincial primary school as her only formal education, she was made the editor of a woman's monthly, the *Arbeiterinnenzeitung*.

In 1892, at a time of industrial slump, she spoke to a mass meeting of unemployed women, flanked by two representatives of the government, namely police captains (*Kommissäre*). The *Neue Wiener Tagblatt* described the speaker's "cream-coloured robe with rich lace trimmings"—which Adelheid had bought second-hand for 2.50 florins. The first appearance of a woman as the main speaker was in itself a sensation, not least because "the uneducated young girl was shaping as a writer", in the words of one of the illustrated papers. When the first mass strike of working women broke out in four suburban factories, the still younger girl who led them fetched Adelheid Dwořak at once, and she coped with the police. And in 1893 she was invited to speak as an expert to the parliamentary commission whose task it was to investigate the factual conditions for a new Trade Charter. She spoke on working hours for women as they were, not on paper but in factories and sweatshops, and produced so many facts that some of the worst evils were put right. The official enquiry by the parliamentary commission was followed three years later by a private one, whose prestige rested on its members. Among them were T. G. Masaryk, then a university professor; the same Rosa Mayreder from whose autobiography I have quoted several times, and who had developed into a feminist and democrat with a sensitive social conscience; Dr. Victor Adler; and Adelheid Dwořak-Popp.

Those early years, when everything she did was the act of a pioneer, must have been fantastic for the young girl, or young woman as she was soon to be. Her mother did not like it. She wanted her to marry and settle down. When Adelheid did marry a man much older than herself, tired and not in robust health, but devoted to her, and a true comrade-in-arms, she had a difficult time with her mother. To be married and have two children, to run almost single-handed a newspaper, even if only a monthly, to be the best woman speaker of her movement and always in demand, to be trying to learn languages and fill the gaps in her general as well as literary knowledge, and to be interrupted by occasional detentions or prison sentences—it needed the full vitality of a forceful woman to answer the multiple demands. But Adelheid had opened up, she had become gay and well balanced, even though her mother would receive her with reproaches on her return home from a gruelling day's work. And the earliest years had their exciting compensations: nearly everything Adelheid did was a première, something without a precedent.

In 1892, when she was still unmarried and working as a clerk at her factory, a Votes-for-Women meeting was called by an association of educated middle-class women, of high intellectual standing and a fine record in public work. The Working Women's Educational Association, not yet two years old, had rejected a merger of the two movements, but sent Adelheid Dwořak to the meeting at the old Town Hall. Two well-known democratic politicians, both in favour of a universal and equal suffrage, spoke first. Then Adelheid asked to speak.

In her account thirty-eight years later, Adelheid Popp lets a faint echo of her old sensations come through: the hangover from seven years of Taaffe's emergency legislation and police rule—the resentment at the way in which working women as a whole had been ignored—"and then, in that circle of elegantly dressed bourgeois ladies, a young working girl asks to be heard". She spoke not only of votes for the women of that ignored category, the working class, but also of a problem which happened to be topical because of new municipal ordinances, prostitution. She argued that those who paid taxes had a right to vote even according to the unjust existing electoral system, and it made no difference if they were prostitutes, humiliated and exploited. She drew on her knowledge of factory girls who had been driven on to the streets, or drifted there, to speak of the underlying causes. It startled the audience, but it impressed them, because the young girl had spoken directly and forcefully; they had not heard anything like it before.

A photograph of Adelheid Dwořak from those years shows her as sturdily handsome, with good strong eyebrows over dark eyes, and a firm set to her lips. There is no sign of the melancholy which had overshadowed her before she had found her purpose and her way. As a mature woman between fifty and sixty, Adelheid Popp still had those dark eyebrows and eyes, not large, but quick to flash and sparkle, her hair was still a dark helmet vigorously springing out from a low, broad forehead. She had broadened out altogether, but with no trace of flabbiness. Her movements were swift and decisive. Her sense of humour could have a touch of malice, but she had warmth and any amount of shrewdness. She liked women to be interested in their clothes and to wear them well, without affectation or pretentiousness, which she hated in any shape and form. What she appeared to appreciate most was courage. She would have rated high in any competition for the most quintessentially Viennese woman of her age—she who had been Adelheid Dwořak, nearly deported from Vienna on the strength of an inhuman clause in an antiquated law, because at fourteen she had exhausted her immature body by four years of hard work, and because neither she nor her parents had been born on Viennese soil. And then she became Viennese, all of her, through her incorporation in a new and positive movement. Vienna—not the city on the map, but the living community of people, linked and divided by economic or social interests, moulded together by the pressures of tradition, a common speech, an inbred attitude at best, an imitative pose at worst, and enfolded by the ever-present landscape—Vienna had received as much from this one woman as it had given her. For she became one of the Viennese citizens who took over the reins when the older social groups had to drop them in 1918.

Adelheid Popp died in the black year of 1939. She had been part of something bigger than herself: both a creator and an incarnation of the workers' movement of Vienna, with the will to master the values of the past and shape the future so that these values should have a new meaning. Her little book of 1930 was rightly called *Der Weg zur Höhe* (*The Road Upward*).

The years immediately before the outbreak of the First World War, which destroyed the foundations of the social establishment of Vienna, were not altogether black years, but they were shot with black. The closer people were to the centre of power, the more they were affected by despondency. Nothing shows this rapid internal collapse—before the outward collapse—as clearly as the political diaries of Josef Redlich, an eminent historian, expert on the history of local government in England and in Austria, and in the years of continual political crises not only a member of the Lower Chamber, as a German liberal-conservative, but also a trusted go-between and adviser of statesmen. From 1908 onwards, when he began to play an outstanding rôle in parliamentary committees and in the wings of successive governmental shows, he kept a diary in which he set down every encounter with official and unofficial people of influence, every conversation, rumour or even joke that seemed relevant to him. His notes were sometimes fresh, outspoken and uncensored, at other times framed as cautiously as if he were already contemplating their future publication. They were published long after his death, without bowdlerising, and are one of the most important sources for the period—but a source tinctured by Redlich's impulsive reactions and changes of opinion.*

It is the upper crust which is mirrored in Redlich's pages: the old aristocracy as far as its members were active in politics and the machinery of the State, or acting as grey eminences, hostesses, and mediators; the great newspaper-owners who made public opinion; a few of the wealthy bourgeoisie, to which Redlich belonged by family connexion

* *Schicksalsjahre Österreichs 1908–1919: Das politische Tagebuch Josef Redlichs*, ed. Fritz Fellner, two volumes, Graz/Cologne, Verlag Böhlau, 1951.

M

(he was born in a Moravian town, the son of a family of Jewish industrialists, but left the Jewish faith himself at an early stage), and in
particular leading bankers; all eminent politicians of the Right and the
centre parties; among writers, those with strong traditionalist leanings
—Hermann Bahr and Hugo von Hofmannsthal. Through his informants, Redlich followed the ins and outs of court intrigues. He collected
opinions on the political attitudes of the old Emperor and his heir
Franz Ferdinand, a formidable despot in the making, with a court of
his own; as well as on the amiable young Archduke Karl who was
next in succession. And though he was no supporter of universal and
equal suffrage, still less a republican democrat, Redlich betrayed in his
jottings a growing inclination to doubt the value of the dynastic principle. As he saw it, the inexorable sequence on the Habsburg throne
was an octogenarian's stubborn refusal to make decisions appropriate
to a changed world—a middle-aged neurotic's ruthless and yet aimless
ambition—a young weakling's blithe ignorance—and all this within a
political frame that was irreparably cracked.

Symptomatic as were Josef Redlich's personal reactions to political
intrigues, there was more significance in the reactions and attitudes of
the political leaders as he recorded them, almost as though preparing
a topography of Austrian politics. Nearly everyone expressed despair
at the state of affairs, hinting that he might, if only he were in the right
place and able to convince the Emperor, form a better cabinet or conduct ministerial business better than the present holder of office; and
nearly everyone in power blamed the character of the Emperor for
his own failures. The round of purposeful talks went on, a round
dance in which friends and foes were constantly changing places.
From time to time one party leader would boast of good relations with the "other place", the court of Franz Ferdinand, but never
for any length of time. One count after another would try his luck, and
lose his chance. After the elections of 1911, Parliament was even harder
to manage than before, because of the sharpening conflicts between
national groups. There was also a constant source of friction in the
periodical negotiations about the *Ausgleich*, the achievement of a
financial settlement with Hungary. Successive governments, despairing
of a safe majority in the House, baulked by the parliamentary obstruc-
tion of radical nationalists, and unable to offer any viable solution of the
gigantic problems, resorted with increasing frequency to the notorious
Article 14 of the Constitution, which allowed emergency decrees to

fill the gap between sessions of the Second Chamber. This backdoor legislation was used almost frivolously, as a game of skill, until it became a matter of life and death during the First World War. But no minister since Ernst von Körber, the clever civil servant who was Premier from 1900 to 1905, could hope to govern bureaucratically and autocratically, by-passing Parliament, unless he secured the formal sanction and backing of the Emperor as the source of his authority. This made the behaviour of old Franz Joseph so important to every candidate—open or secret—for a governmental post that they all watched it like a farmer watching the weather.

Josef Redlich was himself an eternal candidate; he became a minister only for a brief, bitter term at the very end of the Austrian monarchy, one of those who had to prepare the abdication of the last emperor. There were times when he tended towards the Belvedere, the seat of Franz Ferdinand, but he appears never to have established genuine contact with the Archduke. Then came the years of the Foreign Minister Baron Lexa von Aehrenthal, who had engineered the annexation of Bosnia-Herzegovina in 1908. Redlich overrated him sadly, and followed his lead in considering an aggressive policy in the south-east —the Balkans—as a prelude to an "invigorating" war the only way to inject vigour into the ailing body of the Habsburg Empire. Even the possibility of getting involved in a war with Russia seemed a minor evil. The Chief of General Staff, Franz Conrad von Hötzendorf, went further; he, who was Franz Ferdinand's man until he fell into disfavour for offending against the Archduke's bigoted beliefs, advocated a preventive war against Austria's nominal ally, Italy, and would talk about his ideas freely to Redlich. Redlich, though not falling in with Hötzendorf, belonged for several years to the war party. He felt bitter about the Emperor's resistance to anything that might lead to war, and attributed it to senile indecision. On 28 November 1912, for instance, when the Albanian conflict made Austria's entry into a war in the Balkans an acute danger and the Foreign Minister after Aehrenthal's death was the cultured but weak Count Berchtold, Redlich noted a rumour that, some days before, the Emperor had "banged on the table" and exclaimed: "I don't want war, I've always been unlucky in wars—we'd win, but we'd lose provinces." Afterwards the Emperor was supposed to have given in to all his heir's demands. Exactly five months later, on 29 April 1913, Redlich made in his diary the entry:

... That ancient man on the throne, and the weaklings around him, do not see that only the sword can still save Austria. Insurrection is lying in ambush in Dalmatia, Croatia and Bosnia! Sometimes I blame myself for not speaking up for war energetically....

Many, if not most, of Redlich's aristocratic friends were of the same opinion. The conversations with them which he recorded are seldom very interesting; they are limited to gossip on the criss-cross of influences, wire-pulling and clique wars. Redlich was a studiously friendly and sympathetic chronicler; a touch of snobbery often led him to initial mistakes in his assessment of people and their attitudes to him, but he rarely let his criticism of aristocratic circles become explicit, even when he had to revise earlier opinions. Yet the atmosphere his accumulated notes convey is not much different from that in Consuelo Vanderbilt Balsan's description of her visit to the same circles in 1904:

... The aristocratic Austrians I met looked like greyhounds with their long lean bodies and small heads. A polished education tends to bestow a certain ease of manner, and this these Viennese possessed to an eminent degree. It sometimes helped me to forget that they were as a rule more educated than intelligent. It was, I thought, a pity that they could express their thoughts in so many different languages when they had so few thoughts to express.... (*The Glitter and the Gold*, New York, Harper, 1952, p. 82.)

Paucity of thought goes far to explain the blithe war-mongering which Redlich—the brilliant intellectual who courted this well-bred company—recorded time and again. There were, for instance, two countesses Hoyos. The Hoyos were an ancient family of Spanish lineage, made cosmopolitan by intermarriage with foreign aristocratic houses; the men had a long tradition of service in the Austrian Army or the Diplomatic Corps. On 11 July 1913, Redlich noted that Alice Countess Hoyos, whose son was in the Foreign Service, had said that if Count Berchtold, the Foreign Minister, had been a man, he would have intervened in the war between Serbia and Bulgaria "even at the risk of war with Russia". And on 26 July 1914, her daughter-in-law greeted Redlich with effusive joy because he brought her confirmation of the outbreak of war against Serbia. The general public—this, too, Redlich noted—was not enthusiastic on that day.

If an unthinking patriotism, so called, was inbred in the noble ladies, the wish for war among the higher bureaucracy, men drawn from the old gentry, was an outcome of their loss of faith in peace. Redlich recorded a talk with Leopold Baron Chlumecky, an able administrator, who was very depressed because according to his information the old Emperor had asked Franz Ferdinand, with tears in his eyes, not to press for war. In Chlumecky's view, all misfortune in the State sprang from the Emperor, who in his old age had no strength of decision left. On another occasion, Redlich heard the War Minister, Baron Krobatin (who had inherited an unholy mess from his predecessor, one of Franz Ferdinand's protégés), say that Austria had to make war because it was the only way to solve her internal problems.

From November 1911, the government was headed by Karl Count Stürgkh, a poker-faced Styrian aristocrat who had been returned to Parliament in 1891 by the landed property-owners' electoral college. His cabinet started with bad auguries. For the first time a "clerical", Hussarek, was made Minister of Education. Stürgkh himself owed his first ministerial post, also in education, to an *éminence grise*, Rudolf Sieghart, who had been head of the Prime Minister's office for eight important years, until 1910, when his many services behind the scene were rewarded by his appointment as governor of one of the leading banks; Sieghart was a power behind Stürgkh in all financial matters with, in Redlich's opinion, disastrous results for the exchequer. But the links between the old aristocracy and high finance were strong in those years. On 20 December 1912, Redlich made an entry about a luncheon at which everyone except himself had belonged to the *crème de la crème*: all the gentlemen, and even the ladies, had been talking about their ventures on the Stock Exchange, which sounded quite substantial. Redlich for once commented: "A strange form of the degeneration of our high aristocracy!" This was harmless. Sieghart's hidden influence on the Government was not, because he coupled it with the domination of the second-largest bourgeois newspaper, the supposedly liberal *Neue Wiener Tagblatt*. The largest was still the *Neue Freie Presse*, in which Moritz Benedikt endeavoured to make policy; in home affairs, so Redlich found in a conversation with him, Benedikt had no fixed policy except that of being "against Parliament". It meant that in those crucial years, the two most important organs of supposedly enlightened opinion in Vienna backed the Stürgkh government in its anti-parliamentarian course.

The position of Stürgkh's cabinet was precarious from the start. It was well known that he intended to govern with the help of Article 14. For some time it was thought that he would have to go because he was unable to muster a sound parliamentary backing. There were always candidates, in particular the efficient Körber, waiting to succeed him as soon as the Emperor—it must be stressed: the Emperor, not a vote of Parliament—were to dismiss him, or force him to resign. Stürgkh survived, impassively. In March 1914 he suspended the Austrian Parliament, and thus the people of the Austrian half of the Monarchy entered war in 1914 without any democratic representation. (It was Stürgkh's refusal to convene Parliament again, for the discussion of the questions of bread, individual freedom, censorship, the conduct of the war—and peace, which led to his assassination by Victor Adler's son, Dr. Friedrich Adler, on 21 October 1916.)

Before the catastrophe expected by so many, but gauged in its full significance by so few, overtook the Austrian monarchy, Vienna was shaken by several crises on different planes. In 1913 the industrial depression was such that unemployment and bankruptcies rose steeply. The workers had been hit in the preceding years by the rise in food prices, a result of the protectionist policy of various governments intent on securing the support of landowners and big farmers; now the desolate position of industry hit them anew. At the same time, financial equilibrium was endangered by new loans—the nationalisation of the southern railway, for strategic reasons, imposed a heavy burden of compensation—and by the increase of military preparations. The Army was in bad shape, a blatant warning against the warlike policies of its leaders. The scant confidence of the Viennese public in anything under bureaucratic control was further shaken by the *affaire* Redl: in May 1913, a colonel of the general staff was found to have betrayed plans (as it turned out, nothing of substantial importance) to the Russians, under the pressure of heavy debts and of blackmail because of his homosexual private life. The dramatic details—"to save the Army from worse dishonour", as Conrad von Hötzendorf put it to Redlich, the poor sinner Redl was virtually ordered to commit suicide, and two of his fellow-officers guarded the Hotel Klomser until they heard a shot in the room upstairs—caused a sensation. The organisation which was assumed to be the strongest link holding the rickety realm together, the K.K. Army, was as tainted as any other part of the political organism.

In those years, while the public cracked jokes about the old Emperor and his bodyguard of old court officials, the politicians still tried to refer to him, or to invoke his authority, in the face of their own scepticism. Even the aristocrats, who would scarcely have enjoyed the spoils of office in any democratic dispensation, chafed under the very system, the very person, from whom they drew their power; ministers complained that they could never have proper conferences, and always came up against the preconceived notions of the Old Gentleman. (In some cases recorded by Redlich, the very old man seems to have clung to a simpler common sense and humanity than his servants.) After his death on 21 November 1916, Redlich heard an illuminating anecdote from Princess Pauline Metternich-Sándor, who herself had it from her mother, an anecdote that suddenly recalls the enormous span of a life that started in the heyday of Biedermeier, in 1830, and ended in the middle of the First World War. When Franz Joseph became Emperor in December 1848, his first Premier, Felix Prince Schwarzenberg, had apparently told him: "Your Majesty, you're young and I'm old, and I've a great deal of experience. I beg you to promise that in future you will never speak to any minister or general, and so on, about other affairs than those within his competence. This is the only way to protect yourself against intrigues." The young monarch gave his solemn word "as a man and an emperor", and kept it meticulously to the end of his days. The story rings, and may well be, true.

In any case, during the last years of his reign, when Franz Joseph came very near to utter senility and was afraid of it, he was clinging to his rigid rules more than ever. His "ministers and generals" found it impossible to tell him of matters referring to problems outside their special jurisdiction; in particular those who had to deal with the affairs of both halves of the monarchy—the Foreign Minister and the Minister of Defence—acted in a vacuum unless they gathered their information by devious means. This enforced departmentalisation threw the politicians back on something which may well have been to the taste of many of them, to petty intrigues, to small storms in small tea-cups, and to innumerable business meals at Sacher's. (Gone were the days when a man like Billroth would invite Johannes Brahms to an oyster breakfast at Sacher's as a special treat; the famous hostelry had risen, if rise it was, to the rank of a special haunt of nobility and gentry, and the very rich, the very influential or those who wanted to "belong".) It would have been funny, if it had not been a little macabre.

The foreground of the political scene in Vienna was filled with the noise and bluster of parliamentary sessions, as long as Parliament was sitting. The Bohemian Diet was effectively paralysed by the conflict between the two nationalist groups of Czechs and Germans, the Second Chamber was nearly paralysed by it, with other radical nationalists moving in. Even Victor Adler's unified and international Social-Democratic Party was riven by the same nationalist upsurge: the Czech trade unions formed a centre of their own, and after 1911 even the Czech political groups seceded, considering their national ties stronger than their social solidarity. Two great analytical contributions to the problem of the Habsburg multi-national State and the solution of national autonomy in co-existence, one by Karl Renner (*Grundlagen und Entwicklungsziele der österreichisch-ungarischen Monarchie*, Vienna, 1905, published under the pseudonym Rudolf Springer, since Renner was at that time a civil servant), and the other by Otto Bauer (*Die Nationalitätenfrage und die Sozialdemokratie*, Vienna, 1907), helped the Socialist leaders to conduct discussions on a level not reached by any other group, but they provided no solutions acceptable to the raw emotional demands of those who felt themselves cheated out of their national birthright by the German-speaking rulers as well as the German workers.* At least, however, works like these, blending pragmatism with far-sighted international vision as Renner's did, or tempering a lucid theoretical logic by realistic understanding as was the case with Bauer, were to prove of immense value at the moment of collapse in 1918. Those two utterly different men, with different methods—Bauer a pre-Leninist Marxian, Renner in reality closer to John Stuart Mill—forged a good many of the intellectual weapons which were used, not only for debates in the Chamber, but also for the political education which gave to the Austrian, and in particular the Viennese, working-class movement its remarkable cohesion even after the loss of the Czech group (anyway the Viennese Czechs remained in the party). In spite of their republican convictions, the Social-Democrats in Parliament were a constructive opposition, so that they were sometimes mocked as "Black-and-Yellows" by radical nationalists. But they made it clear enough that they, too, believed that the

* Otto Bauer, who was in those years secretary to the Club of Social Democratic Deputies, once told me that after one of many long, fruitless discussions with Czech "separatist" representatives in Parliament, Victor Adler had come out into the passage, shaking his head over the proverbial obstinacy of "the *Bemm*" (*Bemm* is the Viennese idiom for Czechs or a Czech) and then saying: "Well, there's a bit of a *Bemm* in all of us, but to be such *Bemm* as these *Bemm*—that's something only the *Bemm* can manage!"

Habsburg State was doomed, and the society on which the old régime based itself, on the verge of decomposition.

In Vienna, the rot had spread to the ruling party, the Christian-Socials. After Lueger's death, not even their good contacts with the high clergy and with the Archduke Franz Ferdinand could hide the sheer ineptitude of the administrators in the Town Hall. Lueger's heirs would have liked to undo some of the measures of municipalisation—of "municipal socialism", as Lueger at first liked to call his communal enterprises—which had introduced an element of planning. In Parliament, the Christian-Socials played a sorry rôle (their best man in later years, Kunschak, had not yet come to the fore), and the support of Franz Ferdinand was a doubtful asset. He had a talent for alienating even his friends. On the day of his assassination, that hot Sunday of 28 June 1914, Redlich was to wind up a sort of obituary entry in his journal by saying that possibly God had been good to the Austrians in sparing them an Emperor to whom one familiar with him had attributed "the callousness and cruelty of an Asian despot".

The shop-worn slogans of Viennese local patriotism were still repeated *ad nauseam*, but not even the entertainment industry produced new successes to equal Lehár's *Merry Widow* of 1905, or Oskar Straus's *Walzertraum* of 1906. The current operettas were mixtures of sentimentality and *Gemütlichkeit*, often reminiscent of a *Heurigen* mood with their facile tunes, and were clearly devised to please the new lower middle classes. They fitted into the cult of a bogus tradition, and they, too, were an expression of decline.

The two great playhouses, the Opera and the Burgtheater, lived on their repertoires. Gustav Mahler was dead. He had left the directorship of the Opera in 1907, fighting—as Alma Mahler-Werfel explains in one of her autobiographical works—for the acceptance of his symphonies. His revolutionary treatment of Mozart and also of Wagner operas remained, and so did the anti-naturalist settings for which, in the face of many obstacles, he had brought the innovator Alfred Roller to the court Opera. His successors were bent on conserving, not on creating values. Similarly, the greatest actor of the Burgtheater, Josef Kainz, had died; the most original of Burgtheater directors, Max Burckhard, had committed suicide; there remained the technique of an excellent team with many outstanding individual actors, but no genius. Programmes were changing slowly, to include new playwrights with relative daring. But these new playwrights were new only on the stage of the court theatre. They were part of a settled world, even if like Gerhard Hauptmann they had begun as rebels a generation earlier. Single evenings could be enjoyable; but as theatres for Vienna, Opera and Burgtheater signified stagnation in those years.

Nothing could damage the golden tone of the strings in the Philharmonic or, in its other, smaller version, the orchestra of the Opera House. The Philharmonic Concerts, as they had done throughout their history, provided mainly classical fare to compensate their audiences for occasional experiments. The musicians of the Philharmonic shared the customary Viennese conservatism in musical matters (but is it only a Viennese characteristic?). They had not worked happily with Gustav Mahler as their conductor, and he had not lasted long, apparently because he forced them to break with some of their cherished traditions in playing the classics. (Mahler at rehearsals was, as those fortunate enough to have been present never tire of saying, a miracle of inspiring and vivifying strength.) With the elegantly cool Felix Weingartner as Director of the Opera and conductor of the Philharmonic, the concerts returned to their traditional programmes shortly before the outbreak of the First World War. The music they offered has too much timeless life to make talk of stagnation easy, but there was an element of stagnation in the pattern of those great concerts. The foremost orchestra of Vienna ignored the modern composers, not only the French, Spanish and Russian ones, but also the Viennese school which was beginning to attain stature.

For, outside all the established modes of a decaying society, new musicians, new painters, new architects and new writers were fighting for other, meaningful ideas and artistic forms. In music, it was Schönberg and his pupils, Alban Berg and Anton Webern, who broke the old moulds. Schönberg's *Gurrelieder* marked a transition; his *Pierrot Lunaire* of 1912, and Alban Berg's orchestral settings of poems by Peter Altenberg, also of 1912, already represented an independent departure, the "atonal" at its start. I am not qualified to discuss the influences on Schönberg—for instance the question whether Mahler in his last stage, that of the Ninth and the unfinished Tenth Symphony, had not influenced him—but the effect of the first public concerts with a programme of works by him, Berg and Webern is a matter of record —and of tales by those who were present. It is hardly surprising that there was a strong and vocal opposition; these works sounded like a blasphemous attack on hallowed ideals of the beautiful. In any case, the first Schönberg concerts caused less of a scandal in Vienna than did the first performance of Stravinsky's *Sacre du Printemps* in Paris, although Stefan Zweig mentions in his autobiography that at one of Schönberg's premières his friend Buschbeck boxed somebody's ears for hissing and whistling. Rather, it is remarkable that a strong minority of young people, who were brought up in an exclusive tradition of classical symphonies and chamber music, rebelled so strongly against conventional aesthetic norms, against the rule of the "well-tempered pianoforte", that they turned into partisans of a new, no doubt only half understood music. One of that generation has told me that to him and his friends, the first concert of Schönberg, Berg and Webern meant above all a break with the laws of church music, which in their view underlay everything, including the most modern composers such as Mahler. It excited more than convinced them; and it was a form of rebellion which had wider connotations than purely musical ones.

In painting, Oskar Kokoschka—born in an old Lower-Austrian market town, but in his youth at home in Vienna, for a bohemian is at home anywhere—broke, even in his first drawings, illustrations and paintings, with the decorative line still cultivated under the influence of Klimt. In the early years of the century, the *Jugendstil* or *art nouveau* was rampant everywhere, in posters and on vases, on ink-pots and furniture, and of course in fashionable portraits as well. George Grosz defined it in his autobiography (*Ein kleines Ja und ein grosses Nein*, Hamburg, Rowohlt, 1955), as a "veritable spaghetti-orgy of lines", and said that Kolo Moser, the reigning spirit of the *Wiener Werkstätte*, was imposing this style from Vienna. In the middle of it all, Kokoschka rudely destroyed every ornamental pretence and every conventionally respectable surface in his paintings. His poetry and his plays were on expressionist lines; his portraits came increasingly close to psychoanalytical statements. Even while he was living through a time of flaming love and flaming rows with Alma Mahler, the beautiful, self-centred and all-absorbing widow of Gustav Mahler, he painted her without any concession to traditional notions of loveliness. (Alma Mahler-Werfel wrote frankly about her relationship with Kokoscha, and other men of genius whom she drew into her orbit, in her autobiographical books, and was perceptive enough to accept Kokoschka's interpretations of her.) But though rebellion against the insincerity of official Vienna, or of Vienna's bourgeois society, may have been among the forces that drove Kokoschka in his young years, he belonged to the city only in his very beginnings; he left Vienna for Germany on the outbreak of the war. The other angry young man among the painters, Egon Schiele, six years younger than Kokoschka, remained in Vienna till his death. His form of rebellion against Klimt's aestheticism (see p. 325) was as brutal as Kokoschka's; his subjects were mostly concerned with sexual love or its distortion. But he also painted a Viennese suburb: not the romantic, pleasant suburb of the local songs, but a place of waste ground, small one-storeyed houses and bleak taller buildings, perhaps the fringe of Simmering or Ottakring. To judge by his work, Schiele was angry not only for himself, but for all the down-trodden.

Similar notes of social anger sounded in the play *Armut* (*Poverty*), by the young poet Anton Wildgans, but they were embedded in symbol-ism and an attempt to give universal and near-mystical meaning to the acceptance of suffering. In this play the survivors know that every-thing in life is doubly bitter for the "poor", but the poor father who dies is granted—or believes he is granted—a vision of bliss as a reward. Wildgans wrote another lyrical drama during the war, called *Liebe* (*Love*), which was again a blend of realism and symbolism, exploring the humiliations of youth, the sordidness of the business of love, and then turning it all into higher significance—in verse. This best-known Viennese poet of the young generation on the eve of war hovered uneasily between conformism and rebellion. His path led to conform-ism, to the detriment of his poetry.

The two outstanding rebels among writers, in the years before the blood-and-iron curtain of the war came down, were older, and their rebellion was combined with conservative elements. One was Peter Altenberg, an over-sensitised prose poet. He had developed a *pointilliste* technique to catch fleeting moods, and enchanted a closed circle of devoted friends. Originally one of the "Young Vienna" group, he later defined himself as an "anarchist as regards petty lies about life of any sort", and set his ego against the herd to the point of proclaiming "P.A."—his initials—as the best arbiter and reformer of society. Much of what he wrote is now unpalatable—or at least not to my palate—but in its fragmented glitter and its defiance of philistine attitudes to love, women, food, children, or whatever else his imagination trans-formed into a symbol of unsullied life, it corresponded to a minority mood. Sometimes P.A's imagery was startlingly original, bridging apparently disconnected worlds rather in the style of the Spaniard Ramon Gómez de la Serna, who invented the genre of "greguerías" for precisely this expressionist game. But P.A. was of marginal significance compared to Karl Kraus, the poet, essayist, playwright and journalist who through his journal *Die Fackel* waged war on intellectual and moral corruption in Vienna, Austria and—indirectly—the civilisation of our times.

Karl Kraus saw in the aristocratic and bourgeois society which Redlich portrayed in his diaries, and for which Moritz Benedikt wrote his sonorous leading articles in the *Neue Freie Presse*, a humiliating travesty of the human image. He was a moralist, and he discovered immorality—not in the narrow sense given to the word, but in its wider meaning, as lack of moral values—in every hypocritical phrase, every misused word. What he longed for was an aristocratic order of quality, intrinsic and genuine, but independent of external power; he was anti-plebeian, distrustful of mass movements, opposed to a reorganisation of society on socialist lines, and in principle a supporter of a hierarchy. Erich Heller—who admires Karl Kraus far more than I have ever done—compares the "rare fusion of spontaneity and subtlety, of ethical integrity and intellectual complexity" with Kierkegaard, Kafka, and T. S. Eliot, with whom Kraus has in common "the spiritual and ethical situations from which their works spring" (*The Disinherited Mind*, Cambridge, 1952, p. 187). In an incredibly intricate, utterly untranslatable style which mixes puns, literary allusions, cross-references, and fireworks in endless sentences, Kraus seized on a single incident, person or even phrase, disembowelled it, ridiculed it, turned it into a symbol, a farce, a cosmic catastrophe all in one. The murder of a Viennese prostitute would give him an occasion to bare the pudenda of society, and to scourge sexual hypocrisy. Like Altenberg—one of the few writers he tolerated, while he poured scorn on Hofmannsthal and Schnitzler, and even more on Freud—he spoke incessantly of himself: the state of the world around him, of the Viennese, the Austrian, and the entire world, drove him into solipsism, and yet he could not stop preaching, like the Jewish prophet he was by vocation. He preached the coming of the Austrian apocalypse, the "last days of mankind"— this was to be the title of the enormous sequence of scenes which he wrote during the war, a satire cloaking black tragedy.

This, then, was the state of Vienna on the eve of the First World

War: a political void, filled by the petty intrigues of a ruling group which had lost all faith in itself, the system it served, and the State it was supposed to rule—an exhausted old man on the throne, incapable of keeping in touch with the realities of administration—a demoralised bourgeoisie without leadership—a daunted professional middle class, clutching at its precious cultural heritage, but disrupted by the poison of antisemitism—a vast lower middle class, glued together by an artificial legend of Viennese traditions—new beginnings in art and thought on the fringes of society, in rebellion against the "establishment"— scepticism, pessimism and creeping despair among the most respected writers—a working-class movement and party, without any experience of administrative power. Over it all, a deceptive gloss of good nature and enjoyment.

Put like this, it sounds like an over-ripe civilisation doomed beyond any possibility of reprieve. And yet, when the end of the Habsburg Empire came after four years of war, which for Vienna included almost three years of want and unfreedom, and when the capital of a large realm became overnight the capital of a small, isolated, defeated Republic of six million inhabitants, another Vienna rose from the shambles. It was to happen again, twenty-eight years later, after a worse destruction and a worse moral degradation, in the years after 1946. Both times, it was the same section of the Viennese people, and the same political group, which assumed the main responsibility.

After 1918, many of the young generation were quick to believe that the old world had gone for ever, and all things would be built anew. It was a childish illusion and did not last. But it was closer to reality than the belief of the disprivileged who assumed that Vienna was lost, because they themselves had lost their position in the vanished monarchy, or than the disappointment of foreign visitors who came to look for the imperial glitter and glamour of legendary fame, but found a shabby town at work. Much was indeed built anew, and Vienna came alive again, stripped of tinsel and many things that had been pleasant, yet for the many a better place to live in. At last those long years of preparation before the war, when working-class men and women and their allies among the intellectuals had together worked out blueprints for the future, were bearing fruit. The projects for housing, education, child welfare, hospitals for T.B. patients—the plans of men like Adler and Schuhmeier—were turned into reality by the new Social-Democratic administration of the city. For many years,

Vienna gave an example to European capitals in sober matters such as municipal blocks of flats or kindergartens. On each May Day, a quarter of a million marched to the Town Hall, across the Ring from both sides, eight abreast. Until an authoritarian one-party régime and afterwards the Nazi occupation ravaged it, this new Vienna was an island of piecemeal social engineering. In the new tradition that was born, many of the older ones merged. The city was still acting as a melting pot, the Viennese were still sceptical, averse to heroics, self-indulgent, at times evasive, at other times inclined to self-pity, always ready to crack jokes against themselves and everyone, and convinced that their town was unique.

But the strength for renewal was there too. Underneath the flippancy, an inner core of dedication was kept alive through another dark period, and has worked for a second time the miracle of rebirth. The Opera was burnt out, and it stands again. New blocks of flats, whole new suburbs, with playgrounds to please the children and the planners, have changed and yet not changed the face of the town. There are two new streams of immigrants to absorb. Pace and temper have changed as much as elsewhere. But by now there is another fusion of the old and the new. When the guides take visitors from the Town Hall to old, narrow streets lined with baroque façades, and then to plain functional buildings on the outskirts, and finally to the top of the Kahlenberg to look down on the city, the past confirms the present and the future of Vienna.

Bibliography

This is a selective list. It comprises works which are particularly useful, important, or significant as representing a specific point of view, but includes neither all the books consulted and read by the author while preparing the present study nor every title mentioned in the text. In particular, small monographs and specialised articles are not listed here, though quoted in context. Also, the editions of well-known poets and playwrights have been omitted in the Bibliography; the author has used various editions as they came to hand, and referred to the critical and definitive versions no more than occasionally. On the other hand, this Bibliography contains some titles of books that were published—or came to the author's notice—too late to be taken into account in her work, yet are too important to be omitted.

I. B.

Abraham a Sancta Clara: *Mercks Wienn*. Vienna, 1947.

Adler, Friedrich (editor): *Victor Adlers Briefwechsel mit Kautsky und Bebel*. Vienna, 1954.

Adler, Victor: *Aufsätze und Reden*. Vienna, 1929.

Anschütz, Heinrich: *Erinnerungen aus meinem Leben*. 1866.

Aschbach, Joseph von: *Die Wiener Universität im ersten Jahrhundert ihres Bestehens*. Vienna, 1865.

—— *Die Wiener Universität und ihre Humanisten*. Vienna, 1877.

Bach, Alexander: *Geschichte der Wiener Revolution im Jahre 1848*. Vienna, 1898.

Bahr, Hermann: *Wien*. Stuttgart, 1906.

Bauer, Anton: *Hundertfünfzig Jahre Theater an der Wien*. Vienna, 1952.

Bauernfeld, Eduard von: *Aus Alt- und Neu-Wien*. Vol. XII of *Gesammelte Schriften*, Vienna, 1872; reprinted, Leipzig, 1905 etc.

Beer, A.: *Die Finanzen Österreichs im 19. Jahrhundert*. Prague, 1877.

Bierak, Wilhelm: *Das Lebensgefühl des Biedermeier in der österreichischen Dichtung*. Vienna, 1931.

Bourgoing, Jean von (editor): *Briefe Kaiser Franz Josephs an Frau Katharina Schratt*. Vienna, 1949.

Broch, Hermann: *Hofmannsthal und seine Zeit*. Munich, 1954.

Brügel, Ludwig: *Soziale Gesetzgebung in Österreich 1848–1918*. Vienna, 1919.

—— *Geschichte der österreichischen Sozialdemokratie*. 5 vols. Vienna, 1922.

Burgtheater, 175 Jahre. 2 vols. Vienna, 1952.

Burney, Dr. Charles: *The Present State of Music in Germany, the Netherlands and United Provinces*. London, 1775.

Buschbeck, E. H.: *Austria*. London, 1949.

Carner, Mosco: *The Waltz*. London, 1949.

Castle, Eduard (editor): *Geschichte der deutschen Literatur im Zeitalter Franz Josephs I*. 2 vols. Vienna, 1935.

Cloeter, Hermine: *Häuser und Menschen von Wien*. Vienna, 1917.

Corti, Egon Caesar Conte: *Elisabeth, die seltsame Frau*. Salzburg, 1934.

Crankshaw, Edward: *The Fall of the House of Habsburg*. London, 1963.

Czedik, Karl: *Zur Geschichte der österreichischen Ministerien*. 3 vols. Vienna, 1930.

Czeike, Felix, and Lugsch, Walter: *Studien zur Sozialgeschichte von Ottakring und Hernals*. Wiener Schriften II. Vienna, 1955.

Czeike, Helga: *Franz Schuhmeier und der geistige Aufstieg der Arbeiterklasse in Wien*. MS in Archives of the City of Vienna.

Deutsch, Julius: *Geschichte der österreichischen Gewerkschaftsbewegung*. Vienna, 1909.

Deutsch, Otto Erich: *Schubert, a documentary biography*. London, 1946.

—— *Mozart, a documentary biography*. London, 1965.

Ewart, Felicie (pseudonym of Emilie Exner): *Zwei Frauen-Bildnisse zur Erinnerung*. Private ed. Vienna, 1907.

Farga, Franz: *Die Wiener Oper von ihren Anfängen bis 1938*. Vienna, 1947.

Felder, Cajetan: *Meine Erinnerungen*. MS in Archives of the City of Vienna, ed. and transcr. by Felix Czeike.

—— *Erinnerungen eines Wiener Bürgermeisters*. Sel. and ed. by Felix Czeike. Vienna, 1954.

Friedjung, Heinrich: *Österreich von 1848–1860*. 2 vols. Stuttgart, Berlin, 1908.

Funder, Friedrich: *Vom Gestern ins Heute*. Vienna, 1952.

Gentz, Friedrich von: *Staatsschriften und Briefe*. Ed., annot. and introd. by Hans von Eckhardt. Munich, 1921.

Gottlieb-Billroth, Otto (editor): *Billroth und Brahms im Briefwechsel*. Vienna, 1935.

Grimschitz, Bruno: *Johann Lucas von Hildebrandt*. Vienna, 1959.

—— *Ferdinand Waldmüller*. Salzburg, 1957.

Groner, Richard: *Wien wie es war.* Revised edition, ed. by O. E. Deutsch. Vienna, 1934.

Gugitz, Gustav: *Bibliographie zur Geschichte und Stadtkunde Wiens.* 5 vols. and general index. Vienna, 1947 ff.

Hadamowsky, Franz, and Otte, Heinz: *Die Wiener Operette.* Vienna, 1947.

Halsband, Robert: *The Life of Lady Mary Wortley Montagu.* London, Oxford, 1956.

Hannak, Jacques: *Karl Renner und seine Zeit.* Vienna, 1965.

Hanslick, Eduard: *Geschichte des Concertwesens in Wien.* Vienna, 1869.

—— *Music Criticisms 1846–99.* London, 1963.

Harrer, Paul: *Wiener Häuserbuch, Innere Stadt.* MS in Archives of the City of Vienna.

Hoffmann, Edith. *Kokoschka, Life and Works.* London, 1947.

Holzer, Rudolf: *Villa Wertheimstein.* Vienna, 1960.

Jacob, H. E.: *Johann Strauss und das neunzehnte Jahrhundert.* Amsterdam, 1937.

Jahn, Otto, completely revised by Hermann Abert: *W. A. Mozart.* 2 vols. Leipzig, 1919.

Jahrbuch des Vereins für Geschichte der Stadt Wien. Vienna, annually.

Jones, Ernest: *Sigmund Freud, Life and Works,* Vols. I, II. London, 1954–55.

Kaut, Hubert: *Wiener Bilder. Vom Mittelalter bis zur Gründerzeit.* Vienna, 1964.

—— *Wiener Gärten.* Vienna, 1964.

Keller, Otto: *Die Operette in ihrer geschichtlichen Entwicklung.* Vienna, 1922.

Khevenhüller-Metsch, Prinz Johann Josef: *Aus der Zeit Maria Theresias. Journal 1742–1776.* Vienna/Leipzig, 1907.

Kindermann, Heinz: *Hermann Bahr.* Graz, 1954.

Kisch, Wilhelm: *Die alten Strassen und Plätze von Wien.* Vienna, 1883.

—— *Die alten Strassen und Plätze von Wien's Vorstädten.* 2 vols. Vienna, 1888–95.

Klenner, Fritz: *Die österreichischen Gewerkschaften.* Vienna, 1951.

Komorzynski, Eugen: *Emanuel Schikaneder.* Vienna, 1951.

Kralik, Richard: *Lueger und der christliche Sozialismus.* Vienna, 1923.

Kralik, Richard, and Schlitter, Hans: *Wien, Geschichte der Kaiserstadt und ihrer Kultur.* Vienna, 1912.

Kraus, Karl: *Untergang der Welt durch schwarze Magie.* (Selected essays.) Munich, 1960.

—— *Die letzten Tage der Menschheit.* Vienna, 1922.

Kubiczek, August: *Young Hitler, the story of a friendship.* London, 1954.

Kuppe, R.: *Karl Lueger und seine Zeit.* Vienna, 1933.

Laube, Heinrich: *Reisenovellen.* 9 vols. Leipzig, 1834–37.

—— *Das Burgtheater.* Leipzig, 1868.

Leisching, Hugo von. *Der Wiener Kongress.* Vienna, 1893.

Lesky, Erna: *Die Wiener Medizinische Schule im 19. Jahrhundert.* Graz/ Cologne, 1965.

Loos, Adolf: *Sämtliche Schriften,* Vol. I. Vienna, 1962.

Maass, Ferdinand: *Der Josephinismus.* 2 vols. Vienna, 1951–53.

Mahler, Alma: *Gustav Mahler, Erinnerungen und Briefe.* Amsterdam, 1940.

Mahler-Werfel, Alma: *Mein Leben.* Frankfurt, 1960.

Mann, Golo: *Deutsche Geschichte des neunzehnten und zwanzigsten Jahrhunderts.* Frankfurt, 1959.

Matt, R.: *Die Wiener protestantischen Bürgertestamente von 1578–1627.* MS (Thesis) in Archives of the City of Vienna.

—— (same title). Vol. XVII of *Mitteilungen des Vereines für Geschichte der Stadt Wien.* Vienna, 1938.

Mayer, Anton (editor): *Geschichte der Stadt Wien.* 6 vols. Vienna, 1897–1918.

Mayer, Sigmund: *Die Wiener Juden.* Vienna, 1917.

—— *Die soziale Frage in Wien.* Vienna, 1871.

Mayerling-Original, Das: Offizieller Akt des K. K. Polizeipräsidiums. Facsimile der Dokumente. Vienna, 1953.

Mayr, Josef Karl: *Wien im Zeitalter Napoleons.* Vol. VI of *Abhandlungen zur Geschichte und Quellenkunde der Stadt Wien.* Vienna, 1940.

Mayreder, Rosa: *Das Haus in der Landskrongasse.* Vienna, 1948.

Metternich-Winneburg, Fürst Richard: *Aus Metternichs nachgelassenen Papieren.* Vienna, 1880–84.

Mezenseffy, Grete: *Geschichte des Protestantismus in Österreich.* Graz/ Cologne, 1956.

Mitis, Oskar von: *Das Leben des Kronprinzen Rudolf.* Leipzig, 1928.

Mittag, Erwin: *The Vienna Philharmonic.* Vienna, 1950.

Montagu, Lady Mary Wortley: *Letters and Works.* Ed. by Lord Wharncliffe and revised by W. Moy Thomas. 2 vols. London, 1887.

Nadler, Josef: *Grillparzer*. Vienna, 1952.

Neuwirth, Joseph: *Die Technische Hochschule in Wien 1815–1925*. Vienna, 1925.

Noltsch, W. O.: *Bilder aus Wien. Erinnerungen eines Wiener Künstlers*. 2 vols. Stuttgart/Vienna, 1901.

Novotny, Alexander: *1848*. Vienna, 1948.

Oberhummer, Hermann: *Die Wiener Polizei*. Vienna, 1937.

Philippovich, Eugen von: *Wiener Wohnungsverhältnisse*. Berlin, 1894.

Pichler, Karoline: *Denkwürdigkeiten aus meinem Leben*. Ed. by E. K. Blümml. Vienna, 1924.

Pirchan, Emil: *Hans Makart*. Vienna, 1954.

Popp, Adelheid: *Die Jugendgeschichte einer Arbeiterin*. Munich, 1930.

—— *Der Weg zur Höhe*. Vienna, 1930.

Raab, Riki: *Fanny Elssler*. Vienna, 1962.

Rath, R. John: *The Viennese Revolution of 1848*. Austin, Texas, 1957.

Rath, Stefan: *Lobmeyr*. Vienna, 1962.

Redlich, Josef: *Schicksalsjahre Österreichs 1908–1919*. Graz, 1953.

Regele, Oskar: *Feldmarschall Radetzky*. Vienna, 1937.

Renner, Karl: *An der Wende zweier Zeiten. Lebenserinnerungen*. Vienna, 1946.

Reschauer, Heinrich, and Smets, Moritz: *Das Jahr 1848. Geschichte der Wiener Revolution*. 2 vols. Vienna, 1872.

Richter, Josef: *Die Eipeldauer Briefe 1799–1813*. Sel. and ed. by E. von Pannel. Munich, 1918.

Rommel, Otto (editor): *Alt-Wiener Volkstheater*. (Plays.) 7 vols. Vienna, 1917.

—— *Die Alt-Wiener Volkskomödie*. Vienna, 1952.

Schimmer, Karl Eduard: *Alt und Neu Wien*. 2nd ed. 2 vols. Vienna/Leipzig, 1904.

Schmidt, Helga, and Czeike, Felix: *Franz Schuhmeier*. Vienna, 1964.

Schnürer, Dr. Franz (editor): *Briefe Franz Josephs an seine Mutter*. Munich, 1930.

Schönholz, Friedrich Anton von: *Traditionen zur Charakteristik Österreichs, seines Staats-und Volkslebens unter Franz I*. Ed. and annot. by Gustav Gugitz. Munich, 1914.

Sedlmayr, Hans: *Österreichische Barockarchitektur 1650–1740*. Vienna, 1930.

—— *Johann Bernhard Fischer von Erlach*. Vienna, 1958.

Skalnik, Kurt: *Dr. Karl Lueger*. Vienna, 1954.

Srbik, Heinrich Ritter von: *Metternich, der Staatsmann und der Mensch.* 2 vols. Munich, 1925.

—— *Metternich*, Vol. III. Munich, 1954.

Steiner, Herbert: *Die Arbeiterbewegung Österreichs 1867–1889.* Vienna, 1964.

Stockert-Meynert, Dora: *Theodor Meynert und seine Zeit. Zur Geistes-geschichte Österreichs in der zweiten Hälfte des 19. Jahrhunderts.* Vienna, 1930.

Strobl von Ravelsberg, Ferdinand: *Metternich und seine Zeit 1773–1859.* Vienna/Leipzig, 1905.

Suess, Eduard: *Erinnerungen.* Leipzig, 1916.

Technischer Führer durch Wien. Ed. Martin Paul, for Österreichischen Ingenieur-und Architektenverein. Vienna, 1910.

Tietze, Hans: *Alt-Wien in Wort und Bild.* Vienna, 1926.

—— *Die Juden Wiens.* Vienna, 1933.

Trollope, Frances: *Vienna and the Austrians.* London, 1838.

Turnbull, Peter Evan: *Austria.* 2 vols. London, 1840.

Vasili, Comte Paul: *La société de Vienne.* 11th edition. Paris, 1885.

Wien 1848–1888. Sponsored by Gemeinderath der Stadt Wien. 2 vols. Vienna, 1888.

Wingler, Hans Maria. *Oskar Kokoschka.* Salzburg, 1956.

Wurzbach, Konstantin von: *Biographisches Lexikon des Kaisertums Österreich.* 60 vols. Vienna, 1856–91.

Wurzbach, W. von: *Kriehuber, ein Porträtlithograph der Wiener Gesell-schaft.* Vienna, 1859.

Zenker, E. V.: *Die Wiener Revolution von 1848 in ihren sozialen Voraus-setzungen und Beziehungen.* Vienna, 1897.

Zweig, Stefan: *The World of Yesterday.* London, 1943.

Index of Names